Vitali Bartash
Establishing Value

Studies in Ancient Near Eastern Records

Volume 23

Vitali Bartash

Establishing Value

Weight Measures in Early Mesopotamia

DE GRUYTER

ISBN 978-1-5015-1714-3
e-ISBN (PDF) 978-1-5015-1026-7
e-ISBN (EPUB) 978-1-5015-1032-8
ISSN 2161-4415

Library of Congress Control Number: 2019933419

Bibliographic information published by the Deutsche Nationalbibliothek
The Deutsche Nationalbibliothek lists this publication in the Deutsche Nationalbibliografie; detailed bibliographic data are available in the Internet at http://dnb.dnb.de.

Typesetting: Integra Software Services Pvt. Ltd.
Printing and binding: CPI books GmbH, Leck

www.degruyter.com

Preface

This book offers the first comprehensive study of weighing as an economic practice in early Mesopotamia and shows its deep impact on its society. Relying on the data of thousands of cuneiform sources analyzed first-hand, my aim is to provide an integral view on this remarkable phenomenon and to try to answer the questions when, how, and why it appeared, how it changed in the course of the 3rd millennium BC, and how it reflected and affected economic and social practices and relations.

The history of this project goes back to 2010 when I started working on a doctoral thesis in an interdisciplinary research group *Value and Equivalence: The Genesis and Transformation of Values from Archaeological and Anthropological Perspectives* at the University of Frankfurt funded by the German Research Foundation (DFG). I am grateful to my advisors, Thomas Richter and Aage Westenholz, for their manifold support and the knowledge in the "dark arts" of cuneiform scholarship they have bestowed on me. I am indebted to my friends and colleagues in the research group *Value and Equivalence* for the prolific theoretical discussions and its coordinator, Annabel Bockern, for the abiding support.

Although the thesis was completed by the end of 2013, the delay in its publication was due to several factors. First, I was involved in the publication of more than 700 early cuneiform texts, which appeared in monographic form in 2013 and 2017 respectively. Secondly, this hiatus provided me with the opportunity to look at the topic with a fresh eye. As a result, I have written this book anew without using a single sentence from the original thesis and restating numerous arguments and conclusions. This book cites only relevant data and discussions with a view to making it accessible and enjoyable to specialists and the general public alike.

It is my pleasure to thank Gonzalo Rubio for his guidance throughout the publication process and anonymous reviewers for their valuable feedback. In acknowledging the help of others, I would also like to mention the manifold support of the following colleagues: Andrew George, Benjamin Foster, Jöran Friberg, Manfred Krebernik, Manuel Molina, Palmiro Notizia, David Owen, Walther Sallaberger, Martin Schøyen, Horst Steible, and Giuseppe Visicato. Special thanks go to my wife, Volha, for her constant encouragement during the completion of this project.

https://doi.org/10.1515/9781501510267-201

Contents

Preface — V

Abbreviations — X

1 Approaching the topic — 1
1.1 Object and scope — **1**
1.2 Methods — **5**
1.3 Sources — **9**
1.4 Previous research — **10**
1.5 Outline of the contents — **13**

2 From burden to talent — 16
2.1 Introduction — **16**
2.2 GUN_2: The sign and the word — **17**
2.3 Gun_2 as a primitive measure "load" — **20**
2.4 Gun_2 as a standardized weight measure "talent" — **28**
2.5 The fractions of the talent — **32**
2.6 Conclusions — **34**

3 Mina: The cosmopolite — 36
3.1 The etymology of ma-na — **36**
3.2 The earliest use of the mina — **39**
3.3 The fractions of the mina: Two Early Dynastic scribal traditions — **43**
3.4 The "half" of the mina — **49**
3.5 Etymology of šušana and šanabi — **51**
3.6 Šušana and šanabi in time and space — **53**
3.7 Conclusions — **59**

4 Shekel: A tiny axe — 60
4.1 $Gi\hat{g}_4$ "axe" and "shekel": Reading and etymology — **60**
4.2 The early use of the shekel — **63**
4.3 Fractions "one-third" and "two-thirds" of the shekel — **64**
4.4 The fraction "half-shekel" — **66**
4.5 TAR = ku_5 as "half-shekel" — **67**
4.6 The igi-*n*-$\hat{g}al_2$ construction — **68**
4.7 Conclusions — **71**

5 **The missing link: $NINDA_2$ × ŠE + N — 73**
5.1 Introduction — **73**
5.2 Why $NINDA_2$ × ŠE? — **73**
5.3 $NINDA_2$ × ŠE + N: The temporal and local distribution — **75**
5.4 Theories explaining $NINDA_2$ × ŠE + N — **83**
5.5 Many questions – some answers — **90**

6 **Reforms and new measures — 91**
6.1 Introduction — **91**
6.2 The Early Dynastic stage — **92**
6.3 The Sargonic reform — **95**
6.4 The roots of the Neo-Sumerian system — **104**
6.5 The Ur III reform — **105**
6.6 Conclusions — **111**

7 **Stone weights — 112**
7.1 Introduction — **112**
7.2 Na_4 “stone” — **113**
7.3 One-talent stone weights — **115**
7.4 Sets of weights — **120**
7.5 The “correct” standard — **127**
7.6 The silver standard — **131**
7.7 The standard for wool and textiles — **132**
7.8 Foreign standards — **133**
7.9 “Heavy” weights — **134**
7.10 Conclusions — **136**

8 **Weighing scales — 138**
8.1 Introduction — **138**
8.2 Lexical data on balance scales — **139**
8.3 Weighing balance in archival records — **142**
8.4 Conclusions — **150**

9 **Weighmasters and the context of weighing — 152**
9.1 Introduction — **152**
9.2 Weighing and weighmasters — **152**
9.3 Weighmasters in *sensu stricto* — **154**
9.4 Merchants as weighmasters — **159**
9.5 Craftsmen as weighmasters — **161**
9.6 Officials as weighmasters — **163**

9.7 The context of weighing — 165
9.8 Conclusions — 167

10 Weighed goods — 169
10.1 Introduction — 169
10.2 Approaches to express the weight of objects in script — 170
10.3 Copper and silver — 173
10.4 Copper, bronze, and related metals in the production of tools — 183
10.5 Gold and silver for luxury objects — 196
10.6 Resins — 200
10.7 Gems — 214
10.8 Wool and textiles — 215
10.9 The mass of some fabrics and garments — 221
10.10 Ropes, nets, mineral substances — 222
10.11 Conclusions — 227

A retrospect — 230

Bibliography — 238

General index — 253

Signs and Sumerian words — 258

Akkadian words — 263

Cuneiform texts — 264

Abbreviations

General abbreviations

do.	*ditto*, the same
ED I–II	Early Dynastic I and II periods, ca. 3000/2900–2600 BC
ED IIIa	Early Dynastic IIIa ("Fara") period, ca. 2600–2450 BC BC
ED IIIb	Early Dynastic IIIb ("Presargonic") period, ca. 2450–2350 BC
ES	Early Sargonic period ≈ the reign of Sargon of Akkad, ca. 2325–2285 BC
MS	Middle Sargonic period ≈ the reigns of Rimuš, Maništusu, and the earlier part of the Naram-Suen's reign, ca. 2285–2230 BC
MS 0000	siglum of cuneiform documents in the Schøyen Collection, Norway
ca.	*circa*, about, approximately
CS	Classical Sargonic period ≈ the later part of the Naram-Suen's reign and the reign of Šarkališarri, ca. 2230–2180 BC
LS	Late Sargonic or "Gutean" period, ca. 2180–2110 BC
OB	Old Babylonian period, ca. 2000–1600 BC
obv.	the obverse of a cuneiform tablet
P000000	numbers of cuneiform texts in the CDLI database
rev.	the reverse of a cuneiform tablet
Ur III	Ur III period, ca. 2110–2000 BC
Uruk III	= Jemdet Nast period, ca. 3100–3000 BC
Uruk IV	ca. 3350–3100 BC

Bibliographic abbreviations

If not otherwise stated, cuneiform lexical lists and literary compositions are cited according to DCCLT and ETCSL respectively.

AAICAB	Grégoire, Jean-Pierre. 1996–2002. *Archives administratives et inscriptions cunéiformes de l'Ashmolean Museum et de la Bodleian Collection d'Oxford.* Paris: Librarie Orientaliste Paul Geuthner.
AHw	Von Soden, Wolfram. 1959–1981. *Akkadisches Handwörterbuch*. Wiesbaden: Harrassowitz.
AIHA	Rasheed, Fawzi. 1981. *The Ancient Inscriptions in Himrin Area; Results of the Salvage Excavations at Himrin Reservoir.* Himrin 4. Baghdad: The State Organizations of Antiquities and Heritage.
Aleppo	Touzalin, Maryse. 1982. *L'administration palatiale a l'époque de la troisième dynastie d'Ur*. Ph.D. thesis, University of Tours, France.
ARET 2	Edzard, Dietz O. 1981. *Verwaltungstexte verschiedenen Inhalts (aus dem Archiv L.2769)*. Archivi Reali di Ebla, Testi, II. Rome: Sapienza.
ATU 1	Falkenstein, Adam. 1936. *Archaische Texte aus Uruk. Ausgrabungen der Deutschen Forschungsgemeinschaft in Uruk-Warka, Band 2*. Berlin: Deutsche Forschungsgemeinschaft.

https://doi.org/10.1515/9781501510267-202

ATU 3	Englund, Robert K., and Hans. J. Nissen. 1993. *Die lexikalischen Listen der archaischen Texte aus Uruk*. Archaische Texte aus Uruk 3. Berlin: Gebr. Mann.
ATU 5	Englund, Robert K. 1994. *Archaic Administrative Documents from Uruk: The Early Campaigns*. Archaische Texte aus Uruk 5. Berlin: Gebr. Mann.
ATU 6	Englund, Robert K. and Hans J. Nissen. 2005. *Archaische Verwaltungstexte aus Uruk: Vorderasiatisches Museum II*, Archaische Texte aus Uruk 6, Berlin: Gebr. Mann.
AUCT 1–3	Sigrist, Marcel. 1984–1988. *Neo-Sumerian Account Texts in the Horn Archaeological Museum*. Andrews University Cuneiform Texts 1–3. Berrien Springs, MI: Andrews University Press.
BCT 2	Watson, Philip J. 1992. *Catalogue of Cuneiform Tablets in Birmingham City Museum 2*. Warminster: Aris & Phillips Ltd.
BdI 1–2	Pomponio, Fracesco, Giuseppe Visicato, and Aage Westenholz. 2006. *Le tavolette cuneiformi di Adab delle collezioni della Banca d'Italia, vol. I*, and Pomponio, Francesco, Marten Stol, and Aage Westenholz. 2006. *Le tavolette cuneiformi di varia provenienzia delle collezioni della Banca d'Italia, vol. II*. Rome: Banca d'Italia.
BDTNS	Molina, Manuel M. 2002 ff. *Database of Neo-Sumerian Texts* (BDTNS) (http://bdts.filol.csic.es/).
Berens	Pinches, Theophilus G. 1915. *The Babylonian Tablets of the Berens Collection*. Asiatic Society Monographs 16. London: The Royal Asiatic Society.
BIN 3	Keiser, Clarence E. 1971. *Neo-Sumerian Account Texts from Drehem*. Babylonian Inscriptions in the Collection of James B. Nies, Yale University. New Haven, CT: Yale University Press.
BIN 5	Hackman, George. G. 1937. *Temple Documents of the Third Dynasty of Ur from Umma*. Babylonian Inscriptions in the Collection of James B. Nies, Yale University. New Haven, CT: Yale University Press.
BIN 6	Stephens, Ferris J. 1944. *Old Assyrian Letters and Business Documents*. Babylonian Inscriptions in the Collection of James B. Nies, Yale University. New Haven, CT: Yale University Press.
BIN 8	Hackman, George. G. 1958. *Sumerian and Akkadian Administrative Texts from Predynastic Times to the End of the Akkad Dynasty*. Babylonian Inscriptions in the Collection of James B. Nies, Yale University. New Haven, CT: Yale University Press.
BIN 9	Crawford, Vaughn E. 1954. *Sumerian Economic Texts from the First Dynasty of Isin*. Babylonian Inscriptions in the Collection of James B. Nies, Yale University. New Haven, CT: Yale University Press.
BPOA 1	Ozaki, Tohru, and Marcel Sigrist. 2006. *Ur III Administrative Tablets from the British Museum. Part One*. Biblioteca del Proximo Oriente Antiguo 1. Madrid: Consejo Superior de Investigaciones Cientificas.
BPOA 6	Sigrist, Marcel, and Tohru Ozaki. 2009. *Neo-Sumerian Administrative Tablets from the Yale Babylonian Collection. Part One*. Biblioteca del Proximo Oriente Antiguo 6. Madrid: Consejo Superior de Investigaciones Cientificas.
CAD	Oppenheim, Leo et al. 1956–2010. *The Assyrian Dictionary of the University of Chicago*. Chicago: Oriental Institute.
CHEU	Contenau, Georges. 1915. *Contribution à l'histoire économique d'Umma*. Paris: Librarie Ancienne Honoré Champion.

CST	Fish, Thomas. 1932. *Catalogue of Sumerian Tablets in the John Rylands Library*. Manchester: Manchester University Press.
CT 10	King, Leonard W. 1900. *Cuneiform Texts from Babylonian Tablets in the British Museum. Part X.* London: British Museum.
CT 50	Sollberger, Edmond. 1971. *Cuneiform Texts from Babylonian Tablets in the British Museum. Part L. Pre-Sargonic and Sargonic Economic Texts*. London: British Museum.
CUSAS 3	Owen, David I., and Rudolf H. Mayr. 2007. *The Garšana Archives*. Cornell University Studies in Assyriology and Sumerology 3. Bethesda, MD: CDL Press.
CUSAS 11	Visicato, Giuseppe, and Aage Westenholz, 2010. *Early Dynastic and Early Sargonic Tablets from Adab in the Cornell University Collections*. Cornell University Studies in Assyriology and Sumerology 11. Bethesda, MD: CDL Press.
CUSAS 12	Civil, Miguel. 2010. *The Lexical Texts in the Schøyen Collection*. Cornell University Studies in Assyriology and Sumerology 12. Bethesda, MD: CDL Press.
CUSAS 13	Maiocchi, Massimo. 2009. *Classical Sargonic Tablets Chiefly from Adab in the Cornell University Collections*. Cornell University Studies in Assyriology and Sumerology 13. Bethesda, MD: CDL Press.
CUSAS 14	Monaco, Salvatore F. 2011. *Early Dynastic mu-iti Cereal Texts in the Cornell University Cuneiform Collections*. Cornell University Studies in Assyriology and Sumerology 14. Bethesda, MD: CDL Press.
CUSAS 17	George, Andrew R. (ed.). 2011. *Cuneiform Royal Inscriptions and Related Texts in the Schøyen Collection*. Cornell University Studies in Assyriology and Sumerology 17. Bethesda, MD: CDL Press.
CUSAS 19	Maiocchi, Massimo, and Giuseppe Visicato. 2012. *Classical Sargonic Tablets Chiefly from Adab in the Cornell University Collections, Part II*. Cornell University Studies in Assyriology and Sumerology 19. Bethesda, MD: CDL Press.
CUSAS 20	Pomponio, Fracesco, and Giuseppe Visicato. 2015. *Middle Sargonic Tablets Chiefly from Adab in the Cornell University Collections*. Cornell University Studies in Assyriology and Sumerology 20. Bethesda, MD: CDL Press.
CUSAS 23	see Bartash 2013a
CUSAS 26	Westenholz, Aage. 2014. *A Third-Millennium Miscellany of Cuneiform Texts*. Cornell University Studies in Assyriology and Sumerology 26. Bethesda, MD: CDL Press.
CUSAS 27	Milano, Lucio, and Aage Westenholz. 2015. *The "Šuilisu Archive" and other Sargonic Texts in Akkadian*. Cornell University Studies in Assyriology and Sumerology 27. Bethesda, MD: CDL Press.
CUSAS 31	Monaco, Salvatore F. 2016. *Archaic Cuneiform Tablets From Private Collections*. Cornell University Studies in Assyriology and Sumerology 31. Bethesda, MD: CDL Press.
CUSAS 33	Notizia, Palmiro, and Giuseppe Visicato. 2016. *Early Dynastic and Early Sargonic Administrative Texts Mainly from the Umma Region*. Cornell University Studies in Assyriology and Sumerology 33. Bethesda, MD: CDL Press.
CUSAS 35	see Bartash 2017a
DCCLT	Veldhuis, Niek at al. 2003 ff. *Digital Corpus of Cuneiform Lexical Texts* (http://oracc.museum.upenn.edu/dcclt/)
DP	De la Füye, Alotte. 1908–1920. *Documents Présargoniques*. Paris: Éditions E. Leroux.

DPA	Limet, Henri. 1973. *Étude de documents de la période d'Agadé appartenant à l'Université de Liège*. Paris: Société d'Éditions "Les Belles Lettres."
ECTJ	Westenholz, Aage. 1975. *Early Cuneiform Texts from Jena. Pre-Sargonic and Sargonic Documents from Nippur and Fara in the Hilprecht-Sammlung*. København: Munksgaard.
EDPV A	see Civil 2008
EDATŠ	Pomponio, Fracesco, and Giuseppe Visicato. 1994. *Early Dynastic Administrative Tablets of Šuruppak*. Napoli: Istituto Universario Orientale di Napoli.
ELTS	Gelb, Ignace J., Piotr Steinkeller, and Robert Whiting. 1989–1991. *Earliest Land Tenure Systems in the Near East: Ancient Kudurrus*. Oriental Institute Publications 104. Chicago: The Oriental Institute of the University of Chicago.
ETB 2	Oates, David, Joan Oates, and Helen McDonald. 2001. *Excavations at Tell Brak, Vol. II: Nagar in The Third Millennium BC*. Cambridge: McDonald Institute for Archaeological Research.
ETCSL	Black, Jeremy et al. 1998 ff. *The Electronic Text Corpus of Sumerian Literature* (http://etcsl.orinst.ox.ac.uk).
FAOS 15/1	Selz, Gebhard J. 1989. *Die altsumerischen Wirtschaftsurkunden der Eremitage zu Leningrad*. Freiburger altorientalische Studien 15,1. Stuttgart: Franz Steiner.
FAOS 15/2	Selz, Gebhard J. 1993. *Altsumerische Wirtschaftsurkunden aus amerikanischen Sammlungen*. Freiburger altorientalische Studien 15,2. Stuttgart: Franz Steiner.
FAOS 19	Kienast, Burkhart, and Konrad Volk. 1995. *Die sumerischen und akkadischen Briefe des III. Jahrtausends aus der Zeit vor der III. Dynastie von Ur*. Freiburger altorientalische Studien 19. Stuttgart: Franz Steiner.
FTP	Martin, Harriet, Francesco Pomponio, Giuseppe Visicato, and Aage Westenholz. 2001. *The Fara Tablets in the University of Pennsylvania Museum of Archaeology and Anthropology*. Bethesda, MD: CDL Press.
Hirose	Gomi, Tohru, Yoko Hirose, and Kazutaka Hirose, 1990. *Neo-Sumerian Administrative Texts of the Hirose Collection*. Potomac, MD: CDL Press.
HSS 4	Hussey, Mary I. 1915. *Sumerian Tablets in the Harvard Semitic Museum. Part 2: From the Time of the Dynasty of Ur*. Harvard Semitic Series 4. Cambridge, MA: Harvard University Press.
HSS 10	Meek, Theophilus J. 1935. *Excavations at Nuzi conducted by the Semitic Museum and the Fogg Art Museum of Harvard University*. Harvard Semitic Series 10. Cambridge, MA: Harvard University Press.
Imgula 3/1	Sommerfeld, Walter. 1999. *Die Texte der Akkade-Zeit. 1. Das Dijala-Gebiet: Tutub*. Imgula 3/1. Münster: Rhema.
ITT 1–5	Thureau-Dangin, François, Henri de Genouillac, and Louis Delaporte 1910–1921. *Inventaire des tablettes de Tello conserves au musée imperial ottoman*. Paris: Ernest Leroux.
LAK	Deimel, Anton. 1922. *Liste der archaischen Keilschriftzeichen. Die Inschriften von Fara 1*. Wissenschaftliche Veröffentlichungen der Deutschen Orient-Gesellschaft, Bd. 40. Leipzig: J. C. Hinrichs'sche Buchhandlung.
MAD 1	Gelb, Ignace J. 1952. *Sargonic Texts from the Diyala Region. Materials for the Assyrian Dictionary 1*. Chicago: University of Chicago Press.
MAD 3	Gelb, Ignace J. 1957. *Glossary of Old Akkadian. Materials for the Assyrian Dictionary 3*. Chicago: University of Chicago Press.

MAD 4	Gelb, Ignace J. 1970. *Sargonic Texts in the Louvre Museum. Materials for the Assyrian Dictionary 4*. Chicago: University of Chicago Press.
MAD 5	Gelb, Ignace J. 1970. *Sargonic Texts in the Ashmolean Museum, Oxford. Materials for the Assyrian Dictionary 5*. Chicago: University of Chicago Press.
MARI	Mari, Annales de Recherches Interdisciplinaires. Paris 1982 ff.
MC 4	Steinkeller, Piotr. 1992. *Third-Millennium Legal and Administrative Texts in the Iraq Museum, Baghdad*. Mesopotamian Civilizations 4. Winona Lake, IN: Eisenbrauns.
MEE 4	Pettinato, Giovanni. 1982. *Testi Lessicali Bilingui della Biblioteca L. 2769*. Materiali Epigrafici di Ebla 4. Napoli: Istituto Universario Orientale di Napoli.
MSL	Materialien zum sumerischen Lexikon/Materials for the Sumerian Lexicon. Rome: Pontificium Institutum Biblicum, 1937 ff.
MZL	Borger, Rykle. 2004. *Mesopotamisches Zeichenlexikon*. Alter Orient und Altes Testament 305. Münster: Ugarit-Verlag.
MVN 1	Pettinato, Giovanni, and Hartmut Waetzoldt. 1974. *La Collezione Scholmeyer*. Materiali per il Vocabolario Neosumerico 1. Rome: Multigrafica Editrice.
MVN 3	Owen, David. I. 1975. *The John Frederick Lewis Collection Texts from the Third Millennium in the Free Library of Philadelphia*. Materiali per il Vocabolario Neosumerico 3. Rome: Multigrafica Editrice.
MVN 4	Cagni, Luigi, and Giovanni Pettinato. 1976. *La Collezione del Pontifico Instituto Biblico – Roma*. Materiali per il Vocabolario Neosumerico 4. Rome: Multigrafica Editrice.
MVN 5	Sollberger, Edmond. 1978. *The Pinches Manuscript*. Materiali per il Vocabolario Neosumerico 5. Rome: Multigrafica Editrice.
MVN 6	Pettinato, Giovanni. 1977. *Testi economici di Lagaš del Museo di Istambul*. Materiali per il Vocabolario Neosumerico 6. Rome: Multigrafica Editrice.
MVN 7	Pettinato, Giovanni, and Sergio Picchioni. 1978. *Testi economici di Lagaš del Museo di Istambul. Parte II*. Materiali per il Vocabolario Neosumerico 7. Rome: Multigrafica Editrice.
MVN 8	Calvot, Danièle, and Giovanni Pettinato. 1979. *Textes économiques de Ṣelluš-Dagan du Musée du Louvre et du Collège de France. Testi economici dell'Iraq museum – Baghdad*. Materiali per il Vocabolario Neosumerico 8. Rome: Multigrafica Editrice.
MVN 9	Snell, Daniel C. 1979. *The E. A. Hoffman Collection and Other American Collections*. Materiali per il Vocabolario Neosumerico 9. Rome: Multigrafica Editrice.
MVN 10	Grégoire, Jean-Pierre. 1981. *Inscriptions et archives administratives cunéiformes*. Materiali per il Vocabolario Neosumerico 10. Rome: Multigrafica Editrice.
MVN 14	Yildiz, Fatma, Hartmut Waetzoldt, and Hubert Renner. 1988. *Die Umma-Texte aus den archäologischen Museen zu Istanbul 2*. Materiali per il Vocabolario Neosumerico 14. Rome: Multigrafica Editrice.
MVN 16	Yildiz, Fatma, and Hartmut Waetzoldt. 1994. *Die Umma-Texte aus den archaeologischen Museen zu Istanbul*. Materiali per il Vocabolario Neosumerico 16. Rome: Bonsignore Editore.

MVN 20 D'Agostino, Franco. 1997. *Testi amministrativi della III dinastia di Ur dal Museo Statale Eremitage San Pietroburgo – Russia*. Materiali per il Vocabolario Neosumerico 20. Rome: Bonsignore Editore.

NATN Owen, David I. 1982. *Neo-Sumerian Archival Texts Primarily from Nippur in the University Museum, the Oriental Institute and the Iraq Museum*. Winona Lake, IN: Eisenbrauns.

Nik 1–2 Nikol'skij, Mikhail V. 1908, 1915. "Dokumenty chozjajstvennoj otčetnosti drevnej epochi Chaldei iz sobranija N. P. Lichačeva." *Drevnosti Vostočnyja* III/2, V. St. Petersburg [in Russian].

Nisaba 15 Owen, David I. 2013. *Cuneiform Texts Primarily from Iri-Saĝrig / Al-Šarraki and the History of the Ur III Period, 2 Vols*. Nisaba 15. Bethesda, MD: CLD Press.

Nisaba 24 Al-Rawi, Farouk N.H., Franco D'Agostino, and Jonathan Taylor. 2010. *Neo-Sumerian Administrative Texts from Umma Kept in the British Museum, Part Four (NATU IV)*. Nisaba 24. Messina: Di.Sc.A.M.

Nisaba 25 Lecompte, Camille. 2013. *Archaic Tablets and Fragments from Ur (ATFU). From L. Woolley's Excavations at the Royal Cemetery*. Nisaba 25. Messina: Di.Sc.A.M.

Nisaba 26 Al-Rawi, Farouk N.H., Francesca Gorello, and Palmiro Notizia. 2013. *Neo-Sumerian Administrative Texts from Umma Kept in the British Museum, Part Five (NATU V)*. Nisaba 26. Messina: Di.Sc.A.M.

Nisaba 30 Owen, David I. 2016. *The Nesbit Tablets*. Nisaba 30. Winona Lake, IN: Eisenbrauns.

NRVN 1 Çig, Muazzez, and Hatice Kizilyay. 1965. *Yeni sumer çağina ait Nippur hukukî ve idarî belgeleri – 1 = Neusumerische rechts- und verwaltungsurkunden aus Nippur – I*. Ankara: Turk Tarih Kurumu Basjmevi.

NTSŠ Jestin, Raymond. 1957. *Nouvelles Tablettes Sumériennes de Šuruppak au Musée d'Istanbul*. Paris: A. Maisonneuve.

OAIC Gelb, Ignace J. 1955. "Old Akkadian Inscriptions in Chicago Natural History Museum: Texts of Legal and Business Interest." *Fieldiana Anthropology* 44(2): 161–338.

OIP 14 Luckenbill, Daniel D. 1930. *Inscriptions from Adab*. The University of Chicago Oriental Institute Publications, Vol. XIV. Chicago: The University of Chicago Press.

OIP 97 Biggs, Robert D. 1978. "The Cuneiform Inscriptions." Pp. 71–95 in *Nippur II. The North Temple and Sounding E*, ed. by Donald E. McCown, Richard C. Haines, and Robert D. Biggs. The University of Chicago Oriental Institute Publications, Vol. XCVII. Chicago: University of Chicago Press.

OIP 99 Biggs, Robert D. 1974. *Inscriptions from Tell Abū Ṣalābīkh*. The University of Chicago Oriental Institute publications, Vol. XCIX. Chicago: University of Chicago Press.

OSP 1 Westenholz, Aage. 1975. *Old Sumerian and Old Akkadian Texts in Philadelphia Chiefly from Nippur. Part One: Literary and Lexical Texts and the Earliest Administrative Documents from Nippur*. Malibu: Undena Publications.

OSP 2 Westenholz, Aage. 1987. *Old Sumerian and Old Akkadian Texts in Philadelphia Chiefly from Nippur. Part Two: The 'Akkadian' Texts, the Enlilemaba Texts, and the Onion Archive*. Copenhagen: University of Copenhagen, Museum Tusculanum Press.

PBS 9	Barton, George A. 1915. *Sumerian Business and Administrative Documents from the Earliest Times to the Dynasty of Agade*. The University of Pennsylvania, The University Museum, Publications of the Babylonian Section, Vol. IX, No. 1. Philadelphia: University Museum, the University of Pennsylvania.
PDT	Çig, Muazzez, Hatice Kizilyay, and Armas Salonen. 1954. *Die Puzriš-Dagan-Texte der Istanbuler Archäologischen Museen. Bd. 1 (Nrr. 1–725)*. Helsinki: Suomalaisen Tiedeakatemia.
PPAC 1	Zhi, Yang. 1989. *Sargonic Inscriptions from Adab*. Periodic Publications on Ancient Civilizations 1. Changchun: The Institute for the History of Ancient Civilizations.
PPAC 4	Ozaki, Tohru, and Marcel Sigrist. 2010. *Ur III Tablets from Jerusalem: Tablets in Jerusalem – Sainte-Anne and Saint-Etienne (TJSASE)*. Periodic Publications on Ancient Civilizations 4. Changchun: The Institute for the History of Ancient Civilizations.
PPAC 5	Sigrist, Marcel, and Tohru Ozaki. 2013. *Administrative Ur III Texts in the British Museum (AUTBM). Part I: Texts Nos. 1–1010. Part II: Texts Nos. 1011–1785*. Periodic Publications on Ancient Civilizations 5. Changchun: Northeast Normal University.
PSD	Sjöberg, Åke W. (ed.). 1984 ff. *The Sumerian Dictionary of the University Museum of the University of Pennsylvania*. Philadelphia: University Museum.
RIME 1	Frayne, Douglas. 2008. *The Royal Inscriptions of Mesopotamia. Early periods, Vol. 1: Presargonic Period (2700–2350 BC)*. Toronto, Buffalo, London: University of Toronto Press.
RIME 2	Frayne, Douglas. 1993. *The Royal Inscriptions of Mesopotamia. Early Periods, Vol. 2: Sargonic and Gutian Periods*. Toronto, Buffalo, London: University of Toronto Press.
RIME 3/1	Edzard, Dietz O. 1997. *The Royal Inscriptions of Mesopotamia. Early Periods, Vol. 3/1: Gudea and His Dynasty*. Toronto, Buffalo, London: University of Toronto Press.
RIME 3/2	see Frayne 1997
Rosengarten	Rosengarten, Yvonne. 1967. *Répertoire commenté des signes présargoniques sumériens de Lagaš*. Paris: E. de Boccard.
RTC	Thureau-Dangin, François. 1903. *Recueil de tablettes chaldéennes*. Paris: Éditions E. Leroux.
SAT 3	Sigrist, Marcel. 2000. *Texts from the Yale Babylonian Collection, Part II*. Sumerian Archival Texts III. Bethesda, MD: CDL Press.
SCTRAH	Molina, Manuel M. *Sargonic Cuneiform Tablets in the Real Academia de la Historia. The Carl L. Lippmann Collection*. Madrid: Real Academia de la Historia and Ministerio de Cultura de la República Iraq.
SEL	*Studi Epigrafici e Linguistici sul Vicino Oriente Antico*. Verona 1984 ff.
SET	Jones, Tom B., and John W. Snyder. 1961. *Sumerian Economic Texts from the Third Ur Dynasty*. Minneapolis: University of Minnesota Press.
SLT	Chiera, Edward. 1929. *Sumerian Lexical Texts from the Temple School of Nippur*. The University of Chicago Oriental Institute publications, Vol. XI. Chicago: University of Chicago Press.
SF	Deimel, Anton. 1923. *Die Inschriften von Fara. 2. Schultexte aus Fara*. Leipzig: J. C. Hinrichs'sche Buchhandlung. (Reprinted: Osnabrück, Biblio-Verlag, 1969).

STA Chiera, Erward. 1922. *Selected Temple Accounts from Telloh, Yokha and Drehem. Cuneiform Tablets in the Library of Princeton University*. Princeton: Princeton University Press.

StPohl SM 13 Alberti, Amadeo, and Francesco Pomponio. 1986. *Pre-Sargonic and Sargonic Texts from Ur*. Studia Pohl, Series Maior 13. Rome: Pontificio Istituto Biblico.

STTI Donbaz, Veysel, and Benjamin R. Foster. 1982. *Sargonic Texts from Telloh in the Istanbul Archaeological Museums*. Occasional Publications of the Babylonian Fund 5. Philadelphia: University Museum.

Subartu 2 Ismail, Farouk, Walther Sallaberger, Philippe Talon, and Karel Van Lerberghe. 1997. *Administrative Documents from Tell Beydar (Seasons 1993–1995)*. Subartu 2. Turnhout: Brepols.

Syracuse see Sigrist 1983

ŠL Deimel, Anton. 1928–1933. *Šumerisches Lexikon. 2. Teil. Vollständige Ideogramm-Sammlung. Bd. 1-–4*. Rome: Pontificium Institutum Biblicum.

TCTI 1 Lafont, Bertran, and Fatma Yildiz. 1989. *Tablettes cunéiformes de Tello au Musée d'Istanbul datant de l'époque de la IIIe Dynastie d'Ur, I (ITT II/1, 2617–1038)*. Leiden: Nederlands Historisch-Archaeologisch Instituut te İstanbul.

TCTI 2 Lafont, Bertran, and Fatma Yildiz. 1996. *Tablettes cunéiformes de Tello au Musée d'Istanbul – Datant de l'époque de la IIIe Dynastie d'Ur, II (ITT II/1, 2544–2819, 3158–4342, 4708–4713)*. Leiden: Nederlands Historisch-Archaeologisch Instituut te İstanbul.

TEL Lambert, Maurice. 1968. *Tablettes économiques de Lagash (époque de la IIIe dynastie d'Ur) copiées en 1900 au Musée Impérial Ottoman par Charles Virolleaud*. Paris: Impr. Nationale.

TIM 6 Rashid, Fawzi. 1971. *Administrative texts from the Ur III Dynasty*. Texts in the Iraq Museum 6. Baghdad: The Directoral General of Antiquities.

TSA De Genouillac, Henri. 1909. *Tablettes sumériennes archaïques: matériaux pour servir à l'histoire de la société sumérienne*. Paris: P. Geuthner.

TSŠ Jestin, Raymond. 1937. *Tablettes sumériennes de Šuruppak conserves au Musée de Stamboul*. Paris: E. de Boccard.

TUT Reisner, George A. 1901. *Tempelurkunden aus Telloh*. Berlin: W. Spellmann.

UDT Nies, James B. 1920. *Ur Dynasty Tablets: Texts Chiefly from Tello and Drehem Written During the Reigns of Dungi, Bur-Sin, Gimil-Sin, and Ibi-Sin*. Leipzig: J. C. Hinrichs'sche Buchhandlung.

UET 2 Burrows, Eric. 1935. *Ur Excavation Texts II. Archaic Texts*. Philadelphia: British Museum and University of Pennsylvania Press.

UET 3 Legrain, Leon. 1937, 1947. *Ur Excavations Texts III: Business documents of the Third Dynasty of Ur. 2 vols*. Philadelphia: British Museum and University of Pennsylvania Press.

UET 9 Loding, Darlene. 1976. *Economic Texts from the Third Dynasty*: Ur Excavations Texts 9. Philadelphia: British Museum and University Pennsylvania Press.

UTI 4 Gomi, Tohru, and Fatma Yildiz. 1997. *Die Umma-Texte aus den archäologischen Museen zu Istanbul. Band IV (Nr. 2301–3000)*. Bethesda, MD: CDL Press.

UTI 5 Yildiz, Fatma, and Tohru Ozaki. 2000. *Die Umma-Texte aus den archäologischen Museen zu Istanbul. Band V (Nr. 3001–3500)*. Bethesda, MD: CDL Press.

UVB 10 Nöldeke, Arnold, E. Heinrich, and Heinrich Lenzen. 1939. *Zehnter vorläufiger Bericht über die von der Deutschen Forschungsgemeinschaft in Uruk-Warka*

	unternommenen Ausgabungen. Abhandlungen der Preußischen Akademie der Wissenschaften. Philosophisch-historische Klasse, 1939, Nr. 2. Berlin.
VS 14	Förtsch, Wilhelm. 1916. *Altbabylonische Wirtschaftstexte aus der Zeit Lugalanda's und Urukagina's*. Vorderasiatische Schriftdenkmäler der Königlichen Museen zu Berlin. Heft 14. Leipzig: J. C. Hinrichs'sche Buchhandlung.
VS 25	Marzahn, Joachim. 1991. *Altsumerische Verwaltungstexte aus Girsu/Lagaš*. Vorderasiatische Schriftdenkmäler der Staatlichen Museen zu Berlin. Heft 25 (Neue Folge Heft 10). Berlin: Akademie-Verlag.
VS 27	Marzahn, Joachim. 1996. *Altsumerische Verwaltungstexte und ein Brief aus Girsu/Lagaš*. Vorderasiatische Schriftdenkmäler der Staatlichen Museen zu Berlin, Helf 27 (Neue Folge Heft 11). Berlin: Verlag Philipp von Zabern.
WF	Deimel, Anton. 1924. *Wirtschaftstexte aus Fara*. Wissenschaftliche Veröffentlichungen der Deutschen Orient-Gesellschaft, Bd. 45. Leipzig: J. C. Hinrichs'sche Buchhandlung.
YOS 4	Keiser, Clarence E. 1919. *Selected Temple Documents of the Ur Dynasty*. Yale Oriental Series 4. New Haven: Yale University Press.
YNER 8	Snell, Daniel. 1982. *Ledgers and Prices. Early Mesopotamian Merchant Accounts*. Yale Near Eastern Researches 8. New Haven: Yale University Press.
ZATU	Green, Margaret W., and Hans J. Nissen. 1987. *Zeichenliste der archaischen Texte aus Uruk*. Ausgrabungen der Deutschen Forschungsgemeinschaft in Uruk-Warka, Bd. 11. Archaische Texte aus Uruk, Bd. 2. Berlin: Gebr. Mann Verlag.

1 Approaching the topic

1.1 Object and scope

My aim in this book is to offer the first comprehensive analysis of weighing as an economic practice in early Mesopotamia and to see how this cultural phenomenon at the same time reflected and shaped the socioeconomic relations during the 3rd millennium BC.[1] It is an original study that relies on the first-hand analysis and synthesis of data.

In this introductory chapter, I clarify the main concepts, delineate the scope of the study, discuss its principal concepts and methods, provide an overview of the previous research in this area, and concisely present what is found in the following chapters.

First, it is necessary to define the major concepts: *weighing as an economic practice and as a cultural phenomenon.*

Mentioning *weighing* in early Mesopotamia immediately conjures up in people's minds images of cheating with weights and scales in the Bible, duck-shaped weights, or the concept of "metrology." I deliberately use the latter as little as possible in this book. The reason for that is not so much the monstrous Greek-English mongrel "metro(n)+logy" itself as its origins in the scholarly milieu of the "Western world" of the nineteenth century, which obviously had nothing to do with weighing in early Mesopotamia.

Weighing in this book refers first and foremost to an *action* and a *practice* that ancient Mesopotamians performed for some reasons. Clarifying this rationale behind the weighing and the question how did they do it and who were these "they" is the object of this study.

Weighing as a *cultural phenomenon* included various interrelated aspects: units of weight and their system ("metrology") and how they were put in script (writing), goods that were measured by weight, tools that were used for this purpose, people who acted as weighmasters and supervised the process of weighing, the economic significance of the weighing, and, finally, the socioeconomic driving forces behind these factors and their influence on the society, the "why" of the phenomenon.

---

1 The term "Early Mesopotamia" is used in Postgate 1992, the works by Steinkeller, and many others nowadays to refer to the historical period of ca. 3350–2000 BC, that is, from the earliest written records of the Uruk period to the disintegration of the Ur III state in southern Mesopotamia. The term "culture" is used in this book in the broad, anthropological sense.

https://doi.org/10.1515/9781501510267-001

One of the most important parts of the book is concerned with *weight measures and their system*. Traditionally, it is believed that this aspect belongs to the realm of ideas: It is an idea that a unit of weight must have such and such a mass. However, this static view does not consider that a measure was a practical tool and not an abstraction of a learned mind. Besides, the data I discuss indicate the origins of the system of weight measures in unrelated "primitive measures" comparable to the "ell," "cubit," etc. I argue that each measure passed necessarily through evolutional stages in its development: the prototype, the primitive unit, and the standardized unit. We will see that the latter half of the third millennium witnessed several state-run attempts to standardize the weight metrology.

Writing is another aspect of this study. Without writing we would have been left only with actual weights, most of which are very hard to date. In contrast, written records offer precisely datable data sets that cover all the above-mentioned aspects of weighing as a cultural phenomenon.

By ca. 3350 BC, early Mesopotamian accountants of central urban households (traditionally interpreted as "temples") had developed a complicated system of writing that included about 1,000 signs. Originally, they were logograms and numbers only. Logograms represented those parts of objective reality that accountants ("scribes") in these central urban households perceived as valuable and that somehow were related to these households in terms of property or services. These goods had become so abundant due to the communal irrigation-based agriculture and the advanced animal husbandry that a need to record receipts and issues in and out of these households had led to the emergence of writing. As the result, accountants recorded cattle and sheep, human resources, land, grain, tools, cloths, and various types of food. The numbers quantified the amounts of these goods and of people and animals and provided temporal anchoring of the transactions. Some numbers, like our decimal numbers today, referred to the quantity in pieces. The 4th mill. BC texts used sexagesimal and bisexagesimal numerical systems. The 3rd mill. BC written records gradually abandoned the bisexagesimal system and retained only the sexagesimal one, which remained the main system of numeration until the end of the cuneiform tradition.

The 3rd mill. BC records evidence for the first time the use of weight measures, which functioned in the framework of the sexagesimal system of numeration. The texts of each period provide various scribal conventions and idiosyncrasies for writing individual weight measures – the mina, the shekel, etc. – and their fractions. These notations may be very confusing to a newcomer and even to cuneiform scholars of the later periods because these conventions changed repeatedly throughout the 3rd mill. BC. My aim here was to reduce all these idiosyncrasies to several general concepts and, if possible, trace the temporal and regional limits of every scribal practice. However, the main interest in this is not writing in itself but writing as a means to portray the system of weight measures.

Bearing in mind that weighing is an economically driven activity brings us to the rationale behind the weighing. Why would one need weight measures? Of course, they were necessary to measure those types of *goods* that could not have been measured in any other manner. Undoubtedly, ancient Mesopotamians devised measures for grain much earlier than measures for metals. Capacity metrology must be as old as the so-called "Neolithic revolution." In contrast, weight measures are the "children" of a different economic activity. If the measurement of grain may be linked to the communal management of grain in Neolithic villages and towns, the roots of the weighing practice lie elsewhere. The data suggest that metals, wool, and luxury goods triggered the use of weighing in early Mesopotamia. As will be seen in the following, these three types of goods were embedded in various socioeconomic contexts: (a) production, (b) "money," (c) luxury goods and elites, and (d) far-distance trade.

Let us take "money" as an example. This was one of the principal applications of the weight measures in the 3rd mill. BC Mesopotamia. Copper and silver were the metallic goods used for payments of a varying nature. "One shekel silver" meant not simply "8.3 g silver" as a material but represented an exchange means and embodied value. The origins of weight metrology are inseparable from the origins of money in ancient Mesopotamia.

An extra comment on the use of the word "money" in the context of ancient Mesopotamia is unavoidable here. Many scholarly spears have been broken in an attempt to define what money is and how it came about. Many historians of money support the view that Mesopotamians has money as early as the third millennium BC.[2] We probably need to lower the time scale to the late fourth millennium BC certainly in the case of barley.[3] However, other historians and economists are either more cautious or deny this. The same applies in the field of Assyriology. Some scholars interpret silver and barley in Mesopotamia as money. The most prominent among them is Marvin Powell (1996). Others are more cautious and prefer other definitions depending on the context, for example, "financial tools," "measures of value," "means of exchange," etc.[4] I follow

---

2 Ingham 2004: 91–97. Cf. there for the role of debt in the emergence of money.

3 See Monaco 2012 for late fourth millennium barley loans.

4 Van de Mieroop 2004: 60–61 and id. 2014: 24.

Powell who argues that money or, better, monies did exist in ancient Mesopotamia before coinage. Powell speaks about barley as "cheap money" and silver as "expensive money." Considering the data discussed in this book, copper belongs to the same category. This metal was regularly used as a means of payment during the Early Dynastic period.

Everyone who has spent some time studying historical records from Mesopotamia will undoubtedly see that silver and barley and, for some periods, copper and gold appered in the economic life of Mesopotamia in a manner *qualitatively* distinct from other commodities. As the reader will see in Chapter 10, loans around 2400 BC at the city of Umma were issued by a large temple household in silver, copper, and barley but not in any other commodity. This fact is a clear indication that they were monies even if their material representations could be ground, cooked, and consumed as bread or porridge or cast into jewelry or pickaxes. As for the immaterial side, silver and barley often appear in transactions as standard monies to communicate the value of services, property, and goods without being materially present in these transactions. The so-called "balanced accounts" of the Ur III period epitomize this phenomenon.[5] For example, a payment may be calculated in silver but paid in barley. This shows that early monies were "commodity monies" and "virtual" monies alike and resembled in this respect the virtual money on our banking accounts that may be transferred as $, €, £, ¥, etc.

Coming to the *social* aspect of the Sumerian system of weight measures, it is necessary to bear in mind that certain people *required* it for their economic purposes. They were *agents* of weighing. It is impossible to say precisely who arrived, when and where, at the idea of measuring goods by weights and scales. However, the data show us who performed the actual weighing and whose interests this process represented. The archival records are, of course, biased. Most of them present weighing on the level of central households: temples and palaces. Naturally, this process represented the interests of those at the top of the hierarchy of these social organizations that collected, recorded, and distributed goods according to the social proximity of individuals to these "VIP" individuals. However, legal sources (contracts and legal proceedings) show weighing in a different light: as an everyday routine practice.

The problem of the *emergence* and *standardization* of the system of weight measures is central to this study. Terms such as "correct stone" as

5 Hudson (2004) provides an overview of theories on the origins of money in Mesopotamia and concentrates on silver and the role of temples.

early as 2450 BC and two sets of reforms by the Akkadian and Ur III states to reform the weight system are suggestive of attempts to add reliability to the whole economic practice. Obviously, the "state" was the agent that pursued this aim. This should not lead to the conclusion that weighing as an economic activity should be linked to central political authorities. The evidence suggests that the emergence of weighing should be linked in the first place to the advancement of metalworking and the international trade of metals.

Tools and *goods* are two no less important facets of weighing that this study analyzes. The first refers to the implements used to perform weighing. The second includes weighed or weighable goods and objects. My argument is that the need to measure specific sets of goods brought weighing into existence. The aim in the following will be to learn what these goods were.

Writing about early Mesopotamia leads inevitably to the use of the term "Sumerian." As Gonzalo Rubio showed, 3rd mill. BC records exhibit no Sumerian ethnic consciousness whatsoever.[6] Therefore, I use "Sumerian" in this book as a time and region marker, an abbreviation of "4th–3rd BC southern Mesopotamia," and not as an ethnic or linguistic marker. Besides, as the reader will learn from this study, some aspects of early Mesopotamian weight metrology exhibit clear signs of Semitic "influences." Nowadays it is a common opinion that Sumerians and Semites lived in close contact or even together in the earliest periods. Therefore, a form of pidgin Sumero-Akkadian, especially in the sphere of trade and commerce, is highly expected. This allows us to suggest that the system of weight measures was a cosmopolite "child" of the greater Near Eastern society of the 4th or early 3rd mill. BC. Therefore, the "Sumerian" system of weight measures was not an "achievement" of "Sumerian civilization" or Sumerians as an ethnic group.

1.2 Methods

This is a historical study. The historical method, to put it simply, is to uncover how a phenomenon changed over time and why it *existed* in the first place. The sources, the "bricks" for any historical study, are usually written records. The historical method applies diachronic and synchronic approaches to trace the

6 Rubio 2016.

development of the phenomenon and identify its roots. They sources for the present study are cuneiform texts of the late 4th and 3rd millennium BC.

This study of weighing in early Mesopotamia fits well into the broader subjects of social and economic histories. In general, "social history" is not common in the field of cuneiform studies. Traditionally, Mesopotamian history was and is heavily influenced by the narratives of elites found in "royal" and "literary" cuneiform texts.[7] The modern period of the study of the social history of early Mesopotamia is associated with the oeuvre of Igor Diakonoff (1915–1999) and Ignace Gelb (1907–1985). Their work laid the background for all subsequent studies in social and economic history of Sumer. Both scholars combined hard-core cuneiformist skills in deciphering and interpretation of the cuneiform texts with much knowledge about, and interest in, anthropology and social theory. Based on their studies and much new data and new and classic theoretical approaches, the scholars of the following generation offered their interpretations of the early southern Mesopotamian societies. Covering numerous aspects of the social life of early Mesopotamia, many aspects of social and economic relations and structures are hotly debated or remain beyond the scope of the modern scholarship.

Weighing in early Mesopotamia belongs, by and large, to these overlooked subjects. However, as the data and their analysis below illustrate, the significance of this economic practice is hard to overestimate. The study of weighing in 3rd mill. BC Mesopotamia allows us to regard the rising of social and economic complexity from a fresh perspective untainted by clichés.

The points of reference in this study are historical periods: the Early Dynastic, Sargonic, etc. Cuneiform sources often make a more accurate temporal and regional attribution of this or that particular piece of evidence possible. Nevertheless, the discussion and conclusions operate mostly in terms of periods, which is, of course, a necessary simplification.[8] In this sense, some parts of the study are linear and evolutionist: They take a phenomenon and try to figure out what its roots are in the previous periods and how it developed in the following historical epochs. I need to emphasize that I do not relate the evolution of the practice of weighing to any idea of progress. As the example of the Sargonic reforms show, state intrusion into the standardization of metrology led to the creation of a cumbersome and impractical system immediately abandoned after the collapse of the Akkadian state.

7 See Van de Mieroop 1999 and Seri 2005 for the detailed critique of the traditional approaches in writing Mesopotamian history.

8 See Sallaberger and Schrakamp 2015 for the 3rd mill. chronology of southern Mesopotamia.

The following figure explains the terminology of the historical periodization I use throughout the book (Tab. 1.1).

Tab. 1.1: Historical periods and principal cuneiform "archives" used in the study.

Period	Date	Cuneiform archives
Late Uruk (including the archaeological level "Uruk III" = Jemdet Nasr period)	ca. 3350–3000 BC	Lexical and administrative texts from Uruk and Jemdet Nasr; stone legal documents ("kudurrus")
Early Dynastic I–II	ca. 3000–2600 BC	Administrative texts from Ur; "kudurrus"
Early Dynastic IIIa (= "Fara period")	ca. 2600–2450 BC	Administrative, legal, and lexical texts from Šuruppak and Abu Salabikh; "kudurrus"
Early Dynastic IIIb (= "Presargonic period")	ca. 2450–2350 BC	Temple archives from the Umma region (mostly Zabalam) and Ĝirsu, archives from Ebla and Nabada (Tell Beydar) in Syria
Sargonic period (= "Old Akkadian period")	ca. 2350–2200 BC	Palace archives from Adab, Ĝirsu, Umma, and Sagub ("Mesag archive"). State and private documentation from Nippur and Isin
Late Sargonic / Gutean / Lagaš II period	ca. 2200–2100 BC	The central archive of Ĝirsu
Ur III period (= "Neo-Sumerian period")	ca. 2100–2000 BC	Archives from Ĝirsu, Nippur, Umma, Puzriš-Dagan, Irisaĝrig, and Garšana. Legal documents.

The role of the regional context is almost as important in the interpretation of data as the temporal aspect. I tried to place each piece of the "Sumerian system of weight measures" puzzle as precisely as possible in time and space before coming to any conclusions, however trifling they may appear at first. In particular, the careful analysis of the synchronous data from different cities often leads to the identification of local scribal and metrological traditions.

Before any historical evaluation of cuneiform sources begins to be possible, it is necessary to read them. If, as argued by Clifford Geertz, anthropologists do ethnography, Assyriologists read cuneiform texts. This activity is exciting and frustrating at the same time, as anyone who has done it will confirm. Hence, the principal and the most basic approach in the study – the philological approach – comes into play. Like any book in the field of cuneiform studies, this research is based on the "solid data" of primary sources. The original Ph.D. thesis relied on ca. 17,000 individual texts, which I routinely "read" (deciphered) and from which I selected the relevant data, which were then input into a database. I had an opportunity to collate about 3000 documents personally; most of them were not published at that time. Published or not, the study of the texts, their copies, and their editions resulted in a number of improvements. Subsequently, I introduced additional data collected over the years.

These explanations show that this work is both analytic and synthetic. It could not have been a purely synthetic study due to the general lack of previous analytical studies in this area. Several works by Powell in the 70s–90s were the only remedy. Besides, the sources of the study required considerable time and effort investments. This is due to the poor quality of older publications, which required collations of photographs received from colleagues and available in online databases, such as CDLI and BDTNS. Establishing the date and provenance of a text as well as the binding of related texts into "archives" was another task that had to be performed in many cases.

Another challenge of the present study is the fragmentary evidence. For example, the earliest data on the use of weighing and weight measures date to around 2800 BC, the so-called Early Dynastic I–II period from the paleographic perspective. However, the text corpus of this period is the least represented in the whole history of cuneiform writing. Additionally, almost all documents originate from a single city: Ur. Examples of this sort are quite often in the cuneiform scholarship. This leads to the effect that a piece of data pops up and then disappears in the available data, which does not necessarily mean that it has really vanished.

The interpretation of cuneiform sources from the paleographic, philological, and historical perspectives defines this study as a historical and even a positivist one. Any historical study in the field of cuneiform studies is positivistic. The aim of this approach is to fill the gaps in the existing knowledge on a subject, which this study does in the case of weighing in the 3rd mill. Mesopotamia.

Naturally, this work is influenced by other approaches, especially those of anthropology and archaeology. The origins of this book dates back to my Frankfurt years in the interdisciplinary research training group *Value and Equivalence* where I was the only cuneiformist. Theoretical discussions on the essence of these two concepts with historians, ethnologists, archaeologists, sociologists, and economists contributed to the development of the new model to interpret weighing and its relation to the origins of money. Therefore, I need to emphasize structuralism, functionalism, and the theory of agency as the sources of inspiration. I view weighing as an interplay of structural elements of metrology, writing, material culture, economic interest, and social action. Delineating the rationale behind weighing holds a central position throughout the book. Finally, people and their interests and their agency never go out of scope in this study.

This palimpsest of approaches could not have been different because the object of the study is rather ethnographic. I try to revive a segment of the early Mesopotamian social and economic reality relying on written records simulating the ethnographic approach of direct observation and "thick description." Of course, it would be very convenient to have a several-year stay in a Sumerian city to observe how people operated weights and scales, what they measured with them, where these goods came from and went, what the social and economic background of the individuals involved in this practice was, and why they did it in the first place. However, with a reliable time machine still missing, such fieldwork is impossible. Nevertheless, putting scraps of data on these various aspects together and trying to figure out their heads and tails in terms of social action and economic interest brings us to a reasonably comprehensive understanding of weighing as a socioeconomic and cultural phenomenon of early Mesopotamia.

1.3 Sources

The 3rd millennium BC administrative records of central urban households, legal documents concerning private matters, and letters are the main genres of sources used to mine for data in this study. These documents are "historical" since, unlike royal inscriptions, they are (mostly) unbiased by ideology and, unlike literary texts, are synchronous with the period and reality they document. Lexical lists are often helpful in interpreting the data analyzed in this book despite their largely late date. The emphasis of this study lies on the earliest data since they allow to trace the roots of the phenomenon of weighing. This means that the majority of the needle-picking discussions will concern Early Dynastic and Sargonic administrative and legal records.

Coming to the literary sources, proverb collections sometimes mention weighing tools and measures of weight.[9] However, they do not communicate any new or groundbreaking data. Literary texts, mostly in the copies of the Old Babylonian date, are mostly uninformative for the present study too. Jeremiah Peterson has shown that "30 shekels" of several literary compositions is a hoax.[10] Several literary texts mention the process of weighing. The sun god Utu/Šamaš, the divine figure associated with justice, was regarded as a supervisor of the correctness in financial transactions. A composition, *Hendursaĝa A*, informs that Utu fixes the place of weighing (ki ĝeš-rin$_2$-na-ka ... gub) and controls the arm of the balance for the correctness of the transaction (a$_2$ ĝeš-rin$_2$-na-ka ... gi.n).[11] The goddess Nanše is another divine patron of the correct weighing procedure. A literary text, *Nanše A*, edited by Wolfgang Heimpel (1981) describes the misusage of stone weights, in line 142: "taking a small weight instead of a large weight." Lines 234 and 241 mention "a correct stone to weigh silver" (na$_4$-gi-na ku$_3$ la$_2$-e-de$_3$). This text echoes the laws of Ur-Namma, where this king argues that he has standardized weight and capacity measures. Heimpel guesses that *Nanše A* might have been composed in Lagash state during the Gudea dynasty.[12] All this terminology of weights and balances appears in 3rd mill. BC texts. However, it adds nothing to the interpretation of our data.

1.4 Previous research

The study of Mesopotamian weight metrology began in the nineteenth century simultaneously with the archaeological discoveries in Iraq and the decipherment of Akkadian and then Sumerian languages. Naturally, scholars were attracted by duck-shaped stone weights and started immediately to ponder about the masses of each unit and to reconstruct various "norms" and "standards."

The point zero of any modern scholarship in Sumerian weight metrology is an unpublished dissertation, "Sumerian Numeration and Metrology," by Marvin Powell (1971). He discussed all relevant literature pertaining to the topic prior to 1971. Powell dedicated less than a hundred pages to weight metrology and related matters in his study. The positive aspect is that he relied on a

9 Alster 1997: 209, SP 13.20 (na$_4$ "weight" and giĝ$_4$ "shekel"); 92, SP 3.64 (ĝeš-rin$_2$ "weighing scales"); 113 SP 4.3 (sa$_9$(MAŠ) giĝ$_4$ "half-shekel"); 126, SP 5.45 and 214, SP 13.52 (giĝ$_4$ "shekel"); 88, SP 3.38 (ma-na "mina"); 210, SP 13.27 (1/3 or ½ of a mina); 292, N 6119.3 ("50 minas").

10 Peterson 2018.

11 ETCSL c.4.06.1, Segment C, line 32.

12 Heimpel 1981: 67.

critical evaluation of 1st mill. BC lexical sources in his interpretation of the earlier data. On the bad side was an inadequate number of 3rd mill. BC sources at the time of the conception of the thesis. Some periods, such as the crucial Sargonic period, were almost not represented at all. As a result, Powell was not able to identify any weight metrology in the texts predating the Fara corpus, ca. 2600 BC. The most important conclusion of the 1971 thesis is that the Mesopotamian weight metrology is based completely on the sexagesimal system of numeration.[13] His methodological remark on how to study Sumerian weight metrology from a historian's perspective holds true even today: "We must content ourselves with a description of the formal aspect of Mesopotamian practices in measuring mass, rather than attempting to discern concrete and absolute norms" (ib.: 207).

Another work by Powell provided a study of 950 weight specimens from Mesopotamia (all periods) and the problems connected to the analysis of archaeological evidence (Powell 1979). A similar study was attempted by Stefan Karwiese (1990), but it is largely inadequate since it neglects written sources, regards the system as static, and reconstructs nonexistent "norms."

The outcome of Powell's work on the system of weights appeared in a detailed article "Maße und Gewichte" ("Weights and Measures") in the *Reallexikon für Assyriologie*.[14] The most important conclusion was the identification of the "Akkad reform," the first datable attempt to standardize all metrological systems by the Akkadian state. He dates this event to the "Classical Sargonic period" in modern terms. The linkage of the capacity and weight metrologies via the ratio 2 minas = 1 sila as the result of the reform is of special interest for this study.[15] Powell distinguishes several periods in the development of the system of weight measures and its regional variants: "Old Akkadian – Old Babylonian," "Post-Old Babylonian systems," and "North Mesopotamian weight systems." He regards the "Akkad reform" as a starting point in the standardization of the system of weight measures.[16] These conclusions hold now only partially. The present study shows that the Sumerian system of weight units was a single one, but it went through several evolutionary stages: the Early Dynastic, the Sargonic, and the Neo-Sumerian. Additionally, the data in the first stage hint at the attempts to standardize the system much earlier than the Sargonic period.

13 Powell 1971: 210 ff.

14 Powell 1990.

15 Powell 1990: 493, 497–498, 508.

16 Powell 1990: 508 ff.

Since then, several important analytical works pertaining to the early Mesopotamian weight metrology by Jöran Friberg, Alfonso Archi, and Gregory Chambon have appeared. I will discuss them in the respective chapters of this book.

One historiographic question is unavoidable here. I refer to it as the *Late Uruk dilemma*. This is the question as to whether late 4th mill. BC records attest to or not the weight metrology. The pioneer editor of these documents, Adam Falkenstein, proposed that the system of notation, which uses a curious numerical sign N_1+EN, was the representation of the system of weights in these earliest cuneiform accounts.[17] Aizik Vaiman was the first who systematically studied the systems of mensuration of Late Uruk texts. However, he had not gone further than Falkenstein in describing "system E" as a "weight system (?)."[18] The editors of the Late Uruk sign list ZATU are more careful. They name these notations "system E" and are not sure about its application. They state that these writings only appear in 26 texts. All of these documents are of the earliest, Uruk IV layer only.[19] This means that "system E" had been completely abandoned by the Uruk III date, ca. 3100. The system exhibits binary organization of "units," from least to largest: $1N_7(N_1$+EN$) > 4N_8 > 2N_{24} > 2N_1 > 10N_{14}$.[20] As is usual in all Mesopotamian systems of mensuration, the sign N_1 must represent a "basic" unit and N_{14} makes "ten" such units. This means that $N_{24} = 1/2$, $N_8 = 1/4$, and $N_7(N_1$+EN$) = 1/16$ of the basic unit. This progression is completely alien to the system of weight units and their fractions as we know them from the Early Dynastic period on.

Despite this, Friberg follows Falkenstein and identifies "system E" as representing the weight metrology. He argues that factor diagrams of both systems are related and suggests seeing the ratio 1:14 between N_1 and N_7 as the value of gold in silver.[21] However, this is highly speculative. First, the Late Uruk sign TUN_3, which Friberg claims to be the shekel, is unrelated to this measure written $gi\hat{g}_4$ (TUN_3-*gunû*) (see more in Chapter 4). Second, none of the Uruk IV texts – all from Uruk, i.e. local idiosyncrasy – witnessing "system E" are concerned with metal. Finally, as already pointed out by Friberg, most of the texts contain the sign BA, which may refer to the allocation of some unnamed goods. Their recipients are diverse and include various officials as well as simple workers. This detail implies that these goods must have been some commodity in common use,

17 ATU 1: 50.
18 Vaiman 1974; Vaiman 1989: 120.
19 ZATU: 143–144.
20 See figure in Damerow, Englund, and Nissen 1988: 53.
21 Friberg 1999: 129–134.

probably grain or its product. The sign EN may be just a reference that this grain belongs to the *en*, the chief dignitary of the temple household of Inana. Let us take as an example the document ATU 1 218: $1N_7(1N_1{\times}EN_a)$ DU BA $GURUŠ_{b2}$ $MUŠ_{3a}$.[22] The most obvious interpretation is "one . . . measure (of grain belonging to) the *en*: (for) the workers (ĝuruš ?) in service (gub). (Subscript: the household of the goddess) Inana."

The study of Ancient Near Eastern and neighboring Aegean and Indus culture weight metrologies has attracted the interest of many archaeologists in recent decades. Their works concentrate on the study of physical remains of the weight metrology – weights and balances in their archaeological contexts. Naturally, they rely on completely different types of sources and a different methodological tool kit in their analyses and conclusions. I consider and refer to these works only if it appears relevant. The present historical study and the current archaeological research on the topic are the necessary prerequisites for a future comprehensive synthetic study of the weighing in early Mesopotamia.

1.5 Outline of the contents

The following nine chapters center on various aspects of weighing. They share methods and approaches to presenting the material, its analysis, and its synthesis.

Chapters 2–6 are the backbone of the study. They are comprehensive discussions about each weight unit with a concluding chapter that provides a historical reconstruction of how the Sumerian system of weight measures changed during the 3rd mill. BC in various political, economic, and social contexts.

The first four chapters discuss individual measures: the talent, the mina, the shekel, and the little mina. They follow the same structure. Each chapter starts with a discussion about the writing of each unit and the word that is concealed behind it and tries to figure out the *raison d'être* of each unit in the system of weight measures as a whole. Then, each chapter proceeds to the earliest data that illustrate the use of each unit. The question of when, where, and in which context each unit appears is of principal importance. Then, it is the turn of a unit's fractions to be discussed. The same procedure with the earliest data and the context applies here too. This is refined in many cases with the lexical data of the 2nd and 1st mill. BC if necessary. I devote much space to the graphic representation of these data. This includes discussion of the "standard"

22 = ATU 5 pl. 69 (W 9579,bk).

writings and local and temporal idiosyncrasies alike. Another important part of each discussion is the goods that were measured by this or that unit. For instance, this is the mina in the case of copper and wool and the shekel in the case of silver. Each chapter concludes with a summary of the discussion and theoretical deductions. Additionally, I point out the factors and questions that despite all attempts still lack convincing explanations.

Chapter 6 in the "metrological" part of this study uses a pastiche of methods and consequently has a different structure. Whereas the four preceding chapters are a deconstruction of the Sumerian system of weight measures, the chapter about reforms puts the cleaned and oiled parts of the machinery together again. The principal aim is to see how this system evolved during the 3rd mill. BC. Using this opportunity, I discuss all other remaining weight measures – ancient ones, such as the barleycorn, and those that were consciously and artificially introduced into the system by the state, e.g. the little shekel. As a result, I come to the reconstruction of the evolutionary stages of the Sumerian system of weight measures, which included the Early Dynastic system, the Sargonic reform and the resulting logical, albeit cumbersome, system, and the Neo-Sumerian system, which was in a way a full stop in the creation of a standard Mesopotamian weight metrology. One of the key factors is the role of the state in these processes. Did the state control and steer the weight metrology, and if it did, then when and how?

Each of the remaining chapters, 7–10, has a different set of research questions. I would call this part "ethnographic." It is concerned with the material and socioeconomic aspects of the weight metrology as a cultural phenomenon.

Chapter 7 will be appreciated by archaeologists since it is dedicated to stone weights. I apply the historical method to written documentation to trace the use of each kind of weight in time and space. Special attention is paid to large one-talent stone weights. The talent was one of the youngest weight measures and its use revolutionized weighing in Bronze Age Mesopotamia. Then, I proceed to a discussion about sets of weights as they appear in actual accounts and compare these data with the sets of weights that we find in the later lexical tradition. The outcome is that the weight of certain values never existed. Consequently, their identification in archaeological records is not expected. Another important aspect concerns the "standards" or "norms" of the weight measures. The data suggest that there was not a single mina of a certain weight. In contrast, each standard of the mina was related to the actual practice of measuring certain types of goods. This means that the units were not abstract notions prior to the final standardization of weight metrology during the Ur III period; on the contrary, they were inseparably related to well-defined varieties of goods that one needed to measure with weights and scales.

Chapter 8 analyzes the data on weighing balances and related weighing tools. Its structure is in many respects similar to the preceding one. I start the discussion with lexical data on weighing gear with the aim of clarifying the origins of the word ĝeš-rin$_2$, "weighing balance," and its relation to ^{ĝeš}erin$_2$, "yoke." Then, the analysis of the data on scales in administrative and legal records outlines the contexts in which these tools appear. The foremost question here is: Who possessed weighing tools and to what extent was the weighing practice widespread in the urban communities of 3rd mill. BC Mesopotamia?

Chapter 9 is closely related to this question. It is concerned with people involved in weighing. One of the principal questions here concerns the critical interpretation of the written data with the ultimate aim of telling actual weighmasters from those who controlled or supervised weighing. The context of weighing points to a broad social base of weighing. Craftsmen, merchants, and officials could operate scales and weights.

Chapter 10 is the most extensive since it discusses the *raison d'être* of the Sumerian weight metrology: What were the goods that were measured by weight units? This chapter identifies the "core goods" of the system. They are the goods whose measurement has summoned the very idea of weight measurement to life: metals, most importantly copper, wool and cloths, and luxury goods, such as resins and gems. Then, I show how the "family" of "core goods" was expanded during the 3rd mill. BC by introducing new goods previously not measured by weight, and how the reforms and the introduction of new measures contributed to this process.

The final part, an epilogue and a retrospect, provides a synthesis of the study. It presents general conclusions about the origins of the Sumerian weight metrology and its interdependence with other major socioeconomic phenomena such as money, mass production of metal tools and textiles, and international trade. Finally, this part draws attention to the questions this study is unable to answer and envisages new vistas of research of weighing in early Mesopotamia.

The Assyriological conventions used to transliterate cuneiform in this work follow Rykle Borger's *Mesopotamisches Zeichenlexikon* (MZL). The transliteration of complex and unusual numbers corresponds to those used for Late Uruk texts, for which refer to ZATU, page 166. In line with the CDLI practice of transliterating all broken signs in the same manner, I use corner brackets as in ⸢da⸣ instead of [d]a or [d]a. Cuneiform texts are cited generally according to the most recent or relevant publication. The citation follows the pattern "CUSAS 35 1," where the latter number is the number of the text in the 35th volume of the series CUSAS.

2 From burden to talent

2.1 Introduction

Like any standardized system of weight units in human history, the Sumerian one is organized hierarchically. There is always the largest and the smallest unit. A numerical relationship connects them. Going from the upper unit to the lowest, one talent is 60 minas or 3,600 shekels or 648,000 barleycorns. "Sixty" is the factor between the talent and the mina and the mina and the shekel, whereas it is "180" between the shekel and the barleycorn.

The talent is the largest measure in the Sumerian system of weights. Relying on the available weight stones, its weight was about 30 kg. As argued, this weight is an optimal weight for an adult male worker to carry during his working day.[23] Porters in Old Assyrian caravans at the beginning of the 2nd mill. BC carried loads of up to 30 kg.[24] It is hardly surprising that a unit of about 30 kg appears in various historical periods and regions as the largest weight measure.[25]

The name "talent" in the case of the Sumerian measure calques the name of the Greek largest weight measure. In fact, gun_2 means "load, burden" and is equated with the Akkadian *biltum*.[26] Powell argued that the mass of all lower units depended on the mass of the talent.[27] I completely revise this view. As I will argue below, the talent emerged from the primitive unit "load" with a circumstantial mass. The standardization of the "load" and its inclusion in the weight metrology happened only during the Early Sargonic period, ca. 2300 BC. Hence, the talent could not have been the measure that predefined the mass of the succeeding units: the mina, the shekel, and the barleycorn. In contrast, I argue that the system did not have a "unit par excellence" that defined the whole system. This phenomenon was more complex and nonlinear. Most importantly, the units "mina," "shekel," and "barleycorn" played the pivotal role in this process, whose background was the measurement of metals, principally copper and silver. I discuss this in detail in Chapters 3–5.

Coming back to the "load," the crucial difference between it and the talent consisted in the fact that the former was a "primitive measure" of arbitrary,

23 Powell 1979: 87–88.

24 Derksen 1996: 61–63.

25 Gyllenbok 2018 passim.

26 CAD B: 229. Powell 1979: 87 n. 53 observes the same pattern of the Greek and the Latin words for this measure.

27 Powell 1979: 87.

https://doi.org/10.1515/9781501510267-002

variable mass and capacity, whereas the talent that emerged from it was a standardized unit of weight that was divided into 60 minas. The areas of application of these two measures were different as well. This primitive measure was used to record the transportation and storage of reed and other materials of plant origin as well as of fish. In contrast, the talent was applied to measure typical weighable goods: metals, wool, etc.

To name the largest Sumerian unit with the name of its Greek "brother" is, of course, a frivolity. However, no other adequate translation has been suggested in the secondary literature. Therefore, I use the word "talent" as the designation of the largest standardized unit in the Sumerian system of weight measures in order to keep it apart from the "load." The latter never had an exact mass and because of this did not belong to the weight metrology.

The main discovery that I present in this chapter is that *the talent emerged out of the "load" and became a part of the system of standardized units relatively late*, at the beginning of the Sargonic period, when the system had been in existence for at least 500 years. This is not an accident. On the contrary, the definition of "load" as 60 minas, thereby becoming a standardized measure, is a unique historical event. It did not come on its own. It was part of a conscious array of reforms in administration, writing, and metrology that took place during the reign of the first Akkadian kings in Mesopotamia, ca. 2350–2250 BC. In contrast, the origins of other Sumerian units of mensuration lie in earlier, likely prehistoric periods. The case of the Sumerian talent offers a unique opportunity to witness the "birth" of a new unit of mensuration.

Before coming to the discussion of how and why it happened, it is necessary first to discuss the word gun_2 and the primitive measure "load."

2.2 GUN_2: The sign and the word

Both measures, the primitive unit "load" and the standardized weight measure "talent," were written with the same sign, GU_2. More than that, this sign also stands for the Sumerian word gu_2 "neck" – Akkadian *kišādum*.

This alleged polysemy confused Babylonian lexicographers. The earliest lexical evidence on the reading of the sign GU_2 appears in *Proto-Ea* 712–714. GU_2 is gu-u_2, ku, and gu-un.[28] Here the value /gū/ refers to "neck" (*kišādum*) whereas /gun/ is "talent." *Canonical Ea* VIII 29–30 supports this suggestion. Here gu_2 is certainly "neck," whereas the value gun_2 is reserved for "talent":

28 MSL 14: 59.

gu-u = GU$_2$ = gu-u$_2$-nu = *ki-ša$_2$-du* “neck” and gu-un = GU$_2$ = do. = *bil-tum* “load, talent.”[29] The GU$_2$ section of the *Canonical Ea* VIII/1 58–71 is more problematic. It is unsure about the phonemic structure of the Sumerian equivalent of the Akkadian *biltum* and offers both /gū/ and /gun/ for it.[30] Unfortunately no 3rd mill. BC lexical lists, such as the *Ebla Sign List*, provide evidence for the phonemic structure of the word “load, talent.” However, the presence of a final /n/ in the Sumerian word is supported by the word ni$_3$-gun$_2$-na, which has to be analyzed as /niĝ$_2$ = gun$_2$ = a(k)/ “the thing of the load.” It has two meanings: “equipment; utensils” (Akk. *unūtu*) and a variety of tax during the Ur III period.[31]

The writing gu$_2$-un appears for the first time during the Ur III period. However, it always refers to the tribute from foreign lands.[32] It never appears as the writing of the unit “talent,” which is always written simply GU$_2$.

The writing gun$_2$ for “load” and “talent” should not be confused with compound verbs that have an initial element gu$_2$ such as gu$_2$. . .ĝar, “to put on someone’s neck; to mark up” and others. Building compound verbs with words for body parts as initial elements is a characteristic of Sumerian and other structurally similar languages. Therefore, the writing gu$_2$-na should be analyzed as /gu$_2$ = (a)n(i) = a/ “on his neck.”

The sign GU$_2$ has a long history and appears in a multitude of graphemes in 3rd mill. BC texts. However, its origins are obscure. There are no clear examples of GU$_2$ in the earliest, Late Uruk written sources. It appears for the first time in the ED I–II texts, where it is a quite straightforward depiction of a vessel with a pointed bottom[33] (Tab. 2.1):

Tab. 2.1: Sign GU$_2$ in early cuneiform texts.

Early Dynastic I–II, ca. 2800 BC	Early Dynastic IIIa, ca. 2600

29 MSL 14: 477.

30 MSL 14: 491.

31 For words with gu$_2$-na, see Such-Gutiérrez 2003: 399 n. 23. For a discussion of ni$_3$-gu$_2$-na as a “commodity tax,” see Heimpel 2009: 317.

32 See, for example, RIME 3/2.01.04.06 10 for tribute from Anšan.

33 The sign is ZATU233, UET 2 sign list no. 331, LAK544, Rosengarten 355, and MZL176.

Pictographic signs representing vessels and containers abound in Late Uruk–ED IIIa texts. Their importance is explained by the fact that these signs were handy for scribes. They put down a sign that designated a specific vessel or container and inscribed a product that was stored therein. By doing this, the method of storage, the approximate capacity, and the nature of the product were clearly defined with a single sign.

Relying on the form of the sign GU_2 it is tempting to seek the origins of the Sumerian unit "load" in a vessel. Commonly known, the ancient Greek talent was defined as a mass of water in one amphora. Nevertheless, several details reject any relation between a vessel and the primitive unit "load." First, the sign GU_2 represents a relatively small pot.[34] Otherwise, a large pot with a capacity of goods equal to 30 kg would require handles like those of an amphora. However, the strongest argument against the "vessel hypothesis" of the origins of the load lies in the fact that, unlike Greeks, Mesopotamians established a relation between capacity and weight measures only as a result of the Sargonic reform, that is, when the "load" had been in use for many centuries.

The attestation of the sign GU_2 in the Late Uruk texts is equivocal. It remains uncertain whether this sign is indeed GU_2.[35] The sign appears regularly in the ED I–II texts from Ur, for instance in the well-known construction gu_2-an-$še_3$ "total."[36] Sign no. 331 in the UET 2 sign list is a combination of no. 330 and an inscribed number *1*, a "pointed" DIŠ. This reminds us of Late Uruk texts where vessels often appear in combination with "pointed" numerals.[37]

Besides the word for "total" and in a number of personal names, GU_2 appears in post-Late Uruk copies of the lexical list *Archaic Word List C (Tribute)* 32a. Civil interprets it as a compound verb nam-gu_2-$še_3$ . . . ak "to pass on inherited property from an heir to another member of the family." However, it remains unclear which of two Sumerian words – gu_2 "neck" or gun_2 "load" – appears in this expression. Civil argues for the latter.[38] By this, nam-gun_2 refers to possessions and may be compared to ni_3-gun_2-na "utensils."

GU_2-DU_6 appears among cereal products in a record UET 2 4 from ED I–II Ur (obv. i 5). Although Late Uruk texts document a dry cereal product DU_8,[39]

34 Cf. gu_2-zi, Akk. *kāsu*, a bowl for beer and oils of low capacity, for which see Steinkeller 1992: 39.

35 See ZATU: 217 no. 233. Both attestations in P003729 and P000151 are problematic.

36 E.g. in UET 2 21 rev. i 1.

37 See a vessel for beer DUG with an inscribed *AŠ* in Englund 2001: 29.

38 See Civil 2013: 36–39 for a discussion with further references.

39 See Englund 1998: 203.

GU_2 as a measure here is not without problem, since no other cereal products in UET 2 4 have the measure GU_2.

During the following Early Dynastic IIIa period, GU_2 is LAK544 in Falkenstein's sign list LAK. The editors of ZATU claim that LAK61 is also an Early Dynastic successor of ZATU233, which they believe to be a GU_2. Camille Lecompte discussed the sign LAK61, but its meaning nevertheless remains unclear.[40] The frame of GU_2 appears in a number of other Fara period signs, LAK545–551. Only one among them, šembi($GU_2 \times SIG_7$ = LAK547) "kohl," suggests that GU_2 might be a representation of a vessel. Since cosmetics were stored in small containers, GU_2 would not be big enough to be a "load."

In summary, although it is certain that the original meaning of the Sumerian talent is "load," the reason why scribes related this idea with the sign GU_2 is uncertain. Some details allude to GU_2 as a small vessel in very early texts. It is possible that the semantic link between the two was of a purely phonemic nature. In simple words, the word for "load" reminded scribes of the word for a vessel, which scribes notated with a vessel-shaped sign, GU_2.

2.3 Gun_2 as a primitive measure "load"

Gun_2 as a primitive unit "load" predates the talent by at least several centuries. The "load" probably appears in the records of the Early Dynastic I–II period at Ur. In contrast, Early to Middle Sargonic documents are the earliest texts to record the talent.

The term "primitive unit/measure" requires an explanation and a definition. Powell utilizes the term "primitive" in his publications when referring to some containers and vessels. In doing so, he acknowledges the fact that they represented natural measures. My characterization of a "primitive unit" relies on the study of thousands of 4th and 3rd millennia BC administrative documents, and has the following characteristics.

First, a primitive unit originates in a real object: a vessel, a container, or some method of storage or transportation of goods. A classic example for this phenomenon is the Sumerian capacity measure $sila_3$, which was used for grain, flour, oil etc. The sign is a pictographic depiction of the so-called "beveled-rim bowl" of the archaeological Uruk culture of the 4th mill. BC. These bowls were produced in enormous quantities. It is hardly surprising, then, that some modern archaeologists believe that it was the vessel used to measure food allocations to

40 Lecompte 2014: 140–141.

workers during this period.[41] In this particular case, a container of a certain capacity leads to the emergence of a standardized unit.

This leads us to the second characteristic of a "primitive measure." All containers of the same "primitive measure" must be roughly of the same size. Otherwise, one person would starve while another would enjoy a larger share. Nevertheless, in contrast to a standard measure, which is an abstraction, an idea, a "primitive measure" is always something material: a vessel, a reed contained, an armful of flax, a load of rushes, etc.

The third and principal characteristic of a "primitive unit" is that it does not have any lower units. For example, the talent has 60 minas and the mina has 60 shekels. They are standardized units because of these actual mass relationships. The presence of subunits means that this measure must be a standard of some sort.

The primitive unit gun$_2$ "load" fulfills all these requirements. It definitely takes its roots in the practice of carrying goods by humans, not animals. Its weight and capacity were never clearly defined. A "load" of reed might have been about 30 kg for an adult man. The "load" did not have any subunits prior to the Sargonic period. The only exception that I will discuss in detail is six ŠE$_3$-ba-an in one "load" for fish in the archive of the ED IIIb Ĝirsu.

Of no less importance in drawing the line between the talent and the "load" is the nature of goods they intended to measure. Documents of the 3rd mill. BC illustrate that phytogenic materials of low value, such as timber, reed, and grass on the one hand, and fish on the other, were *transported, calculated*, and *recorded* in loads. The same documents provide abundant evidence that the talent was the uppermost measure in the system of weight units. In contrast, it was used to measure metals, wool, etc., but only from the Sargonic period on. Because of that, we will never find "one load of gold" or "one mina of fish" in the texts: These measures belonged to different systems, although both the primitive measure "load" and the standardized talent expressed the same necessity to know "how much." However, "how much of what" plays the crucial part here, since the choice of a mensuration unit depended largely on the value and physical properties of measured goods. The talent, once a part of the weight metrology and equal to 60 minas, measured valuable goods, whereas the "load" appeared with low-value goods throughout the whole 3rd mill. BC.

The scribes were aware of the difference. The talent and the "load" appear differently in script and the syntax shows which is which. The talent, like any other standardized unit of mensuration, appears in the syntactic construction

41 See Pollock 1999: 94–95.

"N MATERIAL gun_2."[42] For example, it is 1 siki gun_2, "one talent of wool." In contrast, the "load" appears in the usual Sumerian regens-rectum construction: "N gun_2 MATERIAL." It is, for example, 1 gun_2 gi "1 load of reeds."[43] Despite this clear-cut difference, which holds for pre-Ur III periods, editions of texts and secondary literature alike abound with confusions of these measures. Scholars recognized long ago that gun_2 with reeds and similar goods had nothing to do with the talent.[44]

Reeds and wood are the most common goods recorded in "loads" in 3rd mill. BC texts. In order to understand the reason for this, it is necessary to visualize the environment of southern Mesopotamia during the period under consideration. Owing to the revolutionary research by Jennifer Pournelle we now know that Lower Mesopotamia was either a temporal or permanent marshland in early historical periods.[45] A British traveler and adventurer, Wilfred Thesiger, who lived among marsh dwellers in southern Iraq in the 1950s, expressed the idea that ancient Sumerian cities were built in the marshes on man-created elevations, i.e. consecutive layers of reed and mud.[46] Now it is known that Mesopotamians built their temples, towns, and cities on the only elevations of the alluvium – the so-called "turtlebacks."[47] Since Sumerian civilization emerged and existed in marshes, reeds and clay were materials for virtually anything: tools, buildings, containers, fodder for animals, firewood, etc. My hypothesis is that the primitive measure gun_2 "load" originated precisely in the practice of transporting and accounting reeds using these measures by the early inhabitants of southern Mesopotamia.

The earliest attestation of wood measured in "loads" that I was able to identify appears in an Early Dynastic I–II text from Ur UET 2 241. Two people appear in connection to deliveries (?) of poplar in this document. The term gun_2 appears in the first line and may refer to all following entries. Each of them records three to 20 "loads of poplar" (gun_2 $asal_x$(LAK212)).

This sort of timber abounds in the Early Dynastic and later sources. The "loads" of poplar appear at Presargonic Ĝirsu.[48] Other types of wood that are measured in "loads" in the earliest sources are date palm (ĝešimmar),[49] apple

42 The only exception is when this is a text written by Semitic-speaking scribes who used the syntax of their language: "number – measure – measured."

43 Documents written in Akkadian language do not adhere to these rules. See ELTS: 11–12.

44 Westenholz 1987: 90 for the Sargonic period and Waetzoldt 1992a: 126 for Ur III.

45 Pournelle 2003.

46 Thesiger 1964.

47 Pournelle 2003: 16–17.

48 DP 59 obv. iii 19 f.

49 VS 25 68 rev. i 8 (ED IIIb Ĝirsu).

tree ($^{\hat{g}e\check{s}}$hašhur),[50] willow ($^{\hat{g}e\check{s}}$ma-nu),[51] fig tree ($^{\hat{g}e\check{s}}$peš$_3$),[52] a variety of fir tree $^{\hat{g}e\check{s}}$še-du$_{10}$,[53] a tree called $^{\hat{g}e\check{s}}$*zirum*,[54] etc. In the case of the apple tree, the document records the issue of 12 "loads" that make up 95 pieces in total. Sometimes documents provide extra information about the size of individual pieces, such as "large" or "small." No early texts deliver a clue to establish the absolute measure of any of these "loads." In all likelihood, these measures were arbitrary.

Various reeds and rushes appear more often than timber in "loads" in early cuneiform texts. The most important among them is gi, *qashab* in Arabic, the species *Phragmites australis*.[55]

The search for the earliest occurrences of gi in "loads" brings us to an interesting discovery. As with any other product, the scribes used the ubiquitous writing N gun$_2$ gi "x loads of reed" in Early Dynastic IIIa and later texts. The numerical system used to notate them was sexagesimal. In contrast, reeds were accounted without mentioning the term gun$_2$ "load" in Early Dynastic I–II sources. Moreover, the numeration in these cases is bisexagesimal. This system of numerical notation was used to record grain in a group of 4th mill. BC accounts.[56] Following the authors of ZATU, it is necessary to stress that the sign "120" (N_{51}) was not an intermediary between the numbers "60" (N_{34}) and "600" (N_{48}) of the sexagesimal numeration. The bisexagesimal system had a different sign for "60," which was N_{34}-*tenû* (a "bariga"-shaped sign); the largest numbers here are also different: "1200" is N_{54} and "7200" is N_{56}.

This detail is essential to account for the evolution of metrology and writing conventions. The bisexagesimal system of notation of reeds made way for the use of the sexagesimal system with the additional use of the logogram for "load." However, what units hid behind the bisexagesimal system in the case of the reeds' notations? Since the bisexagesimal system was used to record a rich variety of goods in Uruk IV–III and ED I–II text, it seems that it was merely a numerical system and each of the measured types of goods required its specific measure, container, vessel, etc. For example, bread is accounted in the bisexagesimal numbers in some Early Dynastic I–II accounts.[57] We know from

50 DP 491 obv. i 2 (ED IIIb Ĝirsu).
51 Genava 26 1 obv. iv 2 = Sollberger 1948 (ED IIIb Ĝirsu).
52 CT 50 72 rev. i 6 (CS Sippar).
53 CUSAS 19 213 (CS uncert.): various timber sorts in "loads."
54 Cripps 2010 no. 41 rev. 5: 10 gun$_2$ $^{\hat{g}e\check{s}}$*zi-ri$_2$-im*.
55 Pournelle 2003: 213.
56 "System B"; see ZATU: 132, 165.
57 UET 2 37 obv. ii 1, 3: 1N_{51} ninda-sag$_8$, and 2N_{51} ninda-gal-gal. For another example with bread, see the list of bread allocation UET 2 55 obv. i 1 f.: 2N_{51} ninda: Nanna-ur-saĝ etc.

later cuneiform sources that the usual practice was to count bread in loaves. Another example: Grain appears in the bisexagesimal numbers in some early grain texts.[58] There must have been a unit of capacity behind this number in this case.

What about the reeds counted in the bisexagesimal system? To cite some examples, WF 146 from ED I–II Šuruppak records 60 (1$N_{34\text{-}ten\hat{u}}$×60) to 720 (5N_{51}×120) "measures" of gi reeds. Another text of the same date, UET 2 37, from Ur records 1200 (1N_{54}) gi reeds in a list of commodities. Relying on the evidence of the ED III and later periods, it is likely that a primitive measure "load" (gun$_2$) or another one, the "bundle" (sa), is hiding behind these archaic numbers in ED I–II texts.

This conclusion holds for early accounts of wood as well. In an ED I–II record of reed, wood, and wood implements, UET 2 25, wood appears in the bisexagesimal system too. Since gi-gal-gal "large reed" is accounted in "loads" in later times,[59] it is suggestive that this method of calculating applied to the timber in this case (obv. i):

8N_1 gi-gal-gal	8 (loads of) large reeds;
1N_{51} 1$N_{34\text{-}ten\hat{u}}$ 3N_{14} ĝeš-MUŠ$_3$-GI	210 (120+60+30 loads? of) . . . wood[60];
1N_{51} 1$N_{34\text{-}ten\hat{u}}$ 6N_1 ĝeš-tur-tur	186 (loads? of) small wood;
2N_{14} 6N_1 $^{\hat{g}e\check{s}}$har	26 wooden logs[61];
2N_1 $^{\hat{g}e\check{s}}$ma-dul$_x$(BU)	2 wooden poles.

In a recent edition of the document WF 146, the authors make a remark that a fishing gear si-NU×U was also accounted in the bisexagesimal system in the early texts.[62] Indeed, many texts from ED IIIa Šuruppak record si-NU×U in the bisexagesimal system.[63] However, other texts from the same archive use the sexagesimal system for the same object.[64] Later Early Dynastic and Sargonic documents illustrate that the same object was accounted in pieces *and* its weight was provided too. For example, 15 si-U-NU-saĝ: ki-la$_2$-bi 3 ma-na, "15 fine *siUNU*-ropes: their weight is 3 minas (= 12 shekels apiece)." This confirms the idea expressed

---

58 For an example with grain, see NISABA 25 6 obv. 1. The number is probably "120."

59 See Molina 2014: 116 no. 103 obv. 1.

60 See UET 2 230 obv. i 1' for 26 large pieces of this timber: 26 ĝeš-gal-gal GI-MUŠ$_3$.

61 For a discussion of $^{\hat{g}e\check{s}}$har(-an), see Molina 2014: 185.

62 Krebernik, Steible, Yildiz 2014: 343–344 for Šuruppak texts of ED I–II that use the bisexagesimal system.

63 DP 36, TSŠ 369, 415, 627, 737, 969.

64 TSŠ 424, 430, 748, WF 142.

above that the bisexagesimal system functioned on the numerical and not on the metrological level. Some goods that were later accounted in "loads," weight, and capacity measures as well as in pieces were counted in the bisexagesimal system during the Uruk IV–III and until the ED IIIa period.

Returning to the use of the "load," rushes $ninni_5$ and "grass" u_2 were also counted in this primitive measure. In an ED IIIa text from Šuruppak FTP 83, a huge number of 480 "loads" of grass appears (obv. i 1). It also appears in loads in later texts.[65]

The number of goods counted in "loads" increases considerably after the Fara period. They belonged principally to two groups. The first includes reeds and grass, timber, vegetables, and greens. The second includes fish and seafood. Many of these records mention other primitive units besides gun_2 "load." They are sa "bundle," a basket kab_2-ku, another sa "net," and a net or a rope for fish $ŠE_3$-ba-an. In the following, I will briefly discuss these primitive units of mensuration in order to show that the "load" did not have any application in the area of weight metrology and goods associated with it.

Sa is "bundle," Akkadian *kiššu*. It should not be confused with another sa "net," Akkadian *šētu*, a method of transportation of fish and onions.[66] In contrast, sa as the "bundle" appears in connection to reed, flax (gu), and branches of various trees.[67]

Westenholz recognized that gun_2 is not a unit of weight in connection to bulbous plants ($šum_2$) in Sargonic texts. In contrast, this measure appears in close connection to sa "bundle" and is not related to the mina or any other weight measure. He suggests that gun_2 is "sackload" and compares it with the Old Assyrian measure *naruqqum* "sack," which was equal to four *karpatum*, "pots," and 120 *qû*.[68] Bearing in mind that this *qû* was less than Sumerian $sila_3$, one arrives at about 60 liters for one *naruqqum*, the rough equivalent of one talent. However, the extrapolation of these data on the earlier periods would be anachronistic. The evidence illustrates that the number of sa "bundles" and sa "nets" in one gun_2 "load" varied. This shows that neither of them was a standardized unit and a high precision of measurement was not required in these cases.

For example, CUSAS 11 240 from Early Sargonic Adab begins as follows: *12* $šum_2$ gu_2 / *40* sa "12 loads of onions: (=) 40 bundles." This makes one "load" of 3 1/3 "nets." A Classical Sargonic account of onions, CUSAS 26 207, has a different

65 Selz 1989/90: 37 obv. iv 1 (ED IIIb Ĝirsu) for 5 gun_2 u_2 and Cripps 2010 no. 41 (Classical Sargonic Umma) for 120 gu_2 u_2.

66 Heimpel 1998: 238 f.

67 Steinkeller 1987a: 93.

68 Westenholz 1987: 90.

ratio: 10 gu_2 $šum_2$-gaz / gu_2-bi *60* sa-ta "10 loads of crushed onions: its load is 60 nets," that is, one "load" has 60 "bundles."

The number of "bundles" in a load varied in Sargonic and Ur III records alike.[69] For example, one "load" has six "bundles" of reed according to the Ur III account MVN 14 471. In contrast, MVN 16 1042 states that 25 "loads" of reed are equal to 20 "bundles," which makes one "bundle" slightly larger than the "load." A similar ratio of "one load = one bundle" appears in another Ur III record, UTI 4 2833: Ten "loads" of ^{ĝeš}ma-nu "willow" represent ten "bundles." A "bundle" almost twice as small is present in UTI 5 3036: 20 "bundles" make 12 "loads" in this case.

Documents provide information about the weight of goods recorded in "bundles" very rarely. A text from Middle Sargonic Adab accounts 270 bundles of flax and states that their weight is four talents (=240 minas).[70] This implies by no means a standardized "bundle" of 0.888 mina.[71] The examples above illustrate that a "bundle" could easily be 60 times more if needed.

Another primitive measure that often appears in context with the "load" is kab_2-ku/-ku_5/-kul/-gul, Akkadian *kabkūru*. According to Steinkeller, this was a container made of wood, reeds, or leather. Its purpose was to store weapons, house utensils, musical instruments, etc.[72] Documents from Presargonic Ĝirsu show that these baskets were produced from twigs of apple tree and poplar.[73] The container kab_2-ku_5 appears to be one of the main means of transportation of bulbous plants ($šum_2$) and coriander (še-lu_2) in the "Onion Archive" from the Sargonic Nippur, which documents horticultural activities.[74] The same onions and coriander that appear in kab_2-ku_5 baskets appear in gun_2 "loads" too.[75] This practice is likely related to the physical properties of the plants. Bulbs are much easier to transport in baskets. It is much handier to carry grass-like coriander and onions with leaves bound in "loads." There is no direct relationship between the "load" and the basket, kab_2-ku_5. The measure that appears in all of the documents of the "Onion Archive" is usually the lid_2-ga. This was the unit of the capacity system equal to 240 $sila_3$/liter. This means that gun_2 "load"

69 See Molina 2014: 115, commentary to no. 100 obv. 1. In no. 102, Molina shows that each "load" had five "bundles." The term sa "bundle" does not appear in the text, though.

70 CUSAS 20 254 obv. 1–2: [180+] 90 gu sa: ki-la_2-bi 4 gun_2.

71 See SCTRAH 116 for 86 bundles of flax fibers measured by a one-talent stone. They weigh two talents, which makes one "bundle" about 1.39 mina.

72 See Steinkeller 1991 with Waetzoldt 1992b.

73 DP 418 obv. i 1 (^{ĝeš}hašhur), Nik 1 282 obv. i 3 (^{ĝeš}$ildag_4$).

74 See Westenholz 1987: 87 f.

75 For example, OSP 2 128, 131–132, 147, 178 (onions), 138, 178 (coriander).

functioned as an auxiliary unit with goods that were measured by the capacity system. This exemplifies the flexibility of any "primitive" unit and of the gun$_2$ "load" in particular. Whereas a standardized measure's application is limited to its own system, a primitive unit finds itself useful in different systems.

The last primitive unit that appears in connection to the "load" is ŠE$_3$-ba-an. It appears only in context with fish and seafood and only in Presargonic Ĝirsu.[76] Gebhard Selz discussed the term and attempted to interpret it in terms of metrology.[77] The striking fact about the "load" and the measure ŠE$_3$-ba-an is that one "load" is uniformly divided into six ŠE$_3$-ba-an units. No other primitive unit had this strictly defined relationship that is a characteristic of standardized measures. This led Selz to regard this "load" as the "talent" of 60 minas and equal to 30 kg. This would produce a ŠE$_3$-ba-an of 10 minas. Further, he compared this alleged measure with the capacity measure ban$_2$. It was equal to six sila$_3$/liters in Presargonic Ĝirsu. He advocated this by suggesting that ŠE$_3$-ba-an could be interpreted as eše$_2$-ba-an /eše$_2$=ban$_2$/, the "rope-ban-measure."

The theory by Selz would provide the earliest known ratio between capacity and weight measures: 10 minas = 6 sila$_3$. However, this is hard to prove, since we need to know the absolute metric values of the Presargonic Ĝirsu sila$_3$ and the mina on the one hand and the standard Akkadian sila$_3$ and the mina of the Sargonic period on the other. The Sargonic evidence shows the ratio 1 sila$_3$ = 2 mina in weight. At Presargonic Ĝirsu, 6 sila$_3$ = 10 mina makes a slightly different but comparable ratio. If the mina's weight was the same in both cases, this would result in a Ĝirsu sila$_3$ 1/5 smaller than the standard Akkadian one. In fact, there is evidence that makes the Ĝirsu sila$_3$ 1/3 larger than its Akkadian peer.[78] Hence, if we stick to the hypothesis by Selz, one ŠE$_3$-ba-an equal to one ban$_2$ (= six Ĝirsu sila$_3$) would be equal to nine standard Akkadian sila$_3$, that is, 9 liters. This would produce a "load" of 54 liters of fish (9 liters × 6 fraction ŠE$_3$-ba-an in a "load"). This fits badly into the talent of 30 kg. Besides, several other considerations do not allow us to conclude

---

76 These fish are ^{ĝeš}ĝeštu$^{\text{ku6}}$-dar-ra and -su-su (FAOS 15/2 66), kin$^{\text{ku6}}$ (DP 284, FAOS 15/2 66, VS 25 50), ubi$_x{}^{\text{ku6}}$-(dar-ra) (DP 283, VS 25 29), and ku$_6$-dar-ra (BIN 8 356, DP 40 and 57, VS 14 172).

77 Selz 1995.

78 Powell 1990: 502 argues that the measure dug "jar" contained 20 Ĝirsu sila$_3$ during the Presargonic period and had been reformed to contain 30 Akkadian sila$_3$ in the course of the Sargonic reform. If we assume that the absolute metric measure of the "jar" in both cases is the same, this would result in a Ĝirsu sila$_3$ 1/3 larger than the standard Sargonic one.

that the "load" of the Presargonic Ĝirsu fish accounts represents the standardized unit "talent."

First, no weight measures appear in these texts. We have only the "load" divided into six ŠE$_3$-ba-an. Second, neither the construction ki-la$_2$-bi "its weight" nor the verb la$_2$ "to weigh" is present. Finally, fish was never measured by weight in early Mesopotamia: It appears either piecewise or in capacity units. Nevertheless, the suggestion to interpret ŠE$_3$-ba-an as eše$_2$-ba-an "rope-*ban*" is probably correct. This relates this unit to capacity metrology and implies a container or other means of transportation made from ropes.[79] It would be a convenient way to carry fish.

This discussion leads to the conclusion that the case of gun$_2$ and ŠE$_3$-ba-an is analogous to the example of gun$_2$ and kab$_2$-ku$_{(5)}$. Gun$_2$ as the primitive measure "load" appeared side by side with other primitive measures and means of transportation of certain goods that were otherwise measured in capacity units. These details portray the role of the primitive unit "load" as a jack-of-all-trades in the Early Dynastic mensuration practices.

2.4 Gun$_2$ as a standardized weight measure "talent"

Gun$_2$ as a standardized measure of weight emerges only at the beginning of the Sargonic period as a result of the Sargonic reforms. This fact has not been recognized so far despite the obvious absence of gun$_2$ in Early Dynastic accounts of metals and wool.[80] These materials were counted in minas as early as the ED I–II and ED IIIa periods, respectively. This predates the use of the talent in the same role by at least several centuries. For a detailed discussion on the Sargonic reform in metrology, see Chapter 6.

The mina was the highest unit in the system of weight measures during the whole Early Dynastic and probably the earliest part of the Early Sargonic periods. The "load" remained unrelated to the mina or any other weight measure. As a result, we find numbers of minas that are equal to or exceed "60," thereby implying that neither the link between the talent and the mina nor its ratio of 1:60 attested from the Sargonic period on existed at that date.

79 Cf. ^{ĝeš}ba-an "(wooden) ban" in *OB Nippur Kagal* 547 and ^{dug}ban$_2$ "(clay pot) ban" in Sallaberger 1996a: 98.

80 This discovery was presented in detail by the author in January 2014 as an invited lecture at the Consejo Superior de Investigaciones Científicas, Instituto de Lenguas y Culturas del Mediterráneo y Oriente Próximo in Madrid, Spain. The author is grateful to Professor Manuel Molina for the invitation and hospitality.

One of the earliest examples of the phenomenon appears in the *Enhegal Tablet* from ED IIIa Ĝirsu, a register of field sales.[81] It records a large number of minas in its total: $1N_{45}$ $3N_{34}$ 40 uruda ma-na, “3820 minas of copper” (rev. i 3). Other amounts of copper in minas in the text are 120, 200, 300, 360, 420, and 720. The term gun_2 is missing in the document.

A critical reader might suggest that the talent might be “hiding” behind the numerical signs N_{45} “3600” (= 60 talents) and N_{34} “60” (= 1 talent). However, clear evidence suggests that N_{34} is the number for “60 minas” without any underlying metrological meaning. For example, a document from Presargonic Ĝirsu provides the following enlightening evidence[82]:

$2N_{34}$ a-ru_{12}-da ma-na	120 minas of copper
$5N_1$ an-na $zabar_3$ ma-na	5 minas of tin (for) bronze

There are no “small” N_1 numbers in the entry with the copper, which would suggest that the “large” number N_{34} stands for the weight unit talent. A supporter of “the hidden measures” theory would expect the writing *$2N_{34}$ a-ru_{12}-da (gun_2), which is not present. The document explicitly states that there are 120 minas of copper. Another Presargonic document, this time from Nippur, is even more convincing. It shows the use of the number N_{34} as “60” with both the “load” and the mina[83]:

$1N_{34}$ $ninni_5$ gun_2	60 loads of *ninni*-rushes
$1N_{34}$ gu-gada ma-na	60 minas of flax fibers

There are other documents that illustrate the high numbers of minas instead of talents during the Early Dynastic and, probably, as late as the Early Sargonic period.[84] Since the talent did not exist during that time, some ambiguous passages in cuneiform text editions should be corrected accordingly.[85]

---

81 ELTS 20; see p. 72 for Steinkeller’s remark on the inadequacy of the copy of the numerical notation in obv. i 2 in the original publication.

82 RTC 19 obv. iv 4–5.

83 ECTJ 91 obv. ii 2–3.

84 DP 171 rev. viii 1, 194 obv. iii 4, 512 obv. i 1 (all ED IIIb Ĝirsu), OSP 1 109 obv. i 2 (ED/ES Nippur), CUSAS 26 265 i 2 (ED/ES uncertain provenance).

85 For example, FAOS 15/1 300 obv. i 1 must be corrected. Instead of [1 gun_2 25] ma-na $^{šim}bulug_x$(ŠIM×$UH_{3\text{-}tenû}$), it must be [85] ma-na $^{šim}bulug_x$.

As for the earliest appearance of the real talent, it is found in the *Maništusu Obelisk* that originates from Sippar or Akkade.[86] "1 talent 2 minas" and "3 talents 33 minas silver (as) the price of a field" appear in B ii 2 and C viii 1. This example is important for the discussion since it allows us to date the earliest appearance of gun_2 as the "talent" of 60 minas. I have cited above several documents that use large numbers of minas instead of the talent, and that may be dated to the Early Sargonic by paleographic considerations. In contrast, other Early Sargonic documents use the talent alongside the mina. This raises a question: When and where exactly did the scribes begin to notate the measure talent in script? The *Maništusu Obelisk* is crucial in this respect since it is the only accurately datable document. The beginning of the paleographic stage "Middle Sargonic" is often associated with Maništusu.[87] The previous paleographic stage, "Early Sargonic," is reserved by some scholars for the reigns of Sargon and his son Rimuš. However, the publication of an Ur III copy of the *Sumerian King List* by Steinkeller mixed all the cards: Maništusu appears as the successor of his father Sargon and hence is the predecessor of his brother Rimuš.[88] It is not the place here to decide which of the two brothers sat on his father's throne first or whether the documents of Maništusu's reign should be related to "Middle Sargonic" script. What is possible here is to create two data sets: the documents in which some goods are measured in minas only on the one hand, and the documents where we find the same goods in talents and minas alike on the other.

Gu(-gada) "(flax) fibers" appears only in minas in Early Dynastic and Early Sargonic texts.[89] However, notations with "talents" abound in the Middle Sargonic accounts of flax fiber from Adab. One among them is dated to the "Early / Middle Sargonic" by the editors.[90] An example with siki "wool" is less equivocal. The mina is the highest unit of mensuration of wool from Early Dynastic IIIa on. Scribes began to notate wool in talents during the Early Sargonic period, which is evident in a number of examples from Adab and Umma.[91] There are several Sargonic accounts from Adab where wool appears in talents and minas that I have attributed to the "Early Sargonic" date in their publication,[92]

86 See ELTS 40 and Westenholz 1999: 47 fn. 138.

87 Maiocchi 2015: 72.

88 Steinkeller 2003: 272.

89 See OIP 14 61 (ED/ES Adab) for 165 and 110 gu ma-na and ECTJ 91 (ED/ES Nippur) for 60 gu-gada ma-na.

90 An Adab document CUSAS 20 18 is ES/MS whereas nos. 255–260 are of the MS date.

91 BdI 1 40 and 42 and Nik 2 52.

92 CUSAS 35 250 and 251.

although they might be somewhat younger. Numerous Middle Sargonic texts record wool in talents and minas alike.[93]

Resins such as eren "cedar," šurmen "cypress," and *supālum* "juniper/pine resin" appear in talents no earlier than the Classical Sargonic period. Accounts of metals are equally unhelpful in the clarification of the "date of birth" of the talent. Zabar "bronze" and ku_3-sig_{17} "gold" are measured in talents not earlier than the Classical Sargonic period.[94] The same applies for uruda "copper": Documents of the Early Sargonic date show that large quantities of copper in minas were not converted into talents.[95]

This discussion shows that the talent appeared in script as a weight measure not earlier than a certain point during the Early or Middle Sargonic period. This event may be synchronous with the reign of king Maništusu. The talent is missing in the "Meskigala tablets" from Adab, which are synchronous with the reign of the founder of the Akkadian dynasty, Sargon.[96] This data allow me to suggest that the *terminus ante quem* of the Sargonic reform in the case of the talent is the reign of the successor of Sargon, be that Rimuš or Maništusu.

Having discussed the "when" of the question, it is time for its "how." One of the Middle Sargonic documents about measuring flax in talents opens with the following passage[97]:

230 la_2 1 gu gun_2	230 minus 1 talents of fibers
na_4 1 gun_2-ta	according to the stone (weight) of 1 talent

This document illustrates the change in the mensuration practice. As mentioned before, gu(-gada) "(flax) fibers" appear only in minas before the Middle Sargonic period even if the number of minas is equal to or exceeds "60." The present text shows that the standardized talent had already been introduced and appears in it. The second line unreservedly states that weighing is the way to measure flax. Additionally, the text alludes to the practice of measuring some bulk goods by weight using large one-talent stone weights and corresponding large balances. Texts from the Ur III period confirm that these tools were not very precise. They document stones of (a) one talent and 1 1/3 mina,

93 For example, CUSAS 20 172 and the following and SCTRAH 59 and the following.

94 Bronze: OAIC 7 obv. 2 (CS Ešnunna), RTC 255 obv. 1 (CS Ĝirsu). A large amount of gold appears in ECTJ 51 obv. 17 (CS Nippur): "1 talent minus 2 ⅔ minas gold."

95 Examples: CUSAS 11 112 obv. ii 1 (ES Adab), BIN 8 100 obv. i 1–5, 309 obv. i 1–2 (ES Umma), OSP 2 44 obv. i 2 (MS Nippur).

96 Cf. Marchesi 2015: 152 on Meskigala.

97 CUSAS 20 256.

(2) one talent and 1 2/3 mina, and (3) one talent and two minas.[98] Wool is a substance that is measured by these stones in all cases. An example from Puzriš-Dagan has the following[99]:

24 gun_2 siki $\hat{g}ir_2$-gul	24 talents of wool from dead sheep:
na_4 1 gun_2 1 2/3 ma-na-ta	(measured) according to the stone (weight) of 1 talent 1 2/3 mina.

I explain this phenomenon in Chapter 7. In brief, large one- and multi-talent stone weights were imprecise and probably very old. Nevertheless, Ur III officials proceeded to use them and marked the mass of these stones in standard minas in order to arrive at the correct quantity of wool measured by these inaccurate stones. One should relate the practice of the use of these Ur III "one-talent plus something" stones to the notation "according to the one-talent stone weight" in Middle Sargonic text from Adab: Sargonic scribes were also conscious that these large weights were imprecise. It is worth noting, however, that the examples of the Ur III "one talent plus something" are always heavier and never lighter than one talent. Additionally, the round numbers of the excessive mass (1 1/3, 1 2/3, and 2 minas) are suspiciously round. Hence, alternative explanation of this remarkable phenomenon are possible.

From the Early Sargonic period on, gun_2 represented two metrological realities. On the one hand, the talent of 60 minas belonged to the system of weight measures. On the other hand, the "load" did not die out: Most of the goods measured in "loads" in previous periods were still measured in "loads" during the Sargonic and Ur III periods, i.e. reeds, fish, etc. We do not find them in minas or lower units in these records. The explanation of this phenomenon is simple. No one needed a precise way to measure goods of low value. As previously mentioned, weight metrology is the metrology of expensive and luxury goods.

2.5 The fractions of the talent

The "load" as a primitive unit did not have fractions since its mass and/or capacity were not clearly defined by their users. The only exception is the "load" in the combination with the measure for fish, $ŠE_3$-ba-an, in Presargonic

98 SAT 3 1274 obv. 2 (1 gun_2 1 1/3 ma-na-ta), AAICAB 1/1 pl. 59 1924–553 obv. 2 (1 gun_2 1 2/3 ma-na-ta), AUCT 3 192 obv. 2 (1 gun_2 2 ma-na-ta).
99 For example, NISABA 30 77 obv. 1–2 (Ur III Puzriš-Dagan).

Ĝirsu. However, this was not a fraction in the strict sense of the word but a separate unit.

The fractions of the talent were only introduced at the end of the 3rd mill. BC, during the Ur III period. Earlier documents never mention fractions of the talent. The reason for that is that there was no practical need for them. One half of the talent appeared as thirty minas, a third was twenty minas, etc. Thirty-mina stone weights appear in Ur III inventories.[100] More often, ten-mina stones appear immediately after one-talent stones, thereby omitting any in-betweens.[101] This shows that the real weighing practice dictated the rules of the game. When there was a need to measure something of about half a talent, the weighmaster took three ten-mina stone weights.

The fractions of the talent that appear in Ur III cuneiform texts correspond exactly to the writing of the fractions of the mina. This means that they were adopted from the mina as a result of the Ur III reform of metrology.[102] Chapter 4 details how the same thing happened to the fractions of the shekel. The Ur III fractions of the talent are:

½ ⅓ ⅔ ⅚

As already noted by Walther Sallaberger, the green fodder reed gi-zi was measured in weight units during the Ur III period.[103] Indeed, the majority of Ur III documents that record the fractions of the talent deal with this commodity. Other goods appear much more rarely. However, there are very few texts where the measure gun$_2$ appears in one entry with other weight measures. In one example, a document has both the fraction ½ of the talent and the unit shekel. The number is large and the precision of measurement of the reed is amazing: 1647 talents 10 shekels of the gi-zi reeds.[104] Nevertheless, as other data discussed in this book

100 CUSAS 3 1372 obv. i 6–7 (Ur III Garšana).

101 AAICAB 1/3 pl. 206–207 Bod S 138 rev. i 1–2 (Ur III Umma) and UET 3 272 rev. vii 10–11 (Ur III Ur).

102 Examples of the talent's fractions: YOS 4 301 obv. 1, 11, CST 207 obv. 1.

103 Sallaberger 1989: 314.

104 AAICAB 1/1 pl. 053 1919–11a–b obv. 1 (Ur III Puzriš-Dagan[?]).

suggest, these bulk goods – even if not being counted in "loads" – were measured by large imprecise weights and balances. The example with calculations of reeds in shekels should be interpreted as accounts not of the actual but of "virtual" calculated totals of reeds. The universal lack of lower weight measures in these texts is suggestive. As a mental experiment, it is worth imagining Ur III weighmasters using one-talent stone weights and large balances while determining the fractions of these imprecise "talents" by eye without any auxiliary mina weights. This suggestion finds support in the fact that valuable materials such as gold, silver, etc. never appear in fractions of a talent.

The materials that appear in the talent's fractions in Ur III records belong to two groups. The first group includes goods that were accounted by weight measures, such as wool and bitumen.[105] Goods that were previously measured in "loads" constitute the second group. Here, the talent and its fractions apply to twigs of willows[106] and poplars,[107] to reeds gi-ru-uš,[108] to wooden planks,[109] and similar goods of plant origins. Additionally, the fractions of talent were applied in Ur III records to goods that were usually measured by capacity units.[110] These are deviations, whose nature still needs to be clarified.

These Ur III data show the expansion in the use of the talent in comparison with the preceding Sargonic period. Additionally, it shows that the primitive unit "load" was almost ousted from usage.

2.6 Conclusions

The talent, a unit of about 30 kg, was the largest measure in the Mesopotamian system of weights from the Sargonic period onwards. The Sumerian word for this measure, gun_2, "load, burden," implies an archaic practice of carrying loads of certain goods. This "load" was a primitive unit during the Early Dynastic period. It did not have a standardized mass. Nor did it belong to any of the standardized systems of mensuration. It appears in the Early Dynastic I–II data and beyond as a means of transportation and storage of certain types of goods: reeds, rushes, grass, brushwood, fish, and onions. Relying on our present knowledge about the ecology of southern Mesopotamia during the 4th mill. BC

105 MVN 16 1226 obv. 1, PDT 209 obv. 1.
106 BIN 3 617 obv. 1.
107 Hirose 322 obv. 6.
108 ITT 2 631 obv. i 2.
109 BPOA 6 997 obv. 3.
110 CT 10 pl. 20–23 BM 14,308 rev. v 9 and UET 3 171 obv. 1.

as a marshy landscape, it is likely that the "load" as the prototype of the later measure "talent" originated in the practice of cutting and transporting various sorts of reeds and "timber," that is, thin stalks and branches of the local varieties of trees.

The clue for the distinction between the "load" and the talent is the division of the latter into 60 minas. The archives of Ebla (ca. 2350–2300) are suggestive in this respect since the talent is missing there as well. While Sumerian scribes counted large amounts of minas in their sexagesimal system of numeration, the Eblaite scribes used their decimal system and recorded *mi-at* "hundreds" of minas.[111]

The weight standard of the talent as the "child" of the Sargonic reform in the earlier part of this period relied on the cumulative mass of 60 standard minas. Originally, only a few materials were measured in talents: metals, aromatic substances, wool, flax fibers, colorants, and glue. Ur III records witness a rapid expansion of the application area of the talent. As a result, the application area of the primitive measure "load" narrowed considerably.

111 See ARET 2 4 rev. ix 1 and passim at Ebla: gu_2:an-$še_3$ 1 mi-at 56 ma-na ša-pi 5 $giĝ_4$-DILMUN "total: 156 ⅔ minas 5 shekels." See Archi 1987: 81–82 for other examples and a discussion of the large quantities of minas in the sums of Eblaite accounts.

3 Mina: The cosmopolite

3.1 The etymology of ma-na

There is much to note about the mina, the second largest unit in the Sumerian system of weight measures. It is the earliest unit that is documented in known written records. It appears for the first time in the Early Dynastic I–II administrative records from Ur and Šuruppak, ca. 2800–2700 BC. I will argue below that the mina, alongside the shekel, stood at the origins of the weight metrology in Mesopotamia.

Unlike all other words for weight measures, the word "mina" is the only word of Semitic origin, along with the words for its fractions. This is striking at first glance. In this chapter, I will concentrate on elucidating this phenomenon, which eventually tells us much about the early use and origins of weight metrology in Mesopotamia.

It is a widespread opinion among Semitists and cuneiform scholars that the Sumerian writing of the unit ma-na is a loanword from the Akkadian,[112] or, rather, early Semitic. This word belongs to one of the earliest layers of Semitic loanwords in Sumerian.[113] Similarly to dam-gara$_3$, the Akkadian *tamkārum* "merchant,"[114] ma-na is a purely phonetic writing with the characteristic /=a/ ending.

The fact that "mina" and "merchant" in Sumerian belong to the same temporal and cultural ("trade") layer is suggestive. These two facts are likely related to the copper (or, more generally, metal) trade with the regions rich in copper and/or run by Semitic-speaking merchants. The analysis of the data in Chapter 10 arrives at the same conclusion. The written records mention the Persian Gulf (Dilmun and Magan), Iran (Elam), and the Indus culture (Meluhha) as the main trading partners of Sumer. Nevertheless, all these written data originated from the most southern cities of Sumer (mostly from Ĝirsu) and are dated to ca. 2400–2000 BC. This means that the written data are biased and indicates only that Ĝirsu got its copper from the East in the second half of the 3rd mill. BC. Cities to the north may have received their copper from other sources. However, most importantly, the use of the mina to measure copper and the words

112 Powell 1971: 210.

113 According to Civil 2007, the earliest Semitic loanwords in Sumerian have the pattern silim; the next layer is the words that have an ending /-a/ and the most recent includes the words with the ending /-um/.

114 See Krebernik 2016.

https://doi.org/10.1515/9781501510267-003

ma-na and dam-gara₃ are older than these Ĝirsu data by at least 400 years. This means that the two facts – the Semitic ma-na and its use to measure copper in ED I–II texts – should not be automatically linked to the copper trade between Sumer and the Gulf. In line with archaeological data of the Late Uruk period ("the Uruk expansion"; Algaze 2008: 68 f.), the trade route via the Euphrates to Turkey may be an alternative explanation of the existence of the Semitic ma-na as a measure for copper in the ED I–II data.

Walter Sommerfeld questions the Semitic origins of the term ma-na in his critical reconsideration of Semitic words in the earliest cuneiform records.[115] He argues that the phonetic writing of the term ma-na does not automatically mean the word was Semitic. His critique centers on the nominal pattern of the word that had bred the Sumerian ma-na. Nevertheless, he does not mention the fact that the mina's fractions one-third and two-thirds are definitely of Semitic origins. Besides, below I dismiss the widespread idea that ma-na originates from *manā'-*, which appears, for example, in the Old Assyrian.

I agree that the presence of the Akkadian verb *manā'um* (later *manû*), "to count," and of the substantive *manû(m)* "mina" does not prove the Semitic origin of the Sumerian ma-na. The basis for this lies elsewhere. It is necessary to consider the possibility that the Akkadian word is not a direct descendant of the original Semitic word but of the Sumerian ma-na instead. In simple terms, there was an early Semitic word that was borrowed into Sumerian, and then this Sumerian word (ma-na) was borrowed back into Akkadian.[116]

Relying on the above-mentioned Akkadian word *manû* "to count; mina," Powell argues that ma-na means "counter." He suggests that it was the fraction "1/60" of a talent, thereby defending his theory that the talent defined the mass of all lower weight measures.[117] However, he stands up for the idea that the mina was the unit "par excellence in the system" in another place.[118]

To begin with the last point, the mina is too heavy to be a "counter." A unit of ca. 500 g would have been unwieldy in real-life trade and financial activities. Merchants needed a smaller unit. The discussion in the next chapter suggests that the shekel must have been much more practical in this respect.

---

115 Sommerfeld 2006: 63–64. See there also for the earliest references to the term from ED I–II Ur. The present author identified these two references independently in 2010 while working on his Ph.D. thesis. Another two references in unpublished documents mentioned by Sommerfeld do not concern the unit mina. It is a personal name in both cases.

116 An alternative possibility would be to derive ma-na from a Semitic word of the pattern *ma-PRaS*. This would require a root with two weak radicals ('^{x}n'^{x}).

117 Powell 1971: 210.

118 Powell 1971: 226.

The analysis in Chapter 10 suggests that the mina was the best way to measure copper, whereas most valuable goods were measured in shekels and barleycorns.

The next issue is the morphological pattern of the early Semitic words behind the term ma-na. Ignace Gelb believed its root to be **mnw* or **mnj*.[119] Semitists reconstruct the originally biliteral root as **man-* "to know, to test, to try." One argues that "the meaning 'test, try' may be the most archaic in this group of words, serving as a source of other meanings connected with intellectual activities as such." In contrast, the Semitic representation of this root is **mnw* with the basic meaning "to count."[120] This makes Powell's interpretation of ma-na as "counter" theoretically possible. The lack of the semantics of weighing or measuring in this word should not be surprising. Other words for weight units lack this semantics as well. The only exception is the Akkadian *šiqlum* "shekel" which means "the weighed." Other Sumerian and Akkadian terms do not have anything to do with weighing or mensuration at all. Both gun_2 and *biltum* "talent" mean "load," $gi\hat{g}_4$ "shekel" is actually "axe," and še and *û* mean simply "barley(corn)."

The reconstruction of the original Semitic word behind the borrowed word ma-na is challenging. It is definitely not the *manû(m)* of the 2nd and 1st mill. BC Akkadian texts. Besides, the form **manā'um* that appears in standard Akkadian vocabularies is nonexistent and should be abolished, since MA.NA is always a logogram in 3rd mill. BC texts. Hence, these writings tell us nothing about the phonemic structure of the word.

The lengthened vowel in the ending of the Akkadian *manû(m)* is a typical feature of Sumerian borrowings into Akkadian. This also suggests that *manû(m)* is not the direct descendant of the original Semitic word.

The *terminus ante quem* for the borrowing of the original Semitic word into Sumerian is the beginning of the 3rd mill. BC. At some point afterward, the word ma-na must have produced the Akkadian word **mana'um* > *manû(m)*. The exact date of this event is difficult to pinpoint since there are no phonetic writings of the word for "mina" in 3rd mill. BC documentation. Note that the verb *manû(m)* "to count" appears no earlier than the Old Babylonian and Old Assyrian times. This allows us to think that the Akkadian word for "mina" and the verb **mana'um* "to count" came into colloquial Akkadian during the Sargonic or Ur III period. This back borrowing must have been borrowed then into Aramaic, Hebrew, Egyptian, and Greek.

119 MAD 3: 179.

120 Orel and Stolbova 1995: 373.

What is the original pattern of the early Semitic word? Taking it at face value, it might belong to the nominal pattern *PaRS-*. Such words in Akkadian are the primary inherited Proto-Semitic substantives such as *kalbum* "dog," *eqlum* "field," *mārum* "son," etc.[121] This would result in **manwum* > **mānum* but not *manû(m)*. This is another argument against the traditional view that the Akkadian *manû(m)* originates directly from the early Semitic word.

The original Semitic word underlying ma-na may not be a primary substantive but a nominalized verbal form instead. The nominal pattern *PiRS-*, as in *šiqlum* "weighed" = "shekel," can be dismissed because of the impossibility to explain the phonetic development **minwum* > ma-na. The pattern *PaR(V)S* seems to be the only choise. Examples are *rapšum* "wide," *damqum* "good," *zīzum* "divided," and *warqum* "green, yellow." The original early Semitic / Akkadian "mina" may have belonged to this pattern. The phonemic structure of the original word is thus **man(V)wum* > **mānum*.

The meaning of this early Semitic word is uncertain. Relying on *zīzum* "divided" and similar words, it may have had a passive meaning. This leads to the interpretation of "the counted" instead of Powell's "counter." What, then, was "counted" in the case of mina? It may have been 60 shekels. Nevertheless, we have too few data currently for any credible suggestion. We know for certain that the mina was the means used to account copper and wool in the first place during the Early Dynastic period.

3.2 The earliest use of the mina

The unit ma-na was written using the sexagesimal system of numeration with its usual "round" signs for "1," "10," and "60" (= N_1, N_{14}, and N_{34}, respectively). "Pointed" numbers for the mina appear simultaneously with the "round" ones in the Early Dynastic period. They are usually oblique. A group of Classical Sargonic texts offers a remarkable exception, a local and temporal idiosyncrasy to notate minas of wool. The numerical sign N_8 appears instead of N_1 for "1" in them.[122]

Previously it was believed that the mina, like any other weight measure, appeared for the first time in the Early Dynastic IIIa documents from Šuruppak. One only hypothesized that the minas could be much older.[123] The sign combination MA NA is present in Late Uruk texts. However, the contexts suggest that

121 Von Soden 1995: 71.

122 CBS 8800 and other CS Nippur texts that record this practice will be published soon by Aage Westenholz as OSP 3.

123 Powell 1990: 508–510.

this was a personal name.[124] Currently, we have data on the mina from the Early Dynastic I–II Šuruppak and Ur.

UET 2 127 is an account of copper, copper objects, and oxen. Its total records a large area of cultivated land, which is followed by the oxen and the unidentified copper objects. This peculiar combination implies that the document concerns the cultivation of land.[125]

obv. i	[2 DUG]-uruda Diĝir-nu-me	[2 copper . . .]: Diĝirnume
	2 DUG-uruda	2 copper . . .:
	Lu$_2$-na-nam	Lunanam;
	60$^?$ uruda-NI ma-na	**60 (?) minas of . . . copper:**
	Kisal-si	Kisalsi;
	10 uruda ma-na	**10 minas of copper,**
	⌜1⌝ anše-DUN.GI	1 horse:
	MA-ZA$_7$	MAZA
	⌜2⌝ DUG-uruda	2 copper . . .:
	[break]	. . .
ii	**53 uruda ma-na**	**53 minas of copper:**
	Kisal-si	Kisalsi;
	2 gu$_4$	2 oxen:
	Aja$_2$-UET 2 no. 48 (=LAK 62$^?$)	Aja. . .;
	2 DUG-uruda	2 copper . . .:
	Aja$_2$-Abzu-si	Aja-Abzusi;
	1 gu$_4$	1 ox:
	Amar-lal$_3$	Amarlal;
	2 DUG-uruda	2 copper . . .:
	Lu$_2$-na-nam	Lunanam;
	1 gu$_4$	1 ox:
	⌜Arad$_2$⌝(⌜NITA$_2$⌝.KUR)-Utu	Arad-Utu;
	3 DUG-uruda	3 copper . . .:
	[break]	[. . .]
iii	2 DUG-[uruda]	2 [copper] . . .,
	1 gu$_4$	1 ox:
	Ušumgal	Ušumgal
	2 DUG-uruda	2 copper . . .:

124 MS 2515 obv. iv 6 (unpublished, Uruk III uncert.), MSVO 4 80 (Uruk III Ešnunna) obv. ii 1–3.
125 Texts that were published in UET 2 are situated in three different museums, the British Museum, the University of Pennsylvania Museum of Archaeology and Anthropology, and the National Museum of Iraq in Baghdad. Unfortunately, the present text belongs to a group of UET 2 texts that were lost or remain unlocated. This excludes the possibility of collating it.

	⌜Mes⌝-gi	Mesgi;
	2 gu$_4$	2 oxen,
	1 DUG-uruda	1 copper . . .:
	[. . .]-si	. . .si;
	20 [uruda ma-na]	**20 [minas of copper:]**
	[. . .]	[. . .]
	2 DUG-uruda	2 copper . . .:
rev. i	[. . .]⌜x⌝ [. . .]	. . .
	2 gu$_4$	2 oxen:
	Ama-bur-si	Amabursi;
	3 DUG-uruda	3 copper . . .:
	Ušumgal simug	Ušumgal, the smith.
	(blank space)	
	⌜aša$_5$ Nanna⌝	The field of (the temple household of the moon god) Nanna.
ii	(blank space)	
	aša$_5$ gu$_2$-an-še	Total: 304 iku cultivated land;
	1(bur$_3$'u) 6(bur$_3$) 2(eše$_3$) 4(iku)	
	APIN	
	5 gu$_4$	5 oxen;
	17 DUG-uruda	17 copper . . .
	(blank space)	

This text is remarkable in many ways. It concerns the cultivation of fields that belonged to the temple household of the city-god of Ur, the moon-god Nanna. Here, this text reminds us of later Early Dynastic documents concerned with the record of subsistence fields allocated to the members of central households. Another detail is that neither the sum of oxen in the main text nor the sum of the copper object DUG-uruda corresponds to the numbers in the total. The totals are less than the sum of individual entries. Besides, neither the horse nor the copper in minas appears in the total. Finally, the individuals who do not appear with the mysterious DUG-uruda objects (probably not to be related to dug "pot") are recorded with the amounts of copper in minas instead. This means that copper and these copper objects were equivalents in some way. The variety of copper uruda-NI (obv. i 4) is otherwise unknown.[126] Each recipient of

126 It reminds us of gag-uruda "copper nails" in later documents. However, there is no way to collate the tablet to check the sign in question.

copper in UET 2 127 appears in the context of 10 to 60 minas. These are considerable amounts. They are comparable to the amounts of copper as prices for fields and houses in the Šuruppak legal documents. Nevertheless, it is hard to say whether the copper was used as money in this document since the administrative procedure behind it is not entirely clear. These minas of copper, copper objects, and animals may have been payments to the temple for the use of the fields.

UET 2 252 is another text from ED I–II Ur that mentions ma-na. Fortunately, this account of sheep is somewhat easier to interpret. Some of the individuals that appear in it are the same as in the previous one. Most people appear in the context of one or two sheep. Two people have as much as six animals. In rev. i 2–3, a certain Munus-kalag$_x$(GIŠGAL) is the only person in the document who appears in the context of a mina of copper (1 uruda:ma-na) instead of sheep. The subscript of the document provides the name Igi-ša$_3$, who is the ugula "overseer." It is likely that UET 2 252 records a receipt of sheep by the temple of Nanna. Munus-kalag$_x$ had no sheep to give and gave a mina of copper as the equivalent. This and, possibly, the previous document may illustrate the role of copper as means of payment in the Early Dynastic I–II period. The documents of the following ED IIIa period confirm this use of copper in early Mesopotamia.

WF 128 from ED I–II Šuruppak may record the unit "mina" in relation to copper as money too.[127] This document is in many ways similar to UET 2 252. It is an account of sheep, a clarified butter in one case, and one mina of copper in three entries. Just as in UET 2 252, individuals without sheep appear with one mina of copper. The document also ends with the personal name of an individual who bears the title "overseer." Editors of this document remain unsure as to whether the text is an allocation of goods.

Another text from Šuruppak Š 692 offers the earliest example of an object whose weight is recorded.[128] This is a copper libation vessel TUN$_3$-la$_2$ weighing five minas. See Chapter 10 for a discussion on this document.

Ma-na appears in numerous documents of the following periods. It is frequent in Early Dynastic IIIa documents from Šuruppak that record land and house purchases. The mina appears very often in the documents – administrative and legal alike – of the Early Dynastic IIIb and succeeding periods of Mesopotamian history. The scarcity of attestations of the mina in Early Dynastic I–II texts should not lead to the conclusion that the system of weight was undeveloped during this time. Considering the meager amount of ED I–II documents

127 Krebernik, Steible, and Yildiz 2014 no. 14.
128 Ib. no. 10.

and the fact that almost all of them come from Ur, the rarity of references to weight metrology is not surprising.[129] Nevertheless, now we know that the system of weight measures is older than was previously believed. Additionally, it is evident that copper belonged to the earliest goods measured by weight. The situation is similar in the following ED IIIa period. The use of the mina and the weight metrology in general was confined to the measurement of two groups of commodities: (1) metals (copper, silver) and their products, and (2) wool, flax, and their products.

The application area of the mina was slightly broader in the following ED IIIb period. Besides the above-mentioned two groups, various resins joined the "family" of goods measured in minas. The Sargonic period did not alter the relatively narrow circle of the goods accounted in minas. The Ur III period added somewhat to the number of commodities measured by weight. Nevertheless, the area of application of the mina remained quite conservative throughout the whole 3rd mill. BC.

The mina remained the highest unit in the system until some point during the Early or Middle Sargonic period.

3.3 The fractions of the mina: Two Early Dynastic scribal traditions

The original fractions of the mina are half, one-third, and two-thirds. The fractions "one-fourth" and "one-fifth" of the mina did not exist in the 3rd mill. BC. There are rare mistakes by ancient scribes that are sometimes incorrectly interpreted as fractions.[130]

The notation of the mina's and the shekel's fractions differed before the Ur III period.[131] All fractions of the mina except "half" employed the initial sign ŠU$_2$ to write the words šušana "one-third" and šanabi "two-thirds" in the ED IIIb period. Earlier writings of these fractions (šu$_2$-1N$_8$-ša-na and 2N$_8$-ša-na-bi/pi) show that the sign ŠU$_2$ was reserved only for the fraction "one-third" as a phonetic indicator. Just as ma-na, šušana and šanabi are loanwords from early Semitic. They appear for the first ime in the texts of the Early Dynastic IIIa period.

---

129 See Bartash 2015a for a discussion on the recent work on these texts.

130 An example is the erroneous interpretation of the sign 2(ban$_2$) as the fraction "1/4" of the mina in the first line of Nik 2 56 by Foster 1982c: 32. La$_2$×2(ban$_2$) is a scribe's mistake. He corrected it afterwards with the notation la$_2$×2. The correct transliteration of this line is 16 ≪la$_2$×2 (ban$_2$)≫ la$_2$×2 ma-na igi-3-ĝal$_2$ "16 minas minus 2 ⅓ (shekels)."

131 See Powell 1971: 131 ff.

However, the existence and use of them and the fraction "half" of the mina in the ED I–II period are very likely.

Kingusila is the word for the fraction "five-sixths" in Sumerian. It is completely missing in the documentation of the previous periods since it was an innovation of the Ur III period. Bram Jagersma proposed a plausible etymology for this Sumerian word: /giĝ$_4$=u=sil=a/ "ten shekels split off," that is, 60–10=50 shekels.[132] The writing of kingusila(ŠU$_2$+3(DIŠ)) follows the scribal logic of šušana(ŠU$_2$+1) and šanabi(ŠU$_2$+2). However, it betrays its artificial nature. The two original fractions use the numbers "one" and "two" after ŠU$_2$ to allude to "one-third" and "two-thirds." The Ur III writing of kingusila as "three-thirds" makes no sense. In addition, the word for the fraction "five-sixths" begins with ku… and not with šu… This shows that the Ur III scribes had no idea why the Early Dynastic scribes had decided to use the sign combination ŠU$_2$+N.

The following figure presents the "standard" writings of the mina's fractions as they appeared in 3rd mill. BC texts. I discuss them in detail below. The transliterations I use for them throughout the book appear in parentheses.

	Early Dynastic IIIa to Sargonic (26–22 c. BC)	**Ur III (21 c. BC)**
Half mina	 (1/2)	 (*1/2*)
One-third mina	 -ša-na ($^{\text{šu2}}1N_8{}^{(\text{ša-na})}$)	 (ša) ($^{\text{šu2}}1N_8{}^{(\text{ša})}$)
Two-thirds mina	 -ša-ba-bi/pi ($^{\text{šu2}}2N_8{}^{(\text{ša-ba-bi/pi})}$)	 (ša) ($^{\text{šu2}}2N_8{}^{(\text{ša})}$)
Five-sixths mina	(did not exist)	 (ša) ($^{\text{šu2}}3N_8{}^{(\text{ša})}$)

The *Early Dynastic Practical Vocabulary B* is the earliest lexical composition that documents weight measures.[133] Its well-preserved manuscripts are SF 20 from

132 Jagersma 2010: 265.

133 See Veldhuis 2014b: 119–123. For a passage with weight measures, see Civil 1982: 5. There are no editions of the complete composition yet. See Civil 1982 for a partial edition.

Early Dynastic IIIa Šuruppak (EDPV B) and CUSAS 12 6.3.1 of the same date but of uncertain provenance (EDPV B_2). Nevertheless, these documents differ considerably in the writing of the fractions of the mina. This suggests their origins in two different scribal traditions. SF 20 offers the Šuruppak or "standard" writings, that is, the way the fractions appear in the most Early Dynastic documents from southern Mesopotamia known to us currently. In contrast, CUSAS 12 6.3.1 presents the writings of the mina's fractions how they appear in the Early Dynastic IIIb texts from the Umma city-state. I subsume these diverging writing habits under the name "the Umma scribal tradition" throughout the book.

Weight measures appear not as abstract units, as in CUSAS 12 6.3.1, but in combination with copper in SF 20. The scribe of SF 20 used this section of the lexical list as a template for everyday administrative work with copper. Obviously, it is no accident that the material in question is copper and not another. This corroborates the data on the importance and use of this material in the early sources discussed in this study.

It is necessary to stress that the list of copper in minas in SF 20 is not the list of actual balance weights. There are indeed lists of weights in 3rd mill. BC lexical and administrative texts alike, which I discuss in Chapter 7. However, weights appear in these sources as na_4 "stone." Additionally, copper weights appear neither in the written nor in the archaeological evidence from early Mesopotamia.

The following is the passage of interest in SF 20[134]:

obv. v 22	1 uruda ma-na	1 mina copper
23	$2N_8$ $ša_4$(DU)-na-bi uruda	⅔ mina copper
24	½ uruda ma-na	½ mina copper
25	$šu_2$-$1N_8$-$ša_4$-na uruda	⅓ mina copper
26	⸢a(ZA)-ru_{12}-da^{uruda}⸣	copper[135]
vi 1	$MUŠ_3^{uruda}$	copper (see Chapter 10)
2	*5* uruda $gi\hat{g}_4$	5 shekels copper
3	*3*$^?$ uruda $gi\hat{g}_4$	3$^?$ shekels copper
4	*2(AŠ.AŠ)* uruda $gi\hat{g}_4$	2 shekels copper
5	*1(AŠ)* uruda $gi\hat{g}_4$	1 shekel copper

134 As in any other ED IIIa and earlier text, the direction of reading is not "left to right." Neither is it strictly "right to left." In the present case, the scribe put first the mark for a lexical entry ("1"). It does not appear in the transliteration. Then he put the number to the left. This is followed by the commodity that was placed to the right. The middle of the entry was filled with the remaining signs.

135 I thank Manfred Krebernik for providing me with his copy of SF 20, which facilitated the interpretation of this line.

The following writing habit that appears in this text applies to administrative and legal texts as well: the term ma-na is missing from the fractions one-third and two-thirds in cases when there are no whole minas. For example, “6 2/3 minas of copper” is written $6N_1$ $2N_8$ uruda ma-na. In contrast, “2/3 minas of copper” is simply $2N_8$ uruda.[136]

Civil (2008: 87) interprets MUŠ$_3^{uruda}$, which also appears in the *Early Dynastic Practical Vocabulary A* 142, as “weight.” However, as the discussion in Chapter 10 shows, this was simply another writing of “copper.” Its appearance in the middle of the list of weight measures with copper must have been a misplacement.

As previously stated, CUSAS 12 6.3.1 represents a different scribal tradition. This results in a considerably different section of weight measures. As in SF 20, the weight measures appear in the context of metals: Metal objects precede and follow the section on the weight measures. However, first, in contrast to SF 20, the weight measures in CUSAS 12 6.3.1 appear without any metal. Second, CUSAS 12 6.3.1 has a considerably longer subsection on the shekel. It meticulously puts down all numbers from “one” to “ten” then followed by “15.” However, the most striking difference lies in the writing of the fractions of the mina (obv. vi 6–8). The following figure compares the writings in CUSAS 12 6.3.1 with those in SF 20[137]:

	ED IIIa Šuruppak (SF 20)	**ED IIIa Umma (CUSAS 12 6.3.1)**
Two-thirds	 ša$_4$-na-bi	 giĝ$_4$ (2N$_8$ giĝ$_4$)
Half	 ma-na	 ma-na
One-third	 -ša$_4$-na (šu$_2$-1N$_8$-ša$_4$-na)	 giĝ$_4$ (šu$_2$-1N$_8$ giĝ$_4$)

136 SEL 19 1–4 obv. i 1 and WF 151* obv. iii 5; both ED IIIa Šuruppak.

137 This peculiarity of CUSAS 12 6.3.1 has been erroneously interpreted as a mistake by Civil. The transliteration of the mina’s fractions is his interpretation and does not show what really appears on the tablet. His commentary in CUSAS 12: 211 6:8 should be taken critically.

The writings of the mina's fractions as they are in CUSAS 12 6.3.1 appear in Early Dynastic documents from the Umma region (cities of Umma, Ĝeša, Zabalam, and KiAN). Its writing for "half" was preserved even in the Sargonic documents from that region, which stresses the persistence of the local scribal "school."

The Umma writings differ from the "standard" writings represented by the Šuruppak tradition in two ways. First, there is a special sign for "half." Second, there are no phonetical complements after the numbers for the fractions "one-third" and "two-thirds" that would facilitate their interpretation as the Sumerian words šanabi and šušana. In contrast, the term $gi\hat{g}_4$ "shekel" appears after these numbers for the mina's fractions. All this concerns the graphics but the latter has metrological implications. The writings with $gi\hat{g}_4$ show that the Ummaean scribes understood "one-third" and "two-thirds" of the mina as twenty and fourty shekels respectively. This must have been a secondary development, an offshoot of the "standard" tradition. Otherwise, the writing $šu_2$-$1N_8$ $gi\hat{g}_4$ makes little sense linguistically since the sign $ŠU_2$ is certainly a phonetic complement facilitating rendering $ŠU_2$-$1N_8$ as šušana "one-third." The writing of gig_4 "shekel" after these numbers indicates that the "Umma" scribes did not know about the original meaning of the sign $ŠU_2$ in this context. Obviously, these Umma writings show the preference by the local scribes to verbalize these writings as "20 shekels" and "40 shekels."

Remarkably, the "Umma" writings of "one-third" and "two-thirds" ($^{šu2}1N_8$ $gi\hat{g}_4$ and $2N_8$ $gi\hat{g}_4$) appear in several Presargonic texts apparently from Adab. The reason is uncertain. The usual Adab writings are $^{šu2}1N_8$ for "one-third" and $2N_8$ ša-na-pi for "two-thirds." However, CUSAS 35 7 obv. ii 10 and iii 2 has $^{šu2}1N_8$ $gi\hat{g}_4$ "1/3 (mina as 20) shekels" and $2N_8$ lagab za:gin_3 $gi\hat{g}_4$ "a lapis-lazuli lump of 2/3 (mina as 40) shekels," respectively. The presence of igi-*3*-$\hat{g}al_2$ $gi\hat{g}_4$ "1/3 shekel" in obv. iv 1 excludes the possibility of interpreting these writings as the fractions of the shekel. Another example of $^{šu2}1N_8$ $gi\hat{g}_4$ as "20 shekels" appears in CUSAS 35 8 obv. ii 8 where it is a part of a person's possessions. Both texts are dated by the reign of two ED IIIb Adab governors. Therefore, their Adab origin is very likely.

The Umma scribal tradition disappears from the script after the Sargonic period. It is definitely related to the decline of Umma as an independent political power after the Early Dynastic period and probably also due to ecological changes in this micro-region.[138]

A somewhat similar idiosyncrasy appears in Presargonic texts from Isin. These writings combine the mina's notations of the fractions "1/3" and "2/3"

138 See Bartash 2015b for a recent overview of the "Umma debate."

with respective phonetic complements with the term giĝ$_4$ "shekel." It is šu$_2$-1N$_8$ ku$_3$ ša-na giĝ$_4$ in two texts, which should be interpreted as "one-third (of a mina as 20) shekels."[139] Another one provides an even odder one: šu$_2$-1N$_8$ igi-*4*-ĝal$_2$ ša-na giĝ$_4$ "one-third (of a mina) and one-fourth of the shekel."[140] It is uncertain whether this idiosyncrasy may be related to similar data from Umma and Adab. If they were indeed related, they represented a tradition parallel to that of Šuruppak, Nippur, and Kiš. If so, we should speak about these data from Isin, Adab, and Umma as representing a different scribal tradition.

The post-3rd mill. BC lexical data provide the writings of the mina, which correspond exactly to the writings on the Ur III sources. This means that the Early Dynastic Šuruppak tradition remained the standard in the whole of southern Mesopotamia during the 3rd mill. BC. The principal lexical sources on weight measures of the later date that has the mina's fractions are the lexical compositions *Ea* and *S^b*. The most complete and important in this respect is *Ea* I 342 ff.[141] The following figure summarizes these data:

Line	**Sum. phonetic writing**	**Sign**	**Akkadian name of the sign**	**Akkadian subcolumn**
342	šu$_2$-u$_2$		*bar-te-nu-u* "An oblique sign BAR"	*e-re-bu ša$_2$* ^{d}*Šamši*(UTU)^{ši} "sunrise."
356	šu^{sic}-ša$_2$-na		MIN *de-eš-še-ku* "an oblique BAR sign (with) a sign DIŠ"	*šu-uš-ša$_2$-an* "one-third"; CAD Š^3: 384.
360	ša$_2$-na-bi		*bar-te-en* min-na-bi "A sign BAR (with a number) 'two'"	*ši-ni-pu* "two-thirds"; CAD Š^3: 43.
366	kin-gu-sil-la		MIN *gi-di-ri-gu-u* "oblique BAR sign with an extra wedge"	*pa-ra-as-rab* "five-sixths," lit. "big part"; CAD P: 164[142].

S^b II 48, 50, and 52 do not provide any further information.[143] The compilers of these 1st mill. BC lexical lists erroneously believed that the basic element in the

139 MVN 3 13 obv. ii 5, iii 2 and MC 4 4 rev. iii' 1' (ED IIIb Isin).

140 Lambert 1979 obv. i 6, x 13; Wilcke 1996: 47–67.

141 MSL 14: 194 ff.

142 The term is opposed by *paras-ṣehru* "one-third" of a shekel (lit. "small part") in later sources.

143 MSL 3: 134.

writing of the fractions was the sign BAR. They mistook it for a part of the number. However, as the earliest lexical evidence (SF 20) explains, ŠU_2 was originally the phonetic complement in the writing of the mina's fraction šušana "one-third."

Relying on this discussion, it is possible to discern several periods in the use of the mina's fractions "one-third" and "two-thirds." The first (ED IIIa, partly ED IIIb) is characterized by a conscious use of the writing ŠU_2-N_8 for "one-third" only. The documents of the second period (ED IIIb on) use this notation indiscriminately for both fractions. This shows that Presargonic scribes in some locations had no idea why and how these fractions were written originally.

3.4 The "half" of the mina

The writing of the fraction "half" is the same for both the mina and the shekel.  ($1N_8$×*DIŠ*) as the "Umma" variant of this sign appears in both the Early Dynastic and Sargonic sources from that region. However, it is missing in the Ur III records. Evidently, this should be related to the reforms of the first kings of this dynasty.

The origins of the "standard" and the "Umma" signs for "half" are obscure. These graphemes appear neither in Late Uruk nor Early Dynastic I–II texts. The Umma "half" is somewhat similar to the Late Uruk sign N_2 in ZATU. However, the latter designated "one-tenth" of a pot of clarified butter and had nothing to do with weight metrology.[144] The numerical sign N_8 ("bariga") designated "half" or "one-tenth" in the Late Uruk sexagesimal and bisexagesimal systems for measuring grain and related products.[145] The same grapheme appears in Early Dynastic texts as half of the area measure iku.[146] Its name is ubu or upu.[147] However, this is not the Sumerian word for "half" par excellence. This word refers to the form of the sign. Note that in 3rd mill. BC Umma texts, ubu as a half-iku had a different form: It is identical to the general Umma variant for "half" ($1N_8$×*DIŠ*).

It is likely that Early Dynastic scribes invented two different signs for "half" of the mina and the shekel ($1N_8$×*AŠ* and $1N_8$×*DIŠ*) to tell them apart from the units and their fractions in other systems of mensuration that were written simply as N_8: the *bariga* of the capacity measures and the half-iku in area mensuration.

144 Englund 1998: 168.
145 Englund 2001: 4.
146 TSŠ 53 obv. ii 3 f. (ED IIIa Šuruppak).
147 See Powell 1990: 480 and *Ea* II 200 = MSL 14: 256 and CAD U/W p. 16 *ubû*.

The standard sign for “half” in its “round” ($1N_8$×*AŠ*) and “pointed” (“MAŠ”) forms appeared in the Early Dynastic IIIa period and beyond.[148] Like all other “round” numbers, the “round” form gradually came into disuse during the Ur III period. The same “round” “half” was used from Early Dynastic IIIa onwards to notate a half of a *sar*, an area unit of ca. 36 m^2.[149] However, I will show below that the origins of this notation should be related to the weight metrology, from where it was borrowed into the notations of other metrological systems.

The earliest attestations of the Umma sign for “half” are synchronous with the standard, Šuruppak writing. Its “round” ($1N_8$×*DIŠ*) and “pointed”  forms also appear in different systems of mensuration.[150] It designated a “half iku” in area mensuration in documents from the Umma region.[151]

Classical Sargonic archives from Sippar and Mugdan use the same Umma writings for the halves of the mina and the shekel.[152] Nevertheless, the scribal practices of these two central Babylonian localities are related neither to each other nor to the Umma scribal tradition of the Early Dynastic period. The Sippar text in question has the “Umma” writing for the half-mina whereas the half of the shekel is written in a standard fashion. This local and temporal idiosyncrasy was likely a conscious choice to differentiate between the halves of these two weight units, which is a unique practice. As for the Mugdan data, I discuss them in the following chapter.

What word hid behind the two writings for “half-mina”? In contrast to its fractions “one-third” and “two-thirds,” whose readings are clearly present in their phonetic complements, the case of the half-mina is not so lucid.

To begin with, it is unknown whether the half-mina and the half-shekel had different words in Sumerian. We know that the fractions “one-third” and “two-thirds” of the mina on the one hand, and of the shekel on the other, were expressed by different means. Hence, the presence of the single word “half” in English does not mean that Sumerian limited itself to the single word too. There were several words for “half.” Their use depended on the context. For example, the word sur/sur$_3$ designated a half of a bread. Powell identified three Sumerian words for “half” in different metrological contexts: šu-ri-a, sa$_9$(MAŠ/

148 See CT 50 9 obv. i 6 (ED IIIa Šuruppak?). However, the “round” form prevails during the Early Dynastic period: see WF 32 obv. iv 6 (ED IIIa Šuruppak) and ELTS 15 obv. i 3 (ED IIIa Adab).

149 MVN 10 82 rev. ii 2 (ED IIIa Šuruppak?).

150 BIN 8 53 obv. i 4 (ED IIIb Umma region) and MC 4 28 obv. ii 1 f. (CS Umma).

151 CUSAS 33 129 rev. ii 2’ (ED IIIb Umma region) and passim in Umma land records.

152 CT 50 72 obv. ii 7 (CS Sippar).

BAN$_2$), and ba$_{15}$(BAR). He reveals inconsistencies in the later understanding of the sign MAŠ/BAR in lexical sources, which were connected to the fact that MAŠ and BAR had the same graphic form in the 1st mill. BC.[153] This writing has an equivalent *mišlu(m)* "half" in Akkadian.[154] Powell illustrated in his later publication that "half-shekel" was expressed by the word *zūzu* in Akkadian from at least the middle of the 2nd mill. BC. Its Sumerian equivalent was likely /ba/.[155] The phonetic spelling ba$_3$(EŠ$_2$) of the shekel's "half" in Ur III and Old Babylonian sources supports this suggestion.[156] The discussion of ba$_{15}$(BAR) as the writing of the shekel's "half" in early texts from Isin in the next chapter corroborates Powell's conclusion. It is, therefore, possible that this Sumerian word originated in the verb ba "to allot, to divide up, to share."[157] However, all these data refer to the "half" of the shekel. No extant evidence alludes to the pronunciation of the "half-mina" in Sumerian. It may or may not be the same as the half-shekel.

3.5 Etymology of šušana and šanabi

Powell argued that the word šušana "one-third" had been used initially for "one-third mina" only. He etymologizes its Akkadian equivalent *šuššān* as "a pair of sixths," which would be the dual form of **šuššum* (<**šudšum*) "one sixth."[158] Wolfram von Soden also interprets Akkadian *šuššān* as "two-sixths." He adds that it is uncertain when and where this word was used.[159] This Akkadian word never appears outside the lexical compositions. Semitic languages have a different word for "one-third" in the context of measures. It originates in the word for "three": for example, it is *šalšu(m)* in Akkadian and *šlṯ* in Sabaean.[160]

Powell strengthens his argument that *šuššān* goes back to the practice of dividing the mina into six parts by noting that "a number of weight specimens having a mass of 1/3, 1/2, 2/3 and 1 mina are marked 2, 3, 4 and 6 respectively".[161] It remains unclear, however, to which time these weights belong. If they are late, they prove nothing. Similar marks appear on the weights from the Palace G at

153 Powell 1971: 138, 155–161.
154 See CAD M/2: 126, lexical section.
155 Powell 1979: 99. Note that according to MZL, the values of BAR and MAŠ are ba$_{15}$ and ba$_7$, respectively.
156 PSD B: 23.
157 PSD B: 2.
158 Powell 1971: 162, 224 f.
159 Von Soden 1995: 116 §70 h.
160 Von Soden 1995: 116 §70 h; Stein 2013: 107.
161 Powell 1979: 104.

Ebla. The study by Alfonso Archi discovered that they designated five (not six) parts in one mina. This mina of ca. 470 g had 50 shekels of about 9.4 g, the so-called "Syrian shekel." However, this mina of 50 shekels never appears in the Ebla documentation. Instead, the same mina of 60 shekels of 7.8 g (the "Phoenician shekel") is used throughout northern Syria and as far east as Mari.[162] The division of the mina into five parts as a characteristic of coastal Syria, Palestine, and Egypt reminds us of the Semitic decimal system. In contrast, several Sumerian systems of mensuration widely use the factor "six": six iku in one eše$_3$ in land mensuration and six še "barleycorns" in one šu-si "finger" in length mensuration.

This shows that even if the division of the mina into six parts ever existed at some point, it would have been a Sumerian invention. As a wild guess, let us imagine that at some point the unit "mina" was a primitive measure unconnected to the shekel or any other weight measure. For example, it might be represented by copper ingots of about 500 g.[163] It would be handy to divide them into two parts and then each piece into three more. This would bring us to the six parts in one mina. However, this mental reconstruction is hard to reconcile with the Semitic word for "one-third" of the mina, **šuššān*. Obviously, both the mina and its fractions "one-third" and "two-thirds" allude to a very old socioeconomic and linguistic reality in Mesopotamia of which we currently know virtually nothing.

What about "two-thirds"? Powell, alongside Akkadian dictionaries and grammars, accepts the suggestion by Goetze and a Hebrew analogy *pī šnaim* to support the interpretation of šanabi as a composite word *šina* + *pûm* "two + mouth" with the difference that he believed it to be "two holes."[164] Neither "two holes" nor "two mouths" have any lucid metrological semantic, although the writing 2N$_8$ of "two-thirds" of the mina does indeed look like two holes. This stands in stark contrast to the word for "one-third" with its clear-cut metrological semantic of six parts in one mina. According to this line of logic, the original Early Semitic word for "two-thirds" of the mina must have meant literally "two twos," that is, the four of six parts in the mina. Such a word appears in Old Babylonian as *šittān* "two twos."[165] This illustrates that the division of the mina into six parts is theoretically possible for some periods of Mesopotamian history. Currently, the theory by Albrecht Goetze that šanabi is a borrowing from Early Semitic instead of Akkadian is the only founded one.[166] I believe

162 Archi 1987: 47–51.

163 See Algaze 2008: 76 for copper axes of roughly the same weight found in the Late "Uruk expansion" outpost Jebel Aruda, which Algaze interprets as ingots.

164 Von Soden 1995: 116 §70 i; AHw: 1242; CAD Š^3: 44; Powell 1971: 225; Powell 1979: 104.

165 CAD Š/3: 134–136.

166 Goetze 1946: 202 n. 81.

that ma-na, šušana, and šanabi share the same origins and date of borrowing somewhere in the late 4th mill. BC. Consequently, similarly to Sum. ma-na > Akk. *manû*, both the Akkadian words *šinipu* "two-thirds" and *šuššān* "one-third" are likely late 3rd mill. BC borrowings from Sumerian into Akkadian.

The idea that šušana means "two-sixths" has an important metrological implication: It refers to an archaic mensuration practice of dividing the mina into six parts. *Šuššu* (**šudšu*) is the Akkadian word for "one-sixth" that appears in the context with the mina. It had been borrowed into Sumerian as šuš.[167] This shows that in contrast to Semitic, Sumerian originally lacked the word for "one-sixth." The construction igi-6-ĝal$_2$ "one-sixth" was used with many measures. However, it was not applied to the mina. Nevertheless, this archaic practice (if it ever existed) is never explicitly referred to in the written data of the 3rd mill. BC: "10 shekels" appears instead of "one-sixth mina."

This does not exclude the possibility that the mina with its fractions has emerged as a primitive weighing practice in the context of the copper trade with Iran and Turkey via Semitic merchants or suppliers during the "Uruk Expansion" of the 4th mill. BC in trading emporia such as Hacinebi Tepe.[168]

3.6 Šušana and šanabi in time and space

As I have already explained above, the earliest writings of the mina's fractions "one-third" and "two-thirds" appear in two scribal traditions in Early Dynastic IIIa lexical and administrative texts. The better-represented, Šuruppak, "standard" tradition used 2N$_8$ ša$_4$-na-bi for šanabi "two-thirds" and šu$_2$-1N$_8$-ša$_4$-na for šušana "one-third." In contrast, the local Umma tradition used the writing 2N$_8$ giĝ$_4$ and šu$_2$-1N$_8$ giĝ$_4$ instead. The subsequent periods document various local and temporal idiosyncrasies in the writing of these fractions of the mina. The most visible trend is the north-south discrepancy.

The documents from a number of cities in northern Babylonia follow the tradition of the Šuruppak lexical lists and keep the original, correct writings during the Early Dynastic IIIb period. In contrast, documents from southern cities use the phonetic complement šu$_2$ indiscriminately for both šušana "one-third" and šanabi "two-thirds." They were simply not aware of the original meaning of the sign ŠU$_2$ and mistook it for a part of the number notations.

167 Goetze 1946: 202.

168 See Algaze 2005: 71, 75–78, 130–131.

Another major observation from the temporal and local overview of the writings of "one-third" and "two-thirds" of the mina is that the first attempt to bring clarity in this matter should be ascribed to the Sargonic reform. The ultimate standardization of these writings happened during the Ur III period: The writing šu$_2$-N$_8$-ša became the standard one for the fractions "one-third," "two-thirds," and the freshly invented "five-sixths." The following figure provides the data for these conclusions. It follows the geographical arrangement: Ebla as the western point of the "cuneiform world" of the 3rd mill. BC and then Mari and northern Mesopotamian cities such as Gasur and Ešnunna, and, finally, cities of central and southern Babylonia. The sites whose archives yield meager or uncertain data are not considered (Fig. 3.1).

	ED IIIa	**ED IIIb**	**Sargonic**
1. Ebla	**(no data)**	**ŠU$_2$+ŠA** **ŠA-PI**[169]	**(no data)**
2. Mari	**(no data)**	**(no data)** **šu$_2$-2N$_8$-ša** (MARI 5 2 obv. ii 6–7)	**(no data)**
3. Gasur (Nuzi)	**(no data)**	**(no data)**	**šu$_2$-1N$_8$-ša** **šu$_2$-2N$_8$-ša** (HSS 10 169 obv. 9–10)[170]
4. Ešnunna	**(no data)**	**(no data)**	**šu$_2$-1N$_8$-ša** (MAD 1 188 obv. i 8) **šu$_2$-2N$_8$-ša-pi** (MAD 4 2 obv. 1)
5. Sippar	**(no data)**	**šu$_2$-1N$_8$** (ELTS 36 obv. v 14) **(no data)**	**šu$_2$-1N$_8$-ša** (CT 50 72 obv. ii 2) **(no data)**
6. Mugdan	**(no data)**	**(no data)**	**šu$_2$-1N$_8$-ša-na** (MAD 5 101 obv. ii' 4) **(no data)**
7. Kiš	**(no data)** **⌜2N$_8$⌝ ša-pi** (ELTS 16a ii 8')	**šu$_2$-1N$_8$-ša** AAICAB 1/1 pl. 8 1928–439	**šu$_2$-1N$_8$-ša** (MAD 5 9) **(no data)**[171]

169 See Archi 1987: 67–83 for the writing of the mina's fractions at Ebla.

170 As fractions of the capacity measure sila$_3$.

171 The reference in MAD 5 52 obv. i 1 as "2/3" of the sila$_3$ is questionable.

(continued)

	ED IIIa	ED IIIb	Sargonic
8. Nippur	**(no data)** **2N$_8$-ša$^!$-na** (OIP 97 2 rev. ii 4)	**šu$_2$-1N$_8$-ša-na** (OSP 1 127 obv. ii 3)[172] **2N$_8$ (ša-na-pi)** (ECTJ 100 obv. 1, 108 rev. ii 7, 149 obv. i 5)	**šu$_2$-1N$_8$-ša-na** (OSP 2 44 obv. i 1) **2N$_8$ ša-na-bi** (OSP 2 59 obv. 1; area measure *sar*). **šu$_2$-2N$_8$ ša-na-bi** (PBS 9 72 obv. 3)
9. Isin	**(no data)**	**šu$_2$-1N$_8$-ša-na (giĝ$_4$)** (BIN 8 37 obv. i 1; MVN 3 13 obv. ii 5, iii 2) **(no data)**	**šu$_2$-1N$_8$-ša-na** **šu$_2$-2N$_8$-ša-na-bi** (MVN 3 1 obv. i 1, iii 11)
10a. Šuruppak (lexical)	**šu$_2$-1N$_8$-ša$_4$-na** **2N$_8$ ša$_4$-na-bi** (SF 20)	**(no data)**	**(no data)**
10b. Šuruppak (administrative and legal)	**šu$_2$-1N$_8$** (WF 139 obv. i 1) **2N$_8$** (SEL 19 1–4 obv. I 1)	**(no data)**	**(no data)**
11. Adab	**(no data)**	Early Dynastic IIIb: **šu$_2$-1N$_8$** (OIP 14 66 obv. I 4 f.) **(no data)** Meskigala's reign (ED/ES): **šu$_2$-1N$_8$** (CUSAS 11 147 obv. ii 2) **2N$_8$ ša-na-pi** (CUSAS 11 77 obv. i 1)	Middle Sargonic: **šu$_2$-1N$_8$(-ša)** (SCTRAH 206 obv. 6) **šu$_2$-2N$_8$(-ša)** (SCTRAH 206 rev. 2) Classical Sargonic: **šu$_2$-1N$_8$-ša** (PPAC 1 752 rev. 1; CS) **šu$_2$-2N$_8$-ša** (PPAC 1 1121 rev. i 2)
12a. "Umma" (lexical)	**šu$_2$-1N$_8$ giĝ$_4$** **2N$_8$ giĝ$_4$** (CUSAS 12 6.3.1)	**(no data)**	**(no data)**

172 See OSP 1 127 obv. ii 3 for an unusual writing of "one-third" mina where šu$_2$ looks almost like 2(ban$_2$).

(continued)

	ED IIIa	ED IIIb	Sargonic
12b. "Umma" (administrative and legal)	**(no data)**	**šu$_2$-1N$_8$** **2N$_8$** (CUSAS 33 171 obv. v 1–2, vi 2; CUSAS 11 15 obv. i 2, ii 3)[173]	**šu$_2$-1N$_8$-ša** (Nik 2 58 obv. 1)[174] **šu$_2$-2N$_8$-ša** (BIN 8 309 obv. 1)
13. Ĝirsu	**(no data)**	**šu$_2$-1N$_8$-ša** (DP 38 rev. i 4) **šu$_2$-2N$_8$-ša** (VS 14 175 obv. i 1)	**šu$_2$-1N$_8$-ša(-na)** (RTC 202 obv. 7) **šu$_2$-*2N$_8$*-ša** (ITT 5 9323 obv. 1) šu$_2$-  -ša (RTC 101 obv. 1)

Fig. 3.1: Local and temporal distribution of the graphemes for "one-third" and "two-thirds" of the mina in the 3rd mill. BC.

The ED IIIa data include the cities Kiš, Nippur, and Šuruppak as the representatives of the "standard" tradition of the lexical list SF 20. The deviant tradition is found in a lexical text allegedly from the Umma region represented by CUSAS 12 6.3.1. Presargonic documents from the Umma region never use the phonetic complements -ša-na or ša-na-pi/bi with the mina's fractions. Neither do they mention ma-na in writings of the fractions "one-third" and "two-thirds." This implies that Umma scribes understood these notations as "20" and "40 shekels" instead of the mina's fractions.

The situation at Ebla is unique since the writings for the mina's fractions are logograms. Their writing ŠU$_2$+ŠA for šušana and ŠA-PI for šanabi show that the Eblaite scribes borrowed these writings likely via Kiš. However, Eblaites were very inventive with these borrowings. First, since ŠU$_2$+ŠA often appears in combination with giĝ$_2$-DILMUN "shekel," it refers not to "one-third mina" but to "20 shekels." Second, they discarded the numerical sign N$_8$ in both fractions. This shows that they understood these writings not as semi-phonetic graphemes but as numerograms of the shekel: ŠU$_2$+ŠA is "20

173 The mention of the goddess Inana, the personal name Gu-u$_2$-u$_2$, and, most importantly, the writing of the half of the mina as 1N$_8$×*DIŠ* (obv. i 3–4, ii 6) favors the ED IIIb Umma region provenance of CUSAS 11 15.

174 In MC 4 27 obv. ii 12' and MC 4 28 obv. ii 8, the fraction ⅓ is written just ŠU$_2$.

shekels" and ŠA-PI is "40 shekels." The only exception appears in ARET 2 3: Rare writings 20 and 40 GIN_2-DILMUN appear instead of the usual $ŠU_2$+ŠA and ŠA-PI. The fact that these were the writings for the shekel is clear from the fact that they (a) appear *after* the writing MA-NA and (b) build ligatures with the "pointed" numbers for shekels. For example, ŠA-PI-*5* is "45" shekels.

Besides the "standard/Šuruppak" and "Umma" traditions, there is a local idiosyncrasy of Ĝirsu from ED IIIb on. Here, the writing $šu_2$-N_8-ša applies to both "one-third" and "two-thirds." The lack of adequate data from Larsa, Uruk, and Ur of the Early Dynastic III date precludes any suggestions about its spread in the southernmost cities of Sumer. The "wrong" writings of the fractions show that, similarly to the Umma tradition, the Ĝirsu one is an offshoot of the standard, correct "northern" tradition represented by the documents from Kiš, Nippur, Šuruppak, and Adab. This distinction is especially clear in the Presargonic documents from Nippur and Adab. They remain faithful to the "northern" tradition and differentiate between $šu_2$-1N_8 for "one-third" and 2N_8 for "two-thirds" sometimes even during the Sargonic period. In contrast, "southern" texts use the phonetic complement -ša with both fractions indiscriminately thus showing that the whole construction $šu_2$-N_8-ša was perceived as a number and not as a phonetic writing. Another vagary that strengthens this idea is that some Presargonic texts from Ĝirsu write a $SILA_3$-like sign instead of the expected ŠA after N_8 numbers.[175]

The documentation from ED IIIb and Sargonic Nippur offers a striking contrast to the ignorance of the southern scribes. Powell was the first to recognize that $ŠU_2$ in $šu_2$-1N_8-ša-na "one-third" in these texts is a phonetic complement to pronounce the word /šuš(š)ana/.[176] It is remarkable how some of the Nippur texts are the only Sargonic documents that avoid the sign $ŠU_2$ in the fraction "two-thirds" and use the older writing 2N_8 instead. By doing this, Nippur seems to have been the keeper of the original tradition after Šuruppak ceased to be a major scribal center during the Early Dynastic IIIa period.

Despite the persistence and correctness of the Šuruppak tradition, the Sargonic reform adopted the corrupt but simplified "southern" writing $šu_2$-N_8-ša for both fractions. This practice is first documented in ED IIIb Ĝirsu. In many cases, the writing is abbreviated as $^{šu2}N_8$. The standardized Sargonic one appears in

175 Nik 1 310 rev. iv 10, v 5.
176 Powell 1971: 133–137.

Early/Middle Sargonic texts, that is, synchronously with the introduction of the standardized talent.

There are some local idiosyncrasies unrelated to the main trends. For example, Classical Sargonic texts from Ešnunna and Ĝirsu write the fraction "two-thirds" with two N_8 signs placed one above the other.[177]

A major phenomenon was the use of the mina's fractions šušana and šanabi to notate the same fractions of basic units in other systems of mensuration as early as the ED IIIa period, which means synchronously with their earliest confirmed use with the mina proper. The most important of them was sar "garden plot" of 36 m^2 in area mensuration. There are ample examples of the use of the writings šu$_2$-1N_8 and 2N_8 as the fractions of the "garden plot" and even lower area units in ED IIIa–b legal, administrative, and metro-mathematical texts.[178]

As suggested by Powell, this usage is secondary.[179] Now it is possible to offer several considerations in favor of this hypothesis. First, the mina and the "garden plot" (sar) share the same lower unit, which is the shekel. Doubtlessly, the shekel was originally a weight measure. The definition of "1 garden plot" as "60 shekels" certainly occurred after both the mina and the shekel existed as measures whose masses were related by the ratio 1:60. The second observation concerns writing. The phonetic complements -ša-na and ša-na-pi/bi are phonetic complements that appear with the mina's fractions but are always lacking in the case of the "garden plot." The writings šu$_2$-N_8-ša for the fractions "1/3" and "2/3" of a basic unit in any mensuration system appear only from the Sargonic period onwards.[180]

The documentation of the succeeding periods illustrates that these writings may be applied to almost any measure, such as šu-si "finger" of the length measures[181] and sila$_3$ "liter" of the capacity measures.[182] These equations allude

177 MAD 1 188 obv. i 4 (CS Ešnunna). STTI 26 rev. ii 3, 107 obv. 3, 162 rev. 2', 181 rev. ii' 1' (CS Ĝirsu); CUSAS 35 500 obv. ii 6 (CS uncert. prov.).

178 MVN 10 85 obv. i 3 and FTP 96 obv. i 3 (ED IIIa Šuruppak). See Friberg 2007: 419–425 (CUNES 50-08-001) for an ED IIIb metro-mathematical text from the Umma region, where the writings of the mina's fractions are used as the fractions of the area unit sar "garden plot" and even its subdivision giĝ$_4$ "shekel." See CUSAS 23 77 for another mathematical text of the same date and provenance that uses the same notations for various units.

179 Powell 1971: 162.

180 For examples with the sila$_3$, see CT 50 137–138.

181 ECTJ 65 obv. 3 (ED IIIb Nippur).

182 CUSAS 23 77 obv. i 6 (ED IIIb Umma region), CUSAS 13 106 obv. ii 15 (CS Adab), CT 50 137 obv. 1–2 (CS Ĝirsu). Sometimes "sila$_3$" is omitted in these notations. This practice is of the same nature as the omission of "ma-na" if there are no complete minas in an entry.

to early attempts to link all measures in a single system that predate the Sargonic reform.

3.7 Conclusions

Previously it was thought that the mina emerged in script for the first time in ED IIIa texts. Relying on the evidence of several texts from Ur and Šuruppak, it is possible now to move this date to at least the Early Dynastic I–II period, ca. 2900–2600 BC. This proves that weight metrology was in active use as early as the beginning of the 3rd mill. BC, suggesting that its roots were in even earlier periods. Copper is the substance measured in minas in all these cases. Some of these data may be interpreted as the use of this metal as means of payment, which is well documented in the following ED IIIa period.

The documentation of the ED and Sargonic periods shows that the mina's area of use was limited to the measurement of metals, wool and textiles, and luxury import goods such as resins. I discuss in detail in Chapter 10 their role as the "core goods" and the hypothesis that the need to measure them has stood behind the emergence of the weight metrology in Mesopotamia.

The fact that large quantities of goods were measured in minas instead of talents before the Early Sargonic period illustrates that the mina had been the highest unit in the system of weight units prior to the Sargonic reforms.

The Semitic origins of ma-na and its fractions šušana and šanabi are of utmost importance. These Sumerian words represent loanwords from Early Semitic. Taken together with the fact that copper is the earliest type of good measured by weight according to the surviving data, this phenomenon alludes to the emergence of the mina as a result of the interregional trade of the 4th mill. BC.

Written data inform about the existence of various standards, local and foreign, of the mina. The discussion of this complex phenomenon is found in Chapter 7.

4 Shekel: A tiny axe

4.1 Giĝ$_4$ "axe" and "shekel": Reading and etymology

The Mesopotamian shekel weighed about 8.33 g. Neither extant weights nor written data allow different mass standards to be identified for this unit in the 3rd mill. BC.[183]

The Sumerian word for "shekel" is giĝ$_4$ "axe." The use of the English word "shekel" to denote the Sumerian unit is, of course, a liberty. The Akkadian equivalent is *šiqlu(m)*, literally "the weighed out (thing)." This word is widely documented in other Semitic languages. The Semitic name for this unit alludes to the measurement of small quantities of valuable substances. The written data confirm that the shekel was the principal unit to measure silver.

We know for certain that giĝ$_4$ was a genuine unit in the weight metrology. However, the reason why the Sumerian word for the shekel is "axe" is not so clear. The Akkadian equivalent of this type of axe is *pāšu(m)*. The usual weight of one giĝ$_4$/*pāšu*-axe was one or two minas (ca. 0.5–1 kg) in the 3rd mill and afterward.[184] Therefore, it is certain that this type of axe is unrelated to the origins of the shekel.

Notably, giĝ$_4$ as an axe appears in the earliest cuneiform documents, both lexical and administrative. The Late Uruk lexical composition *Archaic Metals* records several varieties: giĝ$_4$-gal "large *giĝ*-axe," giĝ$_4$-šu-2N$_{57}$/1N$_{57}$ "two-" and "one-handed *giĝ*-axe," giĝ$_4$-AL, and giĝ$_4$-Dilmun "Dilmun *giĝ*-axe."[185] A number of Late Uruk accounts mention *giĝ*-axes made of various metals or alloys.[186] The appearance of these data in Uruk IV–III texts sometimes leads scholars to the "identification" of the shekel in these early texts.[187] There is, however, no basis for this assumption.

The edition of cuneiform texts and secondary literature alike often mistakenly renders the word giĝ$_4$ "axe" as dun$_3$/du$_5$. The roots of this

183 See Powell 1990: 509 with further references.

184 CUSAS 35 7 (ED IIIb Adab) rev. ii 7 for a giĝ$_4$-zabar^{uruda} weighing a half-mina. For later references, see CAD P: 268.

185 ATU 3: 136. See Englund 1983 for the sign DILMUN in Late Uruk texts that may refer to the land Dilmun. Some scholars relate the latter to the co-called "Dilmun shekel." Uruda giĝ$_4$ Dilmun^{ki} and uruda giĝ$_4$ Ti-a-ma in OB *Ura* (BM 85983; see P247857 and an edition in DCCLT) are likely not related to the shekel. As will be discussed below, the "Dilmun shekel" is a hoax.

186 ATU 6 pl. 27 (W 13,946,a).

187 Friberg 1999: 134.

https://doi.org/10.1515/9781501510267-004

unfortunate practice lie in an outdated idea by Anton Deimel that the early script differentiated between "axe" and "shekel."[188] According to this line of logic, DUN_3 was "axe" whereas GIN_2(DUN_3-*gunû*) designated the shekel. However, the following palaeographic overview shows that these two signs were unrelated (Fig 4.1):.

Sign	Uruk IV–III	ED I–II	ED IIIa	ED IIIb	Sargonic
DUN_3 (not SUG_5)[189]	 ZATU489	 UET 2 sign list no. 280	 LAK666	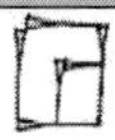 Rosengarten no. 306	 CUSAS 13 sign list no. 836b
AGA_3 GIN_2	 ZATU561  ATU 3 pl. 68 (W 20266,10) obv. ii 5 ff.	 UET 2 sign list no. 339	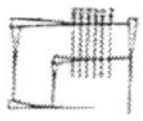 LAK667	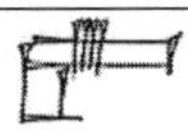 Rosengarten no. 305	 CUSAS 13 sign list no. 836
GIN_2-inverted (a graphic variant)	-	-	-	 MARI 5 2 obv. 5 f. (Mari)	 MAD 4 124 obv. 1 (Umma)

Fig. 4.1: The paleographic evolution of the signs DUN_3 and GIN_2.

The editors of ZATU made the same mistake and named the sign GIN_2 "DUN_3." In contrast, Eric Burrows recognized the difference between the two signs as early as 1935. He stated that DUN_3 is "always with a round corner and distinct from S. 339 [GIN_2]." Manfred Krebernik is also aware of the difference. The two signs are also differentiated in the *Ebla Sign List*.[190]

The similarity of the two signs by the end of the 3rd mill. BC misled Babylonian lexicographers too. The compilers of late lexical compositions did not differentiate between these signs.[191] This resulted in the erroneous interpretation

188 Deimel (ŠL II/4: 1092 no. 595) identifies LAK666(DUN_3) with "Axt" whereas LAK667(GIN_2) with "das Gestell für die Waage," which is incorrect.

189 This value had never existed. It is an invention by W. von Soden. Read DUN $_3$ instead. See Steinkeller 1987c: 192.

190 Krebernik 1998: 277 n. 469.

191 See MZL: 212 no. 836.

^{uruda}du$_5$/dun$_3$/tun$_3$ “axe.” Checking the copies of the 3rd mill. BC documents proves that the sign is GIN$_2$ in all cases when the axe is meant. Therefore, the proper transliteration is ^{uruda}giĝ$_4$.[192]

The reading gin$_2$ of GIN$_2$ is an inaccurate representation of the word’s phonemic structure. Relying on the earliest lexical attestations, von Soden proposed the reading */geĝ/. It appears as giĝ$_4$ in the MZL sign list, and I follow this practice in this book.[193] The value gin$_2$ of GIN$_2$ existed too. It appears in the word še-gin$_2$ “glue” as early as the ED IIIa period.[194] Later lexical lists fail to distinguish the phoneme /ĝ/ and imprecisely render the phonemic structure of the Sumerian equivalent of the Akkadian words *pāšu* “axe” and *šiqlu* as GIN$_2$ = gi-in.

Despite the considerable difference in mass of giĝ$_4$ as an axe and as the shekel, a hypothesis that the shekel originated from the use of miniature axe blades as money remains popular among scholars. Powell argues that “Axe hordes are ubiquitous, and it is virtually certain that these were used as money, and, indeed, axes are on rare occasions attested in cuneiform documents as a money form. Mesopotamians may have begun – at least in part – where we have ended, in representational money.”[195] Julian Reade’s considerations go in the same direction: “. . . it is remarkable that the early Sumerian pictographic or cuneiform sign GIN$_2$, meaning axe, whose shape is originally either oblong (like a hand axe) or L-shaped (like the end of a hafted metal axe), was used for the term ‘shekel’ (Babylonian *shiqlu*). One might compare the Mexican axes that were used for exchange, the copper bar celts of second millennium India, and the suggestion that stone hand axes had a social function, to impress the opposite sex, in many parts of the prehistoric world.”[196]

All these axes are too large to be related to the shekel. Archaeologists do find silver miniature axes in the Near East, however in much later contexts.[197] In earlier periods, one finds miniature copper axes but other tiny copper tools as well.[198] A comprehensive archaeological study of small metal objects of

---

192 For objects written with the sign DUN$_3$, see a skin sack and a container for dry goods dun$_3$ ($^{\text{kuš/ĝeš}}$dun$_3$ = *tākaltum* in later sources). It appears in an ED IIIa account of food TSŠ 515 obv. ii 8–9, iii 1–2: 2 dun$_3$ zu$_2$-lum “2 sacks/containers of dates.” See Selz 1997 for other objects written with the sign DUN$_3$.

193 AHw: 1248; MZL: 212 no. 836. For the lexical references of gi-iĝ$_3$ = GIN$_2$ = *šiqlum* and *pāšum*, see *OB Proto Ea* 718 (MSL 14: 59) and MSL 14: 134 iii 7–8.

194 TSŠ 782 obv. iii 9 (ED IIIa Šuruppak). See *Nabnītu* IV–IVa 361 (MSL 16: 91) for a gloss še-$^{\text{gi-in}}$gin$_2$.

195 Powell 1996: 238.

196 Reade 2002: 249.

197 Moorey 1999: 237.

198 E.g. Kaniuth 2006: 147.

about 8.3 g found in southern Mesopotamia and dated to the 4th and early 3rd mill. BC is required to support or reject the "axe hypothesis" of the origins of the shekel.

4.2 The early use of the shekel

The existing evidence documents the shekel in the ED IIIa and later periods. There are no attestations of this measure in the ED I–II period.[199] However, since the mina was already in use then, the shekel is expected too. In later periods, the shekel appears often in accounts of silver that are missing among the ED I–II texts.

The shekel abounds in ED IIIa sale contracts from Šuruppak, where it appears in relation to silver which, alongside barley and copper, played the role of a means of payment for houses and fields. The shekel appears also in accounts of metals. A receipt of silver and copper by a merchant CT 50 4 obv. i 1 provides an interesting example of the shekel's notation. The number of shekels is inscribed inside the sign GIN_2: 2 ku_3 ma-na $gi\hat{g}_4{\times}2$ "2 minas 2 shekels silver."

The shekel always appears consistently as $gi\hat{g}_4$. Any additional signs to mark morphemes are missing. The editors of FTP 96 (ED IIIa Šuruppak) render obv. i 1 as [n] ku_3-[luh]-ha gin_2-na, which would suggest the genitive marker (gin=a(k)). However, this is a phantom. First, the final consonant is /ĝ/. Second, the sign NA may be an abbreviation for ma-na or the phonetic complement of $šu_2$-N_8-ša-na "one-third." I would reconstruct the passage in FTP 96 as $[^{šu2}1N_8{}^{ša}]^{-na}$ ku_3-[luh]-ha $gi\hat{g}_4$ "⅓ mina of pure silver (as 20) shekels."

The use of the shekel during the ED IIIa period was limited to metals and wool. There are multiple occurrences of either ku_3 "silver" or ku_3-luh-ha "pure/purified silver" in contracts and accounts. For copper, see 15 $gi\hat{g}_4$ uruda-sal "15 shekels of … copper" in TSŠ 60 obv. ii 4 from Šuruppak. In some cases, the term for a metal does not appear at all. For example, TSŠ 860 obv. ii 3–4 records amounts of a metal in minas and shekels in connection to individuals: ½ ma-na $Ša_3$-$KAŠ_4$, 15 $gi\hat{g}_4$ E_2-gid_2. Since the amounts are relatively high, copper is expected here.

Although the number of occurrences of the unit "shekel" in ED IIIb documents is enormous, it rarely appears with materials other than metals. Wool allocations from Presargonic Ĝirsu never mention shekels. However, other types

199 The sign GIN_2 appears regularly in the logogram $PA.GIN_2$ = hursaĝ in personal names during this time: e.g. UET 2 185 obv. i 5.

of documents do. For example, a Ĝirsu document ITT 5 9246 obv. ii 1, 3 records 15 shekels of wool, whereas MLVS 918 has 10 shekels, in obv. i 4 f. The use of shekels with wool exemplifies the accuracy in the measurement of wool as early as the ED period.

In the following Sargonic period, the number of references to the shekel remains very large. Most of the records mention this measure in relation to metals – mostly silver as a means of payment and silver and other metals as material to produce objects – and wool. The latter practice is well documented in the "Mama-ummi file" that records the proceedings of a textile workshop in Middle Sargonic Adab.[200] The Sargonic period offers the earliest examples of the measurement of gems by weighing. They appear in shekels. For example, a text OSP 2 63 rev. ii 7 mentions several shekels of lapis lazuli.

The number of references to materials measured in shekels during the Ur III period is overwhelming. However, the majority of them are the same records of metals, especially of silver, and wool. Various valuables, such as resins and gems, were also measured by weight. The interpretation of other data requires caution. One needs to consider the fact that the shekel had been introduced into the system of capacity measures as the fraction "1/60" $sila_3$. This is especially obvious in the accounting of barley (še), onions ($šum_2$), oils and lards (i_3), potash (naĝa), and some other goods. Capacity measures should not be confused with weight measures in all these cases.

The shekel as "1/60" of a day (u_4) appears in the accounts of labor force in Ur III accounts (a_2). For example, a document from Umma calculates the area of fields and corresponding labor to cultivate it: a_2 $erin_2$-na-bi u_4 43 12 $gi\hat{g}_4$ "its (the field's) labor: 43 and 12/60 days."[201]

4.3 Fractions "one-third" and "two-thirds" of the shekel

The ways in which the fractions of the shekel appear in script are surprisingly numerous. The logic of these graphemes reveals that there had not been a single mastermind behind their origins. The following fractions are known for the shekel: half, one-third, two-thirds, one-fourth, and one-sixth. They are expressed in script differently:

(1) "Half-shekel" has the same notation as "half-mina."

---

200 See SCTRAH and CUSAS 35.

201 Civil 1994: 190 A 4651 obv. ii 4.

(2) "One-third" and "two-thirds" of a shekel use the notations of the respective mina's fractions. The fraction "five-sixths" follows this pattern ($^{šu2}3^{ša}$ = kingusila). However, it appears for the first time in the Ur III period.
(3) However, originally, "one-third" and "two-thirds" of a shekel were expressed by the writing NINDA$_2$×ŠE+N$_1$ ma-na, for which see a detailed discussion in the next chapter.
(4) The construction igi-*n*-ĝal$_2$ expressed the fractions "one-third," "one-fourth," and "one-sixth."

As a result, depending on the period and locality, there were four possible ways to write the shekel's fraction "one-third," for which see the following figure:

	ED IIIa	**ED IIIb**	**ED IIIa–b Umma**	**Sargonic**	**Ur III**
1/3 shekel	NINDA$_2$×ŠE +1N$_1$ ma-na	igi-*3*-ĝal$_2$	šu$_2$-1N$_8$ giĝ$_4$	1 ma-na-tur	šu$_2$-*1*-ša (rarely: NINDA$_2$×ŠE +1(*AŠ*) and igi-*3*-ĝal$_2$)
2/3 shekel	NINDA$_2$×ŠE +2N$_1$ ma-na	NINDA$_2$×ŠE +2N$_1$ ma-na	2N$_8$ giĝ$_4$	2 ma-na-tur	šu$_2$-*2*-ša (rarely: NINDA$_2$×ŠE +2(*AŠ*),)

Fig. 4.2: Graphemes "one-third" and "two-thirds" of a shekel in 3rd mill. BC texts.

As I will argue below, only the construction igi-*n*-ĝal$_2$ was a genuine way to express the shekel's fractions. Other practices were borrowed from other weighing measures, the "little mina" (NINDA$_2$×ŠE+N$_1$ ma-na) and the mina. As explained in the following chapter, the fact that the shekel lacks its own, original fractions "one-third" and "two-thirds" in the ED IIIa period is of utmost importance for understanding the origins of the system of weight measures. The use of the mina's fractions or the unit "little mina" in the case of the shekel's "one-third" and "two-thirds" in ED IIIa–b suggests that the shekel originally lacked any fractions, which alludes to its use as a primitive unit at some point in gray prehistory.

Since I discuss the notation NINDA$_2$×ŠE+N$_1$ ma-na in the next chapter, I limit myself here to the remark that it appears in Šuruppak, Uruk (ED IIIa), Adab, Ĝirsu, and Nippur (ED IIIb). In contrast, the mina's writing of the fractions "one-third" and "two-thirds" ($^{(šu2)}N_8{}^{ša}$) applied to the shekel should be attributed to the ED Umma scribal tradition discussed in the previous chapter. An example of its use is found in a contract recording the purchase of a land plot: $^{šu2}1N_8$ ku_3 $gi\hat{g}_4$ “one-third shekel.”[202] The same practice is found in other early Umma documents.[203]

No phonetic complements -ša-(na) and ša-(na-pi/bi) appear with the writings $^{šu2}1N_8$ as “one-third (shekel)” and $2N_8$ as “two-thirds (shekel).” Exceptions are rare and concern only the complement ^{ša} that appears in the “frozen” standard notation $^{šu2}N_8{}^{ša}$ as the effect of the Sargonic reform. Powell suggested that the term $^{šu2}1N_8{}^{ša(-na)}$ /šušana/ “one-third” “may originally have been applied both to one-third of a mina and one-third of a shekel.”[204] As we see, this is true in the case of Presargonic Umma. However, Powell’s suggestion that the Sumerian */šušana=min/ is the original word for “two-thirds” of a shekel is unconvincing. He doubts it himself in another place.[205] This leaves the following question still open: Does the use of the mina’s fractions in the case of the shekel automatically mean that the words behind these graphemes were the same?

4.4 The fraction “half-shekel”

The mina and the shekel share the same graphemes for the notation of the fraction “half”: $1N_8{\times}$*AŠ* is the usual notation and $1N_8{\times}$*DIŠ* is found in the Umma region texts during the ED and Sargonic periods. The “pointed” variants of these writings are documented as well.[206]

Classical Sargonic documents from Mugdan (Umm el-Jir), 27 kilometers northeast of Kiš, exhibit a remarkable idiosyncrasy. They use both variants of the sign for “half” shekel in accounts of silver.[207] The following rule applies. The usual notation “half” appears when the syntax is N $gi\hat{g}_4$ ku_3 “x shekels of silver.” The Umma variant of the “half” appears when the syntax is ku_3 N $gi\hat{g}_4$ “silver x shekels.” This peculiarity does not appear elsewhere and is not related to the ED Umma tradition.

Another interesting graphic phenomenon is found in Presargonic and Sargonic texts from Isin. Here, the sign BAR misplaces the usual pointed “half”

202 CUSAS 33 224 obv i 5.

203 E.g. CUSAS 33 225 obv. i 6, 228 obv. i 4, 233 rev. i 5’, 236 obv. i 3, P271238 obv. i 4 f.

204 Powell 1971: 219–220.

205 Powell 1979: 100.

206 E.g. BIN 8 53 obv. i 3–4 and CT 50 47 rev. 3.

207 MAD 5 88 obv. 1 and MC 4 48 obv. 1 use the standard form while MAD 5 66 rev. ii 7 and MAD 5 82 rev. 2 use the Umma writing.

(*DIŠ×AŠ*) in context with the shekel.[208] This writing may allude to the pronunciation of the Sumerian word for "half-shekel (and half-mina?)" as /bā/ or /ba'a/, literally "divided." Lexical data confirm that the sign DIŠ×AŠ=MAŠ has this pronunciation.[209] This Sumerian word had been borrowed into Akkadian with the same meaning as *bû, bā'um.*[210]

4.5 TAR = ku_5 as "half-shekel"

Another interesting idiosyncrasy in the notation of the fractions "half-shekel" and "half-mina" appears in several Sargonic texts. It remains uncertain whether they are related.

To begin with, the sign TAR as a notation for "half" is found in the Ebla archives. It designates "half" of a mina and never "half" of a shekel.[211] In contrast to this, southern Mesopotamian texts of the Sargonic period refer to TAR as "half" shekel. This practice appears in Early Sargonic texts from Ur and two ancient "kururrus" allegedly from Sippar of the same date.

Later lexical evidence illustrates that TAR designates "half-shekel." Both the Sumerian word ba-a = ba_3(EŠ) "half" and ½ $gi\hat{g}_4$ "half-shekel" are equated with the Akkadian *zūzu* "half-shekel."[212] The following line in the lexical list provides an equation ½ TAR = *zi-za-nu*, "halved (thing)."[213] Logically, this should be "1/4 shekel." However, the construction igi-*4*-$\hat{g}al_2$ was the usual notation for this fraction.

Powell argued that the writing TAR $gi\hat{g}_4$ may have been read *parras šiqlim* in Akkadian.[214] This may be correct. CAD P: 189 compares *parrasu* "one half" with BAD.DU, which might be read ku_5(TAR)-ra_2 "the cut (thing)," if we assume that post-Sumerian lexicographers confused BAD and TAR. The existence of a special term for "half-shekel" is not unique. It is present, for example, in Hurrian.[215]

---

208 ED IIIb Isin: MVN 3 36 obv. i 4. Sargonic Isin: BIN 8 35 obv. 1 f., 37 rev. i 10, 39 obv. ii 5, 43 obv. 4, MVN 3 59 obv. 9, CUSAS 13 7 obv. 3, 7, rev. 7–9. This notation should not be confused with the term bar "extra" in the accounts of miscellaneous commodities. E.g. bar ½ ku_3 $gi\hat{g}_4$-ka "½ shekel silver extra" in BIN 8 167 obv. 3 (CS Isin) and elsewhere outside Isin.

209 See ba-a = MAŠ in *Proto-Ea* 116 (MSL 14: 36).

210 CAD B: 297; AHw: 116.

211 E.g. ARET 2 11 obv. ii 3: TAR *5 ½* $gi\hat{g}_4$-DILMUN "½ (mina) 5 ½ shekels."

212 CAD Z: 170 *zūzu* A; *Nabnītu* XVII 236, 238 (MSL 16: 162).

213 CAD Z: 149 *zīzānu*.

214 Powell 1971: 218.

215 *Šaḫadnade* corresponds to ½ $gi\hat{g}_4$ and appears, among others, in the *Song of Release*. See Richter 2013: 342–343 sub *šaḫt-*.

At Ur, TAR = ku$_5$ "halved (shekel)" appears in two Early Sargonic documents.[216] It is 3 ma-na ku$_5$ ku$_3$ "1 mina and a halved (unit) of silver" in one case. The editors suggested the interpretation "3.5 minas of silver," although they were aware of "some 'ancient kudurrus'" where the same notation had the value "half-shekel."[217] The interpretation of ku$_5$ as "half-shekel" is definite in the second case: *5* giĝ$_4$ i$_3$ ku$_5$ "5 ½ shekels of lard." This limited data allow the possibility that ku$_5$ was a half of the mina and the shekel alike at Early Sargonic Ur.

The "ancient kudurrus" mentioned by Alberti and Pomponio are the *Maništusu Obelisk* and the *Sippar Stone*.[218] Both texts represent registers of field sales where sellers receive their price in silver and other commodities. All references in the first document have the writing 1 ku$_5$ giĝ$_4$ "1 halved shekel."[219]

In contrast, the *Sippar Stone* implements the writing ½ ku$_5$ giĝ$_4$.[220] Piotr Steinkeller interprets it as "1/4 shekel." The document also has a single example of the usual grapheme "half-shekel" in rev. vi' 12': 7 ½ giĝ$_4$ ku$_3$ "7 ½ shekels silver." This supports Steinkeller's interpretation. Nevertheless, two facts should be taken into consideration in this case.

First, if one weighs the only attestation of ½ giĝ$_4$ against multiple attestations of ½ ku$_5$ giĝ$_4$, in the Sippar Stone, it is likely that the former may be a scribal mistake for ½ <ku$_5$> giĝ$_4$. Second, the document probably has the usual writing for "one-fourth" igi-*4*-ĝal$_2$ in rev. iii' 1'. Finally, the documents from the 3rd mill. BC indicate that the number of "half-shekels" greatly outweighs the number of attestations of "one-fourth" of the shekel. Therefore, ½ ku$_5$ giĝ$_4$ of the *Sippar Stone* may be a haplography of the writing 1 ku$_5$ giĝ$_4$ in the *Maništusu Obelisk*.

The scarcity of the evidence on the practice of the use of TAR as "half-shekel" does not allow any far-reaching conclusions to be drawn. The evidence of Ebla, Ur, and Sippar is likely unrelated. However, it is likely that the idea of TAR as a "half" is due to one of its readings, ku$_5$ "to divide, to split."

4.6 The igi-*n*-ĝal$_2$ construction

The construction igi-*n*-ĝal$_2$, sometimes abbreviated as igi-*n* in cuneiform records, was used to notate the fractions "one-third," "one-fourth," and "one-

---

216 StPohl SM 13 1 obv. i 1 and 22 obv. i 1.

217 StPohl SM 13 25.

218 ELTS 40 and 41.

219 ELTS 40 A ii 10, vi 6, viii 14.

220 ELTS 41 obv. ii 9', v 20', vi 3', rev. iv' 20, left edge 2'.

sixth" of the shekel from the ED IIIb period on. The number is always written in its "pointed" form. Igi-*n*-ĝal$_2$ was also used to build reciprocal numbers.[221]

The etymology of igi-*n*-ĝal$_2$ is obscure. Powell criticizes the previous attempts and comes to the conclusion that the clue to understanding igi-*n*-ĝal$_2$ lies in the semantics of ĝal$_2$. He compares it to the copula /=am/ "it is."[222] He also argues that igi-*n*-ĝal$_2$ is not related to the compound verb igi. . .ĝal$_2$ "to look upon/at."[223] In contrast, he interprets igi as "eye" > "reciprocal," which had been borrowed into Akkadian as *igû*.[224] Powell concludes his discussion:[225]

> "The origin of the term 'the eye is three/four/six' is to be sought in the actual weighing process, which used weight stones of one-sixth, one-fourth, one-third, and one-half shekel to measure shekel fractions. In this context, the term 'the eye is x' must have arisen to designate the number of parts in the whole implied by a mass of one-third or one-sixth of a shekel, and from here the term was attached to the actual mass itself. This is a very theoretical explanation, it is true, but I can see no other means of explaining the term at present."

The philological interpretation of igi-*n*-ĝal$_2$ requires further elaboration. I cannot agree with Jagersma that ĝal$_2$ of the construction is optional and igi "eye" is its focal part.[226] The evidence shows that igi-*n* is an abbreviation that appears later than the original complete writing. Hence, igi cannot be explained without ĝal$_2$.

The Akkadian equivalent of the verb ĝal$_2$ is *bašû* "to be."[227] However, the usage of the verb ĝal$_2$ in Early Dynastic administrative texts suggests the meaning "to be available" in the case of goods, animals, etc. Additionally, the unit of capacity gur-saĝ-ĝal$_2$ "the *gur* over the brim," literally "having a head," allows the semantics "to have" of ĝal$_2$. As the result, igi-*n*-ĝal$_2$ is something like "having *x* (number) in one's eye." This explanation support Powell's suggestion that this construction alludes to the mental process behind the actual weighing practice, where "one-sixth" is highlighted. This reminds us of five parts in one mina as depicted on the Ebla weights discussed in the previous chapter.[228]

Theoretically, igi-*n*-ĝal$_2$ may appear with any number, for example igi-*60*-ĝal$_2$ "one-sixtieth," in later texts and in other systems of mensuration. However, the only possible numbers in the case of the shekel as a weight measure during

221 Friberg 1990: 545–550; Friberg 2007: 67–70.
222 Powell 1971: 222–223.
223 For this verb, see Karahashi 2000: 122 f.
224 Powell 1971: 223; CAD I/J: 45 *igû* A.
225 Powell 1971: 224.
226 Jagersma 2010: 263.
227 See lexical section in CAD B: 144.
228 Archi 1987: 48.

the ED period are 3, 4, and 6. This suggests that the construction igi-*n*-ĝal$_2$ had been devised specifically to express these fractions of the shekel. Afterward, this practice had been adopted by other systems of mensuration. This is a phenomenon of the same nature as $^{(šu2)}$N$_8$^{ša}, which referred originally to the mina's fractions "one-third" and "two-thirds" and was then extended to other areas of metrology.

The construction igi-*n*-ĝal$_2$ does not appear before the Early Dynastic IIIb period.[229] As stated before, the "third" of a shekel appears during the ED IIIa period as NINDA$_2$×ŠE+1N$_1$ (ma-na) in Šuruppak and as ^{šu2}1N$_8$ (giĝ$_4$) in the Umma region. No data suggest how the fractions "one-fourth" and "one-sixth" of the shekel were expressed during the ED IIIa period.

The Presargonic writing igi-*3*-ĝal$_2$ was an innovation. It ousted NINDA$_2$×ŠE +1N$_1$ (ma-na) as "one-third" of a shekel. The grapheme NINDA$_2$×ŠE+2N$_1$ (ma-na) had been reserved for "two-thirds shekel" or "two little minas" from then on. The Umma corpus is the only one that remained faithful to its local tradition during the ED IIIb period: ^{šu2}1N$_8$ (giĝ$_4$) appears instead of igi-*3*-ĝal$_2$ there.

The construction igi-*n*-ĝal$_2$ was used in other systems of mensuration. Early examples include "one-third" of a sar "garden plot." For example, *8* sar igi-*3*-ĝal$_2$ is "8 1/3 garden plots."[230] This is an exception, however. Normally, the fractions "one-third" and "two-thirds" of a sar "garden plot" would have been written using the respective fractions of the mina: $^{(šu2)}$N$_8$^{ša}.

Igi-*4*-ĝal$_2$ seems to be the only productive writing among three possibilities. The reason is the lack of any other adequate means to express the fraction "one-fourth." Thus, while the writing igi-*3*-ĝal$_2$ with sar "garden plot" is an exception, igi-*4*-ĝal$_2$ is a usual phenomenon.[231]

"One-sixth" of a sar "garden plot" was expressed differently. Instead of *igi-*6*-ĝal$_2$, a notation with "shekels" was used. For example, 10 giĝ$_4$ "10 shekels (of area = 1/6 sar)."[232] The "shekel" is not a unit of weight here but designates a fraction "1/60" of the basic unit, sar "garden plot."

From the Sargonic period on, igi-*4*-ĝal$_2$ marks "one-fourth" of the capacity unit sila$_3$: for example, šu-niĝin$_2$ *5* sila$_3$ igi-*4*-ĝal$_2$ i$_3$-nun "total: 5 ¼ *sila* butter."[233] Similarly to sar "garden plot," the fractions "one-third" and "two-thirds" of a sila$_3$ were expressed by the notation of the mina's fractions ^{šu2}N$_8$^{ša}.

---

229 "One-third" of a shekel in the ED IIIb period: DP 513 obv. iii 4; "one-fourth": DP 519 obv. i 1 f.; "one-sixth": DP 513 obv. iii 2 (ED IIIb Ĝirsu).

230 DP 594 obv. i 1. A copyist's mistake of igi-*4*-ĝal$_2$?

231 DP 429 obv. ii 1.

232 For an early example of "10 shekels" of area, see CUSAS 35 2 (ED IIIb Adab) rev. iv 6.

233 BIN 8 340 obv. 7 (CS Umma).

The existence of the fraction "one-fifth" in the shekel's metrology is dubious. Powell denies its existence: "One-fifth of a shekel is not expressed by igi-5-gal$_2$, as one might expect, but by igi-6-gal$_2$+6 še. This method of expression is to be traced back to the process of weighing itself, for which one must presuppose the existence of weight stones in the denominations 1/6, ⅓, and ½ shekel."[234] This should be taken into consideration while interpreting cuneiform texts.[235]

4.7 Conclusions

Sumerian giĝ$_4$(GIN$_2$) designated a measure of about 8.33 g, the shekel. Its origins are obscure. The "axe hypothesis" relates the emergence of this measure to the use of axe-shaped miniature metal objects as means of payment and value storage. However, it lacks any serious evidence for now.

The only definite facts about the shekel are the following. First, this measure appeared first around 2600 BC in script, although it is expected that two centuries earlier it made a companion for the mina.

Second, the fractions of the shekel show that it was divided into three parts from at least 2600 BC and six parts from at least 2450 BC. The use of the "little mina" instead of the fractions "1/3" and "2/3" of a shekel at Šuruppak as opposed to the shekel's fractions that have originated in the mina's notation at Umma is notable. This alludes to the fact that the shekel originally had *no* fractions at all.

Third, the shekel was used mostly to measure smaller amounts of metals and wool, resins, and gems, all of which are luxurious and expensive goods. However, most data portray the shekel in the context of silver as money.

Finally, contrary to some archaeological studies, no written data indicate varying standards of the Mesopotamian shekel. The existence of various standards bound to the measurement of specific goods (Chapter 7) does not necessarily mean that they produced 60 shekels of various masses in each case. For example, the "stone for textiles" representing a heavier mina at Presargonic Ĝirsu was probably never divided into shekels. Its use was to measure wool and textiles, not silver or gold. For that purpose, standard, correct (si-sa$_2$) weights

---

234 Powell 1971: 221.

235 The rendering of the fraction as igi-5-ĝal$_2$ in CUSAS 13 4 obv. 5 (MS/CS Adab) is incorrect and should be replaced by igi-⸢6⸣-ĝal$_2$; this number is clearly visible in the photo. Ku$_3$-bi 5 giĝ$_4$ igi-5-ĝal$_2$ in MVN 3 10 obv. iv 5 (ED IIIb Ĝirsu) should be a scribal mistake.

were used. Hence, we have many minas but only one Sumerian shekel of 8.33 g in cuneiform records of the 3rd mill. BC.

The so-called "heavy," previously "Dilmun," shekel that appears at Ebla and in Early Dynastic IIIb Mari is missing in the documentation from southern Mesopotamia.[236] The interpretation by Alster of a passage in the literary composition *Instructions of Šuruppak* 275 (uruda-)giĝ$_4$-dilmun^{ki}-na sa$_{10}$-še$_3$ TE-ga as "to buy at the (standard of the) Dilmun shekel is a sure loss(?)"[237] is tempting. Since the "Indus/Dilmun" shekel must have had a mass of ca. 13.5 g, this would mean that the buyer using this shekel loses almost two times more silver. However, as pointed out above, (uruda-)giĝ$_4$-dilmun^{ki} of lexical lists refers to a type of axe.

Coming into the realm of hypotheses, it is possible that the establishing of the ratio 1:60 between two primitive units, the mina to measure copper and the shekel to measure silver and other luxury goods, led to the emergence of weight metrology in Mesopotamia. As a result, the mass of the shekel as the more precise unit of the two defined the mass of the "correct" mina. This may indicate that the shekel was the unit par excellence, the point on which the whole system of weight measures was founded. This has parallels in other cultures of the Ancient Near East. For example, the shekel was the only unit with multiples in the system of weight measures in Iron Age Judah. This shekel appears as the "regular shekel" in the Old Testament. It defined the mass of higher units and its writing could be omitted altogether. For example, "n silver" means "n shekels of silver."[238]

236 MARI 5 1 obv. 1; Archi argues that giĝ$_4$-DILMUN means "weighed shekel" relying on the equivalent ^{ĝeš}DILMUN = *ša-qi$_2$-lum* in Ebla bilingual lists (Archi 1987: 86). See also Michalowski 1990: 5–7 and Civil 2008: 17 for this problem. For an alternative explanation, see Chambon 2011: 59–61.

237 Alster 2005: 99.

238 Kletter 2009: 835–836.

5 The missing link: $NINDA_2 \times$ ŠE + N

5.1 Introduction

The case of the grapheme $NINDA_2 \times$ ŠE + N and the metrological units hiding behind it is one of the most intricate in the discussion of the Sumerian system of weight measures. It was in active use during the ED IIIa–Middle Sargonic period and sporadically until the end of the 3rd mill. BC. Depending on time and space, it denoted two metrological units: the little mina and the barleycorn. It is well attested in a number of administrative, legal, mathematical, and metrolexical documents. Despite this, its philological interpretation, origins, and role in the overall system remain challenging.

Two details that require explanation define the discussion of $NINDA_2 \times$ ŠE + N: a paleographic and philological one on the one hand, and a metrological one on the other. First, this metrogram – a logogram with a metrological meaning – was the earliest means of notating *two* measures, the barleycorn and the little mina.

Second, one shekel is divided into 180 barleycorns, or, the other way round, 180 barleycorns make one shekel. This is unique and contradicts the Sumerian numerology of weight measures that centers on the factor "60." One shekel should make 60 barleycorns, which would bring us to a talent of 10.800 g, which was nonexistent.

The two details are related and indicate the common origins of the units "barleycorn" and "little mina." As I argue in the following, this piece of data alludes to the separate origins of the shekel on the one hand and the barleycorn on the other. By this, the definition of a shekel as 180 barleycorns registers the emergence of the standardized system of weight measures. While the same process for the talent took place relatively late, the establishment of the linkage between two primitive units – the barleycorn and the shekel – must have taken place in the late 4th or at the beginning of the 3rd mill. BC.

5.2 Why $NINDA_2 \times$ ŠE?

To understand why the scribes chose $NINDA_2 \times$ ŠE + N_1 ma-na as a writing for a unit of 2.77 g, it is necessary to understand the logic behind its writing. Below, I will discuss the hypothesis that the sign ŠE inside the metrogram may refer to /še/ "barleycorn," a measure of 0.04–0.05 g. However, what was the reason for choosing the sign $NINDA_2$?

https://doi.org/10.1515/9781501510267-005

As is commonly known, the complex sign NINDA$_2 \times$ ŠE has a reading sa$_{10}$(m) "to pay for, to buy, to sell" in Sumerian. This, however, has nothing to do with weight metrology. The sign NINDA$_2$ is a depiction of a seed funnel:

A seed funnel is a piece of equipment installed on a seeding plow. The sower manually poured seed inside it so it could get into the furrow made by the plowshare. /Enda/ is the Sumerian word for this apparatus. *Ittû* is the Akkadian borrowing with the same meaning.[239] *Ebla Sign List* 80 and *Word List D* 3–4 point to the first vocal /e/.[240]

The writing NINDA$_2 \times$ ŠE + N of the weight metrology reminds of the use of NINDA$_2$ with inscribed numbers in the so-called "N-system" in Late Uruk grain accounts. Robert Englund and Peter Damerow ascertained that the sign 1N$_1$ with its variant NINDA$_2 \times$ 1N$_1$ had represented a measure of 25 liter of grain in these late 4th mill. BC accounts. The sign NINDA$_2$ appears in three variants[241] (Fig. 5.1):

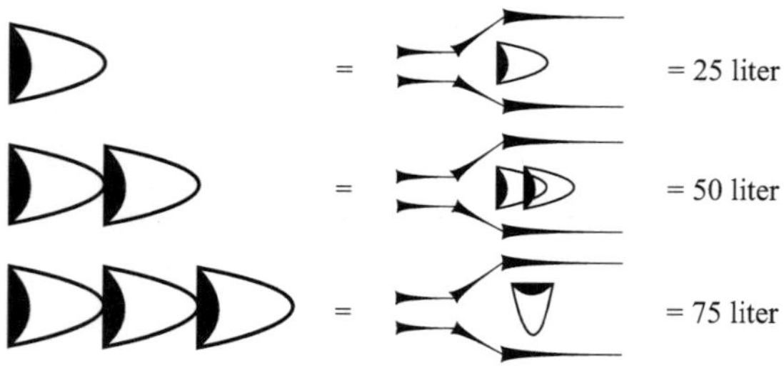

Fig. 5.1: Late Uruk "N-system" of grain mensuration.

These notations fell out of use after the Uruk period. However, scribes knew about their existence during the Early Dynastic times. *Word List D* reflects this vague knowledge. This lexical composition has Sumerian logographic and Eblaite syllabic explanatory versions. The first four lines record measures that resemble the above-mentioned Late Uruk N-system of grain mensuration. The numbers inscribed in NINDA$_2$ vary in the manuscripts. As Civil states, "the disagreement among sources could stem from a lack of understanding of a system that became

239 CAD I: 312 *ittû* B.

240 NINDA$_2$ = en-da-*um* and en-da.

241 See Damerow, Englund, and Nissen 1988: 53 and Englund 2001: 8, 29.

obsolete as early as the time of the Fara tablets."[242] If we combine the repetitive two first entries, we may come to the following reconstruction (Fig. 5.2):

Logographic writing	Syllabic writing	Interpretation
$NINDA_2 \times 3N_1$ (or 10?)	gu_2-sa-ma	"the exchange (sa_{10}.m) gur"
$NINDA_2 \times 2N_1$ ($2N_8$)	en-da	"seed funnel" (enda)
$NINDA_2 \times 1N_1$ ($1N_8$)	en-da sur_x(HUŠ)-ru_{12}	"halved seed funnel"

Fig. 5.2: "N-system" in *Word List D*.

This passage in *Word List D* provides two illuminating details for the discussion of $NINDA_2 \times$ ŠE + N in the weight metrology. First, the "N-System" and $NINDA_2 \times$ ŠE + N_1 ma-na conform to the same logic of dividing a basic unit into three parts. The second detail in *Word List D* is the reference to *gur = sam_2 = a(k) "the exchange gur." I believe that the Early Dynastic scribes failed to see the original idea behind the use of the sign $NINDA_2$ and erroneously related these metrograms to sa_{10}(m)($NINDA_2 \times$ ŠE) "to buy, etc." $NINDA_2 \times$ ŠE as the same capacity measure appears in *Early Dynastic Practical Vocabulary A* 2, where it alternates with ninta (UŠ).[243] The word behind these writings may be related to ^{dug}$ninda_2$, Akkadian *namaddu* "measuring vessel."[244]

This discussion suggests that the Early Dynastic scribes may have relied on their vague knowledge about the archaic capacity measures of the "N-system" in their choice of $NINDA_2 \times$ ŠE to record a weight measure identical to one-third of a shekel. This marks the beginning of the Early Dynastic period as the *terminus ante quem* for the writing $NINDA_2 \times$ ŠE + N_1 ma-na of the weight metrology.

5.3 $NINDA_2 \times$ ŠE + N: The temporal and local distribution

The following figure (Fig. 5.3) with its explanation below offers a systematic overview of the grapheme $NINDA_2 \times$ ŠE + N as it appears in administrative, legal, and mathematical texts. Disregarding local and temporal idiosyncrasies, there are five notations with $NINDA_2 \times$ ŠE + N in total. One expects the sixth possibility – the fraction "two-thirds" of a $NINDA_2 \times$ ŠE + N – because the fraction "one-third" appears in an actual everyday account. A unique metro-lexical text, CUNES 47-12-176, records all possible notations with $NINDA_2 \times$ ŠE + N. I discuss

242 Civil 1982: 5.
243 Civil 2008: 15 no. 2.
244 CAD N/1: 206.

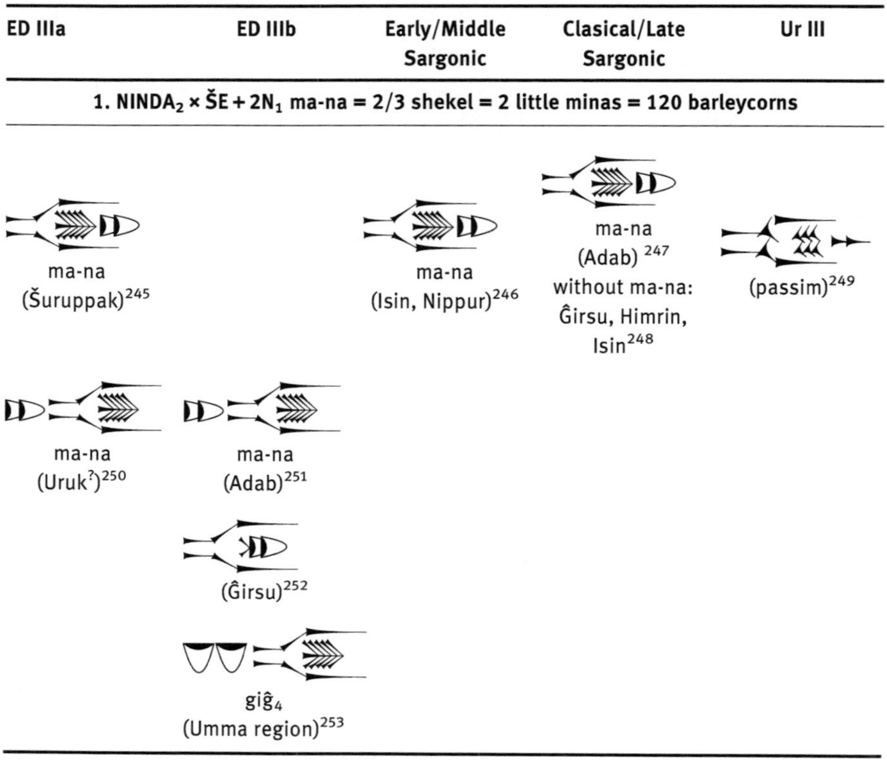

Fig. 5.3: Metrogram NINDA$_2$ × ŠE of weight metrology in time and space.

245 FTP 98 obv. v 2, ELTS 125 rev. i 6 (Šuruppak).

246 BIN 8 43 obv. 2–3 and 175 obv. ii 9 (MS Isin); OSP 2 52 rev. 9 and 59 rev. 9 (MS Nippur).

247 CUSAS 13 2 rev. 12 (MS/CS Adab according to the editor; better: "CS"), OIP 14 157 obv. 1 (CS Adab).

248 AIHA 44 rev. i 1 (CS Himrin area), BIN 8 180 rev. 2–3 (CS Isin), STTI 46 obv. 1, 110 obv. i 6 (CS Ĝirsu).

249 MVN 8 179 rev. vi 8 (Ur III Ĝirsu, Šulgi 48).

250 UVB 10: 13 pl. 26b obv. i 4 (Uruk$^?$); cf. Krebernik 1998: 243 n. 73.

251 OIP 14 49 = ELTS 32 obv. i 3 (Adab).

252 VS 14 175 rev. iii 1 (Ĝirsu).

253 CUSAS 35 419 obv. ii 1–4 (ED IIIb Umma region). The notation is unique and does not appear elsewhere. 2N$_8$ giĝ$_4$ is a usual writing of "2/3 shekel" at ED IIIb Umma.

ED IIIa	ED IIIb	Early/Middle Sargonic	Clasical/Late Sargonic	Ur III
		 ma-na (Nippur)[254]		
		 (Nippur)[255]		
		 ma-na (Adab)[256]		
2. $NINDA_2 \times ŠE + 1N_1$ ma-na = 1/3 shekel = 1 little mina = 60 barleycorns				
 ma-na (Šuruppak)[257]		 ma-na (Adab)[258]		 (passim, mostly Ĝirsu)[259]
	 ma-na (Adab)[260]			

Fig. 5.3 (continued)

254 OSP 1 17 obv. ii 9, 131 obv. iii 4 (ES Nippur).

255 OSP 2 63 obv. ii 11 (MS Nippur).

256 BdI 1 32 obv. ii 7 (ES Adab). The editors of this text claim that ma-na is followed by a -tur. Owing to the friendly collation by Palmiro Notizia in February 2017, it is now certain that this "-tur" is a hoax.

257 RTC 14 obv. v 5, 15 rev. iii 1 (ED IIIa Šuruppak).

258 CUSAS 11 168 rev. ii 3, 254 obv. i 4 (ED/ES Adab, "Meskigala"); P271220 obv. i 10 (unpublished; ES Adab?).

259 Appears rarely; e.g. PPAC 5 279 obv. 3 (Ur III Ĝirsu, Šulgi 44).

260 OIP 14 70 obv. i 4 (1 <$NINDA_2 \times ŠE$> ma-na), iii 2, 6. This document from Adab does not concern weight measures; it is a mathematical tablet about area measures. See Friberg 2007: 357–360 for a discussion.

ED IIIa	ED IIIb	Early/Middle Sargonic	Clasical/Late Sargonic	Ur III
	 giĝ$_4$ (Umma region)[261]  (Ĝirsu)[262]			
		 ma-na (Adab)[263]		
3. $NINDA_2 \times ŠE + 1N_1$ (ma-na) 10 + *5* (giĝ$_4$) = 1/3 shekel (1 little mina) + 15 barleycorns = 75 barleycorns				
	 (ma-na) (giĝ$_4$) (Adab) [264]			
4. $NINDA_2 \times ŠE + 2N_8$ = *2/9 shekel = 2/3 little mina = 40 barleycorns (not yet documented in administrative or legal documents)				
 -ša(-na-bi/pi)				

Fig. 5.3 (continued)

261 CUSAS 35 419 obv. iii 3 (ED IIIb Umma region).

262 VS 14 175 obv. ii 1, 3, 5 (Ĝirsu).

263 CUSAS 35 9 rev. i 8 (ES Adab): *3* ku$_3$ $NINDA_2 \times 1N_1 + ŠE$ giĝ$_4$ ma-na "3 shekels 1 little mina silver."

264 OIP 14 70 obv. i 2 (1 $NINDA_2 \times ŠE$ ma-na 10 + *5* giĝ$_4$), rev. i 2 (1 $NINDA_2 \times ŠE$ 10+*5*).

ED IIIa	ED IIIb	Early/Middle Sargonic	Clasical/Late Sargonic	Ur III
5. $NINDA_2 \times$ ŠE + $^{šu2}1N_8$ = *1/9 shekel = 1/3 little mina = 20 barleycorns				
 -ša(-na)[265]		 -na (Isin)[266]		
6. $NINDA_2 \times$ ŠE + 10 + *5* = *1/12 shekel = *1/4 little mina = 15 barleycorns				
		 (Isin)[267]		

Fig. 5.3 (continued)

it below in connection with the theory of Jöran Friberg. The asterisk marks fractions of the units that did not exist in the Sumerian weight metrology.

This figure illustrates that the earliest examples of the grapheme come from ED IIIa Šuruppak and, possibly, Uruk. The numbers with $NINDA_2 \times$ ŠE are either "one" or "two." The data from later periods confirm that $NINDA_2 \times$ ŠE + N_1 was a standard writing. This shows that Šuruppak texts embody the original, "correct" scribal tradition. A contemporaneous text from Uruk(?) offers a graphic deviation: The numbers appear in front of $NINDA_2 \times$ ŠE.

The writing $NINDA_2 \times$ ŠE + $1N_1$ ma-na was the only means of expressing "one-third shekel" during the ED IIIa period. During the following Early Dynastic IIIb period, scribes introduced the construction igi-*3*-ĝal$_2$ to record one-third of a shekel. In the following periods, it almost ousted the original $NINDA_2 \times$ ŠE + $1N_1$ ma-na, which became extremely rare. I am aware of only one reference to $NINDA_2 \times$ ŠE + $1N_1$ in the ED IIIb corpus.

The way it is written in a ED IIIb text from Ĝirsu tells us that the scribes there were uncertain of the meaning of ŠE inside the sign $NINDA_2$. A simplified ŠE looks more like a KUR_2. Another corrupt writing of weight measures in the Ĝirsu scribal tradition puts it in stark contrast to the diligently correct writings from central Babylonian cities such as Šuruppak, Kiš, Nippur, Isin, and, often, Adab. For example,

265 See a footnote to the fraction "two-thirds."
266 BIN 8 35 obv. 5 (MS Isin).
267 BIN 8 175 obv. ii 11 (MS Isin).

note a meaningless notation that resembles the sign $SILA_3$ instead of the usual phonetic complement ^{ša} in the mina's fraction "one-third" in Nik 1 310.

In contrast to a very rare $NINDA_2 \times ŠE + 1N_1$ ma-na, the writing $NINDA_2 \times ŠE + 2N_1$ ma-na keeps on flourishing during the Presargonic period. It appears at Adab, Ĝirsu, and Nippur. The data from Adab and Nippur deviate from the standard writing. One legal and one mathematical text from Adab follow the ED IIIa example from Uruk(?, probably "Adab" too) and offer the writing $2N_1$ $NINDA_2 \times ŠE$ ma-na.

One of them, the mathematical document OIP 14 70 (A 681), is especially important since it concerns the calculation of area. It shows that the notation $NINDA_2 \times ŠE + N_1$ had been adopted into the system of area measures by then and probably earlier, during the Fara period. $NINDA_2 \times ŠE + N_1$ has a metrological value of "one-third" and "two-thirds" of a "shekel," where the "shekel" is the fraction "1/60" of the basic unit sar "garden plot" of 36 m^2. As a result, one shekel (1/60) of a sar was about 0.6 m^2. "One-third" and "two-thirds" of the "area-shekel" make 0.2 and 0.4 m^2, respectively. Later documents show that this precision was necessary to calculate accurately the area of the houses on sale. Hence, this was not just a mathematical fancy but served practical reasons.

Later Adab texts return to the correct practice of placing the number inside the sign $NINDA_2$. These texts are dated to the office of the governor Meskigala, that is, the time of Lugalzagesi and Sargon (ca. 2350–2300 BC). The writing $NINDA_2 \times ŠE + 1N_1$ ma-na appears in his corpus.[268] $NINDA_2 \times ŠE + 2N_1$ ma-na is missing in the extant data but expected. Classical Sargonic texts from Adab know only the writing $NINDA_2 \times ŠE + 2N_1$ ma-na.[269] Like everywhere during the Sargonic period, igi-*3*-ĝal$_2$ "one-third (shekel)" replaces $NINDA_2 \times ŠE + 1N_1$.

As usual, the case of Presargonic Umma is unique. In the chapter about the mina, I illustrated that the scribal tradition of Umma preferred to use the notation of the mina's fractions for "one-third" and "two-thirds" ($^{šu2}1N_8$ and $2N_8$) of the shekel. This eliminated the need for the grapheme $NINDA_2 \times ŠE + N$ and the unit "little mina" in the Umma region. However, one text from Umma witnesses a remarkable deviation. CUSAS 35 419 uses the idiosyncratic writing $^{šu2}1N_8$ $NINDA_2 \times ŠE$ giĝ$_4$ and $2N_8$ $NINDA_2 \times ŠE$ giĝ$_4$ to record "one-third" and "two-thirds" of a shekel. They are "hybrid" graphemes since they combine the Umma and the "standard" writing traditions. The scribe decided to place the grapheme $NINDA_2 \times ŠE$ between the N_8 number and giĝ$_4$ "shekel." The reason for this vagary was probably to avoid ambiguity, since $^{(šu2)}N_8$ giĝ$_4$ may mean "one/two-third(s) mina" as well as "one/two-third(s) shekel."

---

268 CUSAS 11 168 rev. ii 3, 254 obv. i 4 (ED/ES Adab, Meskigala).

269 CUSAS 13 2 rev. 12 (MS/CS Adab, better "CS"), and OIP 14 157 obv. 1 (CS Adab).

Sargonic documents follow the pattern of the Presargonic ones regarding the use of the grapheme $NINDA_2 \times ŠE + N$. Examples with “one little mina” are extremely rare. The only example known to me is irregular. Here, ŠE and $1N_1$ change positions: $NINDA_2 \times 1N_1 + ŠE$ ma-na.[270]

In contrast, the writing $NINDA_2 \times ŠE + 2N_1$ (ma-na) is common in Sargonic documents, especially of the Early and Middle Sargonic period. A simple explanation of this fact is the absence of another way to convey the shekel’s fraction “two-thirds” before the Sargonic reform that introduced the unit “little mina” for this purpose. Some Sargonic documents provide the full writing $NINDA_2 \times ŠE + 2N_1$ ma-na.[271] Others reduce it to $NINDA_2 \times ŠE + 2N_1$.[272] A noticeable tendency is that Early and Middle Sargonic texts tend to preserve ma-na whereas later texts mostly omit it. Exceptions are found in Classical Sargonic texts from Adab that follow the original writings.[273] A number of irregular graphemes occur with and without ma-na in Early and Middle Sargonic texts from Adab and Nippur.[274]

The presence of $NINDA_2 \times ŠE + 2N_1$ in a number of Classical Sargonic documents is a fact that requires an explanation. As I will show in the next chapter, the Sargonic reform aimed to replace this writing with *2* ma-na-tur. The latter appears as the standard grapheme during the Classical and Late Sargonic periods. However, it has not fully ousted the older writing. This is especially striking if one considers the fact that the notation *n* še “x barleycorns” had completely supplanted the “archaic” writing $NINDA_2 \times ŠE + N_1$ by then. For example, a document from the Sargonic “Lugal-ra archive” from the Lagaš region records $NINDA_2 \times ŠE + 2N_1$ *20* še “2 little minas 20 barleycorns.”[275] This notation is a hybrid of older and new rules: If the scribe followed the norms of the Sargonic reform to the point, the notation must have been **2* ma-na-tur *20* še in this case.

Several texts from Classical Sargonic Ĝirsu illustrate the same idiosyncrasy. They combine $NINDA_2 \times ŠE + 2N_1$ with the post-Reform writings of the barleycorn (še) and the little shekel ($giĝ_4$-tur).[276] This shows a remarkable tolerance of

---

270 CUSAS 35 9 rev. i 8 (ES Adab): *3* ku_3 $NINDA_2 \times 1N_1 + ŠE$ $giĝ_4$ ma-na “3 shekels 1 little mina silver.”

271 BIN 8 43 obv. 2–3, 175 obv. ii 9 (MS Isin); OSP 2 52 rev. 9, 59 rev. 9 (MS Nippur).

272 AIHA 44 rev. i 1 (CS Himrin area), BIN 8 180 rev. 2–3 (CS Isin), STTI 46 obv. 1 and 110 obv. i 6 (CS Ĝirsu).

273 CUSAS 13 2 rev. 12 and OIP 14 157 obv. 1 (CS Adab).

274 $NINDA \times 2N_1 + ŠE$ ma-na in BdI 1 32 obv. ii 7 from ES Adab. Contrary to the editors, there is no “-tur” after ma-na. $NINDA_2 \times ŠE + 2$(“bariga”) ma-na in OSP 1 17 obv. ii 9 and 131 obv. iii 4 (ES Nippur), $NINDA_2 \times ŠE + 2N_8$ in OSP 2 63 obv. ii 11 (MS Nippur).

275 MAD 5 108 obv. 7, rev. 1, 7. See CUSAS 26 175–215 for an edition of the majority of known texts that belong to this archive.

276 $NINDA_2 \times ŠE + 2N_1$ *15* še (ITT 1 1091 rev. 1), $NINDA_2 \times ŠE + 2N_1$ *2* $giĝ_4$-tur (ITT 5 6671 obv. 3’).

Sumerian scribes to $NINDA_2 \times ŠE + 2N_1$ during the later Sargonic and even the Ur III period.

Sargonic texts proceed to use $NINDA_2 \times ŠE + 2N_1$ ma-na in area mensuration. An example of "two-thirds" of an "area-shekel" appears in a Middle Sargonic text from the private "Enlilemaba archive" from Nippur. It records 1 e_2 sar igi-*3* la_2 1 $gi\hat{g}_4$ $NINDA_2 \times ŠE + 2$ ma-na "a house of 1 1/3 *sar* minus 1 shekel and 2 little minas."[277] This makes $(36\ m^2 + 12\ m^2) - (0.6\ m^2 + 0.4\ m^2) = 47\ m^2$.

The Ur III period witnessed another reform of metrology and writing. The grapheme for the mina's fraction "two-thirds" $^{šu2}2N_8^{(ša)}$ mostly replaced the writing $NINDA_2 \times ŠE + N_1$. Nevertheless, sometimes it appears in Ur III documents. These exceptional writings have pointed horizontal numbers placed after $NINDA_2$. The extension "ma-na" never appears. The temporal distribution of the writing $NINDA_2 \times ŠE + 2(AŠ)$ during the Ur III period is more or less even. It does not allow us to suggest that, let's say, some documents from the reign of a certain king or a certain locality tend to use it instead of the standard writing $^{šu2}2^{ša}$.

Several other graphic combinations appear with $NINDA_2 \times ŠE + N$. I discuss $1N_1$ $NINDA_2 \times ŠE$ (ma-na) 10 + *5* ($gi\hat{g}_4$) of a mathematical text from ED IIIb Adab in connection to Friberg's theory below. Another one is a notation of "15 barleycorns" as $NINDA_2 \times ŠE + 10 + 5$ that appears in a number of Middle Sargonic texts.[278] Finally, the metro-lexical text CUNES 47-12-176 discussed below illustrates that the fractions of the little mina correspond graphically to those of the large mina. These writings – $2N_8$ and $šu_2$-$1N_8$ – are placed into $NINDA_2 \times ŠE$. However, only the fraction "one-third" appears in the extant documentation. A Middle Sargonic account from Isin records ku_3 $NINDA_2 \times ŠE$ $^{šu2}1N_8^{\langle ša-\rangle na}$ še *2* "1/3 little mina 2 barleycorns."[279] Here NA is a remnant of the correct original writing of the mina's fraction $^{šu2}1N_8^{ša-na}$. It cannot be <ma->na since this is usually not required in the writings of the mina's fractions "one-third" and "two-thirds."[280]

In contrast, A Classical or Late Sargonic document BdI 1 221 (CUSAS 26 293 = Westenholz 2017) records a silver payment for a field that has a very unusual form (obv. 3'). It is $NINDA_2 \times 2(AŠ)$ NA, where the last sign is the abbreviation of <ma->na. Curiously, the sign ŠE is omitted, which shows that this practice predates the Ur III period when this became the norm.

---

277 OSP 2 55 obv. 14.

278 BIN 8 175 obv. ii 11 (MS Isin), OSP 2 61 rev. i 4 (MS Nippur), BdI 1 88 obv. 1 (MS Adab).

279 BIN 8 35 obv. 5 (MS Isin).

280 See the chapter on the mina for the discussion.

5.4 Theories explaining $NINDA_2 \times$ ŠE + N

Several scholars have suggested their explanations for the phenomenal metrogram $NINDA_2 \times$ ŠE + N and the units behind it. Two facts play a decisive role in these discussions. The first is that $NINDA_2 \times$ ŠE + N (ma-na) is the predecessor of two lexemes that marked the respective weight units še "barleycorn" of 0.04–0.05 g and ma-na-tur "little mina" of še × 60=2.77 g. The common writing $NINDA_2 \times$ ŠE + N suggests common origins or, at least, some sort of relationship between these two weight measures at the onset of the emergence of the standardized system of weight measures. The second fact is that one shekel of 8.33 g makes 180 and not 60 barleycorns, which contradicts the Sumerian weight numerology that centers on the factor "60."

To begin with the first point, what is the philological interpretation of $NINDA_2 \times$ ŠE + N_1 ma-na? What is ma-na here? Why does $NINDA_2$ have an inscribed ŠE?

Marvin Powell was the first to try to resolve these difficulties. He related $NINDA_2 \times$ ŠE ma-na to the Sumerian expression igi-*3*-ĝal$_2$ "one-third (shekel") and "perhaps also mana-tur." He noted: "The existence of this unit as a practical weighing unit is attested by the discovery at Susa of a weight marked 1 MA. NA TUR."[281] In a later publication, Powell suggested that $NINDA_2 \times$ ŠE + N ma-na "must ultimately refer to mana-tur." He defends his claim by citing the writing ma-na-tur in Classical Sargonic documents.[282]

However, this neither proves that (a) the grapheme $NINDA_2 \times$ ŠE ma-na must be read /mana=tur/ nor (b) does it explain the barleycorn-shekel linkage. No lexical or any other data connect the original ED IIIa period writing $NINDA_2 \times$ ŠE ma-na with the Classical Sargonic ma-na-tur. As the overview of the grapheme $NINDA_2 \times$ ŠE + N above shows, the Classical Sargonic ma-na-tur is indeed identical to the original $NINDA_2 \times$ ŠE + N_1 ma-na from the *metrological* point of view. In fact, it is possible that Sargonic scribes invented the term ma-na-tur as they did with many other things in the course of the Sargonic reform. As for the one-little-mina-weight from Susa, it must have originated, alongside all written data from that site, from the Classical Sargonic period.[283] Therefore, strictly speaking, ma-na-tur cannot be taken as the explanation of the logogram $NINDA_2 \times$ ŠE + N.

The next question is the metrological unit behind $NINDA_2 \times$ ŠE + N. Powell elegantly summarizes his explanation: "The Sumerian sexagesimal counting

281 Powell 1971: 217.
282 Powell 1979: 98.
283 Foster 2016: 73–75.

structure is adapted to pre-existing units of mass by defining the 'axe' (shekel) as 180 barleycorns (3 sets of 60)."[284] Although he does not go into detail in explaining his hypothesis, this statement represents a theory that tries to explain the origins of the system of weight measures. It presupposes the existence of originally two independent measuring practices. The first was to measure the weight of goods with real barley grains. The second reflects the measurement of goods by an object of about 8–8.5 g that had something to do with "axes."

The writing $NINDA_2 \times ŠE + \mathit{15}$ appears sporadically in the Middle Sargonic corpus. It is definitely the precursor of the Classical Sargonic–Ur III writing *15* še "15 barleycorns."[285] It never appears with ma-na, which may be interpreted as evidence to interpret the logogram $NINDA_2 \times ŠE$ as /še/ "barleycorn." Another egg in the same basket is the inscribed sign ŠE, which may also allude to the reading of the logogram.

Hypothesizing on the origins of the lowest unit in the Sumerian system of weight measures, its name še "barleycorn" is the only piece of data we have. A grain of barley usually weighs about 0.04–0.05 g. These grains could have acted as primitive weights to measure amounts of goods of very high value: precious metals and gems. The reason for the choice of barley grains instead of other species of cultivated cereals is clear. First, barley was commonplace in Chalcolithic and Bronze Age Mesopotamia. Second, its physical characteristic – the lowest percentage of raw fiber after threshing among grain varieties – could have made these hard, solid grains natural measurement tools.[286] If we accept this theory, the barleycorn must have been originally an independent primitive unit unrelated to the shekel.

The artificial nature of the measure behind the writing $NINDA_2 \times ŠE + N_1$ ma-na in ED IIIa period documents is evident by the numbers with which it appears. The choice of either "1" or "2" in $NINDA_2 \times ŠE + N_1$ and no *$NINDA_2 \times ŠE$+24 ma-na "*24 little minas" or comparable indicates that this was a quasi-measure fulfilling the role of the shekel's fractions "one-third" and "two-thirds."

The suggestion by Powell that $NINDA_2 \times ŠE + N_1$ ma-na allowed a metrological link to be established between the measures "barleycorn" and "shekel" and conform to the Sumerian numerology explains clearly the emergence of the quasi-measure $NINDA_2 \times ŠE + N_1$ ma-na as a by-product of this event. The following hypothetical scenario is one of the possibilities of its reconstruction.

---

284 Powell 1990: 508.

285 BIN 8 175 obv. ii 11 (MS Isin), OSP 2 61 rev. i 4 (MS Nippur), BdI 1 88 obv. 1 (MS) Adab.

286 I thank Aron Dornauer for this suggestion.

The shekel on the one hand and the barleycorn on the other represented originally two independent measuring practices. In the first case, the weighing had something to do with "axes" and the weighing of silver. In the case of the barleycorn, barley grains represented weights for measuring goods that were even more luxurious. At some point, the need arose to link the shekel and the barleycorn. Two questions arise here: how and why? The first one has been answered above. The linkage resulted in the standardization of both measures, which ceased to represent their prototypes: the "axes" and real barley grains.

The "why" question is more intricate. We have at least several possibilities. (A) Merchants established a link between the barleycorn and the shekel on the one hand and between the shekel and the mina on the other to facilitate their trade. (B) Another scenario allows us to believe that the administrators of the central urban households ("scribes") were interested in, and needed, a standardized weight metrology to record incoming and outgoing goods in a precise manner.

Jöran Friberg proposed an interesting hypothesis on the origins of $NINDA_2 \times ŠE + N_1$ ma-na. He understands it literally as $šam_2$-ma-na "exchange mina," whose fraction 1/60 was later explicitly spelled as še "barleycorn." He relates the origins of the ratio 1:180 between the mina and this "exchange mina" to the same value equivalence between silver and copper: 1 mina of copper had the value of $NINDA_2 \times ŠE + 1N_1$ ma-na of silver. He concludes that "it is fairly safe to conclude that the Sumerian system *M(S)* [Sumerian system of weight measures – V.B.] arose as the result of a merger between two systems of weight numbers, one for copper with the main units mina and shekel, another for silver with the main units *exchange mina* and *barley-corn*."[287]

He proceeds with this theory in another place[288] and refines his argument in his ambitious publication of the mathematical texts in the Schøyen collection.[289] First, he adds the talent to the mina and the shekel of the alleged original system of copper measurement. Second, he interprets the writing $NINDA_2 \times ŠE+N$ $gi\hat{g}_4$ that appears in a metro-lexical text, CUNES 47-12-176, as "exchange shekel" equal to 1/60 of "exchange mina" = 1/180 of a shekel. In doing so, Friberg disclaims that the smallest unit was called "barleycorn" prior to the Sargonic period.

As we have seen, the talent was not a part of the weight metrology during the ED period. However, before proceeding to the critique of Friberg's theory, it is necessary to present the key document. CUNES 47-12-176 is the earliest and

287 Friberg 1999: 133.

288 Friberg 2005: 4.

289 Friberg 2007: 427.

most important lexical text to record the grapheme $NINDA_2 \times ŠE + N$. ED IIIa practical vocabularies (SF 20 and CUSAS 12 6.3.1) do not mention it.

Friberg published and edited this remarkable document, which is essentially a metrological list.[290] CUNES 47-12-176 is of uncertain provenance and its date may be established only by relying on its format and paleography. I had an opportunity to collate this document and my impression was that it belongs to the Early or Middle Sargonic period. However, this is certainly not the date of the creation of the *text* behind this cuneiform tablet. The contents of CUNES 47-12-176 suggest that this list was compiled during the Early Dynastic IIIa period at the latest since it epitomizes the notation of weight measures in script as they appear on Šuruppak tablets. Hence, CUNES 47-12-176 is a Sargonic copy of an Early Dynastic original. It is worth noting that the list starts with "10 minas," as all sections of Early Dynastic practical vocabularies do. Another detail is the absence of the talent. This too points to an early date of the text behind CUNES 47-12-176.

The following interpretation somewhat differs from that of Friberg (Tab. 5.1). I leave the interpretation of the graphemes $NINDA_2 \times ŠE + N$ ma-na / $gi\hat{g}_4$ open in the table. The division of the document into sections is for the sake of clarity. It is absent in the original manuscript.

The crucial detail for the interpretation of the grapheme $NINDA_2 \times ŠE + N$ is the writing $gi\hat{g}_4$-tur "little shekel" in rev. i 10. It cannot be identical to $gi\hat{g}_4$-tur "little shekel" of the Classical Sargonic documents for two reasons. First, $gi\hat{g}_4$-tur "little shekel" was introduced during the Classical Sargonic period, which is slightly later than ma-na-tur "little mina" (Middle Sargonic period). Ma-na-tur is missing in CUNES 47-12-176. The original writing $NINDA_2 \times ŠE + N_1$ ma-na appears instead of it. Secondly, the Classical Sargonic "little shekel" was worth three barleycorns (še). In contrast, the metrological value of one $gi\hat{g}_4$-tur in CUNES 47-12-176 is exactly one barleycorn. This means that the measure "barleycorn" was unknown to the author of the text.

$Gi\hat{g}_4$-tur poses another problem. How authentic is this -tur "small"? There are two possible scenarios. First, $gi\hat{g}_4$-tur is an authentic Early Dynastic writing. It suggests that the measure behind the grapheme $NINDA_2 \times ŠE + N$ $gi\hat{g}_4$ had nothing to do with barley grains and was called "little shekel." In this line of logic, $NINDA_2 \times ŠE + N_1$ ma-na is "little mina."

However, $gi\hat{g}_4$-tur is a *hapax legomenon*. It does not appear elsewhere. In contrast, $NINDA_2 \times ŠE + N$ $gi\hat{g}_4$ is documented in another text, OIP 14 70 (Tab. 5.2). It is an ED IIIb mathematical text from Adab that concerns the computation of

290 Friberg 2007: 426–428; see Proust 2010 for a definition of "metrological lists."

Tab. 5.1: Metro-mathematical text CUNES 47-12-176 (Early or Middle Sargonic).

Transliteration		Translation	Metrologic interpretation
		1. Mina	
obv.	[10 ma-na]	[10 minas]	[do.]
	[10 la$_2$ 1 ma-na]	[9 minas]	[do.]
	[8 ma-na]	[8 minas]	[do.]
	[7 ma-na]	[7 minas]	[do.]
	[6 ma-na]	[6 minas]	[do.]
	[5 ma-na]	[5 minas]	[do.]
	⌜4⌝ ma-[na]	4 minas	do.
	⌜3⌝ ma-⌜na⌝	3 minas	do.
	2 ma-na	2 minas	do.
	[1] ma-na	1 mina	do.
		2. Fractions of mina	
	[2N$_8$]^{ša} ma-na	⅔ mina	40 shekels
	[½] ⌜ma⌝-na	½ mina	30 shekels
	[½] ma-na la$_2$ 10 giĝ$_4$	½ mina minus 10 shekels	20 shekels
	[^{šu2}1N$_8$]$^{⌜ša⌝}$	⅓ (mina)	20 shekels
		3. Shekel	
ii	[15 giĝ$_4$]	[15 shekels]	do.
	[14 giĝ$_4$]	[14 shekels]	do.
	[13 giĝ$_4$]	[13 shekels]	do.
	[12 giĝ$_4$]	[12 shekels]	do.
	[11 giĝ$_4$]	[11 shekels]	do.
	10 giĝ$_4$	10 shekels	do.
	10 la$_2$ *1* ⌜giĝ$_4$⌝	10 minus 1 shekel	do.
	8 giĝ$_4$	8 shekels	do.
	7 giĝ$_4$	7 shekels	do.
	6 giĝ$_4$	6 shekels	do.
	5 giĝ$_4$	5 shekels	do.
	4 giĝ$_4$	4 shekels	do.
		4. The shekel's fractions	
	3 giĝ$_4$ NINDA$_2$ × ŠE + *15*	3 shekels 15 (barleycorns)	555 barleycorns
rev. i	*2* giĝ$_4$ NINDA$_2$ × ŠE + *10*	2 shekels 10 (barleycorns)	370 barleycorns
	1 giĝ$_4$ NINDA$_2$ × ŠE + *5*	1 shekel 5 (barleycorns)	185 barleycorns
	NINDA$_2$ × ŠE + 2N$_1$ ma-na	2 (little) minas	120 barleycorns
	½ giĝ$_4$	½ shekel	90 barleycorns

Tab. 5.1 (continued)

Transliteration		Translation	Metrologic interpretation
5	NINDA$_2$ × ŠE + 1N$_1$ ma-na NINDA$_2$ × ŠE + *15*	1 (little) mina 15 (barleycorns)	75 barleycorns
	igi-*3*-ĝal$_2$	⅓ (shekel)	60 barleycorns
	igi-⸢*4*⸣-ĝal$_2$	¼ (shekel)	45 barleycorns
	igi-*6*-ĝal$_2$	⅙ (shekel)	30 barleycorns
	5. Fractions of NINDA$_2$ × ŠE; the "little shekel" (barleycorn)		
	NINDA$_2$ × [ŠE] + 2N$_8^{ša}$	⅔ (little) mina	40 barleycorns
10	NINDA$_2$ × ŠE + ^{šu2}1N$_8^{ša}$ *5* giĝ$_4$-tur	⅓ (little) mina 5 little shekels (= barleycorns)	25 barleycorns
	NINDA$_2$ × ŠE + *15* giĝ$_4$	15 <little> shekels	15 barleycorns
	NINDA$_2$ × ŠE + ⸢*14*⸣ giĝ$_4$	14 <little> shekels	14 barleycorns
	NINDA$_2$ × ŠE + *13* giĝ$_4$	13 <little> shekels	13 barleycorns
	NINDA$_2$ × ŠE + *12* giĝ$_4$	12 <little> shekels	12 barleycorns
15	[NINDA$_2$ × ŠE + *11*] ⸢giĝ$_4$⸣	11 <little> shekels	11 barleycorns
	[NINDA$_2$ × ŠE + *10*] ⸢giĝ$_4$⸣	10 <little> shekels	10 barleycorns
ii	[NINDA$_2$ × ŠE + *10*] la$_2$ *1* giĝ$_4$	9 <little> shekels	9 barleycorns
	[NINDA$_2$ × ŠE+]*8* giĝ$_4$	8 <little> shekels	8 barleycorns
	[NINDA$_2$ × ŠE+]*7* giĝ$_4$	7 <little> shekels	7 barleycorns
	[NINDA$_2$ × ŠE+]*6* giĝ$_4$	6 <little> shekels	6 barleycorns
5	[NINDA$_2$ × ŠE+]*5* giĝ$_4$	5 <little> shekels	5 barleycorns
	[NINDA$_2$ × ŠE+*4*] giĝ$_4$	4 <little> shekels	4 barleycorns
	[NINDA$_2$ × ŠE+*3*] giĝ$_4$	3 <little> shekels	3 barleycorns
	[NINDA$_2$ × ŠE+*2*] giĝ$_4$	2 <little> shekels	2 barleycorns
	[NINDA$_2$ × ŠE+*1*] giĝ$_4$	1 <little> shekel	1 barleycorn
10	[NINDA$_2$ × ŠE+*½*] giĝ$_4$	½ <little> shekel	½ barleycorn

Tab. 5.2: NINDA$_2$ × ŠE + N ma-na / giĝ$_4$ in OIP 14 70 (ED IIIb Adab).

Metrological value	Actual writing in the text	Writing in CUNES 47-12-176
1/3 shekel = 1 "little mina"	1N$_1$ NINDA$_2$ × ŠE ma-na (obv. i 2, iii 2, 6) 1N$_1$ ma-na (obv. i 4) 1N$_1$ NINDA$_2$ × ŠE (rev. i 2)	NINDA$_2$ × ŠE + 1N$_1$ ma-na
2/3 shekel = 2 "little minas"	2N$_8$ ma-na (obv. ii 2)	NINDA$_2$ × ŠE + 2N$_1$ ma-na
15 "little shekels" (barleycorns)	10 + *5* giĝ$_4$ (obv. i 2) NINDA$_2$ × ŠE + 10 + *5* (rev. i 2)	NINDA$_2$ × ŠE + 10 + *5* giĝ$_4$

areas from one square cubit to three square reeds. The units "little mina" and "little shekel" appear as follows in this document (see Tab. 5.2).

This overview shows that the scribe utilized abbreviated writings to economize on space. One "little mina" appears in three variants. The first one is the full writing whereas the two others are shortened to either NINDA$_2$ × ŠE or ma-na. 1N$_1$ NINDA$_2$ × ŠE+10+*5* in rev. i 2 uses the single sign NINDA$_2$ × ŠE for both measures, the "little mina" and "little shekel."

Another interesting detail is the writing of the fraction "two-thirds" of a shekel as 2N$_8$ ma-na. The standard writing for this would be NINDA$_2$ × ŠE + 2N$_1$ ma-na. If we accept the idiosyncrasy of the ED IIIb texts from Adab in putting the number before NINDA$_2$ × ŠE, we must have had 2N$_1$ NINDA$_2$ × ŠE ma-na in the case of OIP 14 70. Why 2N$_8$ ma-na, then? Apparently, the scribe combined two practices. The first is to notate the fractions of the shekel like those of the mina: $^{\text{šu2}}$1N$_8$ "one-third" and 2N$_8$ "two-thirds." The second is to use the grapheme NINDA$_2$ × ŠE + N$_1$ ma-na as the writing for the shekel's fractions. Hence, 2N$_8$ ma-na is actually 2N$_8$ (NINDA$_2$ × ŠE) ma-na. Similar idiosyncrasies appear in other Early Dynastic texts.[291]

Still, there is no sign of giĝ$_4$-tur "little shekel" in OIP 14 70 or elsewhere. This challenges the philological interpretation of both measures, NINDA$_2$ × ŠE + N$_1$ ma-na and NINDA$_2$ × ŠE + *N* giĝ$_4$. The available data show that giĝ$_4$-tur is paralleled by še "barleycorn" in Sargonic records. A parallel to NINDA$_2$ × ŠE+$^{\text{šu2}}$1N$_8$^{ša} *5* giĝ$_4$-tur appears in a Middle Sargonic document from Isin: It is written NINDA$_2$ × ŠE+$^{\text{šu2}}$1N$_8$$^{\langle\text{ša-}\rangle\text{na}}$ še *2* "1/3 (of a little mina) 2 barleycorns."[292]

The merit of the theory of Friberg is that it emphasizes the parallelism of NINDA$_2$ × ŠE + N$_1$ ma-na and NINDA$_2$ × ŠE + *N* giĝ$_4$, a fact previously unknown. His theory of "exchange minas" and "exchange shekels" requires further elaboration. Doubtlessly, one mina of copper was worth one-third of a shekel of silver in the ED IIIa Šuruppak. However, the existence of an original measure of 2.77 g (the Friberg's "exchange mina") does not find proof in the written data. The most commonly documented measure that appears in connection with silver in the Early Dynastic and subsequent periods is the shekel and not the "exchange mina."

The final challenge that I would like to emphasize in connection to the Friberg's theory is the philological interpretation of "exchange mina" and "exchange shekel." The construction *sa$_{10}$-ma-na (*sa$_{10}$(m)=mana=(ak)) contradicts Sumerian syntax. A more plausible form would be *ma-na-sa$_{10}$-ma (*mana=sam$_2$=a(k)) "the mina of the purchase," which, nevertheless, is missing in the extant data.

291 See the text CUSAS 35 419 from the ED IIIb Umma region for similar "hybrid" writings.
292 BIN 8 35 obv. 5.

5.5 Many questions – some answers

The writing $NINDA_2 \times ŠE + N$ ma-na with the metrological values “one-third” and “two-thirds” of the shekel appears in the documentation of the Early Dynastic IIIa. Its use with weight measures and the grapheme ma-na (and $gi\hat{g}_4$ in the case of lexical and mathematical texts) indicates its original purpose of notating weight measures.

The weight measures behind $NINDA_2 \times ŠE + N$ ma-na and $NINDA_2 \times ŠE + N$ $gi\hat{g}_4$/še or simply še “barleycorn” are equal to 1/180 of a mina and 1/180 of a shekel from a metrological perspective. This results in measures of ca. 2.77 g and ca. 0.04–0.05 g, respectively. The first one could not represent an independent one. Its possible writings include only “1” and “2,” which indicates their role solely as the shekel’s fractions “one-third” and “two-thirds.” In contrast, the measure $NINDA_2 \times ŠE + N$ še – albeit extremely rarely documented during the Early Dynastic period – was a genuine measure of 0.04–0.05 g.

The linguistic realization of these measures poses considerable difficulties and hinges principally on later, Sargonic evidence. We know that their Sargonic successors were called ma-na-tur “little mina” and še “barleycorn.” The metro-mathematical text discussed in detail above records a hapax $NINDA_2 \times ŠE + N$ $gi\hat{g}_4$-tur. This supports the alternative hypothesis that these measures were originally called “little mina” and “little shekel.”

The unnatural factor 1:180 between the shekel and the barleycorn may be explained by two originally independent weighing practices represented by two primitive units. The first one of ca. 8.3 g was used to measure metals, principally silver. The second one of ca. 0.05 g was used to measure very expensive goods. Hence, the mass of one shekel being equal to the mass of 180 barleycorns is not because the exchange ratio between silver and copper was 1:180 during the ED period. Rather, the rationale behind this phenomenon was the pre-existence of these unrelated primitive measures. The exchange ratio 1:180 between silver and copper may have been a by-effect of the linkage of these units.

An overview of the history of the grapheme $NINDA_2 \times ŠE + N$ shows that it was poorly understood during the Presargonic period. The scribes introduced the construction igi-*n*-$\hat{g}al_2$ instead of it but were unable to get rid of it completely. The Sargonic reform also attempted to eliminate it by introducing ma-na-tur “little mina” and še “barleycorn.” Despite this, $NINDA_2 \times ŠE + N$ survived into the Ur III period, where it was a rare notation of the shekel’s fractions “one-third” and “two-thirds.”

6 Reforms and new measures

6.1 Introduction

The available data parade considerable differences in the number of weight measures in the system, their names, their writing, and their use in the written data of the different historical periods of 3rd mill. BC southern Mesopotamia. These dissimilarities indicate that the system was in constant change on the one hand. On the other hand, these data allow several succeeding historical stages to be distinguished in the development of the Sumerian system of weight measures. They are *the Early Dynastic, the Sargonic*, and *the Neo-Sumerian* stages. Needless to say, each of them is a *model*, that is, modern constructs for the sake of generalization and tracing trends in this cultural phenomenon. Nevertheless, enough evidence suggests that each of these stages was the result of a conscious set of improvements, a *reform*.

This latter term requires explanation in the present context. *Reform* refers to a systematic innovation of major aspects of the system of weight measures. It should not be linked directly to any central political authority. I do not count local idiosyncrasies and other minor deviations as the signs of a *reform*. Hence, this chapter puts together the discussions in the previous chapters and augments them with still undiscussed ones to delineate the evolution of the weight metrology in southern Mesopotamia relying on the *reforms* as the constructs necessary for the clarity of discussion and the possibility of synthesis.

The data clearly indicate that the innovations in the weight metrology and their representation in script were never isolated events. They were *always* the parts of larger shifts in accounting practices and script. I deliberately avoid mentioning "shifts in metrology" in this context. I argue that what we call "metrology" in the context of Sumerian archival records is actually *accounting*. Inhabitants of the 4th and 3rd mill. BC Near East doubtlessly employed weighing practices to measure certain types of goods *prior* to the conscious choice of Sumerian scribes to "standardize" and introduce weight metrology in script. What we have there are not the pristine everyday weighing practices that arose from the need to measure metals and wool. In contrast, the "Sumerian system of weight measures" is, strictly speaking, an accounting practice. It had been adopted by central urban households – palaces and temples – to record the circulation of goods that fall within the scope of interests of precisely these social organizations and power hierarchies as their frame. Therefore, the documents allow us to examine how the weight metrology had developed throughout the 3rd mill. BC only indirectly: through the myopic spectacles of the scribes. This necessarily puts limitations on this study. *We*

https://doi.org/10.1515/9781501510267-006

cannot see the system of weight measures. We see merely how it was used by a small part of the population at the top of the social pyramid.

The agency aspect is closely related to the political aspect in the case of metrological reforms. An evident pattern is that larger innovations in metrology and script were coincident with major political changes, which is the case with the first kings of the Akkad and Ur III Dynasties, Sargon and Ur-Namma. The question is whether *the Early Dynastic stage* – the earliest shape of the Sumerian system of weight measures we currently know about – was related to some major political events or not is uncertain.

6.2 The Early Dynastic stage

Chapters 3–5 present the analysis principally of the earliest stage of the Sumerian system of weight measures as we find it in written records. The data available to us confirm that this stage was synchronous with the Early Dynastic period in southern Mesopotamia (ca. 3000/2900–2350 BC). Many of its manifestations were still in use during the earlier part of the Sargonic period and because of this coincided with the onset of innovations in accounting and script by the first Akkadian kings.

The Early Dynastic stage is present in full in the ED IIIa period (ca. 2600–2500 BC). However, it is likely at least as old as the ED I–II period. The system at ca. 2600 BC consisted of three units: the mina, the shekel, and a measure of 0.04–0.05 g (the barleycorn; see the previous chapter). A quasi-measure NINDA$_2$×ŠE+N$_1$ ma-na, the predecessor of the Sargonic "little mina," plays the role of the link between the shekel and the barleycorn. The numerical relations of the individual parts in this system are summarized in the following figure.

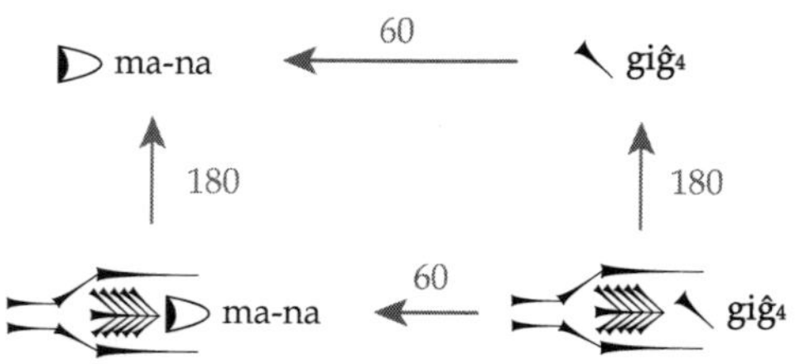

Fig. 6.1: Numerical relations between units in the Early Dynastic (IIIa) system.

This figure is an idealized vision of this system. It is how ED scribes modeled it and what they wanted it to look like. This image does not reflect the actual use of the measures and their fractions in administrative and legal documents, which points to the origins of each unit and the emergence of this system "outside the script."

The real picture is more complex. It allows us to see the artificial link between originally two independent measuring practices and the role of the measure NINDA$_2$×ŠE+N$_1$ ma-na as a bond between them:

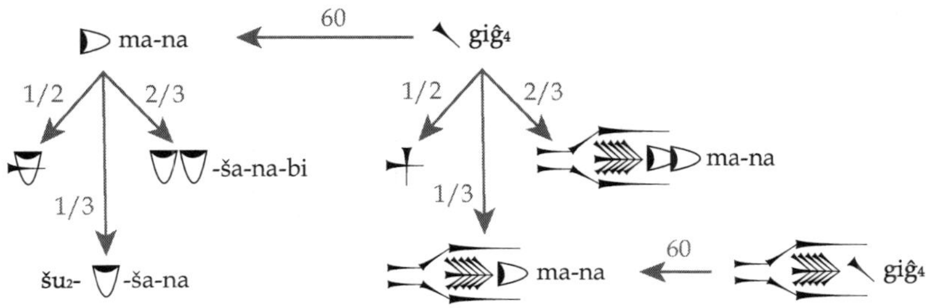

Fig. 6.2: The Early Dynastic (IIIa) system of weight measures.

In the previous chapters, I discussed possible scenarios of how each unit could have emerged, and hypotheses trying to explain the linkage between these units. Since the Early Dynastic stage is the earliest traceable period in the history of the weight metrology in Mesopotamia, the questions surrounding its emergence are the most challenging and the data are meager. However, as the previous discussion and Chapter 10 show, the units "mina," "shekel," and "barleycorn" must have been originally independent measurement practices and the masses of these primitive measures were not standardized. Their area of application was the measurement of copper (the mina), silver (the shekel), and even more precious goods (the barleycorn). We do not know, and probably will never know, how, when, and why these units were united into one system of relations for the first time. However, the factor "60" between the mina and the shekel suggests the origins in the socioeconomic milieu where the Sumerian sexagesimal logic functioned. In contrast, the term for the mina and its fractions indicate that the weight metrology has emerged in the far more cosmopolite and broader context of the Near Eastern interregional trade.

Most of the elements of the Early Dynastic "system" are present in the following, Sargonic stage. Notably, the archaic writing NINDA$_2$×ŠE+2 survived even into the Ur III period as a fraction for "two-thirds" of a shekel. This means that the Early Dynastic stage is the Sumerian system of weights par excellence. It represents its original, pristine form. In contrast, the Sargonic and Neo-Sumerian stages are further improvements of this system.

The linkage of weight metrology to other systems of mensuration is a definite sign of the standardization of measures. It also presupposes a high degree of mathematical knowledge and abstract thinking. The data show that some parts of the weight metrology have been borrowed into other systems of mensuration by the Early Dynastic IIIa period, for example, the area and capacity systems of mensuration. The weight unit ma-na was equated with the basic units in these systems. They are sar "garden plot" of ca. 36 m^2 and $sila_3$ of ca. 1 liter. As a result, the mina, the sar, and the $sila_3$ shared the mina's fractions and were divided into 60 shekels.

It is necessary to emphasize that the linkage of the system of weights to the area and capacity measures via the mina pertains only to the realm of numbers and not metrology. The mina has been equated to the *sar* and the *sila*, the basic unit in each of the systems. This prevents speculation that, let's say, the mass of a mina was equal to the mass of a *sila* of water or whatever. The following example is illustrative.

Powell argued that the metrological link between the mina and the *sila* dated back to the Sargonic reform. He suggested the ratio "one *sila* of water (1 l) = 2 mina (= 500 g × 2)." Powell related this innovation to the use of the water clock, Greek *clepsydra*, Sumerian ^{ĝeš}dib-dib, Akkadian *dibdibbu* and *maštaktu*.[293] Some archaeologists corroborate his suggestion that a *sila* could be about one liter.[294] The use of the water clock is an intricate question. I do not know any references to the use of ^{ĝeš}dib-dib in 3rd mill. BC sources.[295] The reference to this gear in the Old Babylonian lexical tradition suggests that Sumerians did indeed use it and that it was made from wood, which makes it impossible to identify archaeologically.[296]

Other data prove that there was no metrological link between one mina and two *sila* of water prior to the Sargonic period. In contrast, scribes drew a parallel between one *sila* of any liquid and one mina. Obviously, this practice did not involve any elaborate metrological experiments but was done "by eye" for the sake of simplicity of calculations. Early Dynastic documents concerning the preparation of aromatic oils corroborate this suggestion. One took 40 minas of an aromatic substance *algazum* to make one jar (dug) of oil, which is paralleled by 40 *sila* of the aromatic substance šim-gam-gam-ma for the same jar of oil.[297] The correspondence of a mina to a *sila* appears in other ED IIIb "perfume texts." Numbers of minas and *sila* are identical on numerous occasions. It is

---

293 Powell 1990: 509.

294 Senior and Weiss 1992.

295 CAD D: 134 *dibdibbu*.

296 *OB Ura* I 144.

297 VS 14 123 obv. i 1–4 (ED IIIb Ĝirsu): 40 ma-na al-$gazum_x$; i_3 dug-1-kam; 40 $sila_3$ šim-gam-gam-ma; i_3 dug 1-kam.

worth noting that despite the Sargonic reform, Sargonic texts proceed with the same practice to "equate" one mina of weighed aromatics with one *sila* of resins measured by capacity units.[298]

One question is whether this "one mina = one *sila*" ratio had any metrological background. Francesco Pomponio and Giuseppe Visicato believe that one *sila* was about 0.5 liter during the ED IIIa period.[299] Rosemary Ellison also believed the *sila* was less than one liter during the early periods. She connects the fluctuation of the amount of remuneration in barley in 3rd mill. BC archival records to the change in the capacity of the *sila*.[300] However, the question of the capacity of the *sila* goes beyond the scope of the present study. The fact remains that accounts of aromatics tend to record equal numbers of weighed goods on the one hand and of those in capacity measures on the other. My impression is that this practice has no metrological background whatsoever. It is rooted in the desire of the Early Dynastic scribes to avoid complicated calculations and numbers in their accounts. This must have resulted in considerable discrepancies in the actual masses of the weighed goods and the numbers that appeared in the tablets. Indeed, the shekel is relatively rare with any goods but silver in the ED IIIa period. It seems that the ED scribes were content with this modest level of precision, which would horrify pedantic accountants of the Ur III period.

In summary, no data suggest any metrological-based linkage of the weight and capacity metrology in the ED period.

6.3 The Sargonic reform

The Sargonic period (ca. 2350(2325)–2150 BC) brought changes that one cannot overestimate in terms of the history of Mesopotamia. The founder of the Akkadian dynasty, Sargon, created the first territorial state that encompassed central and southern Mesopotamia and laid the foundation of what many believe to have been the first empire in human history. His grandson, Naram-Suen, succeeded in accomplishing this task. This political formation stretched from western Syria to western Iran. It is hard to find any sphere that has not been affected by daring

---

298 See, for example, a Classical Sargonic account of resins CUSAS 35 514 for the proportion 1:1 of the first entries of the weighed and liquid resins: 2 ^{ĝeš}eren gun$_2$ (= 120 minas) and 2(bar-iga) šim-gig (= 120 *sila*) (obv. 1, rev. 1).

299 EDATŠ: 32 n. 4.

300 See Ellison 1981: 38. However, see Sallaberger 1996b: 83 for the same amount of remuneration received by men and women at the Presargonic Nabada (Tell Beydar) and in the Mesopotamian South during the Ur III period.

and often voluntarist innovations of the Akkadian kings. This is the reason why kings-reformers were never forgotten in the Mesopotamian learned tradition and became examples in later literary-political tradition.[301]

The Sargonic period marks a number of innovations in writing and metrology. Due to their systematic and revolutionary nature, they may be subsumed under the title "Sargonic Reform." Powell referred to this event as "the Akkad reform."[302] Since most Sargonic documents available to him were of the "Classical Sargonic" paleographic stage, he linked it with the second part of Naram-Suen's reign, the period after he had defeated the "Great Revolt" of the coalitions of the southern and northern Sumerian cities against the Akkadian rule.

Probably owing to an image of Naram-Suen as a ruthless warrior and dashing innovator in the cuneiform literary tradition, the scholarly community accepted this theory as dogma. However, a careful study of Early, Middle, and Classical Sargonic corpora separately reveals that the so-called "Sargonic reform" was not a snapshot. On the contrary, it was a set of innovations introduced over a considerable period: starting from Sargon's reign to that of his grandson, Naram-Suen.

As we have seen, one of the predecessors of Naram-Suen "introduced" the talent into the family of weight measures. Another innovation that predated this ruler was probably ma-na-tur "little mina." Nevertheless, one should acknowledge the role of Naram-Suen in the Sargonic reforms: the reformed weight metrology in its finished shape appears for the first time in the records of his reign.

An overview of the innovations during the Sargonic reform creates an impression that Akkadian kings and their associates were perfectionists aiming to create flawless administration, taxation, and accounting, elegant writing, and a logical, all-in-one, symmetrical metrology. Sometimes they overdid it. The Sargonic stage of the weight metrology was artificial and unpractical in real life. The reform introduced ma-na-tur for the older $\text{NINDA}_2\times\text{ŠE+N}_1$ ma-na. Obviously, one wanted to avoid a gap between the barleycorn and the shekel that resulted in the ratio 1:180 and to make the system conform to the factor "60." Nevertheless, the most extravagant innovation was probably the creation of a completely new weight unit, the "little shekel" (giĝ_4-tur). This is the only example of this kind in the history of the 3rd millennium. Again, the Sargonic officials wanted this to make the whole system perfectly symmetrical (see fig. below). This longing for speculative knowledge and embellishment is in stark

301 For the Sargonic period in general, see Westenholz 1999 and Foster 2016. See Goodnick Westenholz 1997 for the reception of the deeds by Akkadian kings in the Babylonian literary tradition.

302 Powell 1990: 490 and *passim*.

contrast to the practice-oriented Neo-Sumerian stage of the weight system: Everything that appeared artificial was mercilessly abandoned.

In its finished form by the second half of Naram-Suen's reign, *the Sargonic system* of weight measures had taken the following shape in script:

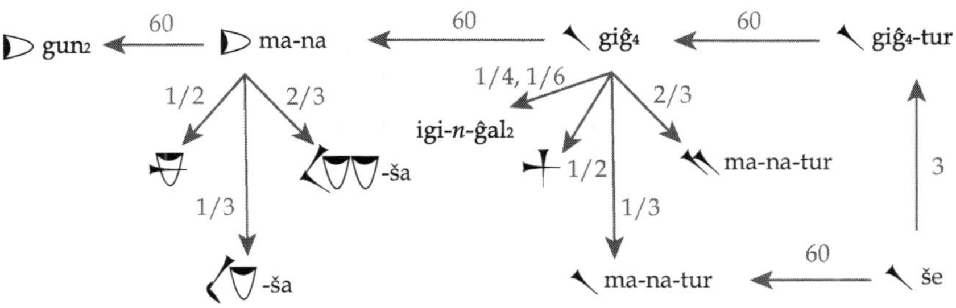

Fig. 6.3: The system of weight measures by the second half of Naram-Suen's reign (Classical Sargonic period).

Turning to the "pros" of the Sargonic reform in respect of weight metrology, the most useful innovation was the standardization of the "load" as 60 minas of ca. 500 g, thereby turning it into a standardized measure we call "talent" (it remained the same "load" for the ancients). This event predated Naram-Suen. The construction igi-*n*-ĝal$_2$ of the shekel's fractions "one-fourth" and "one-sixth" is even older (ED IIIb). In fact, the only certain innovation that may be attributed to Naram-Suen with certainty is the useless "little shekel."

Owing to its extravagance, *the Sargonic system* of weight measures was in use over a relatively short period. Once the capital Akkade lost control over this or that city, their scribes immediately decided in favor of a simplified system, which I name below the *Neo-Sumerian stage*.

6.3.1 New names for old measures 1: še "barleycorn"

The grapheme NINDA$_2$×ŠE+*N* (giĝ$_4$) denoted the unit of 0.04–0.05 g in Early Dynastic texts. As the previous chapter shows, it may have been pronounced as "barleycorn" or as "little shekel," unless NINDA$_2$×ŠE+N giĝ$_4$-tur in the metro-lexical text CUNES 47-12-176 is not an invention of a Sargonic scribe. Be that as it may, the presence of an artificial measure of 2.77 g in the ED IIIa texts confirms that the "barleycorn" had become a standardized unit by that time. This suggests that the barleycorn cannot be the measure that defined the mass of the larger units in the Sumerian system of weight measures.

Several scholars proposed a different view. Stefan Karwiese (1990) and Daniel McDonald (1992) argue in their works that the mass of a barleycorn defined the mass of all higher units in the system. However, their studies do not take into account the role of the earliest written data and the role of the NINDA$_2$×ŠE+N$_1$ ma-na in particular. Some of the ideas expressed by these scholars are purely speculative, which makes their contributions largely unusable.[303] All data suggests that the key "players" in the system – the mina, the shekel, and the barleycorn – were originally independent units. Hence, the emergence of the system was not a linear process, but a multi-source one.

Although the unit NINDA$_2$×ŠE+*N* (giĝ$_4$) of 0.05–0.04 g does not appear in administrative and legal accounts, Early Dynastic scribes were familiar with it since we find it in lexical and mathematical texts. Turning to the Sargonic evidence on this measure, I would like to draw attention to an interesting phenomenon. Middle and some Classical Sargonic texts document the use of še "barleycorn" together with the writings of the shekel's fractions igi-*3*-ĝal$_2$ "one-third" and the "archaic" NINDA$_2$×ŠE+2N$_1$ for "two-thirds."[304] This is an interesting deviation since the Sargonic reform presupposes the use of ma-na-tur "little mina" in both cases. This and similar phenomena discussed below indicate that the spread of reform was not even, which makes the use of these texts to date documents inappropriate: A document may be "Classical Sargonic" and not use ma-na-tur.

The numbers of barleycorns in Middle and Classical Sargonic records are mostly round: 20, 15, and 10. However, lesser amounts are also documented.[305] BIN 8 35 offers an interesting example: The "archaic" fraction "one-third little mina" (NINDA$_2$×ŠE+N $^{\text{šu2}}$1N$_8$$^{\langle\text{ša-}\rangle\text{na}}$) replaces an easier and common writing *20* še to express 20 barleycorns.

Some Classical Sargonic notations with barleycorns require caution to interpret. $^{\text{šu2}}$|1N$_8$.1N$_8$|^{ša} 9 giĝ$_4$ igi-*3*-ĝal$_2$ *2*(ĝeš$_{2'}$u) še ku$_3$ in STTI 26 rev. ii 3 is challenging (if the copy is correct). Here, the pointed sign ĜEŠ'U(*DIŠ*×*U*) cannot be "600" since it would result in an irrational "1200 barleycorns." Instead, it is a scribal error for 20 barleycorns.

---

303 See Karwiese 1990 on nonexistent "egg" and "honey" Mesopotamian weighing norms, etc. See McDonald 1992: 14–15: "the first standard (i.e. the barleycorn) might have been worth 360 barleycorns which might have corresponded to the Sumerian administrative year of 360 days" and other fantastic views.

304 MC 4 69 rev. 5 (MS/CS uncert. prov.): šu-niĝin$_2$ *2*(*AŠ.AŠ*) giĝ$_4$ igi-*3*-ĝal$_2$ *15* še. MAD 5 108 obv. 7 (CS uncert. prov.): igi-*3*-ĝal$_2$ *20* še. Rev. 7: šu+niĝin$_2$ 6 giĝ$_4$ NINDA$_2$×ŠE+2N$_1$ *20* še. ITT 1 1091 rev. 1 (MS/CS Ĝirsu): ku$_3$-bi 15 ½ ma-na 7 giĝ$_4$ NINDA$_2$×ŠE+2N$_1$ *15* še.

305 See OSP 2 183 obv. 1 (CS Nippur) for eight barleycorns, Nik 2 78 obv. i 6' (CS Umma) for four barleycorns, and BIN 8 35 obv. 5 (MS Isin) for two barleycorns.

CUNES 47-12-176 and later metro-lexical and lexical texts record "one-half" of the barleycorn as the bottom line in the weight metrology. The fraction "one-third" in the Ur III records (see below) and of the post-Sumerian lexical tradition is not documented in Sargonic records.[306]

The references to a half of a barleycorn are rare.[307] They become more frequent in Ur III documents. Nevertheless, these Sargonic data are important. They show the elaborateness in the accounting practices of the scribes. However, these fractions may have existed only in script. The insufficient level of technological precision during the Early Bronze Age would not allow such little masses of materials to be controlled.

6.3.2 New names for old measures 2: ma-na-tur "little mina"

The previous chapter discussed the fact that $NINDA_2{\times}ŠE+N_1$ ma-na was the predecessor of the Classical Sargonic ma-na-tur. However, it remains uncertain whether "little mina" is hiding behind the archaic notation. At any rate, the element ma-na points in that direction.

The *Maništusu Obelisk* is the earliest datable document that records both the talent and the writing ma-na-tur "little mina."[308] This means that if this document is authentic, the introduction of the writing ma-na-tur predates the second half of Naram-Suen's reign. Consequently, documents mentioning ma-na-tur should not be interpreted as "Classical Sargonic" par excellence.

In principle, Sargonic scribes did not introduce anything groundbreaking with the writing ma-na-tur. This quasi-measure is as old as the ED IIIa period at the latest. Hence, they "revived" it. This stands in contrast to the impression created by the Presargonic documents of abolishing this quasi-measure in favor of the shekel's fractions. The reintroduction of the unit of 2.77 g in the course of the Sargonic reform was an unprecedented event in the history of Mesopotamian metrology. Sargonic scribes gave the old unit a new and simple phonetic writing and aimed to replace with it the Presargonic igi-*3*-ĝal$_2$ for one-third of a shekel on the one hand and $NINDA_2{\times}ŠE+2N_1$ for two-thirds of a shekel on the other.

The examples of the irregular appearance of ma-na-tur show that the scribes decided for themselves whether to use it or not in some cases or in particular localities. At any rate, the introduction of the unit of 2.77 g and the

306 See MSL 10: 16 l. 452 for the post-Sumerian lexical data.

307 For the Sargonic period, see MAD 5 17 rev. 3 (CS Kiš) and NBC 10,262 rev. 3 (CS$^?$ uncert. prov.; see Foster 1982a pl. 7 no. 7 and Steinkeller 1981a: 130 for an edition).

308 ELTS 40 passim and a similar ELTS 41 ii 7' f.

writing ma-na-tur certainly created confusion among the scribes. Sometimes the little mina appears as just ma-na "mina."[309] Only the context explains its value. Telling the usual mina from the "little" one has become a problem. The writing ma-na-gal "large mina" is documented at least once in the Classical Sargonic corpus as a means of avoiding possible ambiguity.[310] Lexical data do not record ma-na-gal. However, it is present in Old Assyrian documents from the Anatolian trade colony in Kaneš.[311] Nevertheless, it is hard to say whether there is any link between the Sargonic and Old Assyrian data.

Are ma-na-tur and ma-na-gal good Sumerian? In other words, are these words original or are they loanwords from Akkadian? Powell hypothesized that "*mana-tur" originates in "*mana ṣahrum*."[312] The uncertainty of the reading of the Early Dynastic grapheme $NINDA_2{\times}ŠE{+}N_1$ ma-na does not facilitate clarification of this issue. The fact that the later lexical tradition equated Sumerian igi-*n*-$\hat{g}al_2$ with the Akkadian *ma-an ṣa-ah-ru* "little mina"[313] indicates that the knowledge of the Babylonian scribes went no further than the Sargonic period in this case.

Apart from several Early and Middle Sargonic attestations of ma-na-tur mentioned above, it is mostly documented in Classical Sargonic documents. As for the local distribution – from Ešnunna and Mugdan to Ĝirsu – it must have been identical to the borders of Naram-Suen's state. Metals are the goods that are measured in the little mina in all cases. They are silver and gold, and, exceptionally, copper.[314]

Several Classical Sargonic texts witness an idiosyncratic writing of the little mina. It appears as $^{šu2}1N_8{}^{ša}$-tur for "one little mina" and $^{šu2}2N_8{}^{ša}$-tur for "two little minas." It is another example of "hybrid" writing. It takes the mina's notations

---

309 Cf. a remark by Steinkeller in connection to the Sargonic sales of fields from Ešnunna ELTS 43–44: 156: "The sign TUR may have been omitted by the scribe because the context made the meaning of MA.NA as MA.NA.TUR explicit." For this practice in other Ešnunna documents see MAD 1 50 rev. i' 1 and MVN 3 102 obv. 1. Nevertheless, this practice sporadically pops up in documents from other locations.

310 MVN 3 108 obv. 2 (CS uncert. prov.): 1 ku_3-babbar ma-na-gal la_2 5 ku_3-babbar $gi\hat{g}_4$.

311 BIN 6 193 obv. 1, rev. 5', 944 rev. 2.

312 Powell 1979: 99–100.

313 CAD M/1: 219. MSL 10 32 line 97: na_4 ⅓ $gi\hat{g}_4$ = na_4 ma-na *ṣe-eh-[ri]* = *šul-lul-ti* $šiq_2$*-lim* "stone weight of ⅓ shekel = stone of (one) little mina = one-third of a shekel." *Ea* I 358, 362 (MSL 14: 195): [i-gi]-eš-gal "one-third" = 1/3 = *ma-an ṣa-ah-ru* "little mina" and [i-gi-eš-gal]-⸢ma⸣-na-min "two one-thirds" = 2/3 = *ši-na ma-an ṣa-ah-ru* "two little minas."

314 Gold: OSP 2 17 obv. 1, 22 obv. 1, 23 obv. 1, rev. 1 (CS Nippur). Silver: ITT 1 1070 obv. 1 (CS Ĝirsu), MAD 1 166 obv. 1 ff., 195 obv. 2, 5, 303 (ku_3-babbar *el-lum*; CS Ešnunna), MAD 5 86 obv. 1 (CS Mugdan), Imgula 3/1 57 obv. 2 (CS Tutub), CUSAS 27 209 obv. 1 (CS Umm al-Hafriyat). Silver or gold: MAD 5 17 rev. 3; 6 (CS Kiš). Copper: ITT 2 4369 obv. 1 (CS Ĝirsu).

"one-third" and "two-thirds" to designate the respective shekel's fractions. As we have seen, this was the standard practice in the Early Dynastic Umma state. On the other hand, the attribute "-tur" identifies the measure as "little mina."

One may argue that these strange writings represent the fractions of the little mina "one-third" (20 barleycorns) and "two-thirds" (40 barleycorns) instead of the little mina itself. Luckily, the calculations in an account from Ešnunna MAD 1 195 eliminate this doubt. Ignace Gelb erroneously reconstructed ⸢2⸣ in obv. 5 and therefore the sum is not correct in the original publication. The corrected transliteration is as follows.[315]

obv.	⸢15⸣ iku	15 *iku* land:
	sa$_{10}$-*su* ku$_3$-babbar 16 giĝ$_4$ **2 ma-na-tur**	its price is 16 shekels 2 little minas silver:
	Diĝir-*dan*	*'Ilum-dān*.
	1(eše$_3$) iku	6 *iku* land:
5	sa$_{10}$-*su* ku$_3$-babbar 6 giĝ$_4$ **[1] ma-na-tur**	its price is 6 shekels [1] little mina silver:
	[*I$_3$*]-*li$_2$-a-hi*	*'Ilī-'ahī*.
rev.	⸢80⸣ sar	80 *sar* land
	sa$_{10}$-*su* ku$_3$-babbar 1 giĝ$_4$ la$_2$ $^{\text{šu2}}$**1N$_8$**^{ša}**-tur**	its price is 1 shekel minus 1 little mina:
	UD-⸢*kum*⸣	... *kum*.
	(blank)	
	šu-niĝin$_2$ 22 ⸢iku⸣ [20] ⸢sar⸣	Total: 22 *iku* [20] *sar*:
5	šu-niĝin$_2$ $^{\text{šu2}}$1N$_8$$^{⸢\text{ša}⸣}$ [2] ⸢giĝ$_4$⸣ $^{\text{šu2}}$**⸢2**^{ša}**⸣-tur**	Total: 1/3 (mina) [2] shekels 2 little minas.
l. e.	[mostly broken]	

The corrected sum of silver (22 shekels 2 little minas) illustrates that one shekel buys 10 *sar* of land. However, the most interesting detail is the fact that the scribe uses two different notations of the same metrological unit, the little mina. He puts down the standard, "reformed" writing "n ma-na-tur" on the obverse and writes the idiosyncratic $^{\text{šu2}}$N$_8$^{ša}-tur on the reverse. It is hard to explain this extravagance. $^{\text{šu2}}$N$_8$^{ša}-tur appears in another document from Ešnunna, a text from Sippar, and a tablet of uncertain provenance.[316]

315 Photo: P215097.

316 All texts record silver: OAIC 5 obv. 1 (CS Ešnunna), CT 50 83 obv. i 4' (CS Sippar), NBC 10,262 rev. 3 (CS$^?$ uncert. prov.).

The situation with the fractions of the little mina in Sargonic archival documents is the same as with the barleycorn. Only "one-half" of the little mina (30 barleycorns) is documented. It is written not with the usual sign for the "half" but with its "Umma" variant in one document.[317] Since there is no doubt about the provenance of the tablet at Kiš, the basis of this idiosyncrasy lays in the desire of the scribe to avoid possible confusion between the little mina and other units. It is another example that shows that scribes in every corner of the empire looked for ways to avoid ambiguity in the notation of the new unit.

In summary, ma-na-tur is the successor of the archaic quasi-measure written NINDA$_2$×ŠE+N$_1$ ma-na in ED IIIa-period texts. Sargonic scribes revived it and gave it a phonetic writing, something that created considerable confusion among the scribes in Mesopotamia. Owing to its nonpracticality, it existed only for a short period. Neo-Sumerian texts do not use it.

6.3.3 A new unit: giĝ$_4$-tur "little shekel"

One little shekel is three barleycorns (ca. 0.138 g). It appears as giĝ$_4$-tur in Classical Sargonic tablets. Powell suggested that the Akkadian equivalent of giĝ$_4$-tur should be **šiqlum ṣahrum*.[318] However, there are no data whatsoever about this in synchronous or later sources.

As we have seen in the previous chapter, the writing giĝ$_4$-tur is older than the Classical Sargonic period. It is part of the grapheme NINDA$_2$×ŠE+*N* giĝ$_4$ (-tur) in the Early Sargonic metro-mathematical text CUNES 47-12-176. However, it designates the unit of 0.04–0.05 g "the barleycorn" there and is not related to the little shekel of the Sargonic reform.

The fact that ma-na-tur and giĝ$_4$-tur share the same morphological pattern may lead to the conjecture that the latter unit was as old as the former, that is, contemporaneous with the *Maništusu Obelisk*. However, the extant texts confirm that the grapheme giĝ$_4$-tur does not predate the Classical Sargonic period.

In principle, giĝ$_4$-tur is nothing groundbreaking from a numeric perspective. The fraction "1/60" of a shekel dates back to the Early Dynastic period. Friberg edited an interesting Presargonic metro-mathematical text concerning area calculations that probably goes back to the Fara period canon.[319] This text uses the shekel as the fraction "1/60" of the basic area unit *sar*. This "area

317 MAD 5 23 obv. 2, pl. xi (CS Kiš).

318 Powell 1971: 215; Powell 1979: 93; Powell 1990: 510.

319 CUNES 50-08-001 (ED IIIb Zabalam?) = Friberg 2007: 419–425.

shekel" is further subdivided into 60 parts. The writing is not giĝ$_4$-tur as in the Classical Sargonic texts but giĝ$_4$-bi "its shekel" (1/60 of a shekel). This tiny area may be subdivided again: giĝ$_4$-ba-giĝ$_4$ "shekel of its shekel" denotes 1/216,000 of a *sar*. Since the Early Dynastic giĝ$_4$-bi is numerically identical to the Classical Sargonic weight measure "little shekel," the idea of dividing the shekel into 60 parts was not new.

Nevertheless, the little shekel lacks any historical background as a weight measure. Certainly, no primitive unit would lead to the standardized unit of 0.138 g. Additionally, the little shekel is seldom found in Classical Sargonic documents, suggesting that even Sargonic accountants considered it unpractical. The only benefit of this measure was that it made the system of weights symmetrical. It provided a parallel to the shekel: Three little minas made one shekel and three barleycorns made one little shekel. This had nothing to do with the actual weighing. Although the data suggest the accuracy of weighing up to one barleycorn, I know no actual weights that would represent the standard of the little shekel. This measure may have existed only "on paper," and the actual weighing was done – as it had been done since gray times – with shekel and barleycorn weights.

The little shekel appears in the context of gold, silver, and tin. One document records 12 shekels 1 little mina 15 little shekels of gold.[320] Another text records 1 mina minus 5 little shekels silver as the price of two oxen.[321] One damaged account calculates small amounts of a metal, probably silver, in connection with a number of individuals.[322] The shekel, the little shekel, and the barleycorn appear here; remarkably, the shekel's fraction igi-*3*-ĝal$_2$ takes the place of one little mina in this document. Another Sargonic text mentions the little shekel and avoids the little mina.[323] The same document records the fractions "one-half" of a little shekel, ca. 0.069 g. It appears in the context of tin to produce bronze.[324] Another document records three and a half little shekels of silver.[325]

The Classical Sargonic giĝ$_4$-tur was introduced into the systems of area and volume mensuration upon its creation. It was worth 36 square fingers in area

---

320 ITT 1 1070 obv. 1 (CS Ĝirsu).
321 CT 50 73 obv. i 4'(CS Sippar).
322 STTI 170 (CS Ĝirsu).
323 ITT 5 6671 obv. 3', rev. 1 (CS Ĝirsu). It uses the notation NINDA$_2$×ŠE+2N$_1$ instead of 2 ma-na-tur: ku$_3$-bi 4 giĝ$_4$ NINDA$_2$×ŠE+2N$_1$ *2* giĝ$_4$-tur "its silver (=price): 4 2/3 shekels 2 little shekels" and NINDA$_2$×ŠE+2N$_1$ *8* giĝ-tur an-na "2/3 (shekel) 8 little shekels tin."
324 ITT 5 6671 obv. 2', rev. 2 (CS Ĝirsu): 1 ma-<na > la$_2$ *3 ½* giĝ$_4$-⸢tur⸣ zabar-še$_3$ "1 mina minus 3 ½ little shekels (tin) for bronze" and šu-niĝin$_2$ 1 ma-na 5 ½ giĝ$_4$ *5 ½* giĝ$_4$-⸢tur⸣ [an-na] "total: 1 mina 5 ½ shekels 5 ½ little shekels [tin]."
325 MAD 5 84 obv. 1 (CS Mugdan).

mensuration and 5 *sila* in volume mensuration.[326] It is rare in archival records. For example, *11* nindan-DU *1* $kuš_3$-numun multiplied by *1* GIŠ.BAD (= 1 $kuš_3$) *1* zipah.[327] This results in an area of *1 ¼* iku *3* sar *6* $gi\hat{g}_4$ *15* $gi\hat{g}_4$-tur.

In summary, the Classical Sargonic weight measure $gi\hat{g}_4$-tur "little shekel" is the only innovation in the weight metrology that may be dated with certainty to Naram-Suen's reign. This impractical measure appeared in accounts of metals for a short time and then faded away without leaving a trace in later written records.

6.4 The roots of the Neo-Sumerian system

Šarkališarri was the last direct successor of Sargon. The Sargonic state began to crumble under the pressure of Gutians, Amorites, and Elamites. Eventually, Akkad fell into the hands of the Gutians, who established their dynasty with the capital in Adab. The period after Šarkališarri and until the accession of the first ruler of the Ur III dynasty bears the name "Gutian," which lasted about a hundred years.[328] Two polities under the Uruk IV and the Lagaš II dynasties had secured independence in the south. Less than a thousand administrative and legal records survive from this time. The majority of about 600 tablets are from Ĝirsu, the capital of the Lagaš II Dynasty.[329] Its most famous sovereign was Gudea. About a quarter of these archival data have references to weight measures. They attest to a drastic simplification of the system of weight measures.

These documents are in Sumerian. Nevertheless, they witness the Akkadian syntax in the writing of weight measures: "N ma-na ku_3-babbar" appears instead of the correct Sumerian "n ku_3-babbar ma-na."[330]

Another detail is the missing of the Sargonic measures ma-na-tur "little mina" and $gi\hat{g}_4$-tur "little shekel." The unit "talent" is present, though.[331] The fractions of the mina are written in the standardized Sargonic manner as ½($1N_8{\times}$*AŠ*) and $^{šu2}N_8{}^{ša}$ for "one-third" and "two-thirds."[332]

With regard to the shekel, the extant data document only one of its possible fractions, "one-half."[333] The construction igi-*n*-$\hat{g}al_2$ to notate the shekel's fractions

326 Powell 1990: 479, 489.
327 DPA 36 obv. 2 (CS Ĝirsu).
328 See Steinkeller 2015.
329 See Lehmann 2016 for a recent discussion of this textual corpus.
330 ITT 4 7052 obv. 1 f. (Lagaš II Ĝirsu).
331 ITT 4 7560 obv. 8.
332 ITT 4 7052 obv. 1 (1/2 mina), rev. 3 (1/3 mina), ITT 4 7466 obv. 1 (2/3 mina).
333 ITT 4 7441 obv. 7.

"one-third," "-fourth," and "-sixth" does not appear. There are no traces of the fraction "two-thirds" of the shekel. Small amounts of goods are measured in še "barleycorn."[334]

These Ĝirsu documents explicitly mention na_4-si-sa_2, the "correct" mina weight.[335] It appears for the first time in ED IIIb accounts from Ĝirsu, which suggests the stability of the scribal tradition despite the political tumult.

The overall impression of the weight metrology in the Lagaš II texts from Ĝirsu is that it is a radically simplified version of the Classical Sargonic system. In contrast to the learned approach of Sargonic intellectuals, the Neo-Sumerian system of weights shows a practical approach to the matter.

Another conclusion is of great importance for the history of the Sumerian weight metrology. The data from Lagaš II Ĝirsu show that following the collapse of the Sargonic state bureaucracy, the scribes throughout Sumer returned to their local scribal traditions. The fact that the simplified weight metrology in the Ur III records was already in use in southern Mesopotamia prior to the reforms by Ur-Namma, the first king of that dynasty, leads to the conclusion that the simplified *Neo-Sumerian system* of weight measures must have emerged in Sumer following the collapse of the Akkadian empire. We know from the building projects of the Lagaš ruler Gudea that his state may have enjoyed considerable political control over southern Mesopotamia. It is not certain whether the establishment of the new, simplified system of weight notations should be connected to this political factor: We simply do not have any serious amount of datable archival documents from other cities to investigate the matter.

6.5 The Ur III reform

Utu-heĝal, the only king of the so-called fifth dynasty of Uruk according to the *Sumerian King List*, defeated the Gutians and ended their hegemony in central Babylonia. Ur-Namma, the founder of the Ur III state, was one of his generals. His ascension to power is obscure or had been deliberately obscured by the Ur III records. At any rate, he was the founder of the Ur III dynasty and state, 2110–2003 BC. Relying on the ideology of the city of Uruk with the goddess Inana and the hero-king Gilgamesh as key figures, this polity rapidly grew to the size of an empire-like political formation. For the first time, the state was

334 ITT 4 7441 obv. 7, 9.
335 RTC 182 obv. 1 (Lagaš II Ĝirsu).

divided into provinces where officials assigned by the crown, and not the local elites as in earlier times, played the first fiddle.

In the earlier literature, the son and successor of Ur-Namma, king Šulgi, was credited as the reformer of metrology. This was because the 300-*sila gur* called gur A-ga-de_3^{ki} "Akkad *gur*" during the Sargonic period was identical to gur-lugal "king's *gur*" documented from Šulgi on. The latter bears an alternative name gur-^{d}Šul-gi-ra "*gur* of (god) Šulgi" in the written evidence.[336] Walther Sallaberger put the attribution of the Ur III metrological reform to Šulgi in doubt and suggested that this king's role was to advance the innovations introduced by his father.[337]

The most important piece of evidence of the Ur III metrological reform is the prologue to the *Laws of Ur-Namma* (LUN).[338] The passage in question appears in lines 135–149. It concerns the standardization of capacity and weight measures. They are the *bariga* (= 60 *sila*), the ban (= 10 *sila*), and the *sila* in the first case and the shekel and the mina in the second. Of particular interest are the *sila* and the weight measures. Douglas Frayne interprets the passage in question as follows:

> 1 $sila_3$ zabar hu-mu-dim_2 / 1 ma-na-am_3 he_2-ni-ge-en / 1 $gi\hat{g}_4$ ku_3 na_4 / za_3 1 ma-na-e / he_2-ni-ge-en
> "I fashioned a bronze measure of one sila (= c. 1 litre) and standardized it as one mina. I standardized weight stones from the pure one shekel weight to the one mina weight"[339]

Claus Wilcke offers a slightly different interpretation of the passage.[340] The grammatical and the metrological interpretation of this passage is challenging:

(1) Lines 143–4: 1 $sila_3$-zabar hu-mu-dim_2 "I have indeed produced a one-*sila* bronze (vessel)." Dim_2 is a verb that is closely associated with metalworking; cf. a profession ku_3-dim_2 "silversmith." A standardized one-*sila* bronze vessel appears already in Sargonic texts: gur $sila_3$-zabar-ta "*gur* by the bronze (one-) *sila* vessel." This *gur* differed from the gur-saĝ-$\hat{g}al_2$ "*gur* with the head (= over

336 Gomi 1993: 31. Powell was unsure whether the reform was under Ur-Namma or Šulgi; Powell 1990: 493.

337 Sallaberger 1999: 148 with previous literature.

338 For an edition of the prologue, see Frayne 1997: 46–49. See Wilcke 2002 for an edition of the whole text. Civil 2011 is the most recent edition of the law. However, he does not edit or discuss the prologue.

339 Frayne 1997: 48.

340 Wilcke 2002: 309 n. 67–68: "1 $sila_3$(-Gefäss) aus Bronze formte ich wirklich; 1 Pfund (Wasser) – legte ich wirklich darin fest. Einen Ein-Silver-Schekel-Gewichtsstein legte ich wirklich als 1/60 Mine fest."

the brim)."[341] The former was *300* sila and had 5 *bariga* whereas the second was 240 *sila* and 4 *bariga*. Lines 138–142 of the *LUN* indicate that Ur-Namma employed two standards of ban, one of 10 *sila* and another of 6 *sila*, ^{urudu}ba-an si-sa$_2$ lugal-la, "the copper correct king's *ban*." The different number of *sila* in two standards of the *ban* means that they did not influence the capacity of the *sila*. It must be the same in both cases.

(2) Lines 145–6: 1 ma-na-a(m$_3$) he$_2$-ni-ge-en "I have indeed confirmed it in one mina." The verb gi.n "to make firm, to confirm" refers to standardization. The interpretation by Wilcke is correct from the philological perspective: The mass of the mina defines the standard of the *sila*. However, the mass of what exactly? Wilcke suggests water, although this is not mentioned. His suggestion that Ur-Namma's capacity measures *sila* and *bariga* make only the halves of these measures of the Sargonic period is uncritical.[342] Powell argued that the Sargonic reform defined one *sila* as two minas of water. It is very unlikely that the *sila* suffered division in two because of Ur-Namma's reform.

An alternative interpretation is possible. I have shown earlier in this chapter that accounts of aromatic substances tend to equate one mina and one *sila* as early as the Presargonic period. The claim by Ur-Namma that he defined a bronze one-sila measure as one mina makes no sense in this context. He has simply confirmed the practice that had been in use since time immemorial. The question is, what was the capacity of his *sila*? Since it cannot be water, the mass of some other substance defined it. There are no direct clues pointing at a certain substance that would play this role. Hence, let us take barley as the most common commodity measured in capacity units. One liter of barley weighs about 620 g. This means that one mina of barley would produce a *sila* of about 800 cm^3. This roughly corresponds to a *sila* bowl of about 0.85 l of the Presargonic ruler Enmetena.[343] Barley or not, it seems more likely that Ur-Namma used one mina mass of some grain instead of water to arrive at his standardized *sila*.[344]

(3) Lines 147–9: na$_4$ 1 giĝ$_4$ ku$_3$ / za$_3$ 1 ma-na-e / he$_2$-ni-ge-en "I have indeed confirmed one silver shekel, (its) stone weight, to the side of one mina." This is the most complicated and important passage since it concerns the shekel-mina linkage. One detail is the reference to the "silver shekel," a standard shekel to measure metals. The most important, however, is the

341 For example, CUSAS 35 321 obv. 1–3 and 337 obv. 1–2.

342 Wilcke 2002: 296.

343 See Ellison 1981: 38.

344 For a contrasting view that one *sila* was equal to one liter based mainly on later mathematical texts, see Powell 1984: 33, 46.

construction za$_3$ 1 ma-na-e.[345] Wilcke follows in his interpretation Fatma Yildiz. She compared it with the numerical construction za$_3$+NUMBER that conveys fractions "1/nth." Because of this, the number "1" should be changed to "60": za$_3$ 60 ma-na-e. According to this, Ur-Namma claims that he defined one shekel as 1/60 of a mina. However, what should it mean? The written data suggest that there were no other minas but that of the 60 shekels in 3rd mill. southern Mesopotamia. In my view, Ur-Namma states that he has linked the mass of the mina to 60 shekels of the "silver," that is, "correct" metal standard. This is a piece of propaganda: This metrological relation must be as old as the Early Dynastic period.

Unfortunately, the prologue of the *LUN* tells us nothing about the talent and the barleycorn. However, it shows once again the pivotal role of the mina-shekel relationship in the Sumerian system of weight measures. The law code of Ur-Namma is unique since it is the earliest known document where a ruler claims the standardization of the weight metrology. No rulers before him, not even the early Akkadian kings, openly claimed to have reformed the metrology despite the fact that they actually had done so. However, we do not need to overestimate the input by Ur-Namma. As we have seen in the example of the Lagaš II Ĝirsu archival texts, the core of the *Neo-Sumerian system* appears as early as in the economic records of the Lagaš II dynasty.

Nevertheless, the Ur III archival records introduced a number of improvements not observed before. Their motto may be summarized as *simplification and unification*. The Ur III stage in the development of the Sumerian system of weight measures appears in the following figure.

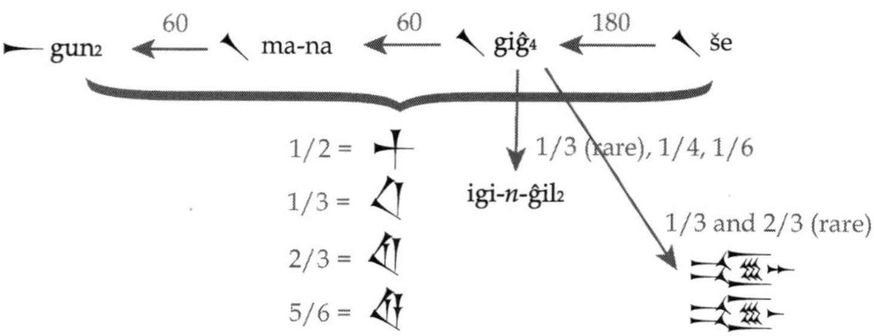

Fig. 6.4: The Neo-Sumerian system of weight measures by the time of Šulgi.

345 Yildiz 1981: 94 n. 34.

The first innovation is restricted to writing. Numbers are exclusively "pointed" from Šulgi on. This phenomenon applies to numbers in general. Some Ur-Namma archival texts still use "round" numbers and resemble Late Sargonic documents.[346] In order to differentiate between measures, the talent is written with a horizontal wedge ("*AŠ*") to tell it apart from the mina.[347]

Another innovation concerns both the writing and the metrology. This is the unified writing of all the fractions of all the units. Historically, the grapheme $^{\text{šu2}}\text{N}_8$ belongs to the mina's metrology.[348] The Ur III reform introduced a unified notation of the fractions "one-third," "two-thirds," and "five-sixths" of any unit. Particularly interesting is a new notation $^{\text{šu2}}3N_8{}^{\text{ša}}$ for kingusila "five-sixths," literally "ten shekels split (from the mina)."

In practice, however, there are a number of exceptions in this well-thought-out simplified system of notations. First, we do not have 5/6 of a shekel. It appears in script as *1* giĝ$_4$ la$_2$ igi-*6*-ĝal$_2$ "1 shekel minus 1/6."[349] The construction igi-*n*-ĝal$_2$ to notate the fractions "one-third," "one-fourth," and "one-sixth" of a shekel proved to be indispensable and remained in active use until the demise of the cuneiform script. As a result, igi-*3*-ĝal$_2$ appears very often as the writing of "one-third" of a shekel instead of the newly introduced writing $^{\text{šu2}}1N_8$.[350]

"Two-thirds" of a shekel appears either as $^{\text{šu2}}2N_8$ giĝ$_4$ or rarely as NINDA$_2$×ŠE+*2*(*AŠ.AŠ*).[351] The latter is an exception. Sometimes, NINDA$_2$×ŠE+*1* (*AŠ*) is used even instead of both $^{\text{šu2}}1N_8$ giĝ$_4$ and igi-*3*-ĝal$_2$ to notate "one-third" of a shekel. Most of the Ur III attestations of NINDA$_2$×ŠE+*N* originated at Ĝirsu. This illustrates the strengths of the local scribal tradition.

"One-fourth" and "one-sixth" of a shekel cannot be expressed in any other way than the construction igi-*n*-ĝal$_2$ and thus appear often in archival records.[352] One should be cautious with the writing igi-*5*-ĝal$_2$. It is indeed

---

346 For example, RTC 263 (Ur-Namma 8, Ur III Ĝirsu). This text uses "round" numbers to designate the talent and "pointed" for the mina.

347 AAICAB 1/1 pl. 45 1911–481 obv. 3–6 (Ibbi-Suen 1/12, Ur III Umma).

348 Early Dynastic IIIb texts from the Umma region employed a deviant practice to use it for the shekel's fractions "one-third" and "two-thirds." Nevertheless, it is an exception.

349 AUCT 1 701 obv. 1 (Šulgi 39/7, Ur III Umma).

350 See Aleppo 439 obv. 1 for igi-*3*-ĝal$_2$ (Šulgi 44, Ur III Puzriš-Dagan?) and AAICAB 1/1 pl. 18 1911–147 obv. 1 for $^{\text{šu2}}1N_8$ giĝ$_4$ (Šulgi 46, Ur III Umma).

351 See NRVN 1 78 obv. 1 for the former (Ibbi-Suen 3/3, Ur III Nippur). For the latter, see the previous chapter.

352 See AAICAB 1/1 pl. 43–44 1911–240 obv. i 6 for igi-*4*-ĝal$_2$ (Šu-Suen 5 us$_2$, Ur III Umma) and pl. 67–68 1924–667 rev. i 22 for igi-*6*-ĝal$_2$ (Amar-Suen 5/11, Ur III Umma).

present in Ur III documentation. However, this writing is used almost exclusively with capacity measures and never with any weight measures. "One-fifth" of a shekel is 36 barleycorns, which is practical neither in calculations nor in actual weighing.

Pedantic precision is a well-known trait of the Ur III accounting. As a result, a "half" of a barleycorn appears quite often.[353] "One-third" and "two-thirds" ($^{šu2}N_8$ še) are much rarer.[354] The fraction "five-sixths" of a barleycorn is not documented and probably did not exist. In contrast, this fraction of the mina and the shekel appears quite often in Ur III records.[355]

The following chart summarizes the possibilities for expressing fractions of weight measures. In short, the Ur III reform promoted the writing $^{šu2}N_8$ to write the fractions "one-third," "two-thirds," and "five-sixths" of any unit. Igi-*n*-ĝal$_2$ remained reserved for "one-fourth" and "one-sixth" of a shekel only. The notation igi-*3*-ĝal$_2$ and the NINDA$_2$×ŠE+*N* of the shekel's fractions "one-third" and "two-thirds" are exceptions. Hence, the mina's fractions dominate and only the shekel tends to preserve its historical fractions during the Ur III period.

	Universal	**Mina as prototype**			**NINDA$_2$×ŠE+*N***		**igi-*n*-ĝal$_2$**		
	1/2	**1/3**	**2/3**	**5/6**	**1/3**	**2/3**	**1/3**	**1/4**	**1/6**
gun$_2$ "talent"	+	+	+	+	–	–	–	–	–
ma-na "mina"	+	+	+	+	–	–	–	–	–
giĝ$_4$ "shekel"	+	+	+	+	+ (rare)	+ (rare)	+ (rare)	+	+
še "barleycorn"	+	+	+	?	–	–	–	–	–

Fig. 6.5: Fractions of weight measures during the Ur III period.

The Ur III system of weight measures and its notation in script has become a standard. Old Babylonian lexicographers introduced it in their compositions. As a result, this stage in the development of the weight metrology becomes the background for its further evolution in the succeeding historical periods in Babylonia, Assyria, and elsewhere in the Near East.

353 AAICAB 1/1 pl. 67–68 1924–667 obv. ii 3 (Amar-Suen 5/11, Ur III Umma).

354 STA 1 rev. i 26 (Amar-Suen 8/7, Ur III Umma) and Englund 1992: 99 no. 1 obv. 15 (Šu-Suen 1, Ur III Umma).

355 AAICAB 1/1 pl. 43–44 1911–240 obv. iii 3 and 7 (Šu-Suen 5 us$_2$, Ur III Umma).

6.6 Conclusions

This chapter offers an overview of how the Sumerian system of weights developed during the 3rd mill. The written data document three historical stages in it: the Early Dynastic, the Sargonic, and the Neo-Sumerian with its refinement by the Ur III administration. Each of these stages goes back to a "reform," a set of conscious innovations in metrology and writing.

One can only speculate where, when, and why the Early Dynastic weight metrology originated. We know only that the Early Dynastic scribes adapted this system to their needs. All stages, and the Early Dynastic stage is no exception, exhibit the signs of a learned, scribal approach to weight metrology. This is especially clear in the case of the Sargonic reform with its superficially "logical" but outspokenly unpractical measure "little shekel." Another example is the reform by Ur-Namma, which tried (only partly successfully) to eliminate any illogical parts of the system and introduce standardized writings.

The example with the Lagaš II Ĝirsu squeezed between the Sargonic and the Ur III reforms of metrology and writing is illustrative since it shows that we do not need to overrate the role of the centralized political power in the maintenance of metrology. In times of tumult, urban communities turn to their local practices of measurement in their daily economic activities and defy all the superficiality and bureaucratization that is a characteristic of complex political systems.

7 Stone weights

7.1 Introduction

You need a weighing balance with scales and weights of different mass to measure goods. Cuneiform records of the 3rd mill. BC document both these types of tools. In this chapter, I will discuss stone weights and reserve the discussion of weighing scales for the next one.

Sumerian archival texts record numerous terms for weights, literally na_4 "stones." In particular, these data indicate the presence of various follow-up terms, some of which refer to the different weighing "standards" of the same unit.[356] No single weighing standard such as the modern metric (Europe) or the customary system (US and UK) existed in Ancient Mesopotamia or any other premodern society. However, as I will show below, there was always an idea of the "correct" standard, which in early Mesopotamia was associated with the weights used to measure metals. However, other standards coexisted, which is especially true for the earliest periods. This phenomenon is documented in later evidence too. As Gregory Chambon illustrated in the example with the Old Babylonian Mari, if one bought metal on the market, the "market weight" was applied. If one brought this metal to the palace, the "palace weight" was used to remeasure the goods.[357]

In the following discussion, I divide the weights attested in Sumerian archival records into several categories. The first group consists of "goods-based" standards, that is, those that were applied only to measure certain types of goods: weights for metals, wool, and textiles. I will show that the unified, "correct" standard has evolved from weights for metals.

The second group consists of foreign standards. Sumerians traded with neighboring and far-off regions throughout their history. As a result, we find Sumerian weights in these regions and foreign weights in Sumer. Archaeologists identify Sumerian and Harappan weights in southern Mesopotamia.[358] We do not find data on the latter weighing system in the 3rd mill. BC written records. However, "the stone of Der" discussed below offers an example of what might have been a foreign standard of the mina.

"Heavy" weights make up the third group. This and similar terms referred not to a distinct standard but to large imprecise one-talent stone weights.

---

356 See Powell 1979: 72 f. and Chambon 2011: 28 f., 44 f. for the "norm."

357 Chambon 2011: 148; Bartash 2013b: 423–424.

358 Rahmstorf 2014: 438.

https://doi.org/10.1515/9781501510267-007

It is important to bear in mind that the most written data omit any clues to the weight standards that were used to measure goods. The references to specific "stones" are rare and may indicate the abnormality of the event: for example, when metals are measured by the weight of the "wool standard."

Another important factor that one needs to be conscious of is that the written records offer the *emic* view of the weighing norms. They show that the ancient dwellers of Mesopotamia distinguished between various "stones." The texts cannot tell us their absolute mass. Hence, their classification will certainly differ from any reconstruction by modern archaeologists, who use the *etic* approach to the same matter.

Stone weights of the 3rd mill. BC Near East have been the object of a number of archaeological studies.[359] However, most of them concentrate on the study of the weight metrology in Early Bronze Age Syria, especially at Ebla and Mari, or on the interconnections between trade systems and weights throughout Eurasia, from the Aegean to India. Unfortunately, a comprehensive archaeological synthetic study of actual weights from early southern Mesopotamia is still lacking. Recent historical studies of weight measures in Mesopotamia and Syria during the Late Bronze Age in the context of trade[360] set a high standard for the investigation of the same phenomenon of the earlier periods.

Besides portraying the emic view on the Sumerian stone weights, I pay attention to their "value" in this chapter. By the latter term, I mean the number of certain units in a stone: for example, "a stone of ten shekels." Fortunately, we have texts that record full sets of weights. Their data will be helpful for archaeologists working with Sumerian weights and, in particular, will save their analyses unwarranted reconstruction. For example, the written data suggest that the chances of the real weights representing "seven minas" and "six shekels" are virtually nil. The number of weights of a certain value in a set is of no less importance. These data allow us to reconstruct what the actual weighing process looked like, and how a weighmaster operated the weights.

7.2 Na_4 "stone"

Weights were produced from stone in 3rd mill. Mesopotamia. The Sumerian and Akkadian words na_4 and *abnu(m)* as "stone weights" are merely partial

359 For example, Ascalone and Peyronel 2006a and 2006b, Chambon 2006 and 2011, Milano 2004, and Rahmstorf 2006, 2010, and 2014.
360 Zaccagnini 2018a and 2018b.

meanings of the general semantics "stone." There was no specific Sumerian term for balance weights. The phrase na_4 ki-la_2(-hi-a) in some texts is not "stone (of) weight = weigh-stone" but "stone weights of various units/values."[361] The Akkadian term *aban šuqulti* "stone weight" does not appear in the 3rd mill. BC corpus.[362]

The sign NA_4 does not appear in the Late Uruk period's corpus. It is an Early Dynastic invention, a composite of the signs NI and UD. Both variants, NI+UD and UD+NI, were in use during the Early Dynastic and Sargonic period before the form NI+UD became standard.[363]

The conventional reading of this sign is na_4. However, later lexical data offer three phonemic variants: /na/, /za/, and /ya/.[364] Margret Green and Hans Nissen suggested that the "na/za" polyphony may be attributed to the pronunciation /^{n}za/ or /n^{z}a/ in Late Uruk times.[365] Piotr Steinkeller criticizes this view and argues that $za_{(2)}$ designates "gemstone, bead" whereas na means "rock, ordinary stone." He believes that the sign NA_4 is a "semantic disjunct of NA, which originally denoted 'stone weight.'"[366] In turn, Miguel Civil criticizes the view of Steinkeller. He argues that the interpretation of the Late Uruk sign ZA as "bead" is a "pictographic etymology." He treats with skepticism the idea that /na/ and /za/ were two different words. Eventually, he comes to the same conclusion as Green and Nissen before him that the first consonant in the Sumerian word for "stone" may have been nasalized.[367] Late Uruk accounts show no relation between the signs NA and stones.[368] This explains why Early Dynastic scribes introduced the sign NA_4. The element UD-NI in personal names from various sites during the Jemdet Nasr and Early Dynastic I–II period is unrelated to stones.[369]

Steinkeller interprets the sign sequence NI-UD in the *Prisoner Plaque* from Kiš vi 6′ as na_4. This would be the earliest reference to this word since the manuscript is of the Early Dynastic I–II period. It is a part of the sign sequence NI

361 UDT 1 rev. 20': 1(*DIŠ*) na_4-1(*AŠ*)-gu_2-na "1 stone weight of 1 talent" and 2(*DIŠ*) na_4 ki-la_2-hi-a "2 stone weights of various weight/mass."

362 CAD Š/3: 334.

363 Krebernik 1998: 282, 286 n. 536; Civil 2008: 52.

364 CAD A/1: 54–55.

365 ZATU: 261 no. 423.

366 Steinkeller 1995: 706–707.

367 Civil 2008: 52.

368 The sign sequence UD-NI(+RU) that appears quite often in the subscripts of the Late Uruk accounts has nothing to do with stones.

369 Compare the names ŠU-NI-UD (CUSAS 31 27 obv. 5b3; Uruk III uncert. prov.), UD-NI-ne-saĝ (UET 2 72 rev. i 4), and UD-NI-MUŠEN (UET 2 47 obv. ii 1; both ED I–II Ur).

UD MUD KIŠ there. According to Steinkeller, this means "the stone (monument) fashioned in Kiš."[370] This may refer to the plaque itself.

7.3 One-talent stone weights

The decision to discuss one-talent stone weights ahead of complete sets of weights dwells on the interpretation of several ED IIIa texts by several authors who identify the measure "talent" in them. This contradicts the conclusions of Chapter 2 that this measure was an Early Sargonic invention.

Miguel Civil interprets gu_2^{zabar} in the lexical composition *Early Dynastic Vocabulary A* 136 as "a talent weight of bronze," which he leaves without any explanation.[371] Several considerations contradict his suggestion. The first is, of course, the lack of any data on the talent prior to the Early or Middle Sargonic period. Second, in contrast to the later periods, weights in the 3rd mill. BC Mesopotamia were produced from stone.[372] Evidently, Civil relies on the *Early Dynastic Practical Vocabulary B* 140 in his idea that gu_2^{zabar} is a one-talent weight. In this lexical composition, the writing $MUŠ_3^{uruda}$ appears in the context of weight measures.[373] However, as I argue in Chapter 10, this is not because weights were made of copper or bronze: $MUŠ_3^{uruda}$ is not a weight at all but a variety of copper. It appears in the context of weight measures because this section of the lexical list records amounts of copper. Finally, the reading gu_2^{zabar} (Civil: gun^{zabar}) that appears only in two copies of the *Early Dynastic Practical Vocabulary A* from Ebla is uncertain. The sign (or two signs) in question is probably not GU_2.

---

370 Steinkeller 2013: 134, 140.

371 Civil 2008: 86.

372 The situation may have been different in other regions of Eurasia in the fourth and third millennia BC. Steinkeller 2016: 128 interprets the so-called "Leopard Weight" (Leopardengewicht) of ca. 3000 BC found in Shahi-Tump on the Pakistan coast as an actual measuring weight and relates this artifact of over 15 kg to the interregional trade of metals. He bases his claim on the fact that this lead object coated with a copper alloy and embellished with shellfish ornaments has a loop to suspend it. However, the original publication does not link this luxurious object to a system of weights (Mille, Besenval, and Bourgarit 2004). The authors emphasize that other artifacts of this kind were made from stone. They, too, had a considerable mass and a loop and were common in the fourth and third millennia in Pakistan, Afganistan, and Iran. The analysis of their masses and the identification of the balance weights of lesser masses are required to prove that the "Leopard Weight" was a *balance* weight.

373 Civil 2008: 87.

Another hoax reference to the talent appears in an ED IIIa account of wool from Šuruppak[374]:

Record of wool TSŠ 725 (ED IIIa Šuruppak)		
obv.	200 siki ma-na	200 minas of wool:
	Unug^{ki}	Uruk.
	100 siki ma-na	100 minas of wool:
rev.	^{ĝeš}UH$_3$^{ki}	Ĝeša ("Umma").
	300 siki ma-na	(Total:) 300 minas of wool.
	na$_4$(UD.NI) LAGAB GU$_2$ DU$_3$ 30	. . .

Piotr Steinkeller suggests reading the final line 30 na$_4$ gun$_2$ ^{ĝeš}gag as "30 (one-) talent stone weights."[375] He bases his interpretation of ^{ĝeš}gag on a surviving specimen of one-talent weight MS 4576.[376] Jöran Friberg notes in his original publication of this stone weight: "Two smaller holes placed symmetrically in the upper part of the front and the rear may have been part of the design of the talent stone, placed there to serve as handles."[377] This allows Steinkeller to remark: "These two holes may have originally held wooden pegs, by means of which the stone could be lifted up with both hands."[378]

Several considerations put Steinkeller's interpretation of TSŠ 725 in doubt. Firstly, there is no lexical evidence for talent stone weights with wooden handles. Secondly, ^{ĝeš}gag as a "handle" is rather unusual: Sumerian šu "hand," a$_2$ "arm," and kul "handle" are the usual terms that designate handles of tools, vessels, mirrors, etc. Thirdly, the signs in the line may designate a term or terms completely unrelated to weights.[379] "30" correlates suspiciously with "300," the sum of wool in minas.[380] Finally, why are there no talents in the main body of the account if there are one-talent stones in the subscript? The final line is the subscript of the document and it must provide general information about these bulks of wool. Had the last line been another entry, it would have given us another city's name.

374 TSŠ 725 (ED IIIa Šuruppak).
375 Steinkeller 2013: 140.
376 CUSAS 17 19.
377 Friberg 2007: 127.
378 Steinkeller 2011: 23.
379 For a sign sequence GU$_2$ GAG and GIŠ, cf. gu$_2$-du$_3$ ^{ĝeš}hašhur "the apple tree . . ." in a list of wooden implements see RTC 239 obv. i 3' (LS Ĝirsu).
380 I thank Horst Steible for the photographs of this tablet.

However, the main argument against the interpretation by Steinkeller concerns the perforation on the top of large stone weights. Friberg and Steinkeller speak about "holes" in the one-talent weight MS 4576. However, there is only one hole. It goes through the top and comes out on the other side. Its diameter is about 12 mm at its narrowest point.[381]

The first thing that comes to mind is that this weight was suspended on a cord that was attached to one of the arms of the weighing scales. However, it would be unwise to suspend a 30 kg stone on a centimeter-thick cord. A metal ring as a mediator between this heavy weight and a firmer rope would be more appropriate for this purpose.

An Ur III account of copper and bronze objects confirms this idea. It records 1 (*DIŠ*) ^{uruda}har na_4 1(*AŠ*) gun_2 "1 copper ring for a one-talent stone weight." Its mass is exactly one mina.[382] This shows that this type of heavy stone weight was provided with a metal ring. This ring allowed the weight to be suspended on an arm of a heavy balance provided with a stable cord. Additionally, the form of the weight in question is not suitable for an upright position. It would fall down.[383]

This discussion leads to the identification of a special type of large weighing balance that was used with heavy weight stones. The next chapter confirms the reality of this weighing gear. It bears the name ĝeš-rin_2 1 gun_2 "one-talent weighing scales." Some of them must have had one arm free of a scale and instead had a weight permanently attached to it. The exact one-mina weight of the ring is not accidental. It signifies that the balance pan attached to another arm was probably of the same weight to achieve equilibrium. The figure below illustrates a reconstruction of this gear.

However, not all Sumerian large stone weights had holes. For example, a two-talent granite weight dated by the ruler Ur-Ninĝirsu of the Lagaš II Dynasty has a duck form and no holes.[384] Large scales of the classic form with a robust balance pan on each arm were required to use this huge weight. In contrast, there are small pierced weights that were suspended on a string or a hook on one of the arms of the scales. See a pierced and marked ten-shekel weight from Nippur for an example.[385]

381 I thank Martin Schøyen for examining the weight MS 4576 for me.

382 CST 570 rev. 1–2 (Ibbi-Suen 4/7, Ur III Umma).

383 A similar one-talent stone weight of a much later date with a hole on the top appears as P388147 in the CDLI database.

384 P201714. For a description and reliable photographs, visit http://www.britishmuseum.org/research/collection_online/ and enter the museum number of the object "104724" into the search field.

385 Hafford 2005: 358, 381 (Ur III or Old Babylonian).

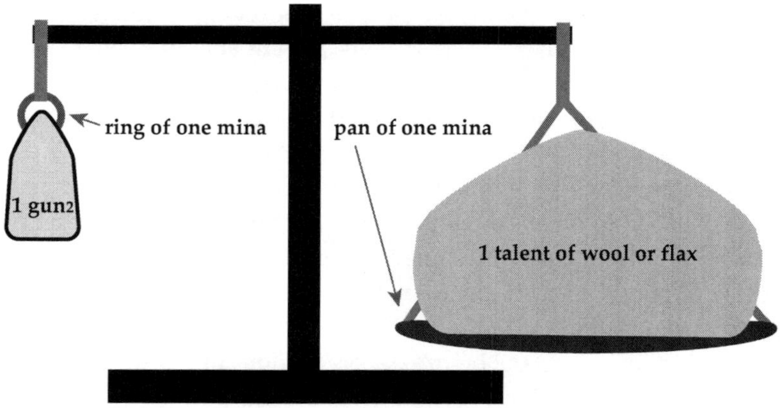

Fig. 7.1: A reconstruction of the "one-talent weighing scales" (ĝeš-rin$_2$ 1 gun$_2$).

Sargonic and Ur III documents specifically refer to the use of one-talent stone weights in measuring flax and wool. These texts may refer to the type of balance I depicted above.

The "Enra dossier" from the Middle Sargonic Adab offers the earliest evidence of their use. It documents the weighing of flax (gu) using one-talent stone weights. Its protagonist, Enra, was the "overseer of the flax (female workers)."[386] The flax is calculated in bundles (sa) and then measured according to a talent stone weight (na$_4$ (1) gun$_2$-ta). Pomponio and Visicato interpret the latter as "[fibres] in bales of 1 talent each."[387] However, several documents explicitly state that these goods were weighed.[388] The form of the verb (ba-la$_2$) designates not an issue or receipt but the process of weighing.[389]

Why was the scribe so particular to mention that these goods were measured by a one-talent stone weight? This detail reflects a weighing practice where the use of the one-talent weight and a special type of balance was crucial. Female workers went into the fields to cut flax. They packed it into bundles and carried it to the city. Enra received them and weighed the flax; the bundles were put on the large weighing scales. The advantage of the use of the one-talent weighing scales is evident: The process of weighing was swift.

386 CUSAS 35 314 rev. 3–4 with commentary. Maiocchi 2016: 94 suggests that geme$_2$-gu are "flax workers" in the Sargonic corpus. Enra appears as the chief administrator of a household (šabra) in BdI 1 139 rev. 3–4.

387 CUSAS 20 255–256, 260.

388 SCTRAH 116 obv. 4, CUSAS 20 260 rev. 1. Pomponio and Visicato erroneously translate it "have been delivered."

389 SCTRAH 115–116.

However, how precise was this mensuration? The reference "according to the one-talent stone weight" answers this question. No mina or shekel weights were used and this type of weighing represents a quasi-norm whose imprecision was evident to the weighmasters and scribes. However, owing to the low value of the goods measured in this manner, this was acceptable. Besides, the process of weighing was considerably accelerated by the use of this weighing gear.

A number of Ur III texts document the same phenomenon. They measure wool using one-talent stone weights that had excessive mass, which the scribes were aware of. They appear as na_4 1 gun_2 1 1/3 (or 1 2/3 or 2) ma-na-ta "according to the stone weight of one talent and 1 1/3 (or 1 2/3 or 2) minas." A detailed discussion of the "heavy stones" below indicates that the use of "heavy" one-talent stones was a norm in Sumer. These stones were used exclusively in the wool and flax industries.

One Ur III document states that one one-talent weight and one thirty-minas-weight belong to a certain building e_2-šu-$šum_2$-ma that is related to the palace according to the text.[390] The wool, the textiles, and the weights are described as the property (ni_3-gur_{11}) of the governor. The context suggests that these two weights were used in textile production.

Another example: A certain Dudu from Ĝirsu had in his household one one-talent weight and two stone weights of various masses.[391] A related text shows that these two weights are a ten-mina stone and a ten-shekel stone.[392] These impressive lists of possessions suggest that Dudu was a person of high rank. The value of the weights – one talent, ten minas, and ten shekels – suggests their use in the textile industry too. The presence of women and children – common laborers in this branch of the Mesoptamian "mass prodution" – at the beginning of the document corroborates this idea.[393]

As we see, the one-talent stone weight appears exclusively in the context of the textile industry and flax processing. This can hardly be an accident. The measurement of metals, resins, and gems required a higher level of precision, which was only possible with sets of weights composed of shekel and barley-corn weights.

390 Maekawa 1997: 291 rev. 3–4 (Ur III Ĝirsu; Amar-Suen 7).

391 UDT 1 rev. 19'–20' (Ur III Ĝirsu): 1(*DIŠ*) na_4-1(*AŠ*)-gu_2-na "1 stone weight of 1 talent" and 2 (*DIŠ*) na_4 ki-la_2-hi-a "2 stone weights of various mass."

392 Berens 89 rev. ii 1–3.

393 For a single one-talent stone weight in a list of goods, see PPAC 4 291 obv. 10.

7.4 Sets of weights

Lexical compositions record lists of weight measures where all possible measuring units and all their fractions appear. The earliest among them are the *Early Dynastic Practical Vocabularies A* and *B*. The most important 3rd mill. BC lexical source is, however, CUNES 47–12-176, which I have discussed in Chapter 5. None of these early sources mention the term na_4 "stone," which means that they do not record actual sets of stone weights.

Later lexical texts take a different approach. They record all possible values of weight measures and their fractions *and* add the term na_4 "stone (weight)." By doing this, Babylonian lexicographers erroneously related these two distinct types of data: how the actual sets of stone weights existed in practice on the one hand, and all possible weight measures as ideal constructs on the other. The most important among these sources are the Old Babylonian and the canonical recensions of the list *Ura* and its late commentary *HAR-gud* (Tab. 7.1).[394]

First to observe is that the writings of measures and their fractions follow the Ur III model. This shows that Old Babylonian and later lexicographers knew nothing about the original Early Dynastic system of weight measures. Second, this portion of the *Ura* does not represent the list of actual weights. Finally, it documents only a single, "correct" weighing norm. The term *aban kitti* "stone of truth" is definitely related to the marking ma-na gi-na "confirmed mina" on Ur III stone weights.

The artificial nature of this list becomes evident through comparison with the sets of real stone weights in the 3rd mill. BC archival texts (Tab. 7.2). Their data show that (a) not all "values" of the weight measures were represented by the actual stone weights, and (b) several standards coexisted during the Early Dynastic period. Unfortunately, no comparable data from the Sargonic period are known currently.

This chart reveals several further interesting details on the actual use of stone weights in Sumer. First, the Early Dynastic "60 minas" become "one talent" in the (Sargonic and) Ur III records, the fact explained in detail in Chapter 2.

Second, some values of weight measures have never existed as actual stone weights: 50, 9, and 7 minas, and 9–6 shekels. A weighmaster could easily do without them. At least one value is not documented but expected as a real weight: one-sixth of a shekel. It is attested lexically but never in actual archival records.

394 MSL 10: 15 f.

Tab. 7.1: Stone weights in post-Sumerian lexical lists.

		Canonical *Ura XVI*			
OB Sippar *Ura*	**OB Nippur *Ura 4***	**line**	**Sumerian**	**Akkadian**	**Translation of Akkadian**
165?	164	413	na_4-ki-la_2	*aban šu-qu-ul-ti*	stone weight
-	-	414	(the entry is not concerned with weights)		
-	-	415	na_4-ki-la_2-tag-ga	*aban šuqulti mah-ṣu*	weighing stone stamped (by authority)
-	-	416	(the entry is not concerned with weights)		
197	178	417	na_4 1 gu_2-un	*aban bi-lat*	(one-)talent stone
198	179	418	na_4 50 ma-na	*aban ha-an-ša-a ma-ne₂-e*	stone of 50 minas
199	180	419	na_4 40 ma-na	*aban ar-ba-a manê*	stone of 40 minas
200	181	420	na_4 30 ma-na	*aban ša-la-ša-a manê*	stone of 30 minas
201	182	421	na_4 20 ma-na	*aban eš-ra-a manê*	stone of 20 minas
202	183	422	na_4 15 ma-na	[...]	
203	184	423	na_4 10 ma-na	[...]	
204	185	424	na_4 5 ma-na	[...]	
-	-	424a	na_4 4 ma-na	-	
-	186	425	na_4 3 ma-na	[...]	
-	187	426	na_4 2 ma-na	-	
-	188	427	na_4 1 ma-na	-	
-	189	428	na_4 ⅔ ma-na	-	
-	190	429	na_4 ½ ma-na	-	
-	191	430	na_4 ⅓ ma-na	-	
-	192	431	na_4 10 $gi\hat{g}_4$	[...]	

Tab. 7.1 (continued)

		Canonical *Ura XVI*			
OB Sippar ***Ura***	**OB Nippur** ***Ura 4***	**line**	**Sumerian**	**Akkadian**	**Translation of Akkadian**
-	193	432	na_4 5 $gi\hat{g}_4$	[. . .]	
-	-	432a	na_4 4 $gi\hat{g}_4$	[. . .]	
-	194	433	na_4 3 $gi\hat{g}_4$	*aban ša-l[a-aš-ti manê]*	stone of 3 minas
-	195	434	na_4 2 $gi\hat{g}_4$	-	
-	196	435	na_4 1 $gi\hat{g}_4$	-	
-	197	436	na_4 ⅔ $gi\hat{g}_4$	-	
-	198	437	na_4 ½ $gi\hat{g}_4$	-	
-	199	438	na_4 ⅓ $gi\hat{g}_4$	*aban ma-na ṣe-eh-ri*	stone of the little mina[395]
-	200	439	na_4 igi-4-$\hat{g}al_2$-la	-	
-	201	440	na_4 igi-5-$\hat{g}al_2$-la	-	
-	-	441	na_4 igi-6-$\hat{g}al_2$-la	*aban par-ras ma-na ṣe-eh-ri*	stone of a half of the little mina[396]
-	202	442	na_4 22 ½ še	-	
-	203	443	na_4 20 še	-	
-	204	444	na_4 15 še	-	
-	205	445	na_4 10 še	-	
-	206	446	na_4 5 še	-	
-	-	447	na_4 4 še	-	
-	206a	448	na_4 3 še	-	
-	206b	449	na_4 2 še	-	

395 *HAR-gud* explains: *šul-lul-ti šiq*$_2$*-lim* "one-third of a shekel."

396 *HAR-gud* explains: *su-ud-d[u-u]* "one-sixth (of a shekel)."

Tab. 7.1 (continued)

		Canonical *Ura XVI*			
OB Sippar *Ura*	**OB Nippur *Ura 4***	**line**	**Sumerian**	**Akkadian**	**Translation of Akkadian**
-	206c	450	na_4 1 še	-	
-	-	451	na_4 ½ še	-	
-	-	452	na_4 ⅓ še	-	
-	-	453	na_4 ^{d}Utu	*aban ^{d}Šamši^{ši}*	stone of (Sun/ justice god) Šamaš
206: na_4 ki-la_2 ni_3-gi	-	454	na_4 ni_3-gi-na	*aban kit-ti*	correct stone
205	-	455	na_4 kuš-na_4	*aban ki-i-si*	a weight of a leather bag for weights
-	-	456	na_4 ni_3-TUR-TUR	*aban ṣe-eh-her-ti*	small stone weights

Third, some weights appear in earlier periods and disappear afterward. These are stones of 15, 8, 6, and 1 ½ mina of the ED IIIb Ĝirsu. Ur III records do not record these values. The most interesting among these ED weights are the values "8 minas" and "6 minas."

Fourth, the ED data from Ĝirsu record only mina stones. In contrast, the Ur III documents record both mina stones and shekel stones.

Fifth, no barleycorn-stones are mentioned in any of the sets of weights. It is easy to jump to the conclusion that there were no real stone weights for barleycorns: Real barley grains could be used instead. However, this is easily questioned if we consider the context of the archival documents that record these sets of weights. All of them come from the context of the wool and textile industry. No barleycorn precision was ever required in this industry. No accounts of wool or cloths document their mass in barleycorns.

Finally, most sets of stone weights have only one weight of a specific value. Rarely are there two or three of them. The latter are the stones that were most commonly used and handy in the wool industry and for wool allocations: one, two, five, and ten minas.

Tab. 7.2: Stone weights in 3rd mill. BC administrative texts.

	Actual stone weights								
	Early Dynastic IIIb Ĝirsu[397]		Ur III						
Measures	**Correct stone (na_4-si-sa_2)**	**Stone for textiles (na_4-$ša_3$-tug_2)**	**Garšana[398]**	**Ur[399]**	**Ur[400]**	**Umma[401]**	**Umma[402]**	**Ĝirsu[403]**	**Irisaĝrig[404]**
60 mina= 1 talent	60 ma-na (1x)		na_4 1 gun_2 (1x) "stone of 1 talent"	^{na4}esi 1 gun_2 (1x) "diorite stone of 1 talent"	[. . .]	na_4 gu_2-na (1x) "stone of a talent"			
The weight of 50 ma-na did not exist									

397 DP 509 and VS 27 34; see Selz 2010: 23 for an edition.
398 CUSAS 3 1372 (Ibbi-Suen 3/8).
399 UET 3 272. The document has another stone weight from hematite. Its value is broken: [. . .]-ga-an u_2 *5* ma-na "*. . .* and 5 minas" (rev. vii 4–5).
400 UET 9 427.
401 AAICAB 1/3 pl. 206–207 Bod S 138 (Šu-Suen 9).
402 Schneider 1930 no. 463.
403 ITT 2 909 (Ibbi-Suen 2/5).
404 Nisaba 15 656 (Ibbi-Suen 1.12d.30).

Tab. 7.2 (continued)

40 mina	+ (1x)	+ (1x)			[. . .]				
30 mina			+ (1x)		[. . .]		+ (1x)		
20 mina[405]					+ (2x)				+ (1x)
15 mina	+ (1x)	+ (1x)				Fell out of use			
10 mina	+ (1x and 2x)	+ (1x and 2x)	+ (1x)	+ (1x)	+ (2x)	+ (2x)	+ (1x)	+ (1x)	
					The weight of 9 ma-na did not exist				
8 mina	+ (1x)					Fell out of use			
					The weight of 7 ma-na did not exist				
6 mina		+ (1x)				Fell out of use			
5 mina		+ (1x and 2x)	+ (1x)		+ (2x)	+ (2x)	+ (1x)	+ (1x)	
4 mina		+ (0x and 1x)	+ (1x)						
3 mina	+ (1x)	+ (1x)	+ (1x)			+ (1x)	+ (1x)		+ (1x)
2 mina	+ (2x and 1x)	+ (1x)	+ (1x)	+ (1x)	+ (1x)	+ (1x)	+ (1x)	+ (1x)	+ (1x)
1 ½ mina	+ (0x and 1x)					Out of use			

405 For an actual Ur III 20-mina duck-weight, see Such-Gutiérrez 2015 §2.02.

Tab. 7.2 (continued)

1 mina	+ (1x)	+ (1x and 3x)	+ (1x)		[. . .]	+ (1x)	+ (2x)	+ (1x)
2/3 mina			+ (1x)	+ (1x)				
½ mina			+ (1x)	+ (1x)		+ (1x)	+ (1x)	+ (1x)
1/3 mina			+ (1x)	+ (≥2x)[406]			+ (1x)	+ (1x)
10 shekels			+ (1x)	+ ([. . .]x)			+ (1x)	+ (1x)
Weights of 9–6 shekels did not exist								
5 shekels			+ (1x)	+ ([. . .]x)			+ (1x)	
4 shekels			+ (1x)					
3 shekels			+ (1x)				+ (1x)	
2 shekels			+ (1x)				+ (1x)	
1 shekel							+ (1x)	
½ shekel			+ (1x)					
1/3 shekel			+ (1x)					
¼ shekel			+ (1x)					
1/6 shekel	Not documented							

406 There is one diorite and at least one hematite one-third mina weights. They belong to two different sets.

Turning to the question of the material of the weight, the majority of the Ur III administrative documents mention diorite, Sumerian ^{na4}esi.[407] One document records diorite and hematite (^{na4}ka-gi-na) weights.[408] A notable detail is that the large, one-talent and the mina stones were made from diorite whereas the shekel weights were from hematite. This is probably linked to the physical properties of these minerals. Diorite is found in big lumps but hematite appears in relatively small crystals. Besides, unlike diorite, a large weight from hematite is easily breakable.

7.5 The "correct" standard

The term na_4-si-sa_2 "correct stone" appears in archival documents of the Early Dynastic, Sargonic, and Lagaš II periods. A related term, ma-na gi-na "confirmed, verified mina," appears on some Ur III weights. Both terms refer to the "correct" mina of ca. 500 g. Its origins lie in the weighing of metals, copper in particular.

The exact meaning of the compound verb si … sa_2 is "to straighten up," Akkadian *ešēru(m)*. Von Soden translates the Akkadian equivalent as "in Ordnung sein, kommen" and refers to the Aramaic *jsr* "to be light."[409] However, the "correct stone" cannot be interpreted as a "light norm" because the Sumerian verb does not have this semantic. Besides, Powell dismisses the old idea of the existence of "heavy" and "light" norms of the same standard.[410]

The name "correct stone" indicates the presence of multiple standards of the mina during the Early Dynastic period and even later. Other standards of the mina had different designations and, eventually, were "outlawed" by the end of the 3rd mill. BC in the course of the Ur III reform.

Two accounts from Presargonic Ĝirsu exemplify the simultaneous use of the "correct stone" with another standard for wool and textiles. Two types of weighing balances – one for copper and another one for wool – clarify the areas of application of these mina standards.

---

407 CUSAS 3 1372 obv. i 25, rev. i 20.

408 UET 3 272 rev. vii 9, 16.

409 AHw: 254.

410 Powell 1990: 508b. Besides, si-sa_2 "correct" appears in the context of other units of measurement that cannot be "light": the capacity measures gur and ban_2 and the length measure gi "reed"; see ib. 463, 498.

VS 27 34 (ED IIIb Ĝirsu): Account of tools for weighing		
obv. i	1 40 na$_4$ ma-na	1 weight of 40 minas
	1 15 na$_4$ ma-na	1 weight of 15 minas
	2 10 na$_4$ ma-na	2 weights of 10 minas
	1 *6* na$_4$ ma-na	1 weight of 6 minas
	2 *5* na$_4$ ma-na	2 weights of 5 minas
ii	1 *4* na$_4$ ma-na	1 weight of 4 minas
	1 *3* na$_4$ ma-na	1 weight of 3 minas
	1 *2* na$_4$ ma-na	1 weight of 2 minas
	3 *1* na$_4$ ma-na	3 weights of 1 mina
	2 ĝeš-rin$_2$-siki	2 weighing balances for wool
	1 ^{ĝeš}UR$_2$×IHA.AI	1 . . . implement
iii	na$_4$-ša$_3$-tug$_2$-kam	These are weights for . . . textiles.
	1 60 na$_4$ ma-na	1 weight of 60 minas
	1 40 na$_4$ ma-na	1 weight of 40 minas
	1 15 na$_4$ ma-na	1 weight of 15 minas
	2 10 na$_4$ ma-na	2 weights of 10 minas
	1 *8* na$_4$ ma-na	1 weight of 8 minas
rev. i	1 *3* na$_4$ ma-na	1 weight of 3 minas
	1 *2* na$_4$ ma-na	1 weight of 2 minas
	1 *1 ½* na$_4$ ma-na	1 weight of 1 ½ mina
	1 *1* na$_4$ ma-na	1 weight of 1 mina
	na$_4$-si-sa$_2$-am$_6$	These are correct weights.
	1 ĝeš-rin$_2$-uruda	1 weighing balance for copper (=metals)
ii	itu udu-še$_3$ še a ^{d}Nin-ĝir$_2$-su-ka-ka	Month . . .
	Ur-du$_6$	to Urdu,
	i$_3$-du$_8$-ra	the doorkeeper,
	En-ig-gal	Eniggal,
	nu-banda$_3$	the supervisor,
	e-na-šid *4*	has counted. The 4th (year).

One interesting detail is the presence of a weight of eight minas that never appears in the subsequent periods. This implies that the standard na$_4$-si-sa$_2$ was *not fully* based on the sexagesimal numerical system at early Ĝirsu.

A similar document from the same archive records the same weights and scales with more details. It identifies the owners of these weights. The balances appear in a separate section.

DP 509 (ED IIIb Ĝirsu): Account of tools for weighing		
obv. i	1 na$_4$ 40 ma-na	1 weight of 40 minas
	1 na$_4$ 15 ma-na	1 weight of 15 minas
	1 na$_4$ 10 ma-na	1 weight of 10 minas
	1 na$_4$ *6* ma-na	1 weight of 6 minas
	1 na$_4$ *5* ma-na	1 weight of 5 minas
	1 na$_4$ *3* ma-na	1 weight of 3 minas
ii	e$_2$-gal-kam	These are (the weights) of the palace.
	1 na$_4$ *2* ma-na	1 weight of 2 minas
	1 na$_4$ *1* ma-na	1 weight of 1 mina
	Sa$_6$-sa$_6$-kam	These are (the weights) of Sasa[411]
	na$_4$-ša$_3$-tug$_2$-kam	These are weights *for weighing textiles*.
	1 na$_4$ 60 ma-na	1 weight of 60 minas
	1 na$_4$ 40 ma-na	1 weight of 40 minas
rev. i	1 na$_4$ 15 ma-na	1 weight of 15 minas
	1 [na$_4$] 10 ma-na	1 [weight] of 10 minas
	1 na$_4$ 8 ma-na	1 weight of 8 minas
	2 na$_4$ 2 ma-na	2 weights of 2 minas
	1 na$_4$ 1 ma-na	1 weight of 1 mina
ii	na$_4$-si-sa$_2$-am$_6$	These are correct weights.
	1 ĝeš-rin$_2$-siki-gal-gal	1 large balance for weighing wool;
	2 ĝeš-rin$_2$-siki-tur-tur	2 small balances for weighing wool;
	1 ĝeš-rin$_2$-uruda	1 balance for copper (=metals);
	1 ^{ĝeš}gab$_2$-il$_2$	1 balance dish.
	En-ig-gal	Eniggal,
iii	nu-banda$_3$	the supervisor,
	e$_2$-gal-ta	from the palace
	mu-de$_6$	has brought (it) out (and)
	En-na-u$_4$-mu	has counted (it to) Enna'umu
	e-na-šid	
	URU-KA-gi-na	URUKAgina,
	lugal	king
	Lagaš^{ki} *1*	of Lagaš. 1st (year).

The compatibility of the ĝeš-rin$_2$-uruda "balance for copper" with the na$_4$-si-sa$_2$ "correct stones" is suggestive. It shows that the "correct" standard was originally the standard to measure metals. Other documents show its use to measure copper and silver.[412] However, there is abundant evidence that weighmasters used

411 The wife of the governor who headed E$_2$-munus, the temple household of the goddess Baba.

412 See VS 27 98 for copper and MVN 3 10 for pure silver (ED IIIb Ĝirsu).

these weights to measure other goods. At least one document records the use of na$_4$-si-sa$_2$ with resins.[413] This is not surprising given the high value of these goods.

What is surprising is that the majority of references to the "correct" standard appear in the context of wool.[414] One of the possible explanations is that na$_4$-si-sa$_2$ had become the standard par excellence by the Presargonic period, which allowed it to be used with all types of goods. A similar phenomenon is observed with the metal standard na$_4$-ku$_3$, the "stone for silver," discussed below.

Another document from Ĝirsu illustrates the use of the "correct stone" for any kinds of goods.[415] It states that a certain trading agent receives an amount of wool and silver that he takes to Dilmun. The wool for three garments is a yearly wool allocation (siki-ba-gal-gal). However, it is issued not using the "stone for wool allocation" (na$_4$-siki-ba) but the "correct stone" instead.

Sargonic references to the weighing of wool using the "correct stone" such as RTC 182–183 allowed Powell to suggest that standards for wool in the ED IIIb Ĝirsu were "largely replaced during the Akkad period by the regular weight standard."[416] However, other standards did not cease to exist because of the Sargonic reform. The document RTC 209 from the II Dynasty of Lagaš dated to the reign of Ur-Ninĝirsu mentions the same na$_4$-si-sa$_2$ "correct stone" in connection to wool. This and the standardization of the mina by Ur-Namma suggest the coexistence of diverging standards throughout the late 3rd mill. BC.

Archeological data suggest the identification of the na$_4$-si-sa$_2$ of the mina with the standard of ca. 500 g. Powell associated an inscribed weight NBC 2565 of 497.5 g with it.[417] However, the term itself does not appear on the weight. The actual inscription is: 1 ma-na Du-du saĝĝa URU×A^{ki} "1 mina, Dudu, the chief administrator of (the city) Arawa." He and all previous scholars incorrectly established the date of the weight. There are two weights of two chief temple administrators (saĝĝa) by the name Dudu. The one in NBC 2565 of ca. 500 g belonged to Dudu, the administrator of Arawa during the Ur III period when this Elamite city was part of the Ur III state.[418] Other Ur III documents record this official.[419] Another Dudu lived several centuries earlier at ED IIIb

413 Nik 1 301 (ED IIIb Ĝirsu).

414 DP 518 and Foster 1997: 54 obv. i 2 (ED IIIb Ĝirsu); CUSAS 33 221 obv. i 5: 10 siki ma-na si-sa$_2$ "10 correct minas of wool" (ED IIIb Umma region); ITT 2 5799, RTC 182 obv. 1, and 183 rev. 1' (CS Ĝirsu).

415 DP 518.

416 Powell 1990: 508.

417 RIME 1: 234; Powell 1971: 255–256.

418 Steinkeller 1982a: 244–246.

419 TCTI 2 2582 seal l. 4: dumu Du-du saĝĝa Arawa^{ki}.

Ĝirsu. His weight was "the mina of wool allocations" (ma-na siki-ba) of 680 g. Powell confused these two individuals.

Hence, the weight NBC 2565 indicates that the mass of the regular mina was 500 g during the Ur III period. A somewhat lighter regular mina of the ED IIIb period may be deduced from a 15-shekel stone weight of Irikagina. Its mass of 119.3 g produces the "correct" mina of ca. 480 g.[420] Despite this, the ED IIIb 480 g and the Ur III 500 g weights represented a single, "correct," or "verified" standard, whose real mass necessarily fluctuated temporally and locally. The latter designation is of the Ur III period: ma-na gi-na "true, verified, confirmed mina." It appears only on weights during this period.[421] Other Ur III inscribed weights also use the verb gi.n to state the correctness of the mina's standard.[422]

7.6 The silver standard

Na$_4$-ku$_3$(-babbar) "stone (to weigh) silver" appears only twice and both texts are of the Sargonic period. An Early Sargonic Adab document records the weight of a garment: [1] 'a$_3$-dam-um^{tug2}, 3 ki-la$_2$-bi ma-na, na$_4$-ku$_3$-kam "[1] *hadamum*-garment; its weight is 3 minas according to the stone for silver."[423] Another document is written in Akkadian. It comes from Classical Sargonic Ešnunna. It records wool: 30 siki ma-na *in* na$_4$-ku$_3$-babbar "30 minas wool according to the stone for silver."[424]

Curiously, both references illustrate the use of "the stone (for measuring) silver" to measure wool and textiles. This exemplifies the phenomenon I have addressed above, which is the use of the weights for metals to measure wool.

The existence of "the stone (to weigh) silver" in several localities is important for understanding how the Sumerian system of weights emerged. This piece of data is in line with the theory by Jöran Friberg discussed in Chapter 5 that copper and silver were measured by different weights at some early historical date. The next chapter delivers data on the "silver balance," corroborating the idea that silver was measured by different gear. Taking into consideration "balances for copper" and "for textiles," it becomes evident that the ancient weighmasters operated several types of balances with the corresponding sets of weights.

420 RIME 1.9.9.13 is in a private collection; see Powell 1971: 260 for this weight.

421 For Ur III weights bearing the marking ma-na gi-na, see BM 94,366 (British Museum, unpublished; 498.5 g according to the online catalogue), RIME 3/2.1.04.22 (Šu-Suen; 5 minas = 2.511 kg; 1 mina = ca. 502 g), and Such-Gutiérrez 2015: 3 for one-half the "true" mina weight of a certain Igimana.

422 For example, RIME 3/2.1.2.50–53 and passim there.

423 CUSAS 11 224 obv. i 1–3.

424 OAIC 36 rev. 4–5.

7.7 The standard for wool and textiles

The stone weights na_4-$ša_3$-tug_2 "stone (for) ... textiles" and na_4-siki-ba "stone for wool allocations" are attested at ED IIIb Ĝirsu. The references to the "correct stone" in the later, Lagaš II documents from Ĝirsu allow us to surmise that both standards were still in use two centuries later. In contrast, we do not have any indications that other standards of the mina existed beside the "verified" one (ma-na gi-na) in the Ur III state. The term ma-na siki-ba in accounts of wool does not refer to a standard but to the allocations of wool.[425]

The weights na_4-$ša_3$-tug_2 at Presargonic Ĝirsu were used together with ĝeš-rin_2-siki, "the balance (to weigh) wool" in DP 509 and VS 27 34. Curiously, no stone weights of the standard na_4-siki-ba are ever mentioned in Ĝirsu records. The references to it appear in accounts of wool allocations, where it is stated that the wool is issued "according to the stone of wool allocations" (na_4-siki-ba-ta).

The exact meaning of the phrase na_4-$ša_3$-tug_2 remains problematic. Powell leaves it without discussion and translates it "weight stone for cloth."[426] Ur III records have several terms for textiles with the element $ša_3$ "heart; inside": for example, $ša_3$-tug_2-nud-da. Waetzoldt leaves them without interpretation.[427] A reference in an Early Sargonic text from Adab exemplifies a possible meaning of $ša_3$-tug_2 as a kind of cover.[428]

The evidence of na_4-$ša_3$-tug_2 is remarkably coherent. All documents record the weighing of garments or fleece by these stones. BIN 8 368 records the fleece of sheep fed with barley or grass measured by these weights. Other texts record three to six textiles that are measured by them.[429] Unfortunately, we do not have any real weights inscribed with na_4-$ša_3$-tug_2, which leaves us no clues as to the absolute mass of this standard. It is not excluded that na_4-$ša_3$-tug_2 and na_4-siki-ba refer to the same standard.

Siki-ba were yearly allotments of wool as part of the "salaries" of employees and dependents in central urban households. In contrast to na_4-$ša_3$-tug_2, we have an actual weight inscribed siki-ba. This weight of 680 g in the Ashmolean Museum has the following inscription: ma-na siki-ba Du-du saĝĝa "a mina of the wool allocations; Dudu, the chief temple administrator."[430] This Dudu

425 For example, 30 ma-na siki-ba PN "30 minas: the wool allocation to PN" (AAICAB 1/1 pl. 19 1911–150; Ur III Umma).

426 Powell 1990: 508.

427 Waetzoldt 1972: 128.

428 CUSAS 11 140 rev. ii 3–4: 1 kuš gu_4, $ša_3$-tug_2 mar $^{ĝeš}gigir_2$ $šum_2$.

429 DP 192–194, VS 14 181, VS 27 9. VS 14 154 records six types of textiles.

430 Powell 1971: 255; Powell 1990: 508; Selz 2010: 24.

was the one from ED IIIb Ĝirsu and was the administrator of the temple household of the god Ninĝirsu.

Numerous accounts from Presargonic Ĝirsu record allocations of wool to workers. However, references to the standard na_4-siki-ba in them are generally rare. VS 25 19 offers an example where a number of individuals receive 70 minas of wool measured by this stone.[431] Nevertheless, most documents are silent about the mina's standard in the case of wool allotments. It is important to note that sometimes wool was issued according to the "correct mina" as early as the Presargonic period.[432] This irregular practice worked the other way. One account records the weighing of axes and other bronze objects produced by the standard for wool.[433] The reasons why the weighmasters used "wrong" weights in these cases is never explained.

The term na_4-siki "stone for wool" at Ebla may represent a related, heavier standard to measure wool. Alfonso Archi translates the term as "stone weight of wool" but, unfortunately, leaves it without further discussion.[434]

7.8 Foreign standards

Foreign weights in Sumer and Sumerian weights in various regions of the Ancient Near East exemplify a well-developed international trade in the 3rd mill. BC. The almost complete silence on foreign weight standards in Sumerian records is surprising in this respect. In particular, the written data never mention the standard of Meluhha, the Indus culture.

Na_4-BAD_3.AN^{ki} "the stone of Der" that appears in several ED IIIb texts from Ĝirsu is an exception. This data suggest the possibility that virtually any locality on the fringes of the Sumerian world may have had its own local standard. This city appears also as Dar-e^{ki} and Ti-$ri_2{}^{ki}$ in written sources and is identified with Tall ʿAqar.[435] Being the gate to the Zagros Mountains and Iranian Plateau, this locality was likely an entrepôt that was important for the whole of Sumer. The trading route may have passed through the city of Keš, since it is also mentioned in one of the documents.

---

431 See VS 25 54 for an almost identical text.

432 DP 518 obv. i 1 (ED IIIb Ĝirsu): 5 ma-na na_4-si-sa_2-ta siki-ba gal-gal "5 minas of big wool allocations according to the correct stone."

433 Nik 1 299 (ED IIIb Ĝirsu).

434 Archi 1988: 132; Archi 2015.

435 Steinkeller 1986: 37; Verkinderen 2006; Edzard, Farber, and Sollberger 1977: 22; Frayne 1992: 59.

Two texts that mention "the stone of Der" also mention the common Sumerian standard, na$_4$-si-sa$_2$ "the correct stone." Silver as a means of payment is the measured substance in both cases. The first document records the purchases of resins and slaves in Der by Ur-Ninmar, a merchant who worked for the temple of the goddess Baba at Ĝirsu.[436] Two types of resins are paid in silver according to the "stone of Der." The prices of all remaining goods, including slaves, are in the "correct stone" of Ĝirsu. The sum of four minas in the total allowed Powell to establish the ratio between the Der and Ĝirsu stones as 3:2.[437] This means that the Der standard was 1.5 higher than the Ĝirsu one. This brings us to the "Der mina" of ca. 720 g (taking the Ĝirsu ED IIIb mina of 480 g). Naturally, the first idea that comes to mind is the Indus culture shekel of 13.65 g,[438] since 720 g divided into 60 shekels brings us to a shekel of ca. 12 g. However, it is important to bear in mind that the number of "shekels" in the "mina" of Der did not necessarily conform to the Sumerian sexagesimal system. For example, the Der system might have been decimal.

Another document that mentions the standard of Der is badly preserved.[439] However, similarly to the preceding, it also refers to "the stone of Der" in relation to the "correct" Ĝirsu standard. The traded goods were resins and horses. Both documents suggest that all goods that were obtained via Der were luxuries.

7.9 "Heavy" weights

Powell discusses the term na$_4$-mah "heavy stones" in Ur III texts about wool.[440] Its weight is first recorded in this "standard" and then recalculated into the regular standard, which lacks any special designation in these texts. One of these documents (UDT 42) has three "heavy stones" of different values: (a) 1 talent 5 and ca. 1/3 mina, (b) 1 talent ca. 6 minas, and (c) 1 talent 6 minas 4 shekels. Powell rightfully argues that na$_4$-mah did not represent a separate standard but referred to large weights with excessive masses. The present state of knowledge show that it is likely that the notation "according to one-talent stone" at Middle Sargonic Adab, the term na$_4$-mah "heavy stone," and the notations "1 talent + x units" represent the same phenomenon, namely the use of imprecise one-talent stone weights to measure wool and flax.

---

436 See Englund 1990: 52 f. for an edition and discussion of this document.

437 Powell 1971: 202–203.

438 Ratnagar 1981: 184–195 and Ratnagar 2003, Roaf 1982, Zaccagnini 1986, Zaccagnini 1993, Ascalone and Peyronel 1999, and Mederos and Lamberg-Karlovski 2004: 208–210.

439 MVN 3 10 = FAOS 15/2: 453–456.

440 Powell 1971: 198–202. E.g. RTC 263 obv. 1 (Ĝirsu, Ur-Namma) and UNT 20 rev. iv 2 (Ĝirsu, Amar-Suen 5).

Another term, na$_4$-gu-la "large stone," may represent the same practice. The term appears on a small lump of clay, probably a student exercise of the Sargonic period.

CUSAS 23 197 (Sargonic, uncert. prov.): A metrological note		
obv.	20 la$_2$×1$^{(ras)}$ na$_4$-gu-la ma-na	19 minas (according to) the large weight
	20 la$_2$×2 <na$_4$>-si-sa$_2$ ma-na	18 minas (according to) the correct <weight>
rev.	(blank)	

The number "1" inscribed into la$_2$ "minus" in the first line is written over an erasure, which suggests that the scribe, probably a student, was unsure about what to write. This memo records the ratio of the regular to the "large" standard. However, there must be a mistake in this note: The "large" standard should be heavier than the "correct" one. Considering this, it must be the other way around: "18 heavy minas are equal to 19 regular minas." This means that the "heavy mina" was ca. 527 g in comparison to ca. 500 g for the regular one (1.05 times more). This mina, of course, never existed. However, this calculation results in a talent of 31.666 g, which fits perfectly the Ur III evidence on the measuring of wool with a talent stone of one talent and two-thirds of a mina.

Coming back to na$_4$-mah, Powell interpreted mah as "heavy," relying on its Akkadian equivalent *kabtu* in the context of weights. However, the term is much older. The *Early Dynastic Practical Vocabulary A* 101 mentions the term (na$_4$-mah$_2$).[441] Civil compares it with the term ĝeš-mah$_2^!$(DILMUN) from another lexical composition, the *Vocabolario di Ebla* 409. Notwithstanding the determinative for wood, this may indeed refer to a weight. The Eblaite translations *ša-gi-lum* /*ṯaqilum*/ "weighed(?)" and *wa-za-nu-um* /*wazzānum*/ "heavy" seem to support this view. Civil also cites an Eblaite archival record where wool is measured according to the "heavy stone," *al* NA$_4$.MAH$_2$. These data refer to the "heavy weight system," according to him.[442] In contrast to Sargonic and Ur III documents, these Eblaite data cannot refer to imprecise one-talent stone weights since we do not have any proof that the talent existed at Early Dynastic Ebla. In turn, they may refer to a heavier standard used for wool, which reminds us of the same situation at Early Dynastic Ĝirsu with its standards na$_4$-ša$_3$-tug$_2$ and na$_4$-siki-ba.

It is important to note that na$_4$-mah$_2$ is not related to the Eblaite measure giĝ$_4$-DILMUN, which some scholars erroneously interpret as "the shekel of

441 Civil 2008: 78–79. The context does not imply the involvement of weights and weighing.

442 Civil 2008: 79; MEE 4: 245.

Dilmun." They relate it either to the system of weights employed in the Indus culture or to the Anatolian shekel of 11.75 g.[443] However, $gi\hat{g}_4$-DILMUN is the writing of the shekel at Ebla par excellence and an example of haplography, "a shekel of weight."[444]

In summary, the Sargonic and Ur III texts that record "heavy/large weights" refer to imprecise one-talent stone weights. Their mass exceeded the mass of the regular talent by several minas. The question that remains here without an answer is why some of these imprecise one-talent weights never have a deficit of weight.

7.10 Conclusions

Weighmasters operated with several weighing standards in 3rd mill. BC Sumer. The following chart illustrates their temporal distribution.

Terms for the "standards" of weights		ED	Sargonic	Lagaš II	Ur III
Mina weights	na_4-si-sa_2 "correct stone" (ca. 480 g)	+	+	+	
	ma-na gi-na (do., ca. 500 g)				+
	na_4-ku_3(-babbar) "stone for silver"	?	+		
	na_4-$ša_3$-tug_2 "stone for textiles"	+			
	na_4-siki-ba "stone for wool allocations" (ca. 680 g)	+	?	?	
	na_4 BAD_3.AN^{ki} "Der stone" (ca. 720 g)	+			
Talent weights	na_4 1 gun_2 "one-talent stone"		+		
	na_4-gu-la "large stone"		+		
	na_4-mah "heavy stone"				+
	na_4 1 gun_2 *x* ma-na (one-talent stone weight with excessive mass)				+

Fig. 7.2: Sumerian terms for stone weights ("standards") in temporal distribution.

443 Stieglitz 1987 and Maiocchi 2005.
444 Civil 2008: 17.

This figure highlights that the written data indicate the existence of two large groups of weight standards: the mina standards and the talent weights. The first two lines indicate that na_4-si-sa_2 and ma-na gi-na refer to the same regular standard of ca. 480–500 g whose origins lie in the practice of measuring metals. Most probably, it was only copper originally.

This standard coexisted with at least two other stones during the Early Dynastic period: the "stone for textiles" and the "stone for wool." The latter was ca. 680 g. The presence of the "stone for silver" in the Early Sargonic texts makes it possible that this standard for measuring silver was different from the standard for copper. Additionally, this standard may have merged with the copper standard by the Early Dynastic times, and the "stone for silver" at Early Sargonic Adab may be identical to the "correct stone" at Early Dynastic Ĝirsu. Another mina of ca. 720(–750) g represented the regional standard of the city of Der. This piece of evidence indicates that new discoveries will undoubtedly bring new data on foreign standards and the complexity of the metrological landscape of the 3rd millennium BC Near and Middle East.

The introduction of the talent into the system of weight measures is reflected in the appearance of large balance weights. Their temporal distribution suggests that all four terms in the table refer to the same phenomenon of weighing wool and flax using imprecise one-talent stones and large weighing balances. The obvious imprecision of this practice forced the Ur III scribes to convert these data into the reliable correct standard.

All these data correlate with the designations of weighing balances that we find in archival and lexical records. The balance for weighing copper was used with the weights of the "correct" standard, the balance for silver was likely used for the silver standard, and the balance for wool for the standard for textiles. We even find a parallel in the balance for one-talent stones with the "heavy" one-talent stones. This suggests that weighmasters operated with multiple sets of weights and various sizes and constructions of weighing balances. This evidence also supports one of the main arguments in this study: that metals and wool were the original goods that were measured by weight.

8 Weighing scales

8.1 Introduction

The simplest type of this gear is *balance scales* or, simply, *the balance*. This gear consists of several parts. The *beam* is the horizontal part of the scales. Each half of this beam is called an *arm*. The balance scales have two *arms*, unlike more sophisticated types such as *bismar* and *steelyard* scales that appeared only later. Each of the arms has a device on the end to which to attach strings or chains, which hold *balance pans*. The beam usually has a hole in the middle by which it is attached to the vertical beam (in the case of large standing scales) or *tassel* (in the case of handheld scales). Some historical examples of the scales simply have a hole with a ring in the middle of the balance beam to suspend them in the air. In contrast, larger scales stood on a *stand*. Ancient Egyptian scales also had an indicator that helped in seeing if the arms were in a perfectly horizontal position. There is no comparable evidence in early Mesopotamia. Smaller balance scales were usually placed in a wooden box for transportation. This box could include a set of weights. Alternatively, weights were carried in a leather or textile bag.[445] This was impossible with the large scales and large weights.

The data of the early cuneiform records and later lexical lists enable identification of all these implements and their parts in Mesopotamia. In general, there were two types of scales in early Mesopotamia: the large and the small ones. The large scales were placed on a stand or a base. A subtype of these scales was scales with only one balance pan. Another arm had a large weight permanently attached to it. In contrast, the light scales were held in the air. The properties and value of the goods dictated the construction and the size of the scales. Additionally, the written records offer numerous terms for the parts of the scales. However, identifying these words with specific parts of the scales is challenging, and the investigation in this direction in this chapter should be regarded as preliminary.

Weighing scales are found more rarely in the archaeological context than stone weights in Ancient Near Eastern cites since they were made of perishable materials. The "bronze disease" destroyed the copper and bronze parts of the instrument. Wooden parts and strings from organic fibers decayed swiftly. Only a few balances from early Mesopotamia survived. Balance pans are more

445 See Kisch 1965: 26–56 for the construction of the balance scales and depictions of them in Ancient Egypt, Mesopotamia, Greece, Rome, and Medieval Europe.

https://doi.org/10.1515/9781501510267-008

numerous.[446] This emphasizes the importance of the data on the scales found in the written records.

8.2 Lexical data on balance scales

Akkadian had three words for balance scales: *gešrinnu(m)*, *mušaqqiltu*, and *zibānītu(m)*.[447] All of them are rare. The last of these is the designation of the constellation *Libra* in Akkadian. In contrast, Sumerian had only one word for the same gear: ĝeš-rin$_2$.

The grapheme GIŠ-ERIN$_2$ had at least three readings: (1) ^{ĝeš}erin$_2$ "yoke," (2) ĝeš-rin$_2$ "scales," and (3) GIŠ+ERIN$_2$, which is one of the graphic variants of the logographically written Akkadian verb *damāqum* "to be good" that appears often in personal names.[448] In contrast, references to balance scales appear in the context of stone weights, wool, textiles, precious metals, and valuable implements in general.

The Akkadian borrowing *gišrinnu* allows the Sumerian word for balance scales to be reconstructed as */ĝešrin(a)/ or */ĝešren(a)/. It is possible that this Sumerian word originates from ^{ĝeš}erin$_2$ "yoke." Both implements have a similar shape and property to balance.[449] Bruno Kisch hypothesizes: "Egyptian monuments and papyri depict persons carrying shoulder yokes with containers attached. This kind of activity would have made men conscious of balancing weights."[450] However, whereas yokes are as old as the Neolithic, balance scales cannot predate the Chalcolithic/Bronze Age in the light of the evidence discussed in this study. These considerations suggest that the idea "scales" was a secondary development of the word /erin/ "yoke."

However, is there one word behind these two meanings (^{ĝeš}erin$_2$) or are these words different (^{ĝeš}erin$_2$ and ĝeš-rin$_2$)? There are pros and cons. Akkadian words such as *gišhummu* "bench" (< ĝeš-hum) imply that ĝeš "wood" was not a determinative but a part of these words. Other examples include "date palm" (ĝišimmar > *gišimmaru*) and "beam" (*gušūru* < ĝeš-ur$_2$). This suggests that ĝeš-rin$_2$ /ĝešrin/ was the word for "yoke" and "weighing balance."

---

446 Steinkeller 1989: 95 n. 276; Hafford 2005: 350–351; Rahmstorf 2006: 18–21; Peyronel 2015; Kulakoğlu 2017.
447 CAD M/2: 260 and AHw: 681, CAD Z: 99–100 and AHw: 1523.
448 See Krecher 1987.
449 See Civil 1968: 9–10, where he argues that ^{ĝeš}šudun meant "yoke of the plow," whereas ^{ĝeš}erin$_2$ referred to "yoke in wagons and chariots."
450 Kisch 1965: 26.

On the other hand, however, we have a borrowing erin$_2$ > *erinnu* "neck stock." In addition, an Ur III document that I discuss below records erin$_2$ ĝeš-erin$_2$ "the yoke (= balance beam) of the balance scales." This suggests that any yoke-shaped implement might have been pronounced */erin/ in Sumerian. Consequently, GIŠ may be an unpronounced determinative, which leads us to ^{ĝeš}erin$_2$ for both "yoke" and "weighing balance." If so, theire is no other way than to interpret the Akkadian *gišrinnu* as a learned word invented by Old Babylonian lexicographers.

Third millennium BC lexical texts do not mention weighing balances. The earliest data appear in the first tablet of the *Old Babylonian Nippur Ura 1*, which is concerned with wooden objects. Lines 436–441 mention ĝeš-rin$_2$ "balance," ĝeš-rin$_2$ lub-lub-bi (see below for an interpretation), ĝeš-rin$_2$ 1 gun$_2$ "balance (to operate) 1 talent (stone weight)," ĝeš-rin$_2$ ma-na "balance (to operate) mina (-weights)," ĝeš-e$_2$-rin$_2$ "box for balance," and ĝeš-dilim$_2$-rin$_2$ "balance pan."

The latter two are clearly corrupt writings. The correct graphemes should be $^{\text{(ĝeš)}}$e$_2$ ĝeš-rin$_2$(-na) "box (lit. "house") of the scales" and $^{\text{(zabar/uruda)}}$dilim$_2$ ĝeš-rin$_2$(-na) "(metal) pan (lit. "spoon") of the scales." The reason for this juxtaposition is clear: All words in the first tablet of the *Old Babylonian Nippur Ura* begin with the sign GIŠ.

The *Canonical Ura* tablet IV lines 108–119 provides additional Sumerian terms for the balance's parts and their Akkadian equivalents. Although some of these data are helpful, others are obviously corrupt and confusing. To begin with, ĝeš-rin$_2$ = *gišrinnu* followed by ĝeš-rin$_2$-gaba = *qablû*, with the latter meaning "median." It is tempting to identify this term with a certain part of scales. However, the 3rd mill. administrative texts discussed below suggest that it was a separate type of balance scales.

The next line in the *Canonical Ura* has ĝeš-rin$_2$-lub-bi, which represents a shortened form of ĝeš-rin$_2$-lub-lub-bi of the Old Babylonian predecessor. The *Canonical Ura* explains the term with Akkadian (1) ditto = *qablû* "median," (2) *libbu* "middle," and (3) *libbu ša zibānīti* "the middle of the *zibanitum* scales."

Lub-bi appears in the literary composition *The Inana's Descent to the Netherworld* 234. Antoine Cavigneaux interprets this term as a "hook(?)" ("peut-être crochu").[451] According to this, the nails of the Netherworld's goddess Ereškigal look like hooks in the latter composition. Miguel Civil disagrees and cites the evidence

451 Cavigneaux 1992. He prefers to read lib-bi and argues that the gloss lu-ub in the lexical data is corrupt.

where $^{ĝeš/uruda}$lub-bi is both a weapon and an agricultural tool. According to him, Ereškigal has nails like "*lub*-axes."[452] I do not see any contradiction in the opinions of the two scholars. $^{ĝeš/uruda}$Lub-bi was a crooked wooden or metal tool that I would compare to the modern weeding hoe used in gardening. It has one or several crooked nails. The author of *The Inana's Descent* was definitely the master of poetical imagery: Ereškigal's hands must have looked like Freddie Krueger's claws.

The idea of being crooked is important in the interpretation of the term ĝeš-rin$_2$ lub-lub-bi. Where are hooks in the weighing scales? There are two on each end of the horizontal beam ("arms"). The ropes that hold balance pans are attached to them. These hooks always look upwards. Otherwise, the stings would slip from them once one of the arms went down. This interpretation fits well the original reduplicated form of the term lub-lub-bi that suggests the plurality or duality of the object. Hence, ĝeš-rin$_2$ lub-lub-bi may mean "balance with hooks" (ĝešrin lub=lub=bi(=da)). We likely owe the abridged form of the term in *Canonical Ura* to the misunderstanding of the term by 1st mill. BC lexicographers. They believed that ĝeš-rin$_2$-gaba and ĝeš-rin$_2$-lub-lub-bi designated the same part of the balance. However, both were separate types of balances and not some parts of a balance.

To proceed with the comparison of the *Old Babylonian* versus *Canonical Ura*, one-talent scales are correctly interpreted in Akkadian as *ša bilat* "those of the talent." The next term is again a corruption in the later tradition. Ĝeš-rin$_2$ ma-na-(la$_2$) "scales (to weigh) mina (stones)" of the Old Babylonian version turns into senseless ĝeš-rin$_2$ ma$_2$-la$_2$ = *ša malallê* of the late sources. Ridiculously, *malallû* is "raft."

The following ĝeš-dilim$_2$-rin$_2$ is a juxtaposed writing of dilim$_2$ ĝeš-rin$_2$ "the pan of the scales." The Akkadian interpretation of the term is correct in the later version of the list, *itqurti gišrinni* "dish of a scale."

The following lines of the *Canonical Ura* prepare another pitfall. Ĝeš-e$_2$-rin$_2$ and ĝeš-a$_2$-rin$_2$ are compared with *kukku* in the first case and *idu* and *ahu* in the second. Then, 1st millennium BC lexicographers compare a term ^{ĝeš}ni$_3$-a$_2$-la$_2$ with all three Akkadian equivalents: *kukku, ahu,* and *idu*. This shows that they believed that e$_2$ and a$_2$ were simply variants of the same term "arm," which is incorrect. First, the correct sequence of signs is e$_2$ ĝeš-rin$_2$ "the box of the scales" and a$_2$ ĝeš-rin$_2$ "the arm of the scales." It is not certain whether *kukku* means "box" or "arm" or anything else because it is a hapax.

452 Civil 1994: 149.

Second, ^{ĝeš}ni$_3$-a$_2$-la$_2$ is interpreted as “arm of scales” (lit. “the (wooden) thing hanging on an arm”) due to a reference in the lexical list *Nabnītu*.[453] This Sumerian term is compared with *(ahu) ša zibānīti* “(arm) of the scales” there. The following line provides the term a$_2$-ĝeš-rin$_2$-na with the same Akkadian interpretation. It is grammatically and lexically correct (a$_2$=ĝešrin=ak). However, ^{ĝeš}ni$_3$-a$_2$-la$_2$ is not so simple. This term literally means “a (wooden) thing of the *ala*.” This *ala* is an irrigation device to draw water and the “thing” (ni$_3$) is the usual term for wooden containers.[454] Hence, this line has nothing to do with the weighing balance that denotes the bucket of the shadoof.

An overview of the later lexical data on weighing scales shows that many Sumerian terms were obscure to Babylonian lexicographers. In contrast, the 3rd mill. BC archival records offer a quite clear image of what the weighing balance looked like and how weighmasters operated with it.

8.3 Weighing balance in archival records

Weighing balances appear relatively rarely in archival records. This should not lead to the conclusion that this gear was a rarity in early Mesopotamia. Containers for measuring grain do not pop up often in texts either, despite the routine nature of this practice. Additionally, some professions – such as merchants and smiths, as the next chapter illustrates – necessarily possessed balances and weights to exercise their work. All this suggests a far broader context of the use of the weight metrology than the 3rd mill. BC texts lead us to believe.

The earliest references to weighing balances appear in the two ED IIIb documents from Ĝirsu that I discussed in the previous chapter: DP 509 and VS 27 34. These documents record stone weights of two standards and the scales to be used with them. The practice of recording weights and scales side by side was common in the 3rd mill. BC archival records.

The types of scales in these texts are (1) ĝeš-rin$_2$-siki-gal-gal, (2) ĝeš-rin$_2$-siki-tur-tur, and (3) ĝeš-rin$_2$-uruda.[455] The first and the second are literally “large wool scales” and “small wool scales.”[456] One of the documents mentions

453 *Nabnītu* E 67–68 (MSL 16: 107).

454 See Civil 1994: 100 n. 9. See CUSAS 3 1372 (Ur III Garšana) for ^{ĝeš}ni$_3$ 3(ban$_2$) (= 30 liters) to ^{ĝeš}ni$_3$ 1 sila$_3$ (= 1 liter) as measuring vessels.

455 DP 509 rev. ii 2–4 and VS 27 34 obv. ii 5, rev. i 6.

456 Cf. siki-TUR-TUR “soft wool” in CUSAS 23 115 (Sargonic Adab). This allows an alternative explanation that may reflect the practice of measuring processed and unprocessed wool with different scales.

simply ĝeš-rin$_2$-siki without the reference to the size. The entry in which it appears comes after stone weights of the "textile standard" (na$_4$-ša$_3$-tug$_2$). This shows that this type of scales was used to measure wool and textiles.

The attributes "large" and "small" require an additional scrutiny. They are written in the reduplicated form even if one weighing balance is recorded, which means that this cannot refer to the plurality of objects.[457] One of the possible explanations is that the reduplication here marks the duality of the object similarly to *pants, scissors*, etc. However, I would expect this with paired objects such as dilim$_2$ "balance pan." Ĝeš-rin$_2$ "balance" (< yoke) is singular. Another possibility is to interpret the reduplication as a comparative: "larger scales" and "smaller scales." In this case, the reduplication is a contextual reference that conveys a comparative semantic: The scribe recorded the fact that one type of balance was larger/smaller than another one.

Be that as it may, two different sizes of weighing balance to measure wool is important for the reconstruction of the process of weighing. It shows that larger weights were used with the larger scales, which was convenient and speeded up the process. In contrast, smaller and more precise balances with smaller weights could have been used, say, to certify the weight of the produced textiles or to measure out wool allocations.

Ĝeš-rin$_2$-uruda, literally "copper scales," is another type of scales that two Ĝirsu texts mention. The attribute "copper" does not refer to the material from which the scales are made. Historical parallels and even some Ur III sources confirm that light balance scales were indeed made of copper or bronze. However, here we have a different phenomenon. A parallel in an Ur III document (see below) shows that uruda "copper" is a reference to the goods that were measured on these scales. The Ur III term is ĝeš-rin$_2$ ku$_3$ la$_2$ "the balance to weigh silver." Hence, the Early Dynastic term should be reconstructed as ĝeš-rin$_2$ uruda (la$_2$) "the balance (to weigh) copper." The term for wool scales is thus *ĝeš-rin$_2$ siki (la$_2$).

Another important detail in the case of the "balance for copper" in VS 27 34 is the fact that it concludes with the list of stone weights of the regular standard (na$_4$-si-sa$_2$). This indicates that there were no separate standards for copper/bronze on the one hand and silver on the other at Ĝirsu. Nevertheless, the value of the stone weights in this document (60 to 1 mina) shows that these implements were useless for measuring precious metals and other valuable goods, which required smaller, shekel weights.

457 Jagersma 2010: 113–117.

DP 509 and VS 27 34 record two more objects that are related to the measurement of goods. The first records a single ^{ĝeš}gab$_2$-il$_2$ in the last entry of the list of weighing implements (rev. ii 5). It comes after the three types of scales I have just discussed. The term ^{ĝeš}gab$_2$-il$_2$ belongs to the frozen voluntative/cohortative verbal forms.[458] It means literally "may I carry/lift it." Civil interprets this passage as a basket "probably to weigh wool."[459] This is a logical suggestion. A large balance to measure wool must have had a large basket suspended by a cord on one of its arms. However, the use of the determinative for wood (^{ĝeš}) instead of the determinative for reed (^{gi}) arouses suspicion.

The context of the same ^{ĝeš}gab$_2$-il$_2$ in VS 27 34 clarifies this mystery. Two pieces of ^{ĝeš}gab$_2$-il$_2$ follow the list of weights of the regular standard and the balance for copper (rev. ii 1). Therefore, ^{ĝeš}gab$_2$-il$_2$ belongs to the sphere of copper weighing and not wool weighing. This explains why these "baskets" were made of wood. Two pieces of this implement with one balance for copper indicates that ^{ĝeš}gab$_2$-il$_2$ was a dish on which large amounts of metals could be placed.

VS 27 34 records another curious implement: ^{ĝeš}UR$_2$×HA.A. It appears after the weights and balances for wool. It is suggestive that this implement belonged to the gear to measure wool. However, this term does not appear elsewhere, which hampers any credible results. Selz discussed the writing without reaching any definite conclusion.[460] Later lexical data provide the phonetic readings /urum/ and /eren(?)/ for a similar grapheme UR$_2$×HA.[461] However, it is not certain if it has any relation to ^{ĝeš}UR$_2$×HA.A in our text. The sign UR$_2$ has the basic meaning "root" and ^{ĝeš}ur$_2$ is a "base" of many wooden objects. This might suggest that ^{ĝeš}UR$_2$×HA.A is a stand for the large balance to measure wool. Ur III texts confirm that there was a special term for such a part (see ^{ĝeš}KIB below).

The Sargonic and the Ur III corpora also have a number of interesting terms for weighing tools. They show that the terminology in this sphere was volatile. Documents from one period often record terms that are otherwise unattested or extremely rare in other periods.

A Sargonic text from Ĝirsu confirms the existence of a special balance to weigh silver. The text records 2 ĝeš-rin$_2$ ku$_3$ e$_2$-ba-an "two pairs of scales (to

458 See Selz 1993: 630 with references.

459 ^{gi}gab$_2$-il$_2$ = *zabbīlu* "basket"; see Civil 1968: 10 with referents to lexical and administrative data.

460 Selz 2010: 24.

461 *Aa* Tablets 35–38 lines 147–148 (MSL 14: 464).

weigh) silver."[462] See below for the same gear in the Ur III material in a full writing ĝeš-rin$_2$ ku$_3$ la$_2$. The writing with e$_2$-ba-an "pair" may confirm the earlier suggestion of interpreting ĝeš-rin$_2$ as a word in a virtual grammatical dual. The context of this text is a temple household since the entry that precedes the scales records one saĝ šu-nir ^{d}Šara$_2$ "the top of the symbol of (god) Šara."

Two pairs of scales appear in a list of the possessions (ni$_3$-gur$_{11}$) of a certain Ursa in a document from the "Lugal-ra archive."[463] Most of the other goods are wool and textiles. Only one entry mentions five shekels of tin for copper. Since the "Lugal-ra archive" records the management of a mid-sized crown or elite estate, this exemplifies the use of weighing gear outside palaces and temples.

Ĝeš-rin$_2$ appears in a Sargonic document from Maškan-ili-Akkade (Umm al-Hafriyat) in a receipt of a rich selection of goods by a certain Al-NI.[464] Three pairs of scales appear after an impressive amount of several minas of gold, three and one-third minas of silver, and 15 minas of copper. An explanation follows the line with the scales: *ša$_4$* A$_2$-*su$_2$-nu la-šu$_4$-a* "(weighing scales) that do not have their 'arms.'"[465] If the interpretation of this line is correct, this is the earliest reference to "arms" as parts of weighing scales. The reverse of the same document records 11 ĝeš-rin$_2$ after two minas of wool (and probably other commodities), which is described as "lost" (*ha-al-qu$_2$-tum*). The high number of this type of tool does not allow them to be identified with the balances. In contrast, they must be "yokes."

The lexical evidence above illustrates that dilim$_2$ was equated with the Akkadian *itqūru* "spoon, balance pan." Dilim$_2$ as "pan" or "dish" of the balance appears for the first time in Sargonic texts. A document from Nippur records 2 dilim$_2$ ĝeš-rin$_2$ kul-sa$_6$-ga-uruda ki-la$_2$-bi ½ ma-na "2 copper pans of scales (made of) *kulsaga* copper: their weight is ½ mina."[466] This document informs that pans were made of copper (and likely bronze). Numerous finds of round dishes with three or four holes in archaeological excavations throughout the Ancient World prove that small pans were made of metal. Each balance pan weighed 15 shekels according to this Nippur document. This "round" number is hardly accidental: This mass allows a pan to act as a weight.

---

462 ITT 5 9276 rev. i 6' (CS Ĝirsu).

463 MAD 5 110 rev. 1 (CS Lagaš region); see CUSAS 26: 148 for the discussion of the archive.

464 CUSAS 13 168 = CUSAS 27 184 obv. 5, rev. 8 (CS Umm al-Hafriyat).

465 The only grammatical problem is that the dual of the relative pronoun and the verbal form stands in contrast to the plural after *yidē*(A$_2$)=*sunu* "their (two) arms."

466 OSP 2 48 obv. i 16–17 (MS Nippur).

As for kul-sa_6-ga as the material of the balance, three Middle Sargonic texts from Adab record a similar term (uruda-)NUMUN-KAL-ga.[467] It appears in the context of expenditures and arrears of metals. It is contrasted with ^{uruda}MUŠ$_3$-luh-ha "pure copper" in these documents. Manuel Molina interprets the former term as ^{uruda}NUMUN kala-ga "'strong' *NUMUN* copper"; other documents show its use in the production of weapons. This type of copper was more valuable than the usual copper.[468] Molina questions the relation of this term to the terms with KUL in two accounts of metal objects from Nippur.[469] However, all these texts refer to the same term but in slightly different writings: sa_6-ga vs. sag_8-ga.

The first Nippur document records 2 BU-uruda-kul-sa_6-ga. BU must designate an elongated object (=gid_2 "long"). Its weight is one-third of a mina. The beginning of the document mentions a similar BU-ku_3 "silver . . ." of ten shekels. Here and in our original Nippur text about the scales, uruda-kul-sa_6-ga must refer to some fine variety of copper. The second text corroborates this suggestion. It adds that kul was a verb that describes a metallurgical process exercised with copper. The text records 22 ha-zi^{zabar} uruda nu-kul-la. Contrary to the edition by Westenholz, it is "22 *hazin* axes (from) not . . .ed copper." The construction uruda nu-kul-la clearly shows that the term should be read kul instead of numun and that this kul is a verbal and not a nominal base.

Kul-sa_6-ga appears as a material to inlay (ĝar) axes ha-zi gu_2-$bir_5$$^{(mušen)}$ in a Sargonic text.[470] The amount is not specified but its price is three shekels of silver.

Now it is possible to interpret the reference to the balance in the Nippur account OSP 2 48. $Dilim_2$ ĝeš-rin_2 kul-sa_6-ga-uruda means "pans of balance scales (made of) premium . . .ed copper." Consequently, the variety of copper in three Adab texts should be interpreted as uruda-kul-sag_8-ga "premium . . .ed copper." In all cases, kul is a verb that refers to a metallurgic or metalworking process with copper. Modern metallurgy knows many ways to strengthen copper by alloying. Alternatively, it may have designated a mechanical hardening by hammering.

Ur III documents provide further data on weighing balances. They often go into details and describe the construction of the scales and the materials they were made of. One document records an inspection of measuring tools in a royal estate in the town of Garšana.[471] The list includes various types of

467 SCTRAH 228 obv. 1, 229 obv. 1, 237 obv. 1.
468 SCTRAH: 139, 180.
469 OSP 2 49 obv. ii 4–5, ECTJ 153 obv. 1.
470 MAD 4 71 obv. 1 (MS Umma?).
471 CUSAS 3 1372 (Ur III Garšana; Ibbi-Suen 2 and 3).

millstones, a set of diorite stone weights with specimens from one talent to one-fourth of a shekel, and a substantial number of flint (^{na4}zu$_2$) measured by volume. Then, seven entries record various types of weighing gear. The list concludes with a section of wooden containers of standard sizes, from one *bariga* to one *sila*. The section on scales appears in obv. i 27–32 and rev. i 22–28:

1 ^{ĝeš}KIB 1 gun$_2$ u$_3$-suh$_5$	1 pine tree base (for a) one-talent (balance)
1 ^{ĝeš}KIB 30 ma-na šinig	1 tamarisk base (for a) 30-mina (balance)
1 ^{ĝeš}KIB 1 gun$_2$ esir$_2$-asal$_2$	1 . . . poplar base (for a) one-talent (balance)
1 ĝeš-rin$_2$ 1 gun$_2$ še-du$_{10}$	1 *šedu* tree "(scale's) yoke" (for a) one-talent (balance)
1 ĝeš-rin$_2$ 30 ma-na še-du$_{10}$	1 *šedu* tree "(scale's) yoke" (for a) thirty-mina (balance)
1 ĝeš-rin$_2$ 1 gun$_2$ esir$_2$-asal$_2$	1 . . . poplar "(scale's) yoke" (for a) one-talent (balance)
1 ĝeš-rin$_2$-gaba hašhur	1 apple tree *chest* balance

The first detail is that these balances are made of two varieties of timber: pine and a variety of poplar. The second fact is that these scales are of two capacities: one talent and 30 minas.[472] The latter detail corroborates our earlier suggestion about the existence of balances of various sizes. This text adds a type of balance for a 30-mina stone to the one-talent balance discussed in the previous chapter.

The interpretation of the gear called ^{ĝeš}KIB is challenging since the reading of the sign is uncertain. It can be neither ^{ĝeš}šennur "plum" nor ul$_3$/hul$_3$ "reins, leash."[473] What is important is the parallelism of the reference to this gear to three large scales. This may allude to the fact that ĝeš-rin$_2$ and ^{ĝeš}KIB were not complete weighing scales their but parts of them. Considering the graphic form of the sign KIB that reminds us of a Christmas tree stand, ^{ĝeš}KIB may be the base for the balance (ĝeš-rin$_2$). I am not aware of pre-Ur III references to a stand for large balance scales. Only one document comes to mind, WF 147 of the ED IIIa date. It records the issue of two types of copper objects to a number of officials and professionals. The first object is LAK610-uruda and the second is a$_2$-GAR-uruda. Similarly to the previous document, the number of these objects is always equal. LAK610 is a sign that resembles the German *Eisernes Kreuz*. Christopher Woods argues that ZATU522(ŠENNUR$_b$) is the predecessor of this

472 See Heimpel 2011: 129 for this interpretation of ĝeš-rin$_2$ in this passage.
473 Woods 2007.

sign and it cannot be KIB.[474] The second term might be interpreted as a_2-uruda-ĝar(-ra) "(balance) arms inlaid with copper" because similar designations appear in Ur III records. However, the identification of LAK610-uruda with ^{ĝeš}KIB of Ur III records is unlikely because LAK610-uruda is a metal object. We know that only lighter scales were made of copper. It is a question of whether some of them required stands or, alternatively, all of them were handheld.

^{ĝeš}KIB appears in other Ur III texts. In one of them, it occurs after a list of 17 diorite stone weights and two other parts of weighing scales[475]:

2 $erin_2$ ĝeš-rin_2 uruda-bi na	2 "yokes" of scales *covered with* copper
1 ^{ĝeš}x ĝeš-rin_2 uruda-da ki-3-am_3 ĝar	1 (wooden) . . . inlaid with copper in three places
1 ^{ĝeš}KIB	1 base (of scales)

This passage shows that scales were taken apart. The first line shows that $erin_2$ refers to the horizontal beam, the balance. It has some copper parts, although the passage is hard to decipher in the photograph.[476] The second term is ^{ĝeš}KIB, probably a stand. The final term is hard to decipher. However, the three metal inlays on this wooden object remind us of a balance pan (^{ĝeš}$utul_2$?).

Ĝeš-rin_2-gaba is the last of seven terms in CUSAS 3 1372. The lexical tradition argues that it was a part of scales ("median"). However, archival documents imply that it was a particular type of balance; otherwise, the term would be *gaba ĝeš-rin_2 "the *chest* of the balance scales." In contrast, ĝeš-rin_2-gaba means "the scales of the breast."

ITT 2 909 from Ur III Ĝirsu offers a context of the use of this type of balance. It appears side by side with seven stone weights – 10, 5, 2, 1, ½, 1/3 mina, and 10 shekels (rev. i 1–8) – in the context of wool and textiles. The subscript of the document informs that these weighing tools belong to a weaving workshop (e_2 uš-bar). This detail and the fact that relatively large stones up to 5 kg were used with ĝeš-rin_2-gaba dismiss the possibility that this balance represented the handheld type. Nevertheless, this document confirms that ĝeš-rin_2-gaba was not a part of the scales but a separate type. Ĝeš-rin_2-gaba was likely a type of balance lighter than the 30-pounders discussed above but more robust than the light scales to weigh silver.

474 Woods 2007: 324–325.

475 HSS 4 6 rev. i 30, iii 14 (Ur III Ĝirsu).

476 P110279.

A number of Ur III documents record balance pans of weighing scales made of copper: ^{uruda}dilim$_2$ ĝeš-rin$_2$. MVN 5 155 records a pair of them in a list of copper objects. There are other isolated references to one or two balance pans in the same context.[477] Other texts mention these dishes in the context of stone weights. One document that registers the production of wool and textiles at the seaport of Gu'abba mentions two pans in the context of one one-talent and one 30-mina weight.[478] This shows that even the large pans that could hold 30 kg could be made of copper.

As we have seen above, some scales, especially the large ones, were made of wood. Balances in the context of wooden tools provide an additional confirmation of this fact. The context of valuable wooden containers and weights (rev. i–ii) in one document shows that ĝeš-rin$_2$ refers to the balance and not to the yoke.[479] This text and the related document UDT 1 record the possessions (ni$_3$-gur$_{11}$) of a certain Dudu. The amount of goods, slaves, and cattle shows that Dudu was a wealthy individual. Moreover, it shows that weights and scales belonged to the "material assemblage" of elite households.

It is necessary to differentiate between large wooden scales with copper parts and completely metallic scales. TEL 21 records one bronze and one copper balance.[480] In contrast, other balances had only metallic parts or inlays. HSS 4 5 obv. iii 20 records one ĝeš-rin$_2$ uruda ĝar-ra dilim$_2$-bi uruda "balance inlaid with copper; with pans from copper." In UET 3 272, two balances appear in the context of weights from one talent to one-third of a mina.[481] The first type is called ĝeš-rin$_2$-ku$_3$-la$_2$-mes-tur zabar ĝar-ra dilim$_2$-zabar si$_3$-ga "small scales to weigh silver (from) mes-timber inlaid with bronze, with bronze pans attached." This indicates that even the lightest scales for measuring silver could have been produced from wood and have only copper inlays. Another type of scales in this document is difficult to interpret: ĝeš-rin$_2$-gaba um-uruda ĝar-ra dilim$_2$-u$_2$-⸢x⸣ si$_3$-ga "*chest* scales inlaid with copper wire with . . . pans attached."

Concluding the discussion of weighing balances in 3rd mill. documents, I would like to draw attention to the fact that they almost never appear in legal accounts. One house sale from the Early Sargonic Umma records a construction

---

477 Ur III Ĝirsu, Amar-Suen 3; obv. iv 1. See Syracuse 452 (Ur III Umma) obv. ii 16, TUT 126 obv. ii 9, and 129 obv. iii 8.

478 Maekawa 1997 no. 15 rev. 1–4: 2 ^{uruda}dilim$_2$ ĝeš-⸢rin$_2$⸣, 7 ^{uruda}⸢HI$^{?}$⸣ ĝeš-⸢x⸣, 1 na$_4$ 1 gun$_2$, 1 na$_4$ 30 ma-na.

479 Berens 89 rev. i 4 (Ur III Ĝirsu; P105800).

480 1 ĝeš-rin$_2$-zabar e$_2$-ba-an, 1 ĝeš-rin$_2$-uruda e$_2$-ba-an (rev. 3–4).

481 Rev. iv 1–20.

ki ĝeš-rin$_2$-bi i$_3$-ak that concludes with a list of witnesses.[482] The price and other payments are in silver in this document. This phrase may refer to weighing as the payment for the house. However, its grammatical interpretation is equivocal.[483] Another example appears in a Sargonic record concerning the purchase of a slave. It states that a merchant held the balance scales during the weighing out of the price: PN dam-gara$_3$ lu$_2$ ĝeš-rin$_2$ dab$_5$-ba-am$_3$ "It was PN, the merchant, who held the balance scales." This statement indicated that the measured amount of silver was correct.[484]

8.4 Conclusions

The 3rd millennium BC cuneiform documents from Lower Mesopotamia offer rich data on weighing balances and their construction. The discussion of the Sumerian word for "balance" (ĝeš-rin$_2$) relates it to the word for "yoke." Therefore, strictly speaking, ĝeš-rin$_2$ is "weighing balance" and not "scale(s)," which is dilim$_2$ in Sumerian.

Six terms designating such balances are documented in 3rd mill. BC records. They differed in their capacity, construction, and the types of goods they were supposed to measure. Hence, one can speak about balances of different "standards" in the pre-Ur III records. This phenomenon emphasizes the fact that the standardization of the weight measures involved not only the regulation of stone weights but also of other weighing gear.

The Presargonic texts from Ĝirsu document two weighing balances: (1) ĝeš-rin$_2$-siki "balance (to weigh) wool" and (2) ĝeš-rin$_2$-uruda "balance (to weigh) copper." The attributes "large" and "small" with the balance for wool refer most likely to their size and, consequently, to their capacity. Weighmasters used the standard weights for textiles and wool (na$_4$-ša$_3$-tug$_2$) to operate the wool scales. The lightest stone was one mina and the heaviest was 40 minas.

The dishes of the copper scales were called ^{ĝeš}gab-il$_2$ in these Presargonic Ĝirsu texts. Weighmasters used these scales together with the weights of the regular standard (na$_4$-si-sa$_2$) of up to 60 minas.

Ur III texts record the balances of the capacities "one talent" and "30 minas." These balances seem to have had only one dish while the second arm was occupied with a permanently attached large weight. Such balances

482 CUSAS 35 427 rev. ii 15 (ES Umma region, the governorship of Šurus-kēn).

483 Ki(=ak) ĝešren=bi=Ø i$_3$=(n)=ak "he has performed the scales of the place" (?). =bi signifies that it is a "free genitive" construction.

484 See Bartash 2017b: 83 with references.

were especially useful in industries where not the precision but the rapid measurement of large amounts of less valuable goods mattered: wool and flax. These heavy scales rested on stands (^{ĝeš}KIB) made from various types of wood.

Ĝeš-rin$_2$-gaba is another type of wool scales that appear in Ur III records. It is certain that it does not designate handheld scales. In contrast, this type is likely hiding behind the term ĝeš-rin$_2$-ku$_3$(-la$_2$) "balance scales (to weigh) silver" that appears in Sargonic and Ur III records.

The terms ĝeš-rin$_2$-uruda(-la$_2$) "balance (to weigh) copper" and ĝeš-rin$_2$-ku$_3$ (-la$_2$) "balance (to weigh) silver" corraborate the theory that these two metals were originally measured by different "standards," using different sets of weights. The Sargonic data on the "stone for silver" discussed before may be another piece of the same jigsaw.

The common term for balance pans was dilim$_2$. Documents tell us that they were made of various types of copper and bronze. In contrast, balances were mostly manufactured of timber and were strengthened with copper or bronze parts, inlays, or wire.

Some terms that appear in the later lexical tradition do not appear in the extant early data. This is the case with ĝeš-rin$_2$ lub-lub-bi (a type of scales), a$_2$ "arm (of the balance)," and e$_2$ "box (of the balance)." However, new data and further work on this topic may change this situation.

The context in which these weighing implements appear is the same as with the stones: large central households and elite private households. The context suggests their use was mostly in the textile industry. We do not have comparable data on their use in metalworking. Meager evidence shows them in the context of trade. However, the next chapter shows that smiths and merchants possessed balances and stone weights and were trained to operate them to perform their craft. This shows that the palace and the temple did not have a monopoly on weighing in Sumer.

9 Weighmasters and the context of weighing

9.1 Introduction

This chapter attempts to answer two related questions. First: *Who acted as weighmasters in Sumer, who performed the actual weighing*? Second: *Where did the weighing take place*? The first looks for an agent, the second for the context.

These important issues usually escape the studies of Sumerian weight measures. Scholars concentrate on the intricacies of the writing and the metrological realities behind them quite forgetting that all these aspects originated in people's activities, agencies, and interests. The person behind the weighing balance was of a certain socioeconomic and legal status and belonged to a certain professional group. Now the time is ripe to meet the archetypal Sumerian weighmaster in person and to see where he performed his task.

The evidence on Sumerian weighmasters and places of weighing is limited. By now, the reader is probably used to the fact that Sumerian scribes only took note of data that were important for *them*. The scribes took notice of them only accidentally since their objective was to record the type and amount of goods, their issue, or receipt.

Both of the aspects that interest us in this chapter are "ethnographic" in their nature. In order to understand how the weighing worked, we must collect the scraps of data the written documents communicate. Their synthesis must be done with utmost care: The written records from the central households mostly lead us to believe that the weighing was concentrated in their hands only, which was not exactly the case.

9.2 Weighing and weighmasters

Weighing of goods is expressed in cuneiform records by the verb "to weigh." It is la_2 in Sumerian and *šaqālum* and, albeit rarely, *hiāṭum* in Akkadian. In the corpus under consideration, we have almost exclusively the verb la_2 and its logogram LA_2 in Akkadian texts to convey this process. The meaning "to weigh" of both la_2 and *šaqālum* is secondary. The original semantic is "to suspend in air." The semantic development "to suspend" > "to weigh" is obvious.[485]

485 See Powell 1971: 139–149 for a discussion of the lexical evidence on la_2 and its compounds.

https://doi.org/10.1515/9781501510267-009

Documents may or may not record the agent of the weighing. We find the construction PN_1=e PN_2=ra *goods* e-na-la$_2$ "PN_1 weighed out the goods to PN_2" with both the agent and recipient marked. This emphasizes the movement of goods, their issue to one individual by another individual or, very often, on its behalf. As we will see below, the agent of the verb la$_2$ in administrative documents is inevitably an official. In contrast, legal documents show that virtually any person could "weigh out" goods for someone. However, this should not be interpreted as evidence that everyone possessed scales and weights and was trained to operate them. La$_2$ in these legal documents means "to weigh out = to pay." Similarly, the cases when an official "weighs out" some goods for someone do not show his role as a weighmaster. They merely record the fact that he authorized the issue of the goods.[486] The identity of real weighmasters in legal contracts and administrative documents remains mostly unknown.

Administrative documents often use impersonal constructions such as ba-la$_2$ "it has been weighed." They refer not to the issue of goods but to the administrative practice of establishing their weight upon receipt, upon production, or in the course of an inventory.

Sometimes, documents provide information about the place where the weighing has happened. These cases, as we will see below, are exceptional. Scribes knew their weighmasters well and the context where the weighing took place. Hence, they did not need to record these details in most cases.

Previously, I have offered a discussion about weighmasters and supervisors of weighing in Early Dynastic and Sargonic Mesopotamia. This contribution includes an overview of previous scholarship on this topic. In this chapter, I rely on additional data to adjust and refine its preliminary conclusions.[487]

We can distinguish four "models" of weighmasters. The first includes *weighmasters* in the proper sense of the word, that is, those people who are plainly identified in cuneiform records as those who performed this task. These people operated weights and scales. *Merchants* make up the second group of those who could operate weighing tools. Obviously, weighing skills were a *sine qua non* for them. The evidence proves this a priori statement. *Artisans*, mostly metalworkers, appear as weighmasters in our documentation too.

The final group includes *officials*. Lorenzo Verderame shows in the example of the Ur III Umma that the governor and other high officials were those

486 The function of the written documentation was not to provide exact details on the identity of the weighmaster in a particular case but to attribute this transaction to the responsibility of a specific official. See Steinkeller 2004a.
487 Bartash 2017b (written and submitted in 2012).

who "weighed" textiles upon their production.[488] Similarly, Franco D'Agostino and Francesca Gorello showed that officials acted as controllers of weighing – literally, in-la_2 "weighed out" – of goods in the metal and textile industries.[489] Hence, the passage "a scribe weighed n minas of goods x to person y" neither describes the process of weighing nor gives any information about a person who held scales. It documents solely the administrative procedure of an issue. The officials in these documents authorized and controlled the receipt and issue of goods in and out of the households under their management. This means that the involvement of officials in the actual weighing process remains questionable in most cases. Nevertheless, limited data suggest that some of them did perform the weighing personally.

9.3 Weighmasters in *sensu stricto*

The existence of a professional in charge of weighing in Sumer has been debated in previous scholarship. Cuneiform documents do provide terms for "weighmaster." However, as will be seen below, "weighmaster" was an auxiliary title applied to well-known occupations. This only illustrates the ability of these professionals to execute weighing. This shows that, strictly speaking, there was no such profession as "weighmaster" in Sumer.

Terms for weighmasters appear for the first time in the lexical composition *OB Proto-Lu*. They were among the professionals associated with trade. The canonical version of this list offers Akkadian equivalents of these terms (Fig. 9.1):

	Sumerian		**Akkadian**
ku_3-la_2	(the one who) weighs silver	*ša-qi-il kas-pi*	weigher of silver
ma-na-la_2	(the one who) weighs (with) mina (weights)	*ša-ma-lu-u*	"assistant, agent of a merchant, trading agent" (CAD Š/1: 291)
dam-$gara_3$	merchant	*tam-ka-ru*	"merchant"
šagan-la_2	merchant's assistant	*ša-ma-lu-u*	(see above)
ga-$eš_8$	seafaring, long-distance trader	*ka-eš-šu*	"traveling merchant" (CAD K: 35)

Fig. 9.1: Terms for weighmasters in the lexical list *Lu* (MSL 12: 58, 137).

488 Verderame 2008.

489 D'Agostino and Gorello 2013: 259.

The two first terms must be the Sumerian words for "weighmaster." However, only the first one appears in 3rd mill. BC documents, both administrative and legal. The second word may be a creation of Old Babylonian scribes, as the following discussion allows us to judge.

The earliest evidence of ku_3-la_2 appears in a Fara period list of personnel published by Giovanni Pettinato and subsequently re-edited by Aage Westenholz.[490] The term is mentioned in connection to two individuals:

obv. iii	1 Ab-ba-tur ⸢muhaldim?⸣	1 Abbatur, the cook(?),
	ku_3-la_2	the silver weigher;
	1 U_2.KA-*il*	1 UKA-*'il*,
	ku_3-la_2	the silverweigher.

Westenholz interprets MU after the first personal name as muhaldim, "cook." This is possible since the personal name *Ab-ba-tur-MU is otherwise unattested. However, professional titles are written in separate entries of personal names, as occurs in this (cf. obv. i 2–3) and other Early Dynastic IIIa texts. Hence, I would expect to find *1 Ab-ba-tur / muhaldim / ku_3-la_2. Therefore, it is uncertain whether Abbatur was indeed a cook. We have no evidence that cooks acted as weighmasters in 3rd mill. BC texts.[491]

Another, more important detail in this attestation of ku_3-la_2 is the use of the term as a professional title. None of the later administrative and legal documents, apart from one odd Ur III record discussed below, uses ku_3-la_2 as a professional designation. As a rule, documents show that a "silver weigher" was either a metalworker, a merchant, or an official.

An Early Sargonic text from Adab shows that ku_3-la_2 is a quasi-professional title complementary to the principal occupation. BdI 1 29 is a list of 45 individuals identified by their professional titles and/or personal names. The document states that they are given to Enlil (rev. ii). Unless it is an abbreviation of a personal name, the document records the assignment of 45 "artisans" (ĝeš-kiĝ$_2$-ti) to the temple of this god. One of the professionals is called "the smith, the weigher of silver" (1 simug ku_3-la_2; rev. i 2). Here, the term ku_3-la_2 specifies that this particular smith could operate scales and weights, and measure silver. Another smith in the document (obv. ii 6) does not have this title.

490 Pettinato 1997 no. 3; CUSAS 26 151. Its prosopography and paleography identify the Umma region as the provenance of the text, as knowingly suggested by Westenholz.

491 However, see CUSAS 35 207 obv. i 5 (ES Adab), where a certain cook receives four minas of copper ($MUŠ_3^{uruda}$).

The term ku_3-la_2 does not mean that these people were concerned with the weighing of silver as goods. On the contrary, the merchants, metalworkers, and officials who were ku_3-la_2 measured silver in the context of transactions with silver as money. This shows that ku_3-la_2 referred to various professionals who acted as controllers, in a somewhat similar role to the Roman *libripens*, in transactions with silver as money.

The earliest document illustrating this phenomenon is a Presargonic sale contract from Adab published and edited by Daniel Foxvog.[492] It records the purchase of a field by a governor of Adab. A "majordomo" (ugula-e_2) acts as a person responsible for measuring the price in silver and barley in this transaction: "Lugalmudakuš, the majordomo, was the one who weighed out silver and the one who measured out barley."[493] This early reference to ku_3-la_2 is also important because it is one of the rare examples where we know for sure that some officials could personally operate scales and weights.

Another pre-Ur III reference to ku_3-la_2 appears in a broken context in a Classical Sargonic document from Ĝirsu STTI 135. It records the assignation of fields to farmers and shepherds. One person is identified as a "silver weigher" (rev. 2′). It is not certain whether he also belonged to one of these professional groups.

Ur III records mention the term more often where it appears as (lu_2) ku_3-la_2 (-a-bi) in sale contracts. The possessive suffix =bi refers to the transaction: "its (the contract's) weighmaster." Dietz Otto Edzard correctly related this term to another construction that identifies weighmasters in 3rd mill. BC texts: "the one who has held the scales (during the transaction)" (lu_2 ĝeš-rin_2 dab_5-ba). Edzard refers to this construction in a text eventually published as MC 4 61. He names lu_2-ku_3-la_2 "a sort of weighmaster."[494]

Discussing purchase practices during the Ur III period, Claus Wilcke interprets lu_2-ku_3-la_2 as the professional comparable to the Roman *libripens* (Lat. *libra* "pound; scales" and *pendere* "to weigh").[495] Piotr Steinkeller also notes the resemblance between the Sumerian lu_2-ku_3-la_2 and the Roman official, who, originally, must have personally weighed amounts of copper as money in transactions. We owe to Steinkeller the first comprehensive discussion of this term in the Ur III material.[496]

However, only very limited data suggest that ku_3-la_2 was a distinct official or professional. Only the earliest reference to ku_3-la_2 in CUSAS 26 151 and an Ur

492 Foxvog 1980.

493 Lugal-mu-da-$kuš_2$ / ugula-e_2 / lu_2 ku_3 la_2-a / lu_2 še $aĝ_2$ (rev. ii 5–8).

494 Edzard 1968: 110.

495 Wilcke 1980: 503.

496 Steinkeller 1989: 92–97.

III document from Ĝirsu suggest this meaning. Steinkeller cites this latter document as support for his idea that the Ur III state administration employed these "professionals" to "weigh silver and to assay its quality."[497] The document in question is as follows: "1 Mandu, the son of Papa, the silver weigher (ku_3-la_2), died (ba-$uš_2$). Ninĝirsu-isa took the assertory oath concerning this."[498] However, this is a unique piece of evidence and the primary title of this person may have been omitted for some reason. It would not have been startling to learn that Mandu was a merchant or a smith.

Steinkeller was the first to identify smiths (simug), goldsmiths (ku_3-dim_2), and merchants (dam-$gara_3$) as professionals acting as "silver weighers" in the Ur III data. In his words, they were "those professionals who owned balances and had the necessary experience to do the weighing accurately."[499] The overview of references to ku_3-la_2 facilitated by Manuel Molina's database BDTNS only corroborates his conclusions. All (lu_2) ku_3-la_2 were either merchants or metalworkers. Steinkeller also makes an important observation that Old Babylonian sale documents from various locations in northern Mesopotamia record smiths as silver weighers in these transactions.

Other contexts of the sign combination ku_3-la_2 in Ur III records are challenging. For example, one document mentions 16 $eren_2$ "16 free royal dependents" and 20 $eren_2$ ku_3-la_2 in the following line.[500] Who would need 20 weighmasters? If they are weighmasters (they are not), why is there no professional title in the first case. Another Ur III document illustrates that (lu_2) ku_3 (nu-)la_2-me, "these are those who are (not) paid in silver," has nothing to do with weighmasters but reflects a practice by the state to remunerate people with silver.[501] Another Ur III document records eight individuals who are described as ĝuruš ku_3-la_2. However, they were not "workmen, weighmasters" but "workmen paid in silver." This document records monthly barley "salaries" to the members of the temple household of a deity ^{d}Ĝeš-bar-e_3 and the people in question received barley as equivalents for the amounts they were supposed to receive in silver.[502]

In summary, (lu_2) ku_3-la_2 was not just a weigher of silver. His role was to weigh silver as money in the context of legal transactions. In doing this, his

497 Steinkeller 1989: 94.

498 Sollberger 1976.

499 Steinkeller 1989: 94.

500 Maekawa 1998: 101 no. 3 rev. i 4–5.

501 For this meaning of ku_3-la_2 in the context of subsistence fields of royal dependents, see MVN 10 93 passim, especially rev. i 3.

502 ITT 2 627 = TCTI 1 627 rev. ii 10–12, obv. ii 13, 20, rev. i 9, 12–14 (Ur III Ĝirsu).

function was not only operational – to use weighing gear and weigh out silver – but included the responsibility of ascertaining the correctness of the procedure and of the amount of silver. In this respect, he may indeed be compared to the Roman *libripens*, as previously suggested by Wilcke and Steinkeller.

The case of another term for "weighmaster," ma-na-la$_2$ "(the one who) weighs (with) mina (weights)," is more challenging. The lexical list *Nabnītu* compares it with a professional *hā'iṭu* "official concerned with the weighing of silver used as currency."[503] A late bilingual copy of the lexical list *Lu* explains all three professional titles – ku$_3$-la$_2$, šagan-la$_2$, and ma-na-la$_2$ – as "silver weigher" (*šāqil kaspi*), which is a simplification. In 3rd mill. BC sources, ma-na-la$_2$ appears only in the term for the large weighing balance ĝeš-rin$_2$ ma-na-la$_2$ "scales to weigh with mina (weights)."[504] No early sources mention ma-na-la$_2$ as a professional title or otherwise.

We do have a professional title GIN$_2$-la$_2$ in the Ur craft archive of the Ur III period. Walther Sallaberger interprets it as giĝ$_4$-la$_2$ "weigher of shekels." He argues that these people represent the first and most important group of craftsmen in this dossier. According to him, they had the right to weigh out precious materials such as gold and silver.[505] Hans Neumann doubts this interpretation and turns to the earliest suggestion by Edzard to understand the term TUN$_3$-la$_2$ as "the one who has instrument TUN$_3$ hanging (on a belt)."[506] The photographs of the document recording this term prove, however, that the sign in question is GIN$_2$ and not T/DUN$_3$.[507] Nevertheless, the interpretation of GIN$_2$-la$_2$-me-eš$_2$ in the Ur III records as "weighers of shekels" is unlikely. Documents in this dossier show that GIN$_2$-la$_2$ was an umbrella term for various professionals. Not all of them were concerned with materials measured by weight. For example, in UET 3 1483, they are metalworkers such as goldsmiths (ku$_3$-dim$_2$), smiths (simug), and other metalworkers (an-dim$_2$-dim$_2$), but also stone artisans (zadim and lu$_2$-za-su$_6$-ma) and carpenters (nagar). Artisans working with stone or timber never appear in the context of weighing.

---

503 MSL 16: 96; CAD Ḫ: 32.

504 It appears in Old Babylonian documents recording the division of property of private households (Kalla 1998: 41).

505 Sallaberger 1994: 138 n. 13.

506 Neumann 2001: 41.

507 E.g. UET 3 1483 obv. 11.

The term lu$_2$-$^{\text{(ĝeš)}}$erin$_2$ in two Classical Sargonic texts from Nippur tentatively interpreted as "recruiter" by Westenholz likely had no relation to weighing.[508] It cannot be "the person (in charge of) the balance."

This discussion leaves us with only one term for a real weighmaster, (lu$_2$-)ku$_3$-la$_2$. Little to nothing suggests its existence as a separate profession. Additionally, (lu$_2$-)ku$_3$-la$_2$ were not Sumerian weighmasters par excellence but a function in legal transactions.

9.4 Merchants as weighmasters

Obviously, a Bronze Age merchant could not do without a balance and a set of weights. These tools had to be of a size to carry with oneself. Sets of small weights in the archaeological context and the terms "bag for weights" and a small "balance (for) silver" in the written data support this assumption.

Ur III sale documents mention merchants, Sum. dam-gara$_3$, quite often as weighmasters: PN dam-gara$_3$ ku$_3$-la$_2$-a-bi "PN, the merchant, the one who weighed its (the transaction's) silver." This means that the agent of the verb la$_2$ "to weigh out" in these documents is not the actual weighmaster (the merchant) but the buyer, which is confusing. The parties in a legal transaction needed a third party, a merchant or some other specialist with weighing tools

[1] saĝ-[x]	1 [male/female] slave;
ni$_3$-sa$_{10}$-ma-ni	its price:
15 giĝ$_4$ ku$_3$-babbar	15 shekels silver.
Lugal-al	To Lugal-al,
dumu Ur-^{d}Ir-[da] išib ^{d}Ir-da	son of Ur-Irda, the išib priest of (god) Irda,
Lugal-engar-[du$_{10}$] ugula e$_2$ ^{d}Inana-[ke$_4$]	Lugalengardu, the overseer of the house (=temple) of Inana,
in-na-la$_2$	has weighed out to him.
Ka-tar dumu Ur-eš$_3$-lil$_2$-la$_2$	Katar, son of Urešlila,
dam-gara$_3$-10 ku$_3$ la$_2$-a-bi	the (head) merchant of 10 (merchants), (is) its (the transaction's) weigher of silver.
[witnesses]	

Fig. 9.2: An Ur III purchase of a slave ELTS 350 = Zettler 1992: 279.

508 See OSP 2 128 rev. ii 18 and 130 rev. ii 3 with commentaries.

and knowledge of weighing to measure the silver as money. An excerpt from an Ur III purchase of a slave illustrates all these points (Fig. 9.2).

Unfortunately, documents of the previous periods mostly do not provide such detailed accounts. Exceptions are rare. For example, one Sargonic document MC 4 61 uses a construction similar to (lu$_2$-)ku$_3$-la$_2$. Here, a merchant acts as a weighmaster too: "It was Enzara, the merchant, who held the weighing scales."[509] Another Sargonic sale document mentions the same construction in connection to a merchant: Ur-li dam-gara$_3$^{ra} ĝeš-rin$_2$-bi ≪ĝeš≫ dab-ba$_5$.[510] However, the earliest text witnessing this phrase is a nonprovenanced document of the Presargonic or Early Sargonic period in the Iraq Museum in Baghdad. Its reverse records a purchase of a person. A merchant acts here as weighmaster: E$_2$-muš dam-gara$_3$, lu$_2$ ĝeš-rin$_2$ dab$_5$-ba.[511]

The discussion until now shows that Presargonic and Sargonic sale contracts used the construction lu$_2$ ĝeš-rin$_2$ dab$_5$-ba "the one who held scales" to identify the weighmaster in these transactions. In contrast, Ur III sale documents switch to the construction (lu$_2$) ku$_3$-la$_2$(-a)-bi "the one who weighed out its silver." Both constructions highlight the socioeconomic practice when merchants and smiths provided their services to private individuals.

Despite the abundance of references to merchants in the ED IIIa texts, the direct evidence of their involvement in weighing is meager. For example, a record of 40 minas of copper from Šuruppak states that a merchant Diĝirnume takes away five to six minas of copper from each individual.[512] It is logical to ask: Who established the weight of this copper? We know from later documents that officials issued metals as money to merchants. These documents portray the socioeconomic role of merchants as mediators between the elites controlling central households and the rest of the population. Thus, the merchants, *not being part* of the top-tier staff of these households, were not entrusted with the measurement of the outgoing goods.

Presargonic accounts from Ĝirsu DP 513 and MVN 3 10 illustrate this point. They record trade of Ĝirsu-based merchants with the city of Der, where a local weighing standard was in use ("the stone of Der"; see Chapter 7). Arguably, the merchants were those who had operated with the Sumerian and the local standard at Der. However, the reference to the Der standard shows the awareness of

509 En-za-ra dam-gara$_3$ lu$_2$ ĝeš-rin$_2$ dab$_5$-ba-am$_3$ (obv. 10–11).

510 Notizia and Schrakamp 2010 obv. 8–9. For another, doubtful reference to the same construction (this time in an administrative text and without a merchant), see CUSAS 13 203 rev. 5–6 with commentary.

511 Westenholz 1995: 535 rev. i 8–ii 1.

512 TSŠ 260 obv. i–ii.

the officials of Baba's temple of the differences between the two standards and their unwillingness to rely on the faithfulness of the Sumerian merchants they entrusted with the task to acquire the luxury goods they were interested in. Unfortunately, nothing in these and similar documents suggests the identity of the actual weighmasters.

9.5 Craftsmen as weighmasters

Ur III sale contracts show the role of metalworkers, such as smiths (simug) and goldsmiths (ku_3-dim_2), as weighmasters in the private context.[513] The already discussed document BdI 1 29 from Early Sargonic Adab mentions a smith who was a "silver weigher" (simug ku_3-la_2). Hence, not all smiths could act as "silver-weigher." Obviously, a smith producing plowshares did not need to operate a weighing balance and stone weights. Apparently, only a portion of smiths possessed the weighing gear.

Third millennium administrative documents often mention that a craftsman "weighed out" some goods to someone or just established their weight in the context of the production. However, as with any attestation of the verb la_2 "to weigh (out)," it is a big question whether it really referred to the agent of the action as the weighmaster in the transaction.

A Sargonic document from Umma CST 11 is interesting in this respect. It records that a number of persons established the weight of copper ore (uruda ni_3-sahar-ra) for its use in the production of metal tools. The procedure is as follows. (1) An amount of ore is mentioned. (2) This is the ore of the land recorder (sa_{12}-du_5-ka-kam). (3) Individuals identified as a chief smith in one case perform its measurement (e-la_2). (4) A person identified by a personal name acts as a controller (maškim) of these actions. Here comes an interesting detail. A chief smith, Dudu, is one of the persons who perform the weighing of copper (rev. 3). No official controls his action. Does this mean that he did it himself? Rev. 4–7 informs that it is a scribe, Dada, who "weighs out" all these amounts to him (e-na-la_2). This shows that, even if Dudu was able to establish the weight of the goods he received, the last word remained with Dada the scribe. However, this does not answer the question of who did the weighing.

Most administrative documents simply record the issue of metals to smiths using the verb la_2. As a result, weighmasters remain unknown. For example, a Presargonic document from Ĝirsu RTC 23 attributes "the weighing" of bronze

513 E.g. Steinkeller 1989: 233–234 no. 57 (simug), 319–320 no. 121 (ku_3-dim_2).

belonging to the chief temple administrator to two smiths. Who weighed this copper? Did these smiths do it? Similarly, a Sargonic document from Nippur ECTJ 153 records the fact that someone weighed out 202 axes to a smith.

The complete lack of interest of administrative records in the identity of weighmasters is striking. However, the presence of a "controller" (maškim) in some transactions with metals and other valuables shows that this official could be responsible at least for the controlling of the weighing process. This presupposes he knew how to do it.

As argued before, the verb la_2 mostly means "to pay" and not "to perform weighing personally." For example, a Sargonic document OSP 2 62 mentions that a smith weighed out an amount of silver to a merchant (obv. ii 1–4). The same document records a gardener (šandana) doing the same to the same merchant (rev. i 5–9). Texts in Akkadian witness the same phenomenon. For example, am Ešnunna document OAIC 10 states (rev. 3–5): *in* E_2 *ši uš-*ta_2*-a-*pi_5*-la a-na si-tim* SA_{10}*-me lu-uš-*qu_2*-ul-kum* "out of the estate to which I have given my consent I will weigh out for you in full."[514] Here, the Akkadian verb *šaqālum* means simply "to pay."

One would naturally expect a flood of information about the professionals who act as weighmasters in the wool and textile industry. However, another disappointment awaits here. A skim through documents recording wool – for example, Middle Sargonic texts published in SCTRAH and CUSAS 20 – shows no interest in the identity of weighmasters. These documents use the impersonal construction "it was weighed (to PN)."

In contrast, some texts recording wool and textiles record the agents of the verb la_2 "to weigh (out)." Most of them are officials. For example, one Sargonic text from Ĝirsu states that "1 tablecloth; its weight: 5 minas 15 shekels wool. AKAdu, the professional tug_2-du_8, weighed it."[515] It is debated whether a professional tug_2-du_8 was a "felter" or not.[516] Anyway, he was in charge of the production. This example would illustrate that a professional involved in the manufacture of a product established its weight all by himself.[517] However, as I stressed before, the presence of an agent of the verb la_2 does not necessarily mean that he operated the balance. A similar document ITT 5 9317 from the same archive states that a governor "weighs" a woolen product, a fact that beggars belief.

---

514 See Sommerfeld 2012: 259 for this interpretation of the first verbal form.

515 STTI 43 obv. 1–rev. 3: 1 tug_2-du_8-a banšur-ra / ki-la_2-bi *5* ma-na *15* $gi\hat{g}_4$ siki / A-KA-du_3 / tug_2-du_8-e / i_3-la_2.

516 Steinkeller 1980; Waetzoldt 2007.

517 See CUSAS 3 706 and related texts for a professional tug_2-du_8 by the name of Ha-NI who "weighed" the goods produced from wool in Ur III Garšana,

9.6 Officials as weighmasters

Numerous administrative documents state that a king (lugal), a governor ($ensi_2$), or their wives "weigh out" goods.[518] Hartmut Waetzoldt illustrated that some rulers had been previously high officials and scribes, which required literacy and, possibly, knowledge of metrology.[519] Nevertheless, it is doubtful that a ruler or his spouse would handle scales and weights by themselves – even if they knew how to do it – instead of commissioning one of their subordinates. Besides, the data on smiths as weighmasters show that *the ability to perform weighing was not related to literacy*. Some officials certainly performed weighing personally. However, this means neither that all of them were literate nor that all of them performed weighing.

Who among the officials could perform weighing? A document from Presargonic Ĝirsu DP 516 may illustrate that a high official *agrig* might have done the weighing all by himself. Obv. i 1 f. states: "*n* minas and shekels of pure silver, PN, the official agrig, weighed *by himself*" (igi-ni-ta e-la_2). There is no doubt that *agrig* was literate and knew metrology.[520] However, the construction igi-ni-ta is the matter of interest here. Gebhard Selz interprets it as "with/by his eye" in his edition,[521] which would mean "personally." This would confirm his role as the actual weighmaster in this transaction. However, Josef Bauer interprets igi-ni-ta as "in his/her presence; under his/her supervision."[522]

Logically, scribes (dub-sar) are among the likely candidates for being weighmasters. Gabriella Spada and Lorenzo Verderame discussed the role of scribes as weighers of wool before it was passed on to weavers and fullers during the Ur III period. Additionally, scribes were present as the authority who controlled the amounts of the materials and objects at each stage of the process of production.[523] Similar evidence is abundant in the previous periods as well. For example, a Sargonic text from Ĝirsu STTI 49 records a delivery of 93 garments by the administrator of a household. A scribe weighs them (i_3-la_2) upon delivery. Another example: an Early Sargonic Umma text Nik 2 56 states that a

---

518 For examples, see DP 192 and 194 for governors' wives as those who "weigh out" textiles to groups of individuals in the context of Baba's temple at Presargonic Ĝirsu. See Nik 1 305, VS 14 30, and passim for the same role of the Lagashite governors. For the same role of the ruler in Presargonic Nippur, see OSP 1 22.

519 Waetzoldt 2009: 252.

520 Visicato and Westenholz 2005: 67; Waetzoldt 2009: 252.

521 Selz 1993: 394.

522 Bauer 1989/1990: 89.

523 Verderame and Spada 2013.

scribe "weighed out" a large amount of silver to Adda, the official ensi$_2$-gal. The same scribe weighs out copper mauls for another scribe and for a smith in BIN 8 332. In the same archive, a messenger (sukkal) "weighs out" an amount of copper for a scribe, Adda (CUSAS 35 451). Nevertheless, all these references do not convince that scribes handled balances and weights personally during these transactions.

Another piece of evidence suggests that the mysterious weighmasters in the textile industry were *illiterate*. We have seen in the chapters on weights and scales that large weights are sometimes designated "a talent and two and two-thirds mina" in Ur III records; these weights deviated from the mass of the ideal, standard talent. However, this was not an obstacle for the weighmasters to use them to measure wool. These anonymous illiterate weighers operated these weights. The role of the literate scribes and other officials was to record the weight discrepancy between the real stone weights and the "virtual weights" in order to arrive at the actual mass of wool. This piece of data illustrates an interesting phenomenon of labor division: Those who do (illiterate weighmasters) and those who control and record (literate officials): in other words, hand labor versus intellectual labor, or skill versus knowledge. We may compare this case with a worker in a car factory who fashions a piece with an engineer who knows that this detail will have a working life of *x* years.

Only occasionally do we know that an official could perform weighing personally, and this happens in the private context of legal transactions. In the above-cited example, the overseer of a household (ugula-e$_2$) acts as a weighmaster in a sale contract in Presargonic Adab.

Indirect evidence suggests that other officials may have operated weighing gear personally: maškim "controller," nu-banda$_3$ "supervisor," and i$_3$-du$_8$ "doorkeeper." I drew attention to the role of the maškim officials in controlling the weighing procedures above. The archive of the Early Sargonic Umma is illustrative in this respect.[524]

Presargonic documents from Ĝirsu exemplify the role of nu-banda$_3$ in the management of the payments in silver called bar-dub$_2$-ba (outgoing payments of an uncertain nature) and apin-la$_2$ (incoming rental payments for fields).[525] For example, RTC 27 records *barduba* payments to a number of shepherds. An overseer (ugula) issues this silver from the Baba temple household (rev. ii). However, it is the nu-banda$_3$ Eniggal who weighs this silver in the household

524 See CHEU 53 and CST 11 for examples.

525 Selz 1989: 524; Marzahn and Neumann 1995: 112.

(rev. iii). Other documents provide similar evidence.[526] Nu-banda$_3$ exercises the same duty in the Early Sargonic documents from Umma Nik 2 60, 62–63. However, these data may, in fact, show the nu-banda$_3$ officials as the controllers and not as weighmasters in the weighing.

In summary, there is very little evidence that officials acted as weighmasters personally in the context of central households' economies. It is likely that this was the task of illiterate professionals such as smiths.

9.7 The context of weighing

Weighmasters performed their duties at a locus. The socioeconomic nature of these places defines the interpretation of the whole transaction. References to the sites where weighing takes place are rare. However, they provide a uniform image: The weighing mostly happened in "house(hold)s" (e$_2$).

Archaeological studies identify various contexts in which stone weights were found. Unfortunately, objects interpreted as early weights from southern Mesopotamia remain largely unpublished and their context has not been determined yet. The duck weights of the Ur III period are the only exception.[527] Lorenz Rahmstorf identifies three contexts of weights in 3rd mill. BC Syro-Mesopotamia: (1) palace/administrative building, (2) temple, and (3) domestic context.[528] The principal merit of his contribution is that he addresses the question of weighing in the domestic context. He states that *the majority of weights are found in domestic areas* in 3rd mill. BC Syro-Mesopotamia.[529] Especially interesting is the case of the Akkadian-date Syrian site of Tell Sweyhat, where the context suggests the use of weights in connection to metalworking, which shows that smiths performed their jobs at home.

As for the written data, the Presargonic archive from Baba's temple *E-munus* is illustrative. Numerous documents record agents of the verb la$_2$ "to weigh out." They have the same structure: PN agent (ruler, his wife, or an official in the ergative) + goods (absolutive) + recipient/purpose (dative) + organization (e$_2$-gal "palace" or *E-munus* itself) + e-(na/ne-)la$_2$ "he/she weighed out (for him/her/them)."[530]

526 Nik 1 295; VS 14 65 and 175.
527 Rahmstorf 2006: 21; Rahmstorf 2014: 430.
528 Rahmstorf 2014: 430–433.
529 Rahmstorf 2014: 432.
530 E.g. see BIN 8 368; DP 192, 194, and 517–18; ITT 5 9231, 9245, and 9247; Nik 1 300 and 305; RTC 25; VS 14 30, 123, 146, 154, and 181; VS 27 9.

The markers of the locative and the ablative cases are used in the synonymous semantic as "issuing weighable goods to someone." Sometimes a document uses the simple form e-la$_2$ and omits a recipient.[531] These cases refer to the administrative practice of establishing the mass of incoming or stored goods. We have every reason to believe that these weighing operations took place *within* the palace or Baba's temple. The account of weighing tools DP 509 registers the inventory of the weights of Sasa, who was the ruler's wife and the "CEO" of Baba's temple on the one hand, and the weights of the palace on the other. This shows that both organizations were well equipped with weighing gear.

The Early Sargonic dossier of metalworking at Umma also illustrates a temple as the place of weighing. Nik 2 55* records the fact that an individual received an amount of copper in the temple called "The Scepter-House" at Umma: e$_2$-ĝidru Umma^{ki}-ka šu ba-ti. The governor Mesag "acts" as the weighmaster in this transaction. Other documents of the same file exemplify the same role of the ruler as a controller in this temple household.[532]

There was a temple called e$_2$-ĝidru at Adab too.[533] A Sargonic document from Adab SCTRAH 221 mentions it in connection with weighing: "(such and such garments): they are old garments (i.e. previously produced) to be weighed. They are in the "Scepter-House."[534] This record shows the temple in the role of the textile production center where these products were also weighed.

Ĝeš-kiĝ$_2$-ti "workshop" is another area within the central economy where weighing takes place. For example, a Sargonic text from Umma Nik 2 51 documents the weighing of 15 sheep fleeces with a mass of 45 minas "in the workshop": ĝeš-kiĝ$_2$-ti-a e-la$_2$.

The final loci where weighing might have taken place in Sumer are private houses of palace and temple officials. We know that similar activities, such as measuring grain, inventories, and (temporary) storage of goods and tools, etc., often happened within these households. For example, ED IIIb documents from the Umma region record the measurement of the "communal" flour in the houses of chief temple administrators (saĝĝa).[535] Early Sargonic texts from Adab show the role of the house of a household's supervisor (nu-banda$_3$) and of other officials as a place for storage and distribution of bread, grain, hides, etc.[536]

531 As in VS 14 30, RTC 27, etc.

532 Nik 2 76–77.

533 See CUSAS 35 302 with a commentary.

534 <. . .> / tug$_2$ libir la$_2$-dam / e$_2$-ĝidru-ka / mu-ĝal$_2$.

535 BIN 8 51 and 109, CUSAS 14 177.

536 CUSAS 11 189; CUSAS 35 88, 134, 169, and 192.

9.8 Conclusions

The legal documents recording private legal transactions are more informative about the social and professional identities of weighmasters in Sumer. Steinkeller's conclusion based on the Ur III evidence that merchants and metalworkers possessed weights and balances has been confirmed by the evidence from earlier periods.

In contrast, administrative documents are generally mute in this respect. The most pitiful example is that of the wool and textile industry. We know by name hundreds of people involved in the processing of wool and the production of textiles. In contrast, we know no one who operated large wool balances and put large imprecise talent weights on their scales.

Another important conclusion concerns the verb la_2 "to weigh (out)." An individual who appears as the agent of this verb does not automatically become a weighmaster. In contrast, the data suggest that he was either (a) a payer (private context) or (b) a controller of weighing (central households: temples and palaces). The real weighmasters are almost never identical to those who are recorded as "he/she weighed out something to someone" in the administrative records.

Another interesting aspect of this topic is literacy. The clearly visible role of metalworkers and merchants as weighmasters suggests that these two spheres were not related.

The final facet is the question of the "private" and the "state" in the social context of weighing in Sumer. In other words, did the state have a monopoly on weighing? The question is a modernization of the social reality in early Mesopotamia. As Steinkeller argues in his influential contribution, artisans and merchants worked "privately" on the one hand and for the "state" on the other. Once they had fulfilled their obligations to the state, they were free to work for themselves. In this way, they possessed their "means of production."[537] This means that weighing as a practice exercised by these individuals was not monopolized by the central households. As D'Agostino and Gorello argue, "it would have been impossible for the state to create the possibility for a person to become a blacksmith. In other words, we do not think that the state built up a 'school' in which smiths could learn the profession. Thus we imagine that some 'families,' intended only in part as a group of relatives, specialized historically in one activity, that of the manufacturing of metal objects being among the most likely of these specialities."[538]

537 Steinkeller 2004b.
538 D'Agostino and Gorello 2013: 261.

This shows a deep contradiction between the written data and the way weighing as a cultural phenomenon must have existed in early Mesopotamia. The weight metrology was inevitably linked to the *actions* of professionals for whom it was a part of their job: smiths and merchants. This shows that the emergence of the weight metrology should not be related to the emergence of the state. The latter was solely responsible for its standardization to maximize the accuracy of accounting of certain types of goods exclusively in those spheres which were under the state's political and economic control.

10 Weighed goods

10.1 Introduction

Now we arrive at the pivotal point of the study. It is obvious that weight measures, their relationships, their standardization, weighing tools, various weighing practices, and the representation of all these objects, ideas, and techniques in script would have never existed without the ultimate aim of the Sumerian system of weight measures – to measure certain goods. So, what were these goods?

It is fascinating how little interest the studies of Sumerian metrology show in this focal topic. Previous scholarship has never thought to link the emergence of the weight metrology and its gradual development and standardization to the need to weigh certain types of goods. In contrast, I argue that the aggregate state of certain goods and their high value and importance in the economy and society of early Mesopotamia are the principal factors in the emergence of weighing. Hence, this chapter contributes more than any other does to the causality of the origins and to the function of the Sumerian system of weight measures.

In this chapter, I discuss the evidence on goods and objects that appear in the 3rd mill. BC cuneiform records as those measured by weight, and consider the possibilities of the existence of these weighing practices in the 4th mill. BC.

Naturally, it is impossible to discuss in detail all goods and objects that were directly measured by weight or first counted in pieces and then weighed in early cuneiform records. This is unnecessary because it would obscure the roots of the measurement metrology. The aim here is to identify the "core goods": those materials whose need for mensuration triggered its emergence, at least in script, in southern Mesopotamia.

How to identify these goods? Two objective factors help: (1) the temporal aspect and (2) the quantitative aspect. The former concerns the analysis of the earliest data where the weight measures appear: for example, it is copper in the documents of the Early Dynastic I–II period. The quantitative aspect relates the frequency of attestations of certain types of goods to their importance in the economy of palace and temple households of Sumerian cities: The more written references we have of a certain type of good – such as silver as a means of payment in the latter half of the 3rd mill. BC – the more important it was to measure by weight to those who were responsible for creating written accounts.

Naturally, this approach does not and cannot consider those goods and practices of weighing that fall beyond the scope of cuneiform records, which,

https://doi.org/10.1515/9781501510267-010

with the exception of legal documents, concentrate on the economies of large "state" households. Therefore, archaeological research on the influx, use, circulation, and amounts of certain weighed goods must be taken into consideration in evaluating their role in the emergence of the Mesopotamian system of weight measures.

Anticipating the discussion that follows below, I identify several groups of "core goods" that played the central role in the early use of the weight metrology in Mesopotamia: (1) metals, most importantly copper and silver, (2) wool and textiles, and (3) luxury materials, such as precious metals, resins, and gems.

Ancient inhabitants of southern Mesopotamia needed copper and bronze to produce strong and durable working tools, utensils, and weaponry. Some metals began to play the role of money as early as the beginning of the 3rd mill. BC. Plentiful flocks produced wool that was then transformed into textiles. The weighing of both types of these goods became obligatory in the central households of 3rd mill. BC Mesopotamia. Finally, the elites required luxury items that maintained their prestige and demarcated them from an average Joe.

The weighing of metals and luxury goods implies that interregional trade played a tremendous role in the emergence of the weight metrology. Despite the scarcity of evidence, it is likely that the export of textiles may have belonged to the same phenomenon.

10.2 Approaches to express the weight of objects in script

Before coming to the discussion of goods and objects that were measured by weight, it is necessary to elucidate how the weight of these goods was notated in cuneiform records. Ambiguous at the beginning of the 3rd mill. BC, the approaches aimed at putting down the mass of goods and object in script have developed very soon in a precise formula that persisted until the end of the cuneiform account keeping.

It is important to draw a line between two sets of data representing two distinct types of physical objects: *substances* (*materials, matters*) and *objects*. This difference was clear to the early Mesopotamian scribes as it is to a modern person. For example, copper, wool, and cedar wood are all substances. It is impossible to count them unless one uses a system of mensuration, which is the system of weight units in our case. We cannot, and neither could Sumerians, say "one wool" or "ten silver." Cuneiform records have "one *mina* of wool" and "ten *shekels* of silver." The measure is explicitly mentioned to make the amount clear to everyone. This practice is found in the earliest references to weighed materials, the Early Dynastic I–II records of copper in minas from Ur and Šuruppak that I discuss in Chapter 3.

Some scholars conjecture that the weight metrology is present in the Late Uruk accounts. They argue that weight measures were not written. For example, "1 wool" means "1 (mina of) wool," etc. There are pros and cons in their interpretations but the data remain ambiguous. What we know definitely is that the weight metrology was used from at least 2800 BC.

Objects make up the second group of weighable goods. They include natural objects, such as pieces of lapis lazuli, and products, such as copper vessels and silver jewelry. Scribes used a different approach to notate the weight of these goods. The available data allow us to reconstruct several historical stages in these notations. The earliest approach is found in the ED I–II and some ED IIIa inscriptions. The scribes used the following syntactical construction to notate the weight of the objects:

NUMBER OF WEIGHT MEASURES – OBJECT – WEIGHT MEASURE

It is easy to follow the logic of the scribes. This practice is a derivation from the usual notation for substances, such as "1 mina of wool." In accordance with this, "1 vessel mina" means "(one) vessel (weighing) 1 mina (of copper or bronze)."

Perhaps the earliest reference to a weighed object uses precisely this construction. It is an Early Dynastic I–II account from Šuruppak. Obv. ii 5 has 5 ma-na uruda TUN_3-la_2.[539] Editors interpret it as "5 Minen Kupfer (für einen) . . .-Becher." However, it should be corrected as "(1) *TUNla* copper vessel (weighing) 5 minas" (5 TUN_3-la_2-⌜uruda⌝ ma-na).[540] This copper vessel weighed about 2.5 kg according to this document, if we presume a standard, "metallic" mina of about 500 g.

A similar entry appears in an ED IIIa text from Šuruppak FTP 84 obv. ii 4': 1 $gi\hat{g}_4$-uruda ma-na. Editors interpret the line correctly as "1 copper ax (weighing) 1 mina" (p. 65). As the discussion in the chapter on the shekel shows, the Sumerian $gi\hat{g}_4$ is equated with the Akkadian word *pāšu*, an axe, in lexical lists. In the same vein, a synchronous text from Nippur records the weight of an *uri* vessel: 3 uri ma-na "(1 copper/bronze) vessel *uri* of 3 minas."[541] Another example from Šuruppak mentions $2N_8$ uruda $\hat{g}iri_2$-sal "(1) thin copper knife (weighing) 2/3 (mina)."[542]

539 Krebernik, Steible, and Yildiz 2014: 342, 370 no. 10.
540 See Selz 1997 with a reference to Braun-Honzinger for this vessel in later texts, a sort of libation cup.
541 OIP 97 2 rev. i 4.
542 WF 151* obv. iii 5.

However, this way of notating the weight of objects was unsatisfactory because it allowed the weight of a *single* object at a time to be recorded. The scribes introduced an improved notation quite soon afterward. It appears in other Early Dynastic IIIa documents and has the following syntax:

NUMBER OF OBJECTS – OBJECT – *NUMBER OF MEASURES* – MEASURE

NTSŠ 154 obv. ii 3–4 from Šuruppak exemplifies this development. It records one bronze cup of a half-mina (?) and one bronze object of three minas (1 zabar ma-na ⸢½$^{?}$⸣; 1 ŠENNUR-x ma-na *3*). Unlike the notations of the weight of substances, the number of minas is written as oblique pointed wedges to tell them apart from the numbers designating the number of objects. The weight of another metal object is notated in the same manner in another Šuruppak document: 1 ni$_3$-saĝ:šu$_2$ ma-⸢na⸣ [*n*] "1 helmet of *n* minas."[543]

However, this notation was imperfect too. To facilitate the correct understanding, scribes decided to introduce the word ki-la$_2$ "weight" into this construction. From then on, any entry in a record that notated the weight of an object or numerous objects of the same type had two parts that usually appear in separate lines. The first line records the number of objects and the lexeme to identify them. The second line specifies their total weight:

(1) NUMBER OF OBJECTS – OBJECT
(2) ki-la$_2$-bi ("its/their weight") – NUMBER OF MEASURES – MEASURE[544]

This construction appears for the first time in the texts of the ED IIIb period and continues until the end of the cuneiform writing. The word ki-la$_2$-bi can refer to a single or to multiple objects of the same type because the Sumerian possessive suffix =bi is used for singular and plural unanimated nouns.

With regard to the translation "weight" versus "mass," Marvin Powell denies the existence of the latter abstract notion among Sumerians.[545] The latter concept is modern. One can clarify the difference between the two with the following example. The *mass* of an object is the same on the Earth and on the Moon. However, it has a different *weight* on each of them due to the difference in gravity. Naturally, we do not find this distinction in cuneiform records. Nevertheless, Sumerian ki-la$_2$ and Akkadian *šuqultum* are the words that designate "weight," the concrete mass of a certain object produced from a certain material.

543 TSŠ 98 obv. ii 3.
544 Some Ur III texts expand this construction by adding the material from which a certain object had been produced: "(a number of textiles); their weight: *n* measures of *wool*."
545 Powell 2000: 344.

The Akkadian word is not documented before the Old Babylonian/Assyrian period.[546] *Šuqultum* originates in the verb *šaqālum* "to suspend; to weigh." Its morphological pattern *pur(u)s-t-* is typical for *nomina actionis* and, sometimes, concrete things.[547]

The Sumerian ki-la$_2$ is a compound noun that combines a nominal stem ki "place" with a verbal stem la$_2$ "to suspend, to weigh." Other Sumerian words share the same pattern with these two stems. For ki+VERB, cf. ki-gub "position" (gub "to stand"), ki-nu$_2$ "bedroom" (nu$_2$ "lie down"). For NOUN+la$_2$, cf. a$_2$-la$_2$ "a drum" (lit. "(the thing that) hangs on arm"), apin-la$_2$ "field rent," dub-la$_2$ "foundation platform."

Ki-la$_2$ "weight" is not related to the compound verb ki . . . la$_2$ = *napalšuhu(m)* "to fall to the ground."[548] Beginning in the Old Babylonian period, ki-la$_2$(-bi) as "(its) weight" appears in lexical lists. The Middle Babylonian *Ura* is speculative about the possessive suffixes after ki-la$_2$. It introduces a hoax form ki-la$_2$-bi-ne-ne *šuqultā-šunu* "their weight."[549] Obviously, the Semitic-speaking compilers of the list introduced their linguistic reality into Sumerian, which, unlike Semitic, uses the same possessive suffix =bi for singular and plural nonanimated nouns. The lexical list *Nabnītu* compares ki-la$_2$ with the Akkadian verb *sanāqum* "to check, supervise, control."[550] However, we do not find this usage of ki-la$_2$ in the 3rd mill. BC texts.

10.3 Copper and silver

10.3.1 Copper as money

As we have seen in the example of four Early Dynastic I–II texts from Ur and Šuruppak, copper is the earliest metal and simultaneously the earliest kind of goods in general that bears witness to the use of the weight metrology in southern Mesopotamia. This is hardly accidental. The importance of copper and its alloys for the societies of the 4th and 3rd mill. BC has led archaeologists to label these periods "Chalcolithic" and "Bronze" Ages, respectively. According to the archaeological evidence, Oman, ancient Ma$_2$-gan^{ki}, was the major source of copper for southern Mesopotamia during the ED IIIa–Ur III periods

546 CAD Š/3: 335.
547 Kienast 2001: 73.
548 CAD N/1: 271.
549 MSL 13: 283.
550 MSL 16: 242; CAD S: 133.

(ca. 2600–2000). In contrast, the evidence of the Uruk III (Jemdet Nasr) and ED I–II periods shows that only about one-fourth of copper from Sumer came from Oman, thereby suggesting other main sources during this time, including Anatolia and Iran. Nevertheless, scholars suggest that the copper trade was the main reason for the contact between Sumer and Oman probably as early as the Middle Uruk period.[551]

This question is closely related to the emergence of weighing in Sumer. As stated throughout this book, the ED I–II cuneiform data show that (a) copper is the earliest material recorded in weight measures and (b) it was measured in "ma-na," a unit with a clearly visible Semitic origin. This is an indication that one of the factors in the emergence of weighing in Sumer was the interregional trade in copper with regions populated by Semites and/or through Semitic-speaking merchants.

The data of the early cuneiform records illustrate two basic functions of copper during the first half of the 3rd mill. BC. The first is the production of reliable and durable metal tools, for which see below. Although copper as a material was the original rationale for its use, I would like to start the discussion with its second function: as money.

As Powell stresses, copper along with silver and barley were the *monies* in Sumer, and not "a sort of money," "exchange means," etc.[552] Metals represented "expensive" monies in Sumer leaving the place of "cheap" money to the easily available barley. Our data suggest that copper embodied value and was used as an exchange etalon in the first half of the 3rd mill. BC in Mesopotamia, which makes it the earliest metallic money in the history of humanity.

Despite the fact that copper was never as valuable as its rivals silver and gold, it was still valuable, rare enough, and, more importantly, useful as a material for producing tools. Consequently, it was more flexible than silver. A person could purchase a field or a house for an amount of copper. Alternatively, he/she could go with it to a smith and let him produce tools used in agriculture or household utensils. The use of stone and clay to produce most basic tools, such as sickles, etc., shows that copper held a position between common goods such as barley and precious metals and other luxury goods. Of no less importance to the relatively high value of copper was the fact that the trade of metals – materials

551 Moorey 1999: 247, Carter 2013: 581, 586, and Laursen and Steinkeller 2017: 12, 19 with references.
552 Powell 1996.

lacking in lowland Mesopotamia – was run by merchants on behalf of central households (palaces and temples) during this period.[553]

Another factor in the value of copper is its physical property and weight. The following rule can be applied to the Mesopotamian monies of the 3rd mill. BC: *The bulkier the money was, the cheaper it was*. This made copper a perfect type of money in the first half of the 3rd mill. BC.

Multiple sale contracts from Early Dynastic IIIa Šuruppak exemplify the use of copper money (passim). UET 2 252 (ED I–II Ur) and WF 128 (ED I–II Šuruppak) suggest the same phenomenon even earlier, ca. 2800 BC.

Uruda is the most common Sumerian writing of copper. A syllabic writing a-ru_{12}(EN)-da^{uruda} or – if one prefers – $uruda^{a\text{-}ru12\text{-}da}$ is found in Early Dynastic Ĝirsu and elsewhere.[554] It is also present in ED IIIa lexical lists, such as in a copy of the lexical list *Early Dynastic Practical Vocabulary A* where it appears after bronze (zabar) and before a variety of copper $MUŠ_3^{uruda}$.[555] The sign URUDA(ZATU602) abounds in the Late Uruk administrative and lexical texts. However, it is unlikely that this sign had the reading uruda "copper" during this period. It appears very often in accounts of animals, personnel, and various food products. This signals its use as a verb or another term of an administrative nature.

Early Dynastic I–II and IIIa sale contracts and administrative documents mention copper almost exclusively in minas, the shekel being the only other measure. Large numbers of minas instead of talents are typical during this period and as late as the Early Sargonic times. A large amount of 3820 minas of copper appears in the total of a register of field sales the *Enhegal Tablet*.[556] For Early and Middle Sargonic examples of copper of more than 60 minas, see CUSAS 11 112 obv. ii 1 for Adab, OSP 2 44 obv. i 2 for Nippur, and BIN 8 100 and 309 for Umma. Not all of these examples illustrate the use of this metal as money: Most post-ED IIIa documents refer to copper as a material for tools.

The earliest attestation of copper in shekels is TSŠ 60 obv. ii 4 from ED IIIa Šuruppak: $gi\hat{g}_4$ 15 uruda:sal "15 shekels ... copper." Later texts mention copper in shekels regularly. Currently, I am unable to find any references to copper in "little minas" ($NINDA_2$×ŠE+N_1) in the ED IIIa data. For copper in "little minas" during the Classical Sargonic period, see ITT 2 4369 obv. 1, where it is written 2 ma-na-tur. Texts of the same date deliver the first references to copper in

553 For ED examples from Ĝirsu concerning the import of copper, tin, and silver, see Prentice 2010: 107–108 with references to specific texts of the *E-munus* temple household.

554 OSP 2 44 obv. i 2 (MS Nippur).

555 OIP 99 33 obv. vi 3'.

556 ELTS 20 (ED IIIa).

talents too.[557] Most of the above-mentioned references to copper refer to it as a material in the production of tools and utensils. Starting from the Sargonic period onwards, copper is mentioned only as a material; it was not used as money any longer.

Scholars repeatedly argue that copper had lost the palm of supremacy as the "expensive" money to silver by the end of the ED IIIa period. This is certainly true in the case of ED IIIb Ĝirsu, where all transactions within the *E-munus* household, if performed in metal money, were performed in silver. However, the recently published documents from the neighboring ED IIIb Umma, which predate Ĝirsu's archive by about 50 years, show copper side by side with silver as metallic monies. Another factor that should be taken into consideration is the context of the transaction and the "genre" of the text. Sale contracts from Presargonic Ĝirsu are rare. The following discussion illustrates that copper money was the "popular" metallic money in the literal Latin sense of the word during the Early Dynastic period. As argued before, this phenomenon should be related to the broad distribution and the intensive use of copper in the societies of early Mesopotamia.

There are several terms of copper varieties or alloys that were used as money during the Early Dynastic period. **Ni$_3$-UD^{uruda}** is one of them.[558] The earliest reference to its use as such appears in the *Lupad Statue*, a Fara period record of land purchases from Ĝirsu.[559] Many similar examples are found in the sale contracts from Zabalam, one of the major settlements in the Presargonic Umma state and the source of the most texts we have from that region. Since ni$_3$-UD^{uruda} is always mentioned in minas – a practice typical for copper as money in ED IIIa texts – it was a quality of copper and/or its alloy. Ni$_3$-UD^{uruda} cannot be simply a regional scribal idiosyncrasy for "copper," since the texts of that corpus document the usual writing uruda side by side with ni$_3$-UD^{uruda}.[560]

Sales of fields, houses, and slaves clearly identify ni$_3$-UD^{uruda} as money.[561] Early Dynastic loan documents from Zabalam do the same. For example, one document shows how ni$_3$-UD^{uruda}, along with barley and silver, was one of the

---

557 See, for example, ITT 5 9257 rev. ii 1 and ITT 5 6670 obv. 1.

558 The term is absent from the lexical tradition. Ni$_3$-UD-ra = *kaspu ša ugāri* "silver (= payment) of the field" in *Nabnītu* XVII 280 (MSL 16: 162) is unrelated to our term. Ni$_3$-UD$^{(uruda)}$ should not be confused with ninda-UD, a type of bread, for which see CUSAS 23 30.

559 ELTS 21 obv. ii 8.

560 See CUSAS 33 226 obv. iii 2 and 256 rev. i 1. The former document records ^{uruda}ni$_3$-UD as well (obv. ii 5, obv. iii 9). Curiously, the term ma-na is missing in both cases.

561 CUSAS 33 220 obv. i 2: 32 minas as the price of a field; 221 obv. i 3: 65 minas as the price of a field; 234 obv. i 1–2: 30 minas as the price of a slave.

monies issued from a central household – probably the Inana's temple household or from the palace – to interested parties.[562] One fact in this text is particularly interesting. Whereas "common" people received loans in barley, individuals connected to seafaring and trade – a sailor and a merchant – got 3 to 35 minas of ^{uruda}ni$_3$-UD. This reminds us of the strong relation between the central households on the one hand and merchants on the other during the Ur III period when silver played the role of the liquid capital.[563]

Other Zabalam loan records document three types of money: barley, ni$_3$-UD^{uruda}, and silver.[564] In BdI 1 13, the amounts of ni$_3$-UD^{uruda} are as large as 38 minas and as small as eight minas. CUSAS 33 240 is perhaps another loan document. However, the amounts are humbler there: the recipients got one to three minas of ^{uruda}ni$_3$-UD.

The nature of the transactions with ni$_3$-UD^{uruda} is not clear in some cases. CUSAS 11 15 pairs ni$_3$^{uruda} with large amounts of silver in a record of an uncertain nature.[565] Editors interpret the term as "copper items," which is logical. However, taking into account the evidence presented above, I would prefer to see in it a shortened writing ni$_3$(-UD)^{uruda}. The context, "this is the ... silver of Inana('s temple) weighed by the field measurer" (obv. ii 5–iii 2), reminds us of the loan documents.[566]

In BIN 8 103, individuals are mentioned together with amounts of 10 to 40 minas of ni$_3$-UD^{uruda}. These recipients (?) are of high status: a priestess nu-gig and a land surveyor. The nature of this record is equally uncertain: It records only a personal name of an official in charge of the transaction.

These data show that the writings ni$_3$-UD^{uruda}, ni$_3$-UD, and ni$_3$^{uruda} refer to (a variety of) copper that was actively used as money during the Early Dynastic period in the Umma region and, probably, elsewhere. Ni$_3$-UD^{uruda} might be identical to either LAM.KUR.RU or MUŠ$_3$^{uruda} of Sargonic Adab texts, for which see below. There is no evidence that would indicate that ni$_3$-UD^{uruda} refers to the form of storage of copper, such as copper objects or copper scrap. Taken at face value, ni$_3$-UD^{uruda} means "whitish matter" with a determinative for copper and bronze tools (ni$_3$-babbar^{uruda}). Salvatore Monaco and Francesco Pomponio

---

562 CUSAS 35 418.

563 See Steinkeller 2004b and Paoletti 2008 for this aspect.

564 BIN 8 46 obv. ii 3: 20 minas of ni$_3$-UD^{uruda}. BdI 1 13 mentions the material in the context of silver and barley. Contrary to the edition, the first line records ⌜30⌝ ni$_3$-UD ma-na and the paleography of the text clearly suggests its "Umma region" provenance.

565 Contrary to the editors, the prosopography and the reference to the Inana's temple household indicates Zabalam as the provenance of this text.

566 Nevertheless, the crucial term (ku$_3$ bar$^?$ si-ga in obv. ii 5) is hard to interpret.

offer a translation "white copper," and they may be correct in this straightforward explanation.[567] According to *A Guide to Working with Copper and Copper Alloys* by the Copper Development Association, NY (p. 26), copper and its alloys have a rich range of shades from "copper red" to "yellow gold" and "pink."[568] Hence, it is possible that Sumerians perceived a copper alloy ni_3-UD^{uruda} as whitish in color in comparison with the usual reddish copper.

The question of what kind of alloy it was is not easy to answer without any metallic objects inscribed with this term. The writing itself suggests that ancient Mesopotamians were conscious that ni_3-UD^{uruda} was not a usual copper (uruda) or bronze (zabar). Ni_3-UD^{uruda} might be brass. James Muhly writes: "[T]he deliberate production of brass should still be considered a development of the Roman period."[569] However, the absence of knowledge on the part of Sumerians about zinc does not exclude their unconscious use of the brass alloy when extracting the material written ni_3-UD^{uruda} from ores high in zinc. Another possibility is that ni_3-UD^{uruda} represented a bronze alloy with a high percentage of lead. Copper-lead alloying was known around 3000 BC at Susa, the practice then rapidly disappearing. Lead makes up to 20% of some early alloys. Finally, a find in the *Riemchengebäude* of the Late Uruk period has a copper alloy with over 25% of silver.[570] This makes it theoretically possible that ni_3-UD^{uruda} "whitish matter" was a copper-silver alloy, where a certain percentage of silver gave this alloy its whitish tint.

Bronze (zabar) never appeared as money in the 3rd mill. BC.

10.3.2 Silver as money

Ku_3-babbar or simply ku_3 is the Sumerian term for "silver," literally "the white (babbar) *metal* (ku_3)."[571] The designation of silver as "white, bright" is common in many languages.[572] In contrast, the Akkadian *kaspum* is derived from *kasāpum* "to break into bits," which is another common idea connected to silver: It exemplifies one of the forms in which this precious metal circulated in the early Mesopotamian society.

567 Monaco and Pomponio 2009: 27.

568 https://www.copper.org/publications/pub_list/pdf/a1360.pdf.

569 Muhly 1993–1997: 121.

570 Moorey 1999: 257 with references.

571 See Moorey 1999: 232–240 and Joannès 2010.

572 Muhly 1993–1997: 130.

William Hallo discussed this and other forms of silver circulation in the latter part of the 3rd mill. BC and subsequent periods.[573] They were scrap silver, silver rings and coils, and ingots. References to scrap and ingot silver are rare in written records. In contrast, we have numerous data on the use of rings, Sumerian har, in transactions with silver. Powell provided a comprehensive discussion of these coils and their weight.[574] Recognized long ago, the sign for silver KU_3 that appears already in Uruk IV texts (ZATU301) is a depiction of a half of a silver coil made from several intertwined silver strings.

The 4th mill. BC witnessed the regular use of silver in the Near East, which scholars attribute to the discovery of an adequate method for its extraction – cupellation from lead ores. During this period, its use was limited to jewelry, embellishment of some architectural elements, and silver vessels. The sources of silver were eastern Turkey, northeastern Iran, and Turkmenistan. Starting from the 34th c. BC – the transition to the Early Bronze Age – silver objects became more numerous and weighty. Barbara Helwing relates this to two factors: the emergence of the first states in southern Mesopotamia and the use of silver as a symbolic expression of prestige by the elites of these polities.[575] This may answer the question by Robert Englund as to why we do not have "any evidence that silver was in any way used in early households in a manner comparable to later, third-millennium usage"[576]: Silver was rare at that time. Additionally, as we have seen above, copper was used as money in the earliest periods.

The identification of silver in the Late Uruk records is problematic. Theo Krispijn argues that KU_3 in the Late Uruk administrative documents refers to silver and gold.[577] In supporting his claim, he compares the Late Uruk and Early Dynastic copies of the lexical text *Metals*. Doubtlessly, KU_3 is the writing of a material of a number of tools that appear in the *Archaic Metals* and administrative records. However, if we compare the two versions of the lists critically, it becomes obvious that the Early Dynastic scribes had no idea what the writing KU_3 in the Late Uruk sources stood for. Krispijn's figure on pp. 6–7 shows that KU_3-NE was the second most used material after the material written AN to produce tools. In the same manner, Monaco and Pomponio are apt to see "precious metals" in the writing KU_3 in Late Uruk texts. They interpret the graphemes KU_3

573 Hallo 1996: 19–21.
574 Powell 1978.
575 Helwing 2014: 413–416.
576 Englund 2004: 24.
577 Krispijn 2016.

UD and KU_3 NE as "pure" and "alloyed."[578] However, there is no evidence for this assumption either. They refer to the same texts as Krispijn about saws and drills made from these metals, but never explain (a) why inhabitants of Late Uruk cities would produce large mundane tools from precious metals and, no less importantly, (b) how practical saws and drills made from very soft pure silver would have been at all.

Obviously, these attempts to interpret the metals of the data are speculative. In my opinion, KU_3 in Late Uruk texts is a writing for metal par excellence. The signs UD "white, bright" and NE "red" refer to its color,[579] which must correspond to neither Sumerian terminology of the Early Dynastic date for metals nor to our modern classification of metals as chemical elements.[580] Besides, as we have seen above, "the whitish matter" (ni_3-UD^{uruda}) was a copper alloy. It is likely that the Late Uruk data refer to various bronzes and qualities of copper.

It is impossible to overlook the professional title GAL $UMUN_2$ KU_3 in the Late Uruk lexical list *Lu A* 32 and synchronous administrative texts side by side with other professional titles.[581] However, one should be cautious about comparing this term to the 3rd mill. BC professional title ku_3-dim_2-gal "chief goldsmith."[582] If we reflect on the whole section of the $UMUN_2$ official in the Late Uruk list (lines 29–33), it may turn out that $UMUN_2$ might have been not a smith at all.[583]

The only definite meaning of KU_3 in the Late Uruk accounts is a half measure of a pot of dairy fat.[584] In summary, although the sign KU_3 is likely a depiction of a half of metal (not necessarily silver) coil, we cannot interpret any passages containing this graphemes as silver, money, or a material of objects in the Late Uruk written data. The theory by Helwing that silver was a prestige good during the Late Uruk period would explain the lack of silver in the 4th mill. BC records.

The 3rd mill. BC written data on the use of metals are in line with another argument by Helwing: that 3rd mill. BC city-states made silver into a currency.[585]

---

578 Monaco and Pomponio 2009: 20: "argento puro" and "argento fuso" (cioè in lega).

579 See Englund 1998: 98 for the designations of colors in Late Uruk texts.

580 Additionally, Krispijn's suggestion that KU_3 marks one shekel silver lacks any evidence. We have no data that would suggest the use of silver as money during the Late Uruk period.

581 E.g. ATU 5 pl. 38 (W 9168,a) obv. ii 5a.

582 See, for example, BIN 8 105 obv. 1 and 107 obv. ii 3; see also MZL: 147 no. 547 for contra /dim/ for $UMUN_2$.

583 Note also the absence of the common goldsmith (*$UMUN_2$ KU_{3a}) in this section.

584 Englund 1998: 52 n. 101, 167 and passim.

585 Helwing 2014: 418.

Her use of the word "currency" is prone to critizism.[586] However, a different matter is important here. One needs to be specific and to ask: when, where, and to what extent did silver become money?

The previous discussion shows that it was copper and not silver that was used as metallic money during the Early Dynastic I–II period. There is no silver as money at all in these texts. During the following ED IIIa period, silver appears side by side with copper as metallic money. This symbiosis of copper and silver as money is also found in the ED IIIb documents from the Umma state (see ni_3-UD^{uruda} above).

A beautifully written sale of a field from ED IIIa Šuruppak CUSAS 35 469 records that a seller (or sellers) received 22 ½ minas of copper as the price of the field (sa_{10} $aša_5$) and 37 minas of copper as an additional payment (ni_3-diri) as well as some barley as a "present" (ni_3-ba). Silver appears in this document only as a payment to the scribe who fixed the deed in script (rev. ii 4). It is two shekels, which were equal then to six minas of copper. This shows that the buyer made the payments for the house in copper, reserving the silver for the scribe.

In contrast, another sale from Šuruppak (CUSAS 35 470) maintains both the price and the additional payment in silver. This shows that some buyers had enough silver on their hands for all purposes. Nevertheless, the available ED IIIa sale contracts from Šuruppak witness more payments in copper than in silver. Two-thirds of transactions in the ED IIIa sales were done with copper and the rest with silver and barley.[587]

This predominant role of copper versus silver as money is also evident in the so-called *kudurrus*, land sales written on stone objects. Some of them have prices in copper and others in silver. In contrast to the ED IIIa sale contract on clay from Šuruppak, these two monies do not appear together in a single document. The distribution shows that copper prevails in ED IIIa documents whereas later deeds were mostly in silver.[588]

The use of silver as money was not limited to purchases of real estate. CT 50 4 (ED IIIa Šuruppak) lists side by side silver and copper issued to a merchant

586 The author she refers to uses a more cautious term "means of payment" (Schrakamp 2013b: 448–449).

587 Cripps 2007: 65.

588 Prices in silver: ELTS 16 and 17 (ED IIIa), 14 and 15 (ED IIIa/early ED IIIb), 27, 30, 30a, 32, 34, and 36 (ED IIIb). Prices in copper: ELTS 17, 20–21, 25 (ED IIIa), 31 (ED IIIb). See ELTS: 252–260 for a chart.

as capital. A related text CT 50 5 records amounts of silver as a pledge (?) in connection with the governor of the city.[589]

The role of silver grew steadily during the following ED IIIb period. Written records of this date show silver as money in the sales of property and slaves as well as various taxes and rental payments. As a parallel, archaeologists record silver hoards during the Early Dynastic III period at Mari, Brak, and other places. This practice represents the storage of goods embodying value.[590]

The data of the following Sargonic period provide no examples of copper as money: If transactions were done with metallic money, it was always silver. The alleged large volume of silver during this period may have been for political reasons. The Sargonic period witnessed the military expansionism of the Akkadian kings who aimed to control the supra-regional network of silver trade.[591]

The use of silver as money during the Ur III period has been the object of several detailed studies, which conclude that silver played the role of money or as a luxury material to produce jewelry and various embellishments.[592]

Let us now consider the actual measures in which silver appears in written records. Minas of silver are rare during the ED IIIa period.[593] The shekel is the most common unit of weight applied to it in the Early Dynastic, Sargonic, and Ur III texts, and the references to this practice are vast. Silver in "little minas" appears for the first time during the ED IIIa too. For example, see FTP 98 obv. v 2 (Šuruppak): ku_3 $NINDA_2{\times}ŠE{+}2N_1$ "2 little minas silver."[594]

The earliest occurrence of silver in talents dates back to the Middle Sargonic period, where it appears in the *Maništusu Obelisk* (ELTS 40). The sides B ii 2 and C viii 1 mention "1 talent 2 minas silver" and "3 talents 33 minas silver," respectively. However, in general, such large amounts were untypical during the Sargonic period, especially as prices. OSP 2 25 obv. 6 from Classical Sargonic Nippur records as much as six talents and 20 minas of silver. This text belongs to a dossier recording the restoration of the main sanctuary in Nippur, the Ekur temple. Therefore, silver here is not money but a material for the embellishment of the building.

589 See commentary in CUSAS 35 386 for the term šu-bad. See Cripps 2007: 97 for the interpretation of CT 50 5 as payments due to the *ensi* as remittance of the corvée.

590 Helwing 2014: 417.

591 Helwing 2014: 413.

592 Paoletti 2008, Mander and Notizia 2009, Ouyang 2013.

593 See, for example, CT 50 4 obv. i 1 for 2 $gi\hat{g}_4{\times}2$ ku_3 ma-na "2 minas 2 shekels silver," a *kudurru* ELTS 15, and another document UVB 10: 13 pl. 26b (ED IIIa Uruk or Šuruppak) obv. i 4.

594 For other examples, see UVB 10: 13 pl. 26b obv. i 4 and RTC 15 rev. iii 1.

Several terms describe physical properties of silver in the 3rd mill. BC sources, its purity, and its forms of circulation. Ku_3-luh-(ha) = *kaspum ellum* "purified silver" is common as early as in the ED IIIa records.[595] The term "pure" also occurs in the Akkadian language.[596] Another attribute applied to silver is $še_3$-be_2-er-tum = *šibirtum* "piece,"[597] which designates scrap silver. A Sargonic sale of a house MAD 4 65 from Umma has in obv. 1–2: 4 ku_3 $giĝ_4$ $še_3$-be_2-er-tum e_2-kam "4 shekels of scrap silver (is the price) of the house." The word must be regarded as a borrowing from Akkadian into Sumerian since the text is written in Sumerian.

Silver rings or coils (har ku_3-babbar) were the most common form the silver money took.[598] Some scholars keep these coils apart from har-hul_3-la = *ḫullum* made from silver or gold. Ingo Schrakamp concludes that it was a kind of pendant, medallion, necklace, or collar.[599] However, CUSAS 35 458 from the ES/MS Umma region puts this interpretation in doubt. It lists silver har-hul_3-la in pairs (e_2-ba) with weights of 14, 15, and 30 shekels. The pairwise record and relatively high mass of these objects exclude the interpretation of har-hul_3-la as a pendant in this text. Here, it is possibly just "ring" and can refer to any such paired objects including bracelets, armlets, or anklets.

Gold never appears as a means of payment during the 3rd mill. BC. For its use as material in the production of luxury items as gifts, see below.

10.4 Copper, bronze, and related metals in the production of tools

Copper as a material for tools was used from at least the 8th mill. BC. A developed copper industry existed in some parts of the Near East by the 5th mill. BC.[600] As we have seen, objects made from various copper alloys appear in Uruk III texts, ca. 3100 BC. These objects were mundane: saws, drills, etc. Their weight was not recorded in these documents. In contrast, the 3rd mill. BC texts

---

595 Sum. luh = Akk. *mesû* "to clean, wash".

596 See MAD 1 303 obv. 1 (CS Ešnunna): 2 $giĝ_4$ 2 ma-na-tur ku_3-babbar *el-lum* "2 shekels 2 little minas of pure silver."

597 CAD Š/2: 379.

598 Michalowski 1978, Powell 1978, Paoletti 2008: 150–152.

599 Schrakamp 2012: 160–161. Molina 2014: 68 follows this interpretation.

600 See Joannès 1993–1997: 96 f., Muhly 1993–1997: 112 f., and Reiter 1997 for overviews and a study of metals in southern Mesopotamian written records of the early periods. See Waetzoldt 1981, Waetzoldt 1984, and Archi 2017 for metals at Ebla.

witness a considerable expansion in the number of objects made of copper and its alloys. Additionally, the documents begin to record their weight from at least 2800 BC.

The 3rd mill. BC texts mention various sorts of copper and its alloys. The example of ni$_3$-UD^{uruda} shows that identifying these Sumerian terms with modern terms for metals is challenging. For the variety of copper uruda-kul-sa$_6$/sag$_8$-ga in Sargonic texts from Adab and Nippur, see Chapter 8.

Uruda-luh(-ha) "pure" or "purified copper" occurs in numerous texts. RTC 23 (ED IIIb Ĝirsu) shows that it was used for bronze: ^{uruda}<a>-ru$_{12}$-da an-na U$_5$-a. The last term remains obscure but it may mean "alloyed." This text shows a 6:1 proportion of copper to tin in the production of bronze.[601]

The variety of copper **uruda-sal** in TSŠ 60 obv. ii 4 mentioned above has parallels in later texts. RTC 24 obv. i 1 (ED IIIb Ĝirsu) records *x* minas and shekels uruda$^{\text{a-ru12-da}}$ sal-la-um-ma la$_2$-a "arrears: (*n* measures) ... copper." The term sal-la-um also appears in a Sargonic document from Umma, where it is interpreted as 1 uruda sal-la-um "1 (piece) of copper wire" relying on the meaning of sal as "thin" and um as "reed rope."[602] Nevertheless, it seems that sal-la-um is a single word. It appears in another Sargonic document in connection with a chair.[603] In a Presargonic document from Ĝirsu, sal-la-um are objects related to wooden objects.[604]

Uruda (ni$_3$-)sahar(-ra). Several Early Sargonic texts from Umma record the term uruda-sahar or uruda ni$_3$-sahar-ra.[605] The translation "copper in grains" has been proposed.[606] However, the term refers rather to "copper ore."[607] BIN 8 101 is illustrative. It contrasts uruda-sahar with uruda-šen-til "pure finished copper." A Presargonic text from Ĝirsu records axes of the *hazin* type produced from either zabar$_3$ "bronze" or sahar-ra,[608] where the latter may refer to a metal smelted from a copper ore and used in the production of tools without a ligation involved.

Arata$_x$(LAM.KUR.RU) appears in Late Presargonic and Sargonic texts from Adab only. Miguel Civil suggests that arata(LAM×KUR.RU) and arata$_x$

601 1 ma-na giĝ$_4$ 15 uruda 7-la$_2$-am$_6$. See Reiter 1997: 82*–83* for this interpretation.
602 CUSAS 35 450 (ES/MS Umma region).
603 OSP 2 48 iii 12. Von Soden's (1990: 136) interpretation "Breitsessel" is groundless.
604 VS 27 24 obv. iii 2, 4 (ED IIIb Ĝirsu),
605 For the latter, see CHEU 53 and CST 11.
606 Foster 1982c: 34.
607 See Akk. *eperu* CAD E: 184, 189, meaning 5: "ore."
608 ITT 5 9249 obv. i 1–2.

(LAM.KUR.RU) are homonym spellings of the well-known uruda "copper."[609] Taking the striking similarity between /arat(t)a/ and uruda (actually, /aruda/ because of the writing a-ru_{12}-da) it seems very likely. Civil discusses early lexical evidence for $arata_x$ as a metal.[610] It is mentioned twice in the *Early Dynastic Practical Vocabulary B*: as arata(LAM×KUR.RU)-zabar and arata side by side with a-gar_5, which is believed to be "lead," Akk. *abāru*.[611] Civil relates arata from this list to a-gar_5-gar_5 "copper" from the *Early Dynastic Practical Vocabulary A*.

The spelling $arata_x$ (in contrast to a variety of copper ni_3-UD^{uruda} at Presargonic Zabalam) never appears together with uruda "copper." This reinforces the argument by Civil. However, the price of $arata_x$ in an Early/Middle Sargonic letter BIN 8 392 is suspiciously high.[612] The author of this letter appealed to an addressee to weigh out (=pay) three and one-third shekels of silver for ten shekels of $arata_x$ (rev. 5–7). This means that silver was only three times more expensive. The document may originate from the merchants' milieu. Another text provides the same silver-$arata_x$ value relationship. It is a Classical Sargonic record of an offering *mašdari'a* by two individuals.[613] The first person dispenses of ten shekels of silver. The second person gives one-third of a mina of $arata_x$ NI-na "tin *arata*." This 1:3 ratio with silver implies that $arata_x$ (NI-na) was not a usual copper or copper at all.

Adab texts record $arata_x$ in minas, shekels, and even barleycorns. The metal appears in the context of the production of tools. The most illustrative data set was published by Manuel Molina in 2014.[614] These Middle Sargonic documents record expenditures and deliveries of various metals to produce weapons and other metal objects. This dossier mentions seven metals and alloys: (1) $zabar^{uruda}$ "bronze," (2) $MUŠ_3{}^{uruda}$ (luh-ha) "(pure) copper," (3) $arata_x$-a NI-na "copper-tin (alloy)," (4) su_3-GAN^{uruda} (an additive to copper), (5) (uruda) kul-sag_8-ga (a type of copper; see Chapter 8), (6) ku_3(-babbar) "silver," (7) and ku_3-sig_{17} "gold."

One needs four minas of $MUŠ_3{}^{uruda}$ and one-third mina of $arata_x$-a[615] NI-na to produce 15 spear points according to SCTRAH 225. These are realistic numbers: Each spear point would have a mass of about 145 g. Molina interprets

609 See commentary to PPAC 1 203 n. 72.

610 Civil 2008: 87.

611 SF 20 obv. vi 6, 10–11.

612 FAOS 19 Um 6. Its provenance may be "Adab(?)" instead of "Umma(?)."

613 OIP 14 111 (CS Adab).

614 SCTRAH 224–238.

615 The writing $arata_x$-a may signify that the latter sign is a phonetic complement: $arata_x$ $(LAM.KUR.RU)^a$.

these materials as "*MUŠ*-copper" and "copper-tin (alloy)," where $arata_x$-a should be "copper" and NI-na is one of the writings for "tin." However, taking into consideration the proportions, $MUŠ_3^{uruda}$ is simply another writing of "copper" whereas $arata_x$-a (NI-na) refers to "tin." This explains the high price of $arata_x$ discussed above.

Although $arata_x$ appears in the context of offerings or issues, it is always a valuable material but never money.[616] A Middle Sargonic text CUSAS 20 396 states the weighing out of one and one-third shekels of silver to buy an unspecified amount of $arata_x$ for the production of bronze (arata$^!$(LAM×KUR) zabar-$še_3$; obv. 7–8). Classical Sargonic OIP 14 157 and an unpublished Middle Sargonic text CUNES 50–04-077 from Adab also record $arata_x$ in relation to bronze. The former mentions 10 $gi\hat{g}_4$ $NINDA_2$×ŠE+$2N_1$ $arata_x$ zabar "10 2/3 shekels of *arata* (for) bronze" received by a chief smith (obv. 1). The latter is even more eloquent: [(x)] $arata_x$ zabar-bi-da "[. . .] *arata* and bronze" (rev. ii '4). Molina argues that $arata_x$ zabar may be identical to $arata_x$-a NI-na, which is likely correct. However, both refer to tin to produce bronze.

CUSAS 11 242 of the Early Sargonic period is of particular interest. This is a list of goods received from rulers (GAR-$ensi_2$) of various localities. The ruler of the city of Marada sends three minas of $arata_x$-BU.[617] An interpretation is still pending.

In summary, $arata_{(x)}$(-a NI-na) appears exclusively in Adab texts and its small quantities and high value prevent it from being identified with copper. Its proportions with $MUŠ_3^{uruda}$ in one text suggest that it was a writing of "tin."

The same document indicates that $\mathbf{MUŠ_3^{uruda}}$, sometimes appearing as luh-ha "pure," is a writing for "copper." $MUŠ_3^{uruda}$ appears in ED IIIa "practical vocabularies" and Presargonic to Middle Sargonic administrative texts from Adab. Then, the terms disappear altogether. $MUŠ_3^{uruda}$ precedes a metal a-gar_5-gar_5 in the *Early Dynastic Practical Vocabulary A* 142. The latter is identical to arata in the *Early Dynastic Practical Vocabulary B*. One manuscript of the composition has the following sequence of copper-related entries: a-ru_{12}-da^{uruda} "copper," $MUŠ_3^{uruda}$ "do.," and $zam_x(UH_3)$-da-ti^{uruda} "scrap metal."[618] Civil interprets $MUŠ_3^{uruda}$ in the *Early Dynastic Practical Vocabulary B* (SF 20 obv. vi 1) as "weight," which is unsupported. The fact is that this and the preceding line a-ru_{12}-da^{uruda} appear in the context of copper of various weight measures. This

616 CUSAS 11 111 (ES; issue of one mina of $arata_x$ controlled by an official maškim).
617 Incorrectly deciphered "sud_3-gid_2" in the original publication.
618 OIP 99 33 obv. vi 3'–5'; Civil 2008: 87.

may be confusing for a modern scholar but certainly not for an ED IIIa scribe for whom "weighing" and "copper" were naturally related matters, as they belonged to the same cultural domain.

The data of the Adab administrative texts illustrate that $MUŠ_3^{uruda}$ was used in the production of weapons, helmets, and vessels.[619] For example, SCTRAH 229 mentions one mina ten shekels of pure *MUŠ* copper ($MUŠ_3^{uruda}$-luh-ha) side by side with a comparable amount of copper uruda kul-sag_8-ga. They are both used to produce axes and helmets. SCTRAH 228 mentions both materials together.

Two texts identify $MUŠ_3^{uruda}$ with a variety of copper. An unpublished Late Presargonic or Early Sargonic document from Adab records trade activities and economic transactions with the city of Ĝirsu.[620] One entry records the fact that a Ĝirsu merchant gave 20 minas of $MUŠ_3^{uruda}$ to an Adab reed worker. The value of this metal is ten shekels of silver (obv. iii 4–iv 3). This indicates the value ratio 1:120 between copper and copper $MUŠ_3^{uruda}$. This shows that silver has become 1/3 cheaper in relation to copper since the ED IIIa period.[621]

In summary, $MUŠ_3^{uruda}$ was another writing of uruda "(pure) copper." Both writings were used at Adab.[622] The reading of the logogram $MUŠ_3^{uruda}$ still requires explanation.

zabar "bronze." The writing is of a mixed logographic-syllabic nature that is typical of the Early Dynastic orthography: zu_2:bar_6^{bar}(UD.KA.BAR).[623] The discussion in this chapter suggests that zabar was one of the copper alloys, the copper-tin variety. By the Ur III period, the writing zabar had subsumed all previously known spellings for copper alloys. The term often appears as $zabar^{uruda}$, where the latter is a determinative for copper and its alloys in the pre-Ur III times. It should not be confused with a homograph that refers to a copper or bronze cup. Civil argues that zabar is a loanword from the Akkadian *siparrum* "bronze."[624]

Zabar appears in the *Early Dynastic Practical Vocabulary A* as a material of figurines of animals, of a lunar crescent, beads, vessels, and sharp and cutting

619 Molina 2014: 178.

620 P271223.

621 Steinkeller interprets a passage in a Classical Sargonic text from Ĝirsu documenting the import of copper from Magan to Ĝirsu ITT 1 1422 "1 ma-na la_2 10 $gi\hat{g}_4$ (ku_3-babbar), saĝ uruda 3 gun_2 20 ma-na-$še_3$, e_2-gal-$še_3$ mu-de_6-a" as an indication of the price ratio "1:240" between silver and copper (Laursen and Steinkeller 2017: 37–38).

622 See CUSAS 35 261 (ES Adab) for uruda.

623 Correct the commentary to CUSAS 35 364 obv. ii 3 accordingly; also: "The sign for *bronze*."

624 Civil 2007: 22.

tools of all sorts.[625] This writing is lacking in the lexical list *Metals*. This indicates that bronze was spelled differently in the Late Uruk texts: The writing zabar is an Early Dynastic innovation. A variant spelling $zabar_3$((KA×UD).BAR) appears in ED IIIa–b texts.[626]

Given the abundance of bronze objects in lexical and administrative evidence, it is surprising how rarely bronze in weight measures appears in the texts of the Early Dynastic period. In addition, its amounts are mostly relatively low.[627] In contrast, some Sargonic and Ur III texts record talents of bronze, sometimes equal to several tons.[628] Daniel Potts argued that the expression an-na $zabar_3$ at Presargonic Ĝirsu was not "tin (for) bronze" but "tin bronze."[629] However, this is uncertain. First, five minas of an-na $zabar_3$ appear in RTC 19 obv. iv 5 together with 120 minas of copper as a delivery to the wife of the ruler of Adab. This discrepancy in amounts reminds us of tin and copper. Second, another Ĝirsu text records one mina of an-na $zabar_3$ for a ruler of the Elamite city of Arawa.[630] A mina of bronze would be a humble present. This suggests that an-na $zabar_3$ at ED IIIb Ĝirsu and $arata_x$(-a) NI-na at MS Adab designated the same matter: tin to ligate with copper to produce bronze.

An-na, NI-na "tin." The *Early Dynastic Practical Vocabulary* A 145–146 records both variants, an-na and NI-na, of the word for "tin." Both variants are also found in administrative texts. The phonemic shape of the Sumerian word for "tin" is debated.[631]

Considerable amounts of tin appear in Presargonic texts from Ĝirsu. VS 14 43 records an issue of 24 minas of tin (an-na) together with 120 minas of copper and other merchandise (ni_3-sa_{10}-ma-$še_3$) to a merchant working for the palace. The ratio 1:6 alludes to the production of tin bronze. During the Classical Sargonic period, another additive was added to these two components. One document records

625 104–118, 122, 125–126, 133–140.

626 CT 50 8 obv. ii 1 (ED IIIa Šuruppak?) and Presargonic Ĝirsu passim.

627 BdI 1 95 rev. 2 (MS Adab; 3 minas 16 shekels), OIP 14 156 rev. 3 (CS Adab; 12 minas minus 12 shekels), RTC 100 rev. 9 (CS Ĝirsu; 2 minas). CUSAS 13 48 obv. 2 from CS Adab records 2 minas 16 shekels bronze ($zabar^{uruda}$; contra the edition where it is interpreted as "copper (cast in) a mirror").

628 Sargonic Nippur: OSP 2 32 rev. 11'; Sargonic Ešnunna: OAIC 7 obv. 2; Ur III Umma: AAICAB 1/1 pl. 46 1911-483 obv. 10 (10 talents 40 minas).

629 Potts 1999.

630 Nik 1 310 rev. iv 4.

631 See Sjöberg 1965: 258 and Civil 2008: 87. For tin in Mesopotamia, see Muhly 1993–1997: 131 f. and Reiter 1997: 206 f.

20 minas 6 shekels of pure copper, 2/3 mina 6 shekels of tin, and a number of shekels of the additive su_3-GAN, for which see below.[632] Other contemporaneous data from Ĝirsu record equally small amounts of tin. STTI 107 rev. 1' has 9 barleycorns (ca. 0.4 g) of tin and ITT 5 6671 rev. 1 has $NINDA_2$×ŠE+$2N_1$ 8 $gi\hat{g}_4$-tur an-na "2 (little minas) 8 little shekels of tin."

PA-na is an attribute that appears with an-na "tin" in this CS Ĝirsu "dossier." ITT 2 5728 obv. 1 has 12 ma-na uruda an-na PA-na "12 minas of copper . . . ed (with) tin." It is tempting to interpret the verb written PA as "to alloy." Taking into consideration the final consonant of this verb, the only fitting interpretation is kun_2-na, where kun_2 is *nabāṭum* "to shine brightly." However, other interpretations are possible. At any rate, uruda an-na kun_2-na was a variety of tin bronze. Other texts record the same phrase but without uruda "copper." Hence, an-na kun_2-na refers to tin-copper alloy, bronze.[633]

A Classical Sargonic Adab text PPAC 1 666 mentions two objects with NI-na "tin" as an attribute. Two KU(tukul$^?$)-si-sa_2 "straight weapons(?)" weigh 48 and 36 shekels, respectively. One tin helmet (saĝšu NI-na) weighs a half-mina. A merchant is credited with the delivery of these weapons and armor, which were probably of foreign origin. Archaeologists argue that, in principle, an-na and NI-na may refer to tin and lead at that time. Besides, tin is useless in the production of objects since it breaks easily.[634] Therefore, NI-na in this text likely refers to the copper-tin alloy, bronze, too.

An additive for bronze **su_3-GAN** is often interpreted as antimony, although clear evidence is still lacking.[635] Another Sumerian term associated with "antimony" is lu_3-lu_3, written AK-AK at Ebla. This had been borrowed into Akkadian as *lulû*.[636] We know that antimony was rarely used as a material for objects.[637] Nevertheless, it is not clear which of the Sumerian writings, if any, refers to it.[638] Waetzoldt and Bachmann (1984) suggest a mineral borax as a possibility for su_3-GAN. Curiously, su_3-GAN is not present in lexical tradition but appears as a weighable material and an additive for bronze. In contrast, lu_3-lu_3 is

632 ITT 5 6676 obv. 1–3.

633 ITT 5 6670 obv. 1–2 (CS Ĝirsu): 4 talents 11+x minas of copper are recorded, which is followed by 29 minas an-na kun_2-na. ITT 5 9276 mentions 3 1/3 shekels of an-na kun_2-na with another small amount of an additive uruda su_3-GAN in obv. ii' 6'–7'.

634 Moorey 1999: 297–298.

635 Muhly 1993–1997: 119.

636 Civil 2008 no. 147.

637 Moorey 1999: 240–242.

638 See Reiter 1997: 327–333 for su_3-GAN in Ur III and Old Babylonian sources.

present in lexical lists as early as *Archaic Metals* 60 but never occurs as a material in administrative texts. This mutual exclusion may suggest that su_3-GAN and lu_3-lu_3 designate the same material. Note a writing KU_3-GAN of *lulû* in the later lexical tradition.[639]

All references to su_3-GAN originate from the Middle and Classical Sargonic periods. The amounts of metal are relatively small and never exceed several minas. In BdI 1 181, ⅓ mina 4 shekels of su_3-GAN appear in an uncommon context with a rush ^{u2}ninni$_5$ and the minerals alkali (naĝa) and gypsum (im-babbar$_2$). In contrast, other documents illustrate the use of su_3-GAN in the production of bronze tools.[640]

a-gar$_5$/-bara$_2$ "lead." Despite the fact that we find this metal in the earliest lexical tradition,[641] archival records are mostly silent about the use of lead and the weight of lead objects. Leaden rings (har a-gar$_5$) covered with gold were not recorded by weight in Ur III texts.[642] The same archive mentions humble amounts of lead of about a half-mina.[643] One text mentions as much as 15 minas of uruda a-bara$_2$ "lead-copper," which probably refers to an alloy. No comparable data predated the Ur III records. It is hard to say whether we should attribute this lack of written records to the limited circulation and use of lead in early Mesopotamia. Peter Moorey (1999: 257) draws attention to bronze objects, including seals, from around 3000 BC with a high percentage of lead. Cf. a recently published bronze cylinder seal of the Jemdet Nasr date from Uruk with only 2.5 % of lead and 2 % of arsenic.[644]

Above, I have given some examples of copper objects, mostly vessels, whose weight we know from documents dating to 2800–2600 BC. The following list based on later 3rd mill. BC data gives an overview of the masses of some widespread and mundane copper and bronze objects (Tab. 10.1).

639 CAD L: 243.

640 ITT 4 7634 = MVN 7 34 (CS Ĝirsu; as an additive to produce spear points), BIN 8 135 obv. 5 (CS Sagub(?); an additive for the production of daggers and vessels). Other references to su_3-GAN: ITT 5 9276 (list of commodities) and 9260 (with other metals).

641 *Archaic* and *ED Metal* 60 (a-gar$_5$), if it was indeed lead and not copper or copper alloy at that time.

642 UET 3 496 obv. 1–3 (Ur III, Ibbi-Suen 15/5/23).

643 UET 3 1498 obv. v 21, rev. iii 9; 494 obv. 1.

644 Jendritzki and Martin 2018.

Tab. 10.1: Some copper and bronze objects with the known mass.

Object	Interpretation	Weight	References
^{uruda}alal$_x$(ŠEN)	drainage pipe (Steinkeller 1981b; see also ^{uruda}šen below)	17 m.	STTI 8 rev. 3'–5' (CS Ĝirsu)
		7 m.	ITT 5 9286 obv. 4'–5' (CS Ĝirsu)
BU^{uruda} kul-sa$_6$-ga / zabar	uncertain; a rod or pole; the same object made of silver weighs three times less. See below.	1/3 m.	OSP 2 49 obv. ii 4–5 and 65 rev. 5–6 (MS Nippur)
dilim$_2$ ĝeš-rin$_2$ kul-sa$_6$-ga^{uruda}	pan of the balance (made of) . . . copper (see Chapter 8)	15 sh.	OSP 2 48 obv. i 16–17 (MS Nippur)
dur$_{10}$-tab-ba	axe with one blade and several spikes on the opposite side (Civil 1987c: 22–23)	3 m. minus x sh. 2/3 m.	Nik 1 298 = FAOS 15/1 298 obv. i 1–2, ii 1–2 (ED IIIb Ĝirsu)
eme-ĝiri$_2$-zabar	blades of plowshare	134 p. = 1 t. 37 ½ m. minus 1 sh. (= ca. 43.6 sh. each)	MVN 5 155 rev. i 16–17 (Ur III Ĝirsu)
gab$_2$-la$_2$^{uruda}	(uncertain) (Selz 1993: 630 ("hook"); too weighty for that)	8 m.	OSP 2 45 obv. i 11–12 and 48 obv. i 14–15 (MS Nippur)
$^{(uruda)}$gag	(1) point (of a spear or an arrow)	1 m.	ITT 5 6789 (Ur III Ĝirsu)
	(2) blade (Schrakamp 2006: 171)	55 sh. (HAR.AN^{uruda})	OIP 14 106 (CS Adab)
		1/3 m. (a knife)	OIP 14 106 (CS Adab)

(continued)

Tab. 10.1: (continued)

Object	Interpretation	Weight	References
^{zabar}gu$_3$-zi	goblet, bowl (Steinkeller 1992: 39, 54; Civil 2008: 98–99)	1 1/3 m.	ITT 1 1370 obv. 1–2 (CS Ĝirsu)
ĝiri$_2$-udu-šum^{uruda}	knife to butcher sheep	1 ½ m.	NATN 852 obv. 20–21 (Ur III Nippur)
ha-zi-(in)^{uruda}	axe used both as a weapon and in agriculture (Civil 2008 no. 166)	2 p. = 9 "wool" m.	Nik 1 299 obv. ii 1–2 (ED IIIb Ĝirsu)
		22 p. = 60 m.	ECTJ 153 obv. 1, 6 (ES Nippur)
		55 sh.	CUSAS 35 364 obv. i 4–6 (ES Isin)
		10 p. = 20 m.	BdI 1 93 obv. 1–2 (MS Adab)
		1 ½ m.	BdI 2/1 57 obv. 1'–2' (CS Isin)
		2 m., 1 ½ m.	AAICAB 1/2 pl. 104 1937–062 obv. 1–4 (Ur III Umma)
		54 sh.	MVN 20 86 obv. 4–5 (Ur III Umma)
^{uruda}ha-bu$_3$-da	a hoe	40 and 50 sh.	AAICAB 1/2 pl. 104 1937-062 obv. 5 and MVN 1 236 passim (Ur III Umma)
HAR.AN^{uruda}	a pointed tool (cf. Molina 2014: 185)	8 p(ieces) = 21 1/3 m.	OIP 14 106 (CS Adab)
igi/gu$_2$ ĝeš-gid$_2$-da	spear point (Schrakamp 2006: 167–169)	42 p. = 11 m. 40 p. = 10 1/3 m. 5 sh. (1 p. = ca. 15.7 sh.)	Nik 1 298 obv. ii 4 – iii 1; iii 3–4 (ED IIIb Ĝirsu)
		84(?) p. = 41 m. (1 p. = ca. 30 sh.)	ECTJ 151 obv. 1–2 (ES Nippur)

^{uruda}kin/gur$_{10}$	sickle (blade)	25 p. = 1 m. *x* sh.	Aleppo 496 obv. 5–6 (Ur III Umma)
ma-šum^{uruda}	(uncertain)	7 m.	OSP 2 45 obv. i 9–10 and 48 obv. i 12–13 (MS Nippur)
NAM^{uruda}	sieve (?) (FAOS 15/1: 533)	<15 sh.	CUSAS 20 26 obv. 5–6 (ES/MS Adab), CUSAS 35 204 (ES Adab)
NI-GAM^{uruda}	(uncertain)	[1? p.] = ½ m.	OSP 2 49 obv. i 12–ii 1 (MS Nippur)
ni$_3$-gul^{uruda}	maul (Foster 1982c: 46; Civil 2008 no. 167)	6 ½–7 m.	CUSAS 11 276 (ES Adab)
		4 m. 15 sh.–5 2/3 m.	Nik 2 60–62 (ES Umma)
ni$_3$-luh^{zabar3}	washing basin	2 m. 12 sh.	MAD 4 50 obv. 2 (MS/CS uncert. prov.)
^{uruda}SAG×NI LAGAB×*U* 6-la$_2$	uncertain; in the context of weapons (cf. Steinkeller 1992: 48: cup or bowl).	1 m.	MC 4 21 rev. 1–2 (MS Umma)
^{uruda}šen	kettle (Civil 2008: 84; see also ^{uruda}alal$_x$ above)	3 m.	OSP 1 95 obv. 2–3 (ES/MS Nippur)
		7 m.	BIN 5 1 rev. 10 (Ur III Umma)
		23 m.	CT 50 72 obv. i 8–9 (CS Sippar)
		38 m.	AUCT 1 954 obv. 1–2 (Ur III Puzriš-Dagan)
šen-da-la$_2$/li$_2$^{zabar}	a kind of bronze kettle (Owen 2013: 38).	5/6 m.	BIN 5 2 rev. 2–3 (Ur III Umma)
$^{(uruda)}$šen-gam-(e) (-zabar)	do.	3 m. 10 sh.	Nik 2 422 obv. 2 (Ur III Umma)
		2 ½ m.	Nisaba 24 34 rev. ii 7–8 (Ur III Umma)
		1/3 m.	BCT 2 87 rev. 2–3 (Ur III Umma)

(continued)

Tab. 10.1: (continued)

Object	Interpretation	Weight	References
^{uruda}šen-šu$_2$	a kettle with handle(s)	6 1/3 m. 5 sh.	AAICAB 1/2 pl. 165 1975-292 rev. i 3–4 (Ur III Umma)
		18 m.	Maekawa 1996: 167 rev. i 6–7 (Ur III Ĝirsu)
^{uruda}dur$_2$ šen	copper stand for a *šen* kettle	2 1/3 m. 5 sh.	BdI 1 215 obv. 3–rev. 1 (CS Adab)
		2 t. 23 ½ m.	Paoletti 2012 pl. 2 NBC 07494 obv. 1–2 (Ur III Puzriš-Dagan)
šu-la$_2$^{uruda}, šu-ša-la$_2$-zabar	a small vessel or container (Steinkeller 1992: 48; Schrakamp 2013a: 214)	1 m.	CUSAS 20 26 obv. 3–4 (ES/MS Adab)
		5/6 m.	UET 3 703 obv. i 14–15 (Ur III Ur)
šum^{uruda} (1)	saw	3 p. = 6 m. 7 sh. (ca. 2 m. each)	CUSAS 11 113 (ES Adab)
šum^{uruda} (2)	sickle with serrated edge (Civil 2008 no. 157)	64 p. = 16 ½ m. 4 sh. (= ca. 15.5 sh. each) and 20 sh.	SCTRAH 231–232 (MS Adab)
		12 p. = 3 m. 10 sh. (ca. 15 sh. each)	BIN 8 310 obv. 1–2 (CS uncert. prov.)
		17 sh.	MVN 8 246 (Ur III unc. prov.)
umbin gu-za sal e$_2$-ba-an (zabar)	a pair of (bronze) thin furniture legs	7 sh.	RTC 233 (Lagaš II Ĝirsu)

uri^{uruda}(-zabar)	a bronze vessel (Civil 2008 nos. 129–130)	4 m.	OSP 1 95 obv. 4–5 (ES/MS Nippur)
		2 p. = 17.5 m.	STTI 8 rev. 6'–8' (CS Ĝirsu)
		6–7 m.	Ur III passim.
zabar^{uruda}	a cup and/or mirror (Steinkeller 1987b: 347–349; Westenholz 2010: 475–478[645])	30 p. = 15 m. 5 sh. (ca. ½ m. piece)	ECTJ 150 obv. 1–2 (ES/MS Nippur)
		7 p. = 2 m. (ca. 17 sh. piece)	OSP 2 45 obv. i 6–8; OSP 2 48 obv. i 9–11 (MS Nippur)
		64 p. = 35 m. 50 sh. (ca. 33.5 sh. piece)	BdI 1 215 (CS Adab)
zabar-šu	a bronze cup or mirror with a handle (cf. above)	13 and 17 sh.	MVN 10 137 obv. 1–2 and MVN 6 88 obv. 2–3 (CS Ĝirsu)
^{uruda}za-ri$_2$-in	An axe made of copper/bronze of the lowest quality.	22 p. = 8 ½ m. 2 sh.	Aleppo 496 obv. 1–2 (Ur III Umma)
^{uruda}zi-ir	a pot	8 m.	Maekawa 1996: 164 no. 7 obv. i 8–9 (Ur III Umma)

645 Joan Goodnick Westenholz regarded zabar as a determinative, which is incorrect since the determinative for copper and bronze objects is ^{uruda}. Besides, zabar-šu ku$_3$-luh-ha "*zabaršu* from pure silver" indicates that zabar cannot be the indication of the material either. However, I agree with Westenholz that zabar(-šu) may be "cup" and not "mirror" in many cases. Cf., for example, a commonplace sila$_3$-zabar-ta "(grain measured) according to the bronze *sila* vessel."

Many Ur III records deal specifically with copper and bronze objects measured by weight.[646]

The construction ki-la$_2$-bi "its/their weight (is)" is the common means to record the mass of these bronze and copper objects in the ED IIIa–Ur III data. Very occasionally, a document may use another way to notate the weight of an object: NUMBER MEASURE OBJECT-kam. For an example, the BdI 1 215 mentioned in the table: "2 ⅓ minas 5 shekels (bronze) is for a stand of the šen vessel."

Some of these examples may refer not to an object but the material to produce it. For example, one document records the material for the production of a stand for an *uri* vessel: 6 ^{šu2}1N$_8$^{ša} ma-na 3 giĝ$_4$ zabar; dur$_2$^{uruda} uri-še$_3$; dim$_2$-me-de$_3$ "6 ⅓ minas 3 shekels of bronze in order to produce a stand for an *uri* vessel."[647] We can only guess how the mass of the material could have correlated with the mass of the product. A considerable loss of material is documented in Ur III records.

There is a limited number of bronze objects whose relatively small weight and high numbers forced scribes to record them without the construction ki-la$_2$-bi. The most obvious example concerns nails (gag), which one should differentiate from more weighty points of weapons. Two and a half minas minus 4 shekels and up to 6 minas minus 3 shekels of nails appear in BIN 8 72 (ES Umma). In later periods, the measurement of *sikkātu(m)* "nail" in the units of weight was common too.[648]

Another example of the same practice is found in OSP 1 97 obv. 1 (ES Nippur): 65 ½ la$_2$ 1 giĝ$_4$ ^{uruda}igi ĝeš-gid$_2$-da ma-na "65 ½ minas minus 1 shekel copper spear points." If we take the usual weight of a single spear point as ca. 15.6 shekels (see above), we come to the perfectly round number of 250 pieces.

10.5 Gold and silver for luxury objects

Gold appears in archaeological records in Mesopotamia from the late Ubaid period on. Its modern sources lie in Turkey, Egypt, South Arabia, Transoxiana, and Afghanistan.[649] Its exact sources in 4th and 3rd mill. BC Sumer are

646 E.g. see the detailed accounts TIM 6 19 and AAICAB 1/1 pl. 34 1911-225.
647 ITT 2 2852 obv. 1–3 (CS Ĝirsu).
648 CAD S: 247 f.
649 Moorey 1999: 217–232.

debated. The ruler Gudea of Lagaš (ca. 2150 BC) states in one of his inscriptions that he brought gold from the mountains of Hahhum and Meluhha, that is, from Turkey and Pakistan.[650]

Gold appears as small pieces of jewelry, sheet gold on vessels, luxury tools, weapons, and cylinder seals in the ED IIIa royal tombs at Ur. Analyses show that much of the Mesopotamian gold was in reality not pure gold but electrum,[651] for which there was no Sumerian word. In contrast, Ur III material distinguishes three grades of gold according to its purity: a pure "red" gold (huš-a), a less pure, "mixed" gold (HI-da), and a normal gold (si-sa$_2$). Their exchange ratio to silver differs and lie in the range from 21:1 to 6.5:1.[652]

The Sumerian ku$_3$-sig$_{17}$(GI), literally "yellow *metal*," is the only standard writing for gold, Akkadian *ḫurāṣum*. The data confirm the reading /sig/ "yellow" of the last sign.[653] Currently it is impossible to identify gold in Late Uruk records. The earliest references to ku$_3$-sig$_{17}$ appear in the lexical lists *ED Metals* 121–122 and *EDPV A* 37 and 102 as the material of necklaces and statuettes.

Early Dynastic archival texts rarely mention gold. Even if they do, its weight does not exceed several shekels. A bulla-like tablet ECTJ 198 (ED/ES Nippur) mentions an amount of gold in shekels: [n] ⸢ku$_3$-sig$_{17}$⸣ giĝ$_4$ "... shekels of gold." Another example is the fragment OSP 1 96 (ED IIIb Nippur), which mentions three shekels of gold (obv. i' 5').

Most references to golden objects of the Early Dynastic period do not record their weight since these objects were not purely golden but adorned with gold using various metalworking techniques, such as beads and ear jewelry covered with gold.[654]

Monumental inscriptions often state that rulers adorned temples with gold and silver. The exact amounts or any precise details are absent. At least the weight of one golden object is known in the ED records. Several Presargonic documents from Ĝirsu mention an object ŠEN-šu-e$_3$, whose identification is challenging.[655] At any rate, it is not a vessel šen(-šu$_2$),[656] since the mass of ŠEN-šu-e$_3$ was very small. VS 14 176 is the most illustrative in this respect. It seems to be a

650 Archi 2017b: 163.

651 Moorey: ib.

652 Waetzoldt 1985b, Paoletti 2012: 153.

653 See Sjöberg 1988: 174 contra the reading guškin, and Reiter 1997: 15–17 for syllabic writings of the term.

654 DP 72 ii 1, 74 i 2, ii 6, 75 obv. iv 3 f. (ED IIIb Ĝirsu), CUSAS 33 241 obv. i 8 (ED IIIb Zabalam), CUSAS 35 7 obv. v 1 (ED IIIb Adab).

655 VS 14 176, DP 75 rev. i 1–2. See Steinkeller 1981b: 244 n. 5 for further occurrences of this term.

656 Paoletti 2012: 149.

list of presents to a number of VIP persons from Ĝirsu and other cities. Each individual receives two to 20 ŠEN-šu-e$_3$. Their weight is notated in each case: There are four instances of one shekel, 12 of ½ shekel, and one of ¼ shekel. This means that ŠEN-šu-e$_3$ was a small luxury object. It is tempting to relate ŠEN to dur$_{10}$ "axe," Akkadian *pāštu*. This would be perhaps the only piece of evidence, besides the word giĝ$_4$ "axe," that little axe-shaped objects from precious metals could have contributed to the emergence of the measure "shekel."

The number of references to gold accurately recorded in weight measures grows considerably in the Sargonic and especially in the Ur III texts. These data illustrate the same functions gold played in the preceding periods: as a material for luxury goods and as luxury gifts. CUSAS 11 109 from Early Sargonic Adab mentions a golden lion and a dog produced by a smith from the city of Kiš. The weight of both objects is only 1/6 of a shekel, which is only ca. 1.5 g.[657]

Several texts from Classical Sargonic Adab illustrate the use of gold as gifts. CUSAS 13 46 and CUSAS 35 360 record allocations of gold to a number of individuals, mostly high officials. The amounts range from one-half to five shekels. The second text is dated to the year when Naram-Suen defeated Azuhinnum. It is possible that the practice of sporadic giving of presents by the king to his loyal supporters was somehow related to the political situation. These and other Classical Sargonic texts document for the first time the amounts of gold in minas.[658]

Coming to the question of the quantity, gold appears in considerable amounts in the far-off Syrian city of Nagar (Tell Brak) in the Classical Sargonic period.[659] This is not to mention the impressive quantities of gold in the Early Dynastic Ebla, sometimes as much as a thousand minas.[660] The data from Sumer also suggest that gold was plentiful in the hands of the central households. The Classical Sargonic texts from Nippur concerned with the rebuilding of the Ekur temple are the earliest references where gold is measured in talents. ECTJ 51 rev. records "1 talent minus 2 ⅔ minas gold." This gold was used to produce a large number of cult objects and adornments: 100 "large crescents" (iti-gal) and 100 "large divine suns" (^{d}Utu-^{d}Utu-gal). Each piece would weigh about 17 shekels, ca. 140 g. This interesting dossier reminds us of the biblical description of the adornment of the Jerusalem temple by Salomon.

---

657 Aage Westenholz suggested in a personal communication that this object might represent sheet gold with the incised pictures of the lion and the dog, which was eventually mounted on an object.

658 Other examples: CUSAS 13 47 (CS Adab) rev. 4' (a half-mina), CT 50 52 (CS Umma) obv. i 1 (x mina(s)).

659 ETB 2 72 obv. 3: 3 ma-na ku$_3$-sig$_{17}$.

660 Archi 2017b: 164–165.

Tab. 10.2: Some silver objects with the known mass.

Object	Interpretation	Weight	Reference
bi_2-za-za	(silver) frog	1/3 sh.	OSP 2 76 obv. 3 (MS Nippur)
BU-ku_3	uncertain; a piece of jewelry(?)	10 sh.	OSP 2 49 obv. i 2–3; 65 obv. 3'–4' (MS Nippur)
$^{tug2}gu_2$-gil_2(LAGAB) ku_3-babbar	silver collar (Cripps 2010: 126)	1 m.	Cripps 2010 no. 47 (CS Umma?)
ĝeštug(-ku_3)	silver earring	1 sh.	OSP 2 76 obv. 2 (MS Nippur)
har-hul_3-la ku_3 e_2-ba	a pair of silver bracelets (see discussion above)	14, 15, 30 sh.	CUSAS 35 458 (ES/MS Umma region)
ki-li-lum ku_3-babbar	silver wreath, headband	15, 20 sh.	Maništusu Obelisk (ELTS 40)
su-ga-nu ku_3-babbar *maš-ka_3-na-at*	. . . overlaid with silver	15 sh.	Maništusu Obelisk (ELTS 40)
urin-ku_3	silver eagle	1/3 sh.	OSP 2 76 obv. 4 (MS Nippur)
zabar ku_3(-babbar / luh-ha)	silver cup and/or mirror (see discussion above)	20 sh.	VS 14 176 rev. v 11–12 (ED IIIb Ĝirsu)
		12 sh.	CT 50 52 obv. i 2–3 (CS Umma), STTI 148 rev. iii 2'–3' (CS Ĝirsu)

The largest amount of gold mentioned in Sargonic records is ITT 2 4598 (CS Ĝirsu) obv. 1, where "10 talents of gold" appear. However, this text is a school exercise, as has been suggested by Benjamin Foster.[661] Nevertheless, the court at Akkad could easily have been in possession of this amount of gold at that time. Note that the huge amount of gold at Ebla appears in the context of war tribute paid to Mari. In the same manner, the Akkadian kings may have required the tribute from the conquered lands in gold. The Akkadian king Rimuš explicitly stated that gold constituted the booty he had taken on one occasion.[662]

Classical Sargonic texts witness the earliest attestations of gold in barleycorns. For example, STTI 107 (CS Ĝirsu) obv. 1: [n] $gi\hat{g}_4$ *10* še ku_3-⌜sig_{17}⌝ "... shekels minus 10 barleycorns gold." Another Ĝirsu text introduces both the little mina and the little shekel in connection with gold: 12 $gi\hat{g}_4$ 1 ⌜ma⌝-[na-tur] 15 $gi\hat{g}_4$-tur ku_3-[sig_{17}] "12 shekels 1 little mina 15 little shekels gold."[663]

References to gold in Ur III records are vast. Nevertheless, this gold played the same roles of a luxury material and gifts. Paola Paoletti (2013) analyzed the techniques used in the production of jewelry from gold and silver. Another study of hers, that of the royal treasury in Puzriš-Dagan, offers much data on the production techniques and weights of numerous jewelry pieces and other objects.[664] Many golden objects were not made from gold but covered (ĝar) with this precious metal. A study by David Owen adds new items made of gold and silver or covered with them, which were stored in the "sacristies/cupboards" ($^{(\hat{g}e\check{s})}$$gu_2$-ne-saĝ-$\hat{g}a_2$) in temples and shrines of the city of Irisaĝrig.[665]

Tab. 10.2 gives a general idea of the mass of some luxury objects made from silver in pre-Ur III texts. Most of these texts use the ki-la_2-bi construction to record the mass of these objects. It is omitted only rarely and usually in cases of tiny jewelry.

10.6 Resins

Perfume has always been a sign of status, style, luxury, and wealth. Since later texts state explicitly that resins were an import in Sumer,[666] this type of

661 Foster 1982b.
662 RIME 2.1.2.6 p. 55 line 131 (30 minas gold).
663 ITT 1 1070 obv. 1.
664 Paoletti 2012.
665 Owen 2013.
666 Silver to buy aromatics is recorded in DP 513 obv. (ED IIIb Ĝirsu).

merchandise was expensive. The earliest, Late Uruk lexical texts document a sign DUG×UH_3.[667] This may be identical to a perfume substance $bulug_x$ (ŠIM×UH_3) of the Early Dynastic and Sargonic texts.

Records of aromatic substances are largely uniform throughout the whole of the 3rd mill. BC. The variation concerns mostly the diachronic and regional distribution of their writings. Ancient Mesopotamians used these fragrant substances to prepare aromatic oils, which is explicitly stated in these texts. These documents provide the proportions of individual ingredients in these oils.[668] Hartmut Waetzoldt discussed oil plants and oil in 3rd mill. BC Mesopotamia.[669] A recent discussion of aromatic substances with the emphasis on Ur III records is offered by Hagan Brunke and Walther Sallaberger (2010). Michael Jursa (2009) offers a discussion of aromatic substances in later Babylonian sources, which were also used to prepare incenses to burn.

Some resins were measured by weight and others by capacity measures. This distinction implies a difference in their aggregate state: liquid vs. dry. I will discuss only weighed aromatics, their usual amounts, and measures used to record them. I will concentrate on the earliest evidence in the following discussion.

The measurement of resins by weight began simultaneously with their regular appearance in ED IIIb cuneiform sources. Most of them list these resins in minas. This should not be interpreted as reflecting the abundance and cheapness of these luxury goods. The reason for their relatively large numbers in these accounts should be attributed to several factors. First, they record large deliveries as the outcome of the interregional trade subsidized by the elite members of the palace and temple households, and the resins were acquired in bulk quantities for further distribution. Second, the large amounts appear in the context of the preparation of large amounts of perfumed oil: for example, ten pots and more.

The following is a short description of each variety of the resins that were measured by weight. Tabs. 10.3–4 at the end of this section provide their overview and offer a comparison of several typical lists of these resins.

$^{(\text{šim/ĝeš})}$ad$_2$ "myrtle." This is *Myrtus communis*, Akkadian *asu*. See Pascal Attinger (2005: 263–264) and Miguel Civil (2008: 104 nos. 220, 261) for a

---

667 ZATU123 in the lexical list *Archaic* and *ED Vessels and Garments* 50–51. Late Uruk administrative accounts do not document this sign.

668 For example, see DP 514 (ED IIIb Ĝirsu), where a subscript "these are resins for ten pots of oil" (šim i_3 dug 10-kam; rev. i 1) follows the list of the resins.

669 Waetzoldt 1985a.

discussion. This fragrant plant should not be confused with the allograph u$_2$-kiši$_{17}$(GIR$_2$-*tenû*) > Akk. *ašāgu* that is interpreted variously by scholars.[670]

al-gazum$_x$(ZUM×LAGAB) = /*arganum*/. The latter complex sign cannot be read /garig/ since this is a word for "comb." It appears in the context of combing wool.[671] Al-gazum$_x$ is the correct reading of this spelling, which is documented in the ED and ES texts from Ĝirsu and Adab. The reading of LAGAB×ZUM relies on variant spellings in other texts: ^{šim}ar-ga-num$_2$ passim in Ur III texts, ^{šim}[*ar*]-*gu-zum* and $^{\text{(šim)}}$*ar-ga-nu-um* in Nippur Old Babylonian lexical fragments,[672] ^{šim}mar-gu-zum, ^{šim}mar-gu$_3$(KA)-zi, ^{šim}mar-ku-zi in Ur III and later sources,[673] and ^{šim}a-a$_2$-zum.[674] The lexical list *Ura* III 116–119 lists four "Sumerian" names for one Akkadian *ar-ga-an-nu*: $^{\text{ĝeš.šim}}$MIN$_3$-nu, $^{\text{ĝeš.šim}}$ar$_2$-gan-nu, $^{\text{ĝeš.šim}}$mar-gu-nu, and $^{\text{ĝeš.šim}}$mar-gu-zum.[675] All of them probably referred to the same plant.

The phonemic structure of the word /algazum/ is interesting. There is at least one more word beginning with /alga-/ in Sumerian: /algameš/ "a stone." This stone appears in similar pronunciations in Egyptian, Hebrew, and Ugaritic.[676] The =um ending of /algazum/ may point to its Semitic origins. Both words may have belonged to the "wandering words" in the Near East quite early. The factor behind this process was evidently the same as with the word for the measure ma-na "mina": the international trade networks in the late 4th–early 3rd mill. BC.

It is tempting to suggest that /algaz/num/ designates the tree and the nuts of *argan* (*Argania spinosa*), the oil of which is still used in modern Morocco as food and cosmetics. Nowadays this species is found in Morocco and Israel.

$^{\text{(šim)}}$*am-ru-um*. This unidentified aromatic substance should not be confused with /*kuk(ku)rum*/, for which see MAD 3: 143 sub *KKR*, Jursa 2009: 162, and Brunke and Sallaberger 2010: 51. The difference lies in (a) the writing and (b) the fact that /*amrum*/ is measured by weight and /*kuk(ku)rum*/ by capacity measures. The latter term was written gug$_2$-ru-um, ^{šim}ku-ku-ru-um, and

---

670 It is a borrowing from Sumerian with a metathesis of the consonants. For identification and discussion, see CAD A/2: 408 f., Civil 1987a: 47, Maekawa 1990: 124, De Maaijer and Jagersma 2003/2004: 351.

671 Reiner and Civil 1967: 210–211, Waetzoldt 1972: 115–116.

672 N 4808 obv. i 3', N 3951, N 4808.

673 CAD M/1: 279 *margūṣu*. These words represent reborrowings into Sumerian: Sum. /algazum/ > Akk. *argazum* > Sum. /(m)arguzum/ and /(m)arguzi/.

674 MAD 1 286 rev. i (CS Ešnunna).

675 MSL 5: 103.

676 Civil 2008: 71 no. 70.

$^{(\text{šim})}$gu$_4$-ku-ru during the 3rd mill. BC.[677] In contrast, the resin accounted by weight is always $^{(\text{šim})}$*am-ru-um*. In addition, a CS Ĝirsu text CUSAS 13 162 records both substances: 14 ½ minas of *am-ru-um* and a certain capacity of ^{šim}gug$_2$-ru. Considering the sequence in which aromatic substances occur in the resin texts, it is not excluded that *amrum* is the Akkadian equivalent of the Sumerian šim-IM (see Tab. 10.4).

^{šim}an/en-HAR. The identification is uncertain. These writings appear in the documents of the Umma region only.[678] It has the variation of the first sign in Classical Sargonic texts, whereas the Ur III documentation retains only the spelling ^{šim}en-HAR. This resin appears at the end of the lists of the weighed resins. The mass of ^{šim}an/en-HAR is usually humble.

$^{(\text{šim})}$bulug$_x$(ŠIM×UH$_3$) = *ballukkum* and *baluḫḫum*. As mentioned before, the sign DUG×UH$_3$(ZATU123) appears as early as in the 4th mill. lexical lists, where it may have had the same meaning. As already noted by Rykle Borger, the value šembulug$_x$ is a hoax,[679] and bulug$_x$ is a correct one.[680] *Ballukku* is the Akkadian equivalent of the Sumerian word in some later lexical lists.[681] There is a similarly written aromatic substance *baluḫḫum*. It is spelled ^{šim}*ba$_{(5)}$-lu-ḫum* (Sargonic), ^{šim}*bu$_3$-lu-ḫum*, and ^{šim}*bu-lu-ḫu-um* (Ur III). It is compared with ^{šim}buluh(HAL) in the later lexical tradition.[682] Steinkeller and Civil argue that these Akkadian words designated the same resin, which is bulug$_x$ in Sumerian.[683] Relying on a Sargonic list of resins ITT 2 4461, Brunke and Sallaberger argue that bulug$_x$ is *ballukkum*, whereas *baluḫḫum* should be kept apart from it. However, as Tab. 10.4 below illustrates, this text is an exception. In all other sources, bulug$_x$ and *baluḫḫum* are mutually excludable, which speaks in favor of their identity. The amounts of bulug$_x$ are usually considerable. An Early Sargonic account of perfumed oils mentions one pot of the *bulug* oil among other single-ingredient oils.[684]

---

677 *Kuk(ku)ru* has been confused in the later lexical tradition with šim-gam-gam of ED sources; see Civil 2008 no. 224.

678 Brunke and Sallaberger 2010: 50.

679 MZL: 524.

680 Steinkeller 1992: 57–58. They interpret the inscribed sign UH$_3$ as a phonetic complement.

681 The lexical tradition provides ^{šem}bu-lu-ug, ŠIM×IGI, ŠIM×BULUG for *ballukku* (CAD B: 64).

682 CAD B: 74 interprets *baluḫḫu/buluḫḫu* as “a tree and its resin, possibly galbanum.” It is $^{\text{ĝeš.šim}}$buluh(HAL) in *Ura* III 106 f.

683 Steinkeller 1992: 57; Civil 2008: 105.

684 CUSAS 35 227 obv. 1 (ES Adab): 1 i$_3$-bulug$_x$(ŠIM×UH$_3$) dug.

Several passages in accounts of resins introduce šim diri-*um* in minas.[685] It is not a distinct resin. In contrast, it should be interpreted as "resins in excess," where diri corresponds to the Akkadian *watrum*.

$^{(\text{šim})}$dam-še-lu-um. This unidentified aromatic substance does not appear before the Ur III period. Another writing is dam-še/ši-lum. Brunke and Sallaberger (2010: 50) proposed an identification with ^{šim}tal$_2$-tal$_2$.

du$_{10}$-gan. Two administrative records mention this term. In a Sargonic text from Sagub, an amount of du$_{10}$-gan in minas opens the section of resins followed by ba-lu-hum. Steinkeller interprets obv. 4 as "leather bags,"[686] which is impossible here. Another reference is found perhaps in a Sargonic document from Adab.[687]

$^{(\text{šim/ĝeš})}$eren(-UD(.UD)) "cedar (resin/wood)" was widely used as an ingredient in aromatic recipes and in carpentry of luxury items. As the resin, it appears often as eren-UD.(UD). This is usually normalized eren-babbar$_{(2)}$ "white cedar," relying on the comparison to *tijāru* in later lexical data. However, the same *tijāru* "conifer" is equated with other Sumerian terms for trees such as ^{ĝeš}mes-babbar.[688] Miguel Civil conjectures that UD may be a reflection of an earlier phonetic complement ERIN$_2$ for erin "cedar."[689] He points to the similarity between the signs ERIN$_2$ and UD. Here, UD is actually ERIN$_2^{!}$(UD) misinterpreted by ancient scribes. Therefore, the spelling should be normalized eren^{erenx}(UD). The addition of the second UD may be likewise a misinterpretation of the Early Dynastic scribes.

It has been suggested that eren represented pieces of wood for incenses.[690] One Presargonic text mentions 245 minas of cedar wood in three lumps.[691] However, it is impossible to use wood directly in the preparation of oils because the wood must be distilled by steam first. The smallest amounts of eren are less than one mina and as much as 420 minas appear in one Presargonic document. The talent appears in connection with cedar wood/resin in Middle Sargonic documents. One record witnesses as much as 6 talents 44 minas of cedar (406 minas). Ur III records begin to use the shekel and its fractions in recording the weight of cedar.

685 CUSAS 35 514 obv. 7 and Nik 2 88–89 (CS Umma).
686 MC 4 43 obv. 4 (CS Sagub); ib.: 79.
687 CUSAS 13 162 (CS Ĝirsu) rev. 3: 6 ⸢ma-na⸣ [du$_{10}$]-GAN.
688 ^{ĝeš}eren-UD = *ti-ja-lu* "white cedar"; CAD E: 274 *erēnu* and CAD T: 399 *tijāru*.
689 Civil 2008: 103 no. 218.
690 Brunke and Sallaberger 2010: 49.
691 3 ĝeš-lagab eren-UD.UD ki-la$_2$-bi 245 ma-na (DP 514 obv. i 1–2; ED IIIb Ĝirsu).

gi-i$_3$ "sweet reed." It is also ^{šim}gi or simply gi in the accounts of aromatics. Its equivalent is *qanû ṭābu* "sweet reed" in later texts.[692] "Sweet reed" appears in considerable amounts in minas during the Presargonic period, where it takes the proportion 1:10 in relation to cedar. Sargonic texts mention humbler amounts, usually several minas.

^{šim}hi(-ib). This resin pops up in the later lexical tradition after ligidba,[693] the nig̃$_2$-ib of the Presargonic sources. The amounts of ^{šim}hi(-ib) range from 10 shekels to 12 minas. This writing does not appear prior to the Sargonic period.

$^{\text{(šim)}}$kur-gi-rin. Both known references where this substance appears in weight measures are in the Presargonic documents from G̃irsu RTC 20–21. One of the documents mentions 10 minas of ^{šim}kur-gi-rin side by side with 27 minas of ^{šim}ad$_2$ "myrtle." Both are among the commodities procured in Elam. The second document lists the goods that were delivered to the palace as a result of the "running trade with Elamite ships."[694]

Other texts indicate that kur-gi-rin was a garden plant. One Sargonic text mentions its roots obtained in the garden of the *en* priest.[695] ^{šim}kur-gi-rin in these records is identical to $^{\text{u2}}$kur-gi-rin$_{(2)}$-na in lexical lists. This was borrowed into Akkadian as *kurkānû* "a medicinal plant."[696] Note also the equation kur-gi-rin-na^{nisig} = *kur-ka-nu-u* = *pi-ri-za-⌜ah⌝* in a lexical commentary.[697] The latter is a Kassite word.[698] Süel and Soysal observed its resemblance to the word for "leek" in Latin, Greek, and Turkish.[699] Heimpel suggests that ^{šim}kur-gi-rin is a conifer and relates it to the above-mentioned *kuk(ku)ru*.[700] However, the latter was measured by capacity measures only. In contrast, both the Sumerian $^{\text{(šim)}}$ kur-gi-rin and the Akkadian *kurkānû* were measured by weight.

nig̃$_2$-ib = /*nikiptum*/. Hartmut Waetzoldt discusses numerous Ur III writings of two similar-sounding words: *liKtum*, which he identifies with a mineral tanning agent "alum" (hydrated double sulfate of aluminum and potassium) measured by capacity units, and the substance *niGitum* measured by weight.[701] The older and original writing of the latter term is nig̃$_2$-ib. The word had been

692 CAD Q: 85, 88–89.
693 SLT 12 rev. i 8' (OB Nippur).
694 nam-ga:eš$_8$-ak ma$_2$-Elam-ka-kam (RTC 21 obv. ii 2–3).
695 ITT 1 1282 obv. 1–2 (CS G̃irsu): 2 kur-gi-rin ur$_2$; $^{\text{g̃eš}}$kiri$_6$ en.
696 CAD K: 560 f. The placement of the term kur-gi-rin-na^{nisig} among the terms of the garden greens is suggestive (OB Nippur *Ura*, MSL 10: 122 Section C 17).
697 MSL 10: 105.
698 CAD P: 403 *pirizaḫ*.
699 Süel and Soysal 2003: 359.
700 Heimpel 1987: 72, n. 175.
701 Waetzoldt 2010: 297.

borrowed into Akkadian as the feminine *nikiptum*,[702] although the Sargonic and Ur III writings sometimes fail to write the closing consonant of the penultimate syllable, thus *niki(p)tum*. This word was reborrowed into Sumerian as ligidba (ŠIM.^{d}NIN.URTA) with the obvious metathesis /*pt*>db/: /niĝib/ > *nikiptum* > ligidba. The Akkadian term appears in the later lexical tradition accompanied by the determinatives ^{ĝeš} or $^{\text{u2}}$, thereby pointing to its plant nature.[703] This substance was used in the preparation of an oil, i$_3$-ligidba.[704]

Seven and 60 minas of niĝ$_2$-ib appear in the same Presargonic documents from Ĝirsu RTC 20–21 with ^{šim}kur-gi-rin. A roughly synchronous text from Adab records 30 minas of the same substance in a different, Akkadian writing ^{šim}*ni*-⌜*kib*$_3$(GIG)⌝-*tum*.[705] Together with 30 minas of the aromatics ^{šim}*(h)ululum*, 16 minas of /algazum/, 20 minas of šim-IM, and other luxury goods it is a *mašdari'a* gift to a certain Lugalkinedudu, who is likely identical to the well-known ruler of the city of Uruk.[706]

In Sargonic sources, we find 10 minas of ^{ĝeš}*ni-ki-tum* together with 29 minas of bulug$_x$, and a piece of *supālum* conifer tree a "cubit" and a "hand" long.[707] The writing ^{šim}*ni*$^{!}$(IR)-*gi*$_4$-*ip-tum* appears in another Sargonic record among other resins to prepare seven jars of perfumed oil.[708] For Lagaš II and Ur III writings and references, see Brunke and Sallaberger 2010: 50 and the abovementioned work on oils by Waetzoldt.

šim-IM. The reading of the sign IM, not to be confused with NI$_2$, in this term is not certain and neither is the identification of the resin. It appears mostly at the end of the sections on the resins' accounts concerned with those among them measured by weight. This indicates that its proportion in fragrant oils was the lowest. As conjectured above, šim-IM may be identical to *amrum*.

Šim-IM is calculated only in minas in the ED and Sargonic records. One hundred and five minas of šim-IM is one of the types of merchandise that were brought from the border city of Der as depicted by the account DP 513 from Presargonic Ĝirsu. The price of this commodity is relatively low: one shekel of silver for 25 minas of šim-IM. For comparison, seven minas of ^{šim}ad$_2$ "myrtle" were worth one and one-third of a shekel. Another interesting fact is that šim-

702 Heimpel 1987: 72 n. 175.

703 CAD N/2: 222 *nikiptu*.

704 MSL 11: 112 T = N 5543 obv. i 4.

705 CUSAS 11 68 obv. ii 1 (ED IIIb Adab). Collated by the author.

706 RIME 1.14.14.

707 ITT 2 4573 obv. 3 (CS Ĝirsu).

708 CUSAS 13 162 obv. 9 (CS Ĝirsu).

IM was measured with the "correct stone" (na$_4$-si-sa$_2$-ta) in Presargonic Ĝirsu. In Ur III records, šim-IM appears for the first time in shekels.

šim mar-tu "the Amorite resin." A half mina of it appears in several Ur III texts. Nothing definite is known about this resin besides its alleged origins in the West and its procurement from the Amorite tribes.

šim-MI(giggi?). The only attestation appears among other aromatic substances in the above-mentioned list of gifts to Lugalkinedudu in CUSAS 11 68 obv. ii 3 from ED IIIb Adab. An Old Babylonian copy of the lexical list *ED Vessels and Garments* 60 mentions šim-MI$^{\text{ši-im-mi}}$, which may be identical to the substance in our document.[709] Since the ED version has šembi$_3$(DUG×IGI-*gunû*)-babbar(UD) before šembi$_3$(DUG×IGI-*gunû*)-giggi(MI), šim-MI of the ED Adab text may be actually šim-giggi "black resin."

šim naĝa$_3$(GAZ)$^{\text{ĝa2}}$ "*potash-resin.*" Two-thirds of this mysterious resin appears in a single Ur III document concerning far-distance trade.[710]

šurmen "cypress." The substance /šurmen/[711] is identified with "cypress" and has the equivalents *šarmīnum* in Ebla and *šurmēnum* in Akkadian.[712] For example, it is written ^{šim}*su-me-num*$_2$ in the Sargonic account MAD 1 286. Similarly to eren "cedar," cypress was delivered in large blocks. DP 514 records a block (lagab) weighing 100 minas. Like eren, /šurmen/ is written either with the determinative for perfumes or for wood. It is usually the second-ranked substance in lists of ingredients, which signifies its high proportion in oils. As a result, ED texts record considerable amounts of /šurmen/ and always in minas. Classical Sargonic documents have talents instead. The Ur III data provide the writing šu-ur$_2$-me and the earliest attestations of the substance in shekels.

^{šim}tal$_2$-tal$_2$ "fennel." The reading ^{šim}tal$_2$-tal$_2$ is identified by Miguel Civil who compared the Eblaite spelling ^{ĝeš}RI(tal)-RI(tal) with the one from Abu Ṣalabikh ^{ĝeš}PI(tal$_2$)-PI(tal$_2$)^{nisig}. Previously believed to be anise, it is probably fennel.[713] The word should not be confused with the medical plant aš-tal$_2$-tal$_2$ = *ardadillu*.

---

709 SLT 11 obv. iii 8.

710 NINDA$_2$ or KUM according to the copy. The reading relies on a similar writing in obv. 15 of the same document, YNER 8 24.

711 The quality of the last vowel is clear by the use of the phonetic complements: $^{\text{šu-me}}$EREN = šurmen, ^{šu}EREN^{me}, and EREN$^{\text{šu-me}}$ = šurmen$_{\text{x}}$.

712 Civil 2008 no. 217; CAD Š^3: 349 f.

713 EDPV A 223; Akk. *urânu*: CAD U/W: 206. Cf. *Antagal G* explaining the reading: $^{\text{ta-al-MIN}}$PI×PI$_{\textit{tenû}}$ = ^{d}*E*$_2$*-a ni-me-qi*$_2$ EN *ha-si-si* (MSL 17: 228 line 287).

$^{\check{s}im}$tal$_2$-tal$_2$ was the usual component in ED IIIb Ĝirsu oil recipes. It is always measured in minas and the amounts never come close to 60 minas. However, this writing does not appear outside this corpus.

$^{\check{s}im}$*u$_9$-lu-lum*. Probably *(h)ul(l)ulum* or *(ḫ)ul(l)ulum*, this Semitic word for a resin appears in two texts from Adab. The first is the Presargonic list of gifts to Lugalkinedudu discussed above. Together with *nikiptum*, it has the largest amount: 30 minas. If we take this fact at face value, *(h/ḫ)ul(l)ulum* may be an Akkadian equivalent of the Sumerian eren "cedar" or šurmen "cypress." The second text is of the Middle Sargonic period, where 11 minas of $^{\check{s}im}$*u$_9$-lu-lum* and eight pieces of flitch appear in the context of a chief merchant, which implies the import of this resin.

A similarly sounding plant is *ullulu* of the later lexical data. It is compared with a no less obscure plant *ḫabšallurḫu*.[714] It is uncertain whether the early *(h/ḫ)ul(l)ulum* is identical to the latter *ullulu*.

$^{\hat{g}e\check{s}}$u$_3$-suh$_5$ = *ašūhu* "a pine" and $^{\hat{g}e\check{s}}$za-ba-lum = *supālum* "a juniper." Civil observes that Sargonic and Ur III za-ba-lum takes the place of $^{\hat{g}e\check{s}}$u$_3$-suh$_5$ in the Early Dynastic accounts of resins.[715] However, these are two different plants. Whereas $^{\hat{g}e\check{s}}$u$_3$-suh$_5$ is a variety of pine,[716] $^{\hat{g}e\check{s}}$za-ba-lum is a variety of juniper.[717] Both terms appear in the *Statue B* of Gudea, where he boasts that he brought juniper and large pines from Uršu and the mountains around Ebla.[718] The reason why the accounts of aromatic substances use /usuh/ "a pine" and /zabalum/ "a juniper" as synonyms remains unclear. Especially interesting in this connection is the writing $^{\hat{g}e\check{s}}$eren zu$_2$-ba-lum "the *zubalum* cedar" in CUSAS 35 514 that appears alongside the usual cedar.

The resin "juniper/pine" was measured during the Presargonic period in minas only, even if its quantity exceeded 60 minas. From the Classical Sargonic period on, the talent was used. The largest amount exceeded three talents. As usual, Ur III records offer examples of /zabalum/ measured in shekels.

Tab. 10.3 gives examples of the resins' masses in the texts of the Early Dynastic, Sargonic, and Ur III periods.

---

714 A hapax in *Uruanna* III 102–103; CAD U/W: 84. CAD H: 18 *habšallurhu*.

715 Civil 2008 no. 216.

716 See Powell 1992: 116–117, 122 for a tentative identification with *Pinus brutia*.

717 Along with other sorts of juniper such as dup-ra-an and $^{\hat{g}e\check{s}}$li (Old Babylonian): Van de Mieroop 1992: 158–160.

718 RIME 3/1: 33 lines 55–56.

Tab. 10.3: Aromatic substances measured by weight, ca. 2400–2000 BC.

$^{(\text{šim/ĝeš})}$**ad$_2$** "myrtle"	7 m.	DP 513 obv. iii 3 (ED IIIb Ĝirsu)
	27 m.	RTC 20 obv. i 5 (ED IIIb Ĝirsu)
	40 m.	TSA 6 obv. ii 3 (ED IIIb Ĝirsu)
	28 m. for 7 jars of oil	CUSAS 13 162 obv. 5 (CS Ĝirsu)
	30 m. for 7 jars of oil	CUSAS 35 514 obv. 4 (CS Umma)[719]
al-gazum$_x$(ZUM×LAGAB)	42 m.	VS 27 86 rev. i 1 (ED IIIb Ĝirsu)
(a resin)	4 m.	CUSAS 13 162 obv. 8 (CS Ĝirsu)
$^{(\text{šim})}$***am-ru-um*** (a resin)	14 ½ m.	CUSAS 13 162 obv. 10 (CS Ĝirsu)
	30 m.	STTI 27 rev. 2–3 (CS Ĝirsu; "1 *gurdub* container of *amrum* aromatic substance; its weight is 30 minas")
^{šim}**an/en-HAR** (a resin)	1 and 3 m.	BIN 8 300 obv. 5, Nik 2 88 obv. 1 and 319 rev. 2 (CS Umma)
	1 m.	Nisaba 26 33 obv. 10 (Ur III Umma)
$^{(\text{šim})}$**bulug$_x$(ŠIM×UH$_3$), ^{šim}ba-lu-kum, $^{(\text{šim})}$ba$_{(5)}$-lu-hum, ^{šim}bu$_3$-lu-hum, ^{šim}bu-lu-hu-um** (a resin)	85 m.[720] (^{šim}bulug$_x$)	Nik 1 300 obv. i 1 (ED IIIb Ĝirsu)
	30 m. (^{šim}ba-lu-ḫum)	CUSAS 35 514 obv. 6 (CS Umma)
	13 m. (^{šim}ba$_5$-lu-ḫum)	ITT 2 4461 obv. 4 (CS Ĝirsu)
	10 m. (^{šim}ba-lu-kum)	MAD 1 286 rev. 2 (CS Ešnunna)
^{šim}**dam-še/ši-lu-um/-lum** (a resin)	1 and 3 m. ($^{(\text{šim})}$dam-še-lu-um)	Nisaba 26 33 rev. 1, MVN 9 215 obv. 10 (Ur III Umma)
	8 m. 3 1/3 sh. (dam-še-lum)	MVN 4 61 obv. 7 (Ur III Umma)
	2 m. (dam-ši-lum)	NATN 618 obv. 13 (Ur III Nippur)
du$_{10}$-gan (a resin)	*x* and 6 m.	MC 4 43 obv. 4 (CS Sagub), CUSAS 13 162 rev. 3 (CS Ĝirsu).

719 The attribution of the provenance is based on the similarity of the resins' sequence to BIN 8 300 and 319 from CS Umma.

720 The large amount of 85 minas can be deduced from the price in silver. Since the measure "talent" did not exist in the ED period, FAOS 15/1 300 must be corrected: Instead of [1 gu$_2$ 25] ma-na šimbulug$_x$ there must be [85] ma-na ^{šim}bulug$_x$.

Tab. 10.3: (continued)

$^{\text{(geš.šim)}}$**eren(-UD)** "cedar (resin)"	420 m. 6 t. 44 m. 5 m. 8 2/3 sh.	VS 27 86 obv. ii 3 (ED IIIb Ĝirsu) CUSAS 20 263 (MS Adab) AAICAB 1/3 pl. 248 Bod S 304 obv. 3 (Ur III Umma)
gi-i$_3$, $^{\text{(šim)}}$gi "sweet reed"	42 m. (gi-i$_3$) 30 m. (^{šim}gi) ½ and 2 m. (gi)	VS 27 86 obv. iii 5 (ED IIIb Ĝirsu) CUSAS 35 514 obv. 5 (CS Umma) CUSAS 35 317 obv. 9, rev. 4 (MS Adab)
^{šim}**hi(-ib)** (a resin)	2 m. 12 m. 10 sh.	ITT 5 9293 rev. 1 (CS Ĝirsu) SET 282 obv. 7 (Ur III Umma) UET 3 1060 obv. ii 3 (Ur III Ur)
$^{\text{(šim)}}$**kur-gi-rin** (a resin)	10 m.	RTC 20–21 (ED IIIb Ĝirsu)
niĝ$_2$-ib, ^{šim}*ni-kib$_3$-tum*, ^{ĝeš}*ni-ki-tum* (a resin)	7 and 60 m. (niĝ$_2$-ib) 30 m. (^{šim}*ni-kib$_3$-tum*) 10 m. (^{ĝeš}*ni-ki-tum*)	RTC 20–21 (ED IIIb Ĝirsu) CUSAS 11 68 obv. ii 1 (ED IIIb Adab) ITT 2 4573 obv. 3 (CS Ĝirsu)
šim-IM (a resin)	105 m. 1 m. 1 m. 3 1/3 m. 5 2/3 sh.	DP 513 obv. ii 4 (ED IIIb Ĝirsu) DP 511 obv. ii 1 (ED IIIb Ĝirsu) BIN 8 300 obv. 4 (CS Umma) AAICAB 1/3 pl. 248 Bod S 304 obv. 19
šim mar-tu (a resin)	½ m.	BIN 5 292 obv. 10 (Ur III Umma), YNER 8 24 obv. 10 (Ur III uncert.)
šim-MI (a resin)	20 m.	CUSAS 11 68 obv. ii 3 (ED IIIb Adab)
šim naĝa$_4$(KUM)$^{\text{ĝa2}}$ (a resin)	2/3 m.	YNER 8 24 obv. 10 (Ur III uncertain)
$^{\text{(ĝeš)}}$**šurmen(ŠU.ME.EREN), ^{ĝeš}šurmen$_x$ (EREN.ŠU.ME) ^{šim}šu-me, ^{šim}*su-me-num$_2$*, šu-ur$_2$-me** "cypress"	120 m. (šurmen) 1 t. (^{ĝeš}šurmen$_x$(EREN.ŠU.ME)) 1 t. 2 m. (^{šim}šu-me) 25 (m.) (^{šim}*su-me-num$_2$*) 11 m. 14 sh. (šu-ur$_2$-me)	VS 14 131 obv. i 7 (ED IIIb Ĝirsu) CUSAS 35 514 obv. 2 (CS Umma) ITT 2 4587 obv. 3 (CS Ĝirsu) MAD 1 286 obv. 2 (CS Ešnunna) AAICAB 1/2 pl. 158-159 1971-406 obv. i 4 (Ur III Umma)

Tab. 10.3: (continued)

^{šim}tal$_2$-tal$_2$ "fennel"	11 and 42 m.	VS 27 59 obv. ii 1 and 86 obv. iii 4 (ED IIIb Ĝirsu)
^{šim}u$_9$-lu-lum (a resin)	30 m.	CUSAS 11 68 obv. i 6 (ED IIIb Adab)
	11 m.	CUSAS 20 305 obv. 2 (MS Adab)
^{ĝeš}u$_3$-suh$_5$, ^{ĝeš}eren zu$_2$-ba-lum, ^{šim}zu$_2$-ba-lum, *$^{\text{(ĝeš)}}$za/zu-ba-lum, ^{šim}zu-pa$_2$-^{lu}lum* "pine" and "juniper"	80 ma-na u$_3$-suh$_5$	TSA 6 obv. i 2 (ED IIIb Ĝirsu)
	x m. (za-ba-lum)[721]	CUSAS 20 267 obv. 2 (MS Adab)
	1 t. (^{ĝeš}eren zu$_2$-ba-lum)	CUSAS 35 514 obv. 3 (CS Umma)
	3 m. (za-ba-lum)	BIN 8 300 obv. 3 (CS Umma)
	3 t. 17 m. *^{šim}su$_2$-pa$_2$-lum*	ITT 2 4587 obv. 2 (CS Ĝirsu)
	1+n t. 40 m. (*$^{\text{[šim]}}$su$_2$-pa$_2$-lum*)	CUSAS 13 168 rev. 11 (CS Umm al-Hafriyat)
	25 (m.) (*^{šim}su$_2$-pa$_2$-^{lu}lum*)	MAD 1 286 obv. 3 (CS Ešnunna)
	5 m. 8 2/3 sh.	AAICAB 1/3 pl. 248 Bod S 304 obv. 4 (Ur III Umma)

Tab. 10.4 compares several illustrative accounts of resins. The numbers preceding each entry refer to the place each resin occupies in a given document.

In summary, about a half of all resins that were used in the preparation of luxury perfumed oils were measured by weight. The Presargonic archival texts record their weight for the first time. They use exclusively minas and the amounts are usually large. Many contexts explicitly suggest that these resins were Elamite imports. The situation remains largely the same in the Sargonic period with the only difference that the talent had been introduced. The Ur III records offer measurements that are more precise: They use the measure "shekel." The cumulative data on the resins of 2400–2000 BC illustrate that the palace and temples used the system of weight measures to document a vibrant import of these luxury goods that were procured with the help of trading agents in far-off regions.

721 Collated by the author in 2011.

Tab. 10.4: Exemplary lists of resins, ca. 2400–2000 BC.

Nik 1 301 (ED IIIb Ĝirsu)	**TSA 6 (ED IIIb Ĝirsu)**	**CUSAS 11 68 (ED IIIb Adab)**	**CUSAS 13 162 (CS Ĝirsu)**	**STTI 27 (CS Ĝirsu)**	**ITT 2 4461 (CS Ĝirsu)**	**BIN 8 300 (CS Umma)**	**BIN 8 319 (CS Umma)**	**CUSAS 35 514 (CS Umma)**	**Parr 1974: 100 (Ur III Umma)**
		1. ^{šim}*u$_9$-lu-lum*							
		2. ^{šim}*ni-kib$_3$-tum*	9. ^{šim}*ni$^!$-gi$_4$-ib-tum*						
					1. bulug$_x$				
1. eren-UD			[1. eren]	[1. eren]		1. eren-UD	1. eren-UD	1. ^{ĝeš}eren	1. eren
2. šurmen	3. šurmen		[2. šurmen]	[2. šurmen]		2. šurmen	2. šurmen	2. ^{ĝeš}šurmen$_x$ (EREN$^{\text{šu-me}}$)	3. šu-ur$_2$-me
3. u$_3$-suh$_5$	2. u$_3$-suh$_5$		4. za$^?$-[ba-lum]			3. za-ba-lum	3. za-ba-lum	3. ^{ĝeš}eren zu$_2$-ba-lum	2. za-ba-lum
	4. ^{šim}ad$_2$		5. ad$_2$	4. ^{šim}ad$_2$	2. ^{šim}ad			4. ^{ĝeš}ad$_2$	10. ad$_2$
4. ^{šim}bulug$_x$	1. bulug$_x$		6. *ba-lu-hum*	3. *ba$_5$-[lu]-⸢hum⸣*	4. ^{šim}*ba$_5$-lu-hum*		4. bulug$_x$	6. ^{šim}*ba-lu-hum*	11. bulug$_x$
5. gi-i$_3$			7. gi		3. ^{šim}gi		5. gi	5. ^{šim}gi	5. gi
6. al-gazum$_x$		3. al-gazum$_x$	8. al-gazum$_x$	5. al-gazum$_x$					8. *ar-ga-num$_2$*
7. ^{šim}tal$_2$-tal$_2$									

8. šim-IM					4. šim-IM	6. šim-IM	6. šim-IM
					5. ^{šim}an-HAR	7. ^{šim}an-HAR	
		10. ^{šim}*am-ru-um*	6. *am-ru-um*				
				5. ^{šim}hi-ib			4. ^{šim}hi
	4. šim-MI						
		11. du_{10}-gan					

10.7 Gems

Precious stones have always been the luxury objects par excellence. We find various gems in the Early Dynastic and possibly even in the 4th mill. BC texts. However, the practice of recording their weight is relatively late and irregular. It dates back to the Sargonic period. These data appear in two contexts. First, there is the circulation of gems in the economies of the central households: palaces and temples. Second, and more rarely, we find gems in a private context: in lists of private possessions, records of private transactions, and legal records.

Perhaps it is appropriate to begin with one of the most praised and valued gems in the Ancient Near East, **lapis lazuli** (Sum. ^{na4}za$_{(7)}$-gin$_3$, Akk. *uqnû*). As is commonly known, this gem was procured in Afghanistan. The trading route went westward as far as Egypt. The importance of this gem can be seen by its prime place among other minerals in the *ED Practical Vocabulary A*.[722] However, the occurrences where this gem in its raw state (lumps) is recorded by weight are rare in early records. In contrast, objects from lapis lazuli appear often. Like other gems, lapis lazuli reached Mesopotamia in its natural form, in pieces of geological material. A document from Early Sargonic Nippur mentions "a block of lapis lazuli of (value) 13 shekels of silver."[723]

Probably the earliest data on the weighing of lapis lazuli are found at Ebla. The Middle-Euphrates city of Mari was the only source of this gem for Ebla emphasizing the east-to-west direction of the trade route. The price of lapis lazuli in silver was not fixed and ranged from 3.5:1 and less.[724]

Sargonic records begin to mention the weight of lapis lazuli. A document from the "Enlilemaba archive" from Nippur mentions a certain amount of shekels of lapis lazuli.[725] More often, this gem appears as (parts of) luxury objects: jewelry, cylinder seals, etc. For example, one text records a small lapis lazuli plaque (dib) weighing two and a half shekels.[726] A text from Nippur records a lapis lazuli and a golden seal (kišib$_3$) weighing two and one and two-thirds shekels, respectively.[727] The same text mentions two lapis lazuli gems mounted in an object.[728] Two texts from the same archive mention five beads (za-us$_2$)

722 EDPV A 1–47 for lapis lazuli objects.

723 OSP 1 17 obv. ii 4 (ES Nippur): lagab za-gin$_3$ 13 ku$_3$ giĝ$_4$-kam.

724 Archi 2017a: 37.

725 OSP 2 63 rev. ii 7 (MS Nippur).

726 BdI 2/1 61 obv. 2 (CS uncert. prov.).

727 OSP 2 49 obv. i 4–7 (MS Nippur).

728 OSP 2 49 obv. ii 6–8 (MS Nippur): 2 saĝ za-gin$_3$ ab-dab$_5$.

weighing five shekels, that is, ca. one shekel each.[729] Similar evidence appears in Ur III records.

^{na4}an-zu-gur$_4$-me. The reading has been possible due to the comparison with ^{na4}an-zu$_2$-gul-me of the *OB Nippur Ura* 4 Seg. 1 line 125. Lexical data indicate that seals were made from this stone as well. However, this gem remains unidentified.[730] A Sargonic text from Ĝirsu mentions a piece of this stone weighing 13 shekels, ca. 100 g.[731]

Another Sargonic text records the weight of numerous **nir$_3$** = *ḫulālu(m)* "agates (?)" and **gug** = *sāmtu(m)* "carnelians."[732] Four long (gid$_2$) agates weigh three shekels. Three hundred and forty small carnelians amass only to ten shekels, that is, a quarter of a gram apiece. References to these and other gems in Ur III records are numerous. Usually, they record only the fact that this or that "lucid," "small," etc. gem is set into a luxury object.

Ur III texts mention other precious stones that sometimes appear with their weight. Manuel Molina (1989) discussed these data in detail. On pages 86–87 one finds a useful map and a list of regions from where these gems were imported into Sumer. As with resins, everything points to the eastward-bound trade with the Gulf, Iran, and the Indus culture.

10.8 Wool and textiles

Wool and its products, woolen fabrics, are one of the most important and frequently documented goods measured by weight. In this section, I will discuss their earliest measurement practices and evaluate their role in the emergence of the Mesopotamian system of weight measures.

Wool, being a material, was measured directly in units of weight. In contrast, fabrics and garments produced from them were counted in pieces. Their weight is usually introduced then by the construction ki-la$_2$-bi "its weight." All this holds for linen and linen clothes and garments. However, being luxurious products, they appear more rarely than wool and its products.

The "Fiber" or "Textile Revolution" formulated in Ancient Near Eastern archaeology in recent decades remains an influential concept and multiple

729 OSP 2 51 obv. 4–5 and 52 obv. 8 (MS Nippur).

730 See Schuster-Brandis 2008: 396 for a discussion of this unidentified stone AN.ZA.GUL.ME = Akk. *za-aš$_2$-k/qi-tum*.

731 ITT 5 9276 obv. ii 4'–5' (CS Ĝirsu): 1 ^{na4}an-zu-gur$_4$-me: ki-la$_2$-bi 13 gig$_4$.

732 YBC 16676 = Foster 1983 no. 18 (CS uncert. prov.). See Schuster-Brandis 2008: 413–414, 436 for these stones.

scholars and research centers devote their efforts to deepening the understanding of when, how, and why humankind began to use plant and animal fibers to produce fabrics and clothing.[733]

Written, archaeological, and image sources document a highly developed wool and textile production in the Ancient Near East with a tangible intensification by the Late Uruk period.[734] It is a widespread opinion that luxury textiles were one of the main southern Mesopotamian exports in return for lacking goods from neighboring regions.[735] Others see the export of textiles as perhaps the only possible way to acquire foreign goods peacefully in the following 3rd mill. BC Mesopotamia.[736]

However, we are still lacking any substantial data indicating that textile surpluses were exported and that these surpluses existed at all in early Mesopotamia. It seems that all textiles were consumed locally during the Late Uruk period.[737] Additionally, we do not know whether southern Mesopotamian central households of the 4th mill. BC were involved in wool and textile production as they were in the second half of the 3rd mill. BC. Archaeologists suggest that the nature of the Late Uruk economy was tributary. Besides, the monumental structures interpreted as "temples" of the Late Uruk period do not exhibit any signs of textile production.

In contrast, both archaeological and written records indicate clearly that palace and temple households were centers of the mass textile production in the 3rd mill. BC. Nevertheless, the export of these goods is a problematic issue in respect to the earlier part of this period. First, the textiles may have been (nearly) fully consumed locally within the *oikos* economies of these organizations in the form of wool and textile allocations to its members.[738] Some scholars try to trace back the phenomenon of these distributions or try to identify the writings of these production centers in the Late Uruk administrative accounts.[739] However, much new analytical research needs to be done to arrive at

733 For example, the "Centre for Textile Research," the University of Copenhagen (Marie Louise Nosch et al.) and the research group "Textile Revolution" in the Excellence Cluster TOPOI in Berlin (Becker et al. 2016).

734 Algaze 2008: 77.

735 Crawford 1973: 236, Zagarell 1986: 417, Algaze 2005 [1993] passim, Algaze 2008: xvii, 96.

736 Fink 2016.

737 McCorriston 1977: 533, see ib. 539 for a suggestion by Andrew Sherratt that the Uruk influence in the 4th mill. BC Susa can be explained by the dependence of southern Mesopotamia on the import of wool *from there*. This suggestion is much more realistic than the still unconfirmed export of textile surpluses or luxury textiles from Sumer abroad.

738 Pollock 1999: 117 f.

739 Szarzyńska 2002: 43; Charvat 2014.

a credible interpretation of these data. Second, the appearance of textiles in relation to central urban organizations (temples) in Late Uruk Sumer may be alternatively interpreted in the vein of Susan Pollock: The deliveries of textiles into these "households" may represent obligations of individual households as producers towards these central urban organizations (= tribute).[740]

These considerations do not automatically mean that the "invisible" export of textiles in 4th and 3rd mill. BC southern Mesopotamia was a nonexistent export. Nevertheless, the frequency of the sign SIG_2, possibly "wool," in the Late Uruk accounts is *much lower than that of other goods*. For example, it is almost twice as low as dairy fat.[741] Hence, the export of textiles in 4th mill. Sumer seems very unlikely presently.

The situation in the 3rd mill. BC may have been different. However, no decisive data documenting the textile trade have been identified so far. The texts depict the circulation of textiles in two contexts. First, wool, cloths, and garments appear in the context of the allocations ("salaries") to the dependents and employees of central households. Second, luxury textiles appear in records that originate in the milieu of the gift exchanges among the intra-Sumerian and interregional elites. Examples where the outbound trade with textiles is explicitly mentioned are extremely rare.[742] 2nd and 1st mill. texts deliver much more data in this respect. However, their simple extrapolation on the earlier periods would be ahistorical.

Let us consider the earliest written data on wool and textiles in order to see whether the need to measure these goods could have been one of the factors that triggered the emergence of the system of weight measures in Sumer.

Wool is siki(SIG_2) in Sumerian. The sign SIG_2(ZATU452) appears in the 4th mill. BC administrative accounts. Margret Green assumes that it had the same meaning "wool" then. She relies on the terms UDU-SIG_2, U_8-SIG_2, and UDU-NITA-SIG_2 that should be "wool sheep/ewe/ram."[743] This is possible, since the term udu siki "wool sheep" appears in later, Early Dynastic texts too. However, considering the 4th mill. BC lexical data, the identification of SIG_2 with later siki "wool" is not without questions.[744]

740 Pollock 1999: 103–104.

741 Englund 1998: 70–71.

742 Prentice 2010: 111–112.

743 Green 1980: 4. See Englund 1998: 149 for the terminology of domestic animals in Late Uruk texts.

744 There are only references to tug_2 "textiles" in *Archaic Vessels and Garments* 90–116. The only entry with SIG_2 is 89 (EN-SIG_2). It is paralleled by the writing $eše_2$(-EN) "… rope" in *ED Vessels and Garments*. SIG_2 in *Archaic Metals* 8 has a parallel banšur "table" in the *ED Metals*.

$SIG_{2(b-e)}$[745] is one of several goods that belong to the semantic domain "wool and textile" of the Late Uruk administrative accounts. Other goods include TUG_{2a} (tug_2 "textile, cloth"), $DARA_{4c}$ (= $dara_4$ "red/dark (wool?)"), $ŠU_2$ (a cloth), $GADA_a$ (gada "linen (cloth)"), and TUG_{2a}+BAD+BAD (a cloth). Sometimes, these texts go into particulars and inform us that this or that cloth is white (UD), black (GI_6), yellow/green (GI), red/brown (NE_a), or speckled (GUN_3).[746]

I would like to draw attention to the fact that Sumerian tug_2 = Akkadian *ṣubātu(m)* is "cloth, fabric." This is a point of much misinterpretation of Sumerian accounts. Tug_2 does not refer to any type of garment, a finished product made from cloth. As we will see, the original way to measure cloth in Mesopotamia hardly differed in any way from its measurement in other cultures. Fabrics were, and still are, measured in "bolts," rolls of cloth. Naturally, the width of the cloth depends on the breadth of the loom. In contrast, the length of a bolt varied.[747] Cuneiform texts record cloths in pieces as discrete objects, and, sometimes, use fractions like "one and a half of a ... cloth." Nevertheless, this method is sometimes unsatisfactory in accounting when it is necessary to know a more precise "measure" of cloth. We use now the length measurement to measure a piece of cloth in a bolt. The accountants of the early Mesopotamian central households used a different approach. They recorded cloth in "pieces" (bolts) and then notated their weight. As the figure below shows, a usual piece or bolt of cloth weighed about three minas. It is hard to say whether this was 1.5 kg or not in every case since wool and cloth were measured by a heavier mina during the Early Dynastic period (see Chapter 7). Nevertheless, it is certain that the mass of these bolts was more or less the same in a given data set.

The fact that cloths and wool were counted in pieces using the sexagesimal system in the Late Uruk accounts often confuses modern scholars. Robert Englund suggests that some mensuration units are hiding behind these simple notations. He exemplifies his argument with the metrology of beer and fats, where discrete objects (pictograms of jars) are divided into smaller units.[748]

745 See Englund 1998: 153 n. 354 for SIG_{2a1-4} counted in the bisexagesimal system, and thus representing a grain product, versus SIG_{2b-e} and $DARA_{4c}$ as types of wool counted in the sexagesimal system in Late Uruk texts. The grain product SIG_{2a} of the Late Uruk texts appears in an ED IIIa document from Šuruppak in the writing TUG_2. Here, it is not a textile but a forage measured in the capacity system and allocated to male donkeys (TSŠ 924 rev. i and colophon for 33+x TUG_2).

746 Englund 1998: 153.

747 See Peyronel 2014: 133.

748 Englund 1998: 153.

Although there are no fractions in the context of $SIG_{2b\text{-}d}$ or any other textile product in the Late Uruk accounts, the fractions of "garments" do appear as early as ca. 3000 BC. Nevertheless, the data discussed below suggest that these fractions represent the fractions of bolts of cloths and not the fractions of the units of weight, the mina, or any other. In addition, the sexagesimal numbers with SIG_2 for usual wool and $DARA_4$ for dark wool may refer to "fleeces," which is a yearly yield of fleece of about 1 kg of one sheep according to Englund.[749] Early Dynastic and Sargonic sources suggest about 2–2.5 "textile" minas (na_4-$ša_3$-tug_2) or three (regular) minas (1.5 kg).[750] The data from the Syrian Nabada (Tell Beydar) mentioned below are in line with this.

Let us consider the evidence. The *Blau Plaque* (ELTS 11) is a stone document of the Uruk III period that may records a sale of land ("kudurrru"). Two allegedly similar numerical notations attract attention: $2N_1^!$ SIG_2 (obv. ii 8) and $1N_1$ $1N_8$ UŠ. BUR.TUG_2 (rev.). Piotr Steinkeller interprets them as two minas of wool and a garment weighing one and a half mina. He relies on another "kudurru," ELTS 13 of the ED IIIa or of an earlier date where a similar notation N_1 N_8 tug_2:ni_3-lam_2 is interpreted as "a *lamaḫuššûm* garment (weighing) 1½ (pounds)" (p. 42). This would (a) suggest the existence of the mina as early as ca. 3000 BC, which is very likely, and (b) confirm the suggestion by Englund that a unit of measurement is hiding behind the purely numerical sexagesimal notations in the Late Uruk texts. Supporting his suggestion, Steinkeller cites two Ur III texts where a type of cloth has a notation "2 ½."[751] However, the fractions with tug_2 in Ur III texts refer not to garments but to pieces of cloth.[752] These cloths were then additionally measured by weight. For example, an Ur III document from Umma records 3 ½ cloths that have a weight of 7 5/6 minas and 4 ½ shekels.[753] Relying on this, the "garments" of the *Blau Plaque* and the other "kudurrus" were various types of woollen cloth measured in bolts. As we will see below, the notation "1 ½" of a cloth is a typical trait of the ED IIIa records.

Therefore, although it is theoretically possible, and even likely, that the unit mina (in fact, "minas" of various standards) already existed around 3000 BC, we do not have any certain evidence that wool and textiles were measured in minas.

The question of the wool mensuration in the Late Uruk accounts is challenging. Its accounting in "fleeces" is probable. The 3rd mill. BC sources

749 Englund 1998: 151.

750 BIN 8 368 obv. i 1 f. (ED IIIb Ĝirsu) and Nik 2 51 obv. 1–2 (ES Umma).

751 Waetzolds 1972: 227 obv. i 22, 242 rev. i' 6.

752 Waetzoldt 1972: 84 n. 345.

753 AAICAB 1/2 pl. 117 1951-81 obv. 7–8.

confirm that wool was sometimes counted in fleeces with a subsequent measurement by weight. However, relying on the theory of the tributary nature of the Late Uruk economy, it is logical to surmise that the temples required from the population not wool but its finished products: cloths. What would the temples do with wool if they did not have any facilities to transform it into something useful? The home-based production of textiles during the Uruk period questions the possibility of wool mensuration in minas during the 4th mill. BC.

The notation of a half of a cloth's bolt with the sign N_8=½ has a history. Although its earliest attestation is found in the *Blau Plaque* dated to around 3000, we find the same notation in ED IIIa administrative documents (ca. 2600 BC).[754] These accounts record various goods, including cloths and copper. Importantly, whereas copper always appears with the term ma-na "mina," that is never the case with cloths. This is hardly accidental. The fabrics are recorded in them by an identical notation $1N_1$ $1N_8$ tug_2 "one and a half cloth." This uniformity is interesting in itself and still lacks a credible explanation. Be that as it may, the data of these ED IIIa accounts confirm that the sexagesimal numbers in the context of cloths had nothing to do with the weight metrology.

A unique way to notate cloths directly in the units of weight appears in CUSAS 11 59 (ED IIIb Adab). This document records a receipt of one to 11 minas of tug_2 "cloth." The writing N tug_2 ma-na in some ED IIIa sale documents is an abbreviation of N siki ma-na / tug_2 "x minas wool (instead of) cloth."[755] The standard practice was, however, to record cloths and textiles in pieces and then notate their weight using the ki-la_2-bi construction.

Proceeding to the measurement of wool, we find two approaches in the ED IIIa texts. The first practice resembles that of the Late Uruk texts. The wool appears with regular sexagesimal numbers: 1(N_1), 10(N_{14}), and 60(N_{34}). For example, one document records *1* siki-ud_5. The editors of the document understand this as "1 (measure of) goat hair."[756] The same text mentions the weight of an axe in minas. This excludes the interpretation "one (mina of) wool." Other texts follow the practice and record various sorts of wool solely with numbers.[757] The

754 CT 50 8a obv. i 1 ($1N_1$ $1N_8$ tug_2), 9 obv. iii 2–3 ($2^?$ ½^{sic}), and 15 obv. ii 1 ($1N_1$ $1N_8$ tug_2); TSŠ 348 obv. 1 ($1N_1$ $1N_8$ tug_2), 732 obv. i 1, 5, ii 1 ($1N_1$ $1N_8$ tug_2).

755 Steible and Yildiz 1996: 149–159 obv. i 5: ELTS 123 obv. ii 3–4.

756 FTP 84 obv. i, 1, ii 1' (ED IIIa Šuruppak).

757 Siki-sa_6-ga "premium wool," siki-us_2 "wool of the following (quality)," siki-$sila_4$ "lamb's wool": WF 132 with a total of 220 "measures." Other texts that mention wool in "numbers": CT 50 16 (2–10 "wools" per person), 17 (2–25 "wools" per person), 18 (5–10 "wools" per person), RTC 9 (270 "wools" issued to a number of individuals), 10 (2–5 per person), 11 (1169 "wools" in total; 10–120 per capita). All these documents are of the ED IIIa date but their provenance is uncertain.

second way to record wool is by weighing in minas (ED IIIa on) and shekels (ED IIIb on).[758] This means that two practices to record wool coexisted during the ED IIIa period.

The only clear omission of the unit ma-na in the accounts of wool is documented in the archive from Nabada (Tell Beydar) in northern Syria. Walther Sallaberger refers to this unit as "wool mina."[759] This archive is synchronous with the ED IIIb period in southern Mesopotamia. In contrast, a some forty years later archive from Ebla records wool in minas.

The ED IIIa period texts are the earliest certain attestations of the unit mina in the context of wool. The accounts of the following ED IIIb period document the shekel. For example, a document from Ĝirsu records 15 shekels of combed wool issued to, or received from, three individuals.[760] As expected, the talent is missing in the Early Dynastic accounts. Even if the amounts of wool are large, the unit is always the mina. The colophon of DP 171 mentions 736 minas of wool. Talents of wool appear from the Early Sargonic period on (Chapter 2). Ur III documents sometimes witness enormous amounts of wool. One well-known example is the vast amounts of wool in the textile mills in the town of Gu'abba in the Lagaš province. The texts of the same period begin to employ the unit barleycorn to record the amounts of wool. As little as ten barleycorns (ca. 0.5 g) are documented.[761] However, it is doubtful that these notations are anything but perfectionist mathematical calculations. Using small silver balances to measure wool would require unnecessary time and labor investments on the part of the administration of the central households.

10.9 The mass of some fabrics and garments

Cuneiform records provide a rich terminology for cloths, garments, and their parts. They often provide their weight too. Benjamin Foster (2010) discussed garments in the Sargonic textual documents and visual art. Richard Firth and

758 Wool in minas: TSŠ 411 (460 minas; two people are entrusted with it: šu ba_4-$šum_2$), 725 (100, 300, and 320 minas: for various localities), 751 (40 ma-da_5 instead of ma-na; a weaver entrusted with this amount: tug_2-du_8 / šu $šum_2$); all ED IIIa Šuruppak.

759 Subartu 2 6, Sallaberger 2004: 20, and Sallaberger 2014: 101 n. 31 for "one single fleece weighing 2 (minas)" (siki-bar-dili 1 ki-la_2 2).

760 ITT 5 9246.

761 AAICAB 1/3 pl. 203 Bod B 8 (115) obv. 2 (Ur III Ĝirsu).

Marie-Louise Nosch studied several widespread terms for textiles in the Ur III records: ^{tug2}guz-za, ^{tug2}ni$_3$-lam$_2$, ^{tug2}uš-bar, and ^{tug2}bar-dul$_5$. Jacopo Pasquali (1997) and Maria Giovanna Biga (2010) offered their discussions of the Semitic terms for textiles and wool in Ebla texts.

Cloths and garments are often hard to tell apart in cuneiform records. The writings are mostly the same but there are small details that help to tell them apart, at least in some cases. For example, there is a garment aktum^{tug2}. A Gudea period text mentions two tug$_2$ aktum guz-za us$_2$ "2 aktum tufted cloths of secondary quality" weighing one talent.[762] The writing with a tug$_2$ at the beginning and the mass exclude the possibility of interpreting it as garments. A person would be uncomfortable in an outfit weighing 15 kg.

Tab. 10.5, which is far from being exhaustive, illustrates the weight of garments and cloths that appear in cuneiform records. Contrary to the common view, I believe that most tug$_2$ entries refer not to the finished garments but to the bolts of cloth. The usual weight of one tug$_2$ in our sources is two to three minas. It is hard to imagine a person being comfortable wearing a single piece of dress weighing over one kilogram. For comparison, a heavy sweater made of a wool-cotton mix fabric weighs less than 0.5 kg. A Kashmir wool sweater has an even smaller mass. It is logical to suggest that only those tug$_2$ goods that were equal to or less than one mina represented garments.

10.10 Ropes, nets, mineral substances

Metals and wool as well as their products constituted the "core goods" measured by weight in early Mesopotamia. Nevertheless, there are several other groups of materials and objects measured in such a fashion. First, there are ropes, straps, and nets produced from wool, flax, and hides. They would be measured by length and not by weight nowadays. The second group consists of mundane minerals, such as bitumen and gypsum. They were used in the production of common tools. Some of them were usually measured by capacity or measures rather than weight units. This suggests that these practices were added to the "core" afterwards.

To begin with the ropes and the like, eše$_2$ "rope, thong, string" = Akk. *eblu(m)* is their generic term. It is also a determinative ^{eše2} for these type of objects. Although there is vast evidence on ropes in the corpus, the cases when they are measured in weight units are rare. Usually, they were simply counted in pieces.

762 ITT 4 7522 rev. 6–7 (Lagaš II Ĝirsu).

Tab. 10.5: Cloths and garments with known weight, ca. 2400–2000 BC.

Term	Interpretation	Weight	Textual reference
'a$_3$-dam-um^{tug2}	a garment or cloth (MAD 3: 19 'xDM)	3 m. according to the stone for silver (na$_4$-ku$_3$-kam)	CUSAS 11 224 obv. 2–3 (ED/ES Adab)
bar-si(g$_9$) sa-dab$_6$	a sash with laces to wrap around (Molina 2014: 134)	5 sh.	CUSAS 35 301 (MS Adab)
$^{(tug2)}$bar-dul$_5$	an outer wrap-around garment (Foster 2010: 129). A cloth too?	2.5 m.	CUSAS 11 61 obv. i 1–2 (ED IIIb Adab)
bar-dul$_5$ uš-bar	*b.*-garment/cloth of *ušbar* quality	3 m.	CUSAS 11 60 obv. i 1–2 (ED IIIb Adab), CUSAS 35 201 rev. 10–11 (MS Adab)
^{tug2}bar-dul$_5$ tab-ba	double *b.*-garment/ cloth	3 m. 15 sh.	OIP 14 181 obv. 5–6 (CS Adab)
^{tug2}bar-dul$_5$ DU$_{gunû}$-ma	a variety of *b.*-cloth	7 m.	ITT 5 9274 obv. 1–2 (CS Ĝirsu)
tug$_2$ gu$_2$-da$_5$	a cloth	3 m.	ITT 5 9317 obv. 1'–2' (CS Ĝirsu), ITT 5 6713 obv. 7–8 (Ur III Ĝirsu)
^{tug2}*ḫa-la-um*	a garment/cloth (MAD 3, 127 HL'x)	2.85 m.	ECTJ 104 obv. ii 1–2 (ED IIIb Nippur), SCTRAH 212 (MS Adab)
ib$_2$-(ba)-du$_3$^{tug2}	skirt/kilt (Foster 2010: 129) (the cloth is written tug$_2$ ib$_2$-ba-du$_3$)	ca. 1 m.? 14 sh.	CUSAS 13 36 obv. (MS Adab); NATN 553 obv. (Ur III Nippur)
$^{tug2/gada}$*na-aš$_2$-pa$_{(2)}$-ru-um*	a garment	<1 m.	Nik 2 86 obv. 5–7 (CS Umma)
ni$_3$-la$_2$^{tug2}	a bandage(?) (Foster 2010, 129) cf. the next entry	3 2/3 m.	CUSAS 20 244 rev. 1–2 (MS Adab)
tug$_2$ ni$_3$-la$_2$ gu$_2$ anše	a neck band for donkeys	3 2/3 m.	CUSAS 20 241 obv. 6–7 (MS Adab)

Tab. 10.5: (continued)

Term	Interpretation	Weight	Textual reference
tug_2 ni_3-lam_2 (uš-bar)	a cloth and a garment = *lamaḫuššû* "a precious garment made of wool"	3 m. (a cloth) 1 m. (a garment: tug_2 ni_3-lam_2 gid_2-da)	CUSAS 35 304 (MS Adab); VS 14 154 rev. i 6–7(ED IIIb)
^{tug2}$ša_3$-ga-du_3	a waist cloth (Steinkeller 1982b: 362; Foster 2010: 134)	50 sh.–1 m.	OIP 14 145 obv. 3'–4', 146 obv. 1–2, 181 obv. 1–2 (CS Adab)
^{tug2}$ša_3$-gi-da_5	a long toga-like garment (Steinkeller 1992: 48; Foster 2010: 133)	1 m.	CUSAS 26 212 obv. 3–4 (CS "Lugal-ra archive")
tug_2-bur_2	a garment	13–20 sh.	OIP 14 153 rev. 2'–3', 181 obv. 3–4 (CS Adab)
tug_2 du_8-a banšur-ra	a tablecloth	5 m. 15 sh.	STTI 43 (CS Ĝirsu)
tug_2 guz-za (of various qualities)	tufted cloth (CAD A/2: 179 *(ḫ)apparrû*)	ca. 4 m. and more	passim Ur III
tug_2-mug (of various qualities)	a cloth from low-quality wool	1 2/3 m.	ECTJ 104 obv. i 1–2 (ED IIIb Nippur)
		3 m. and more	Ur III passim
^{tug2}uš-bar	a garment/cloth (Civil 2008 no. 176)	2 m.	CUSAS 26 212 obv 1–2 (CS "Lugal-ra archive")

For example, a Sargonic text CUSAS 35 515 records straps to attach front and rear oxen to a plow, neck ropes, and similar objects. Their weight amounted to several minas each. Exceptionally, other leather goods that appear in the same context were measured by weight. For example, another Sargonic text SCTRAH 269 records one strap weighing two minas and a pair of sandals weighing one-third of a mina. There are other Sargonic and later texts delivering similar data.

A **si-NU×U** was a tool used in fishery, probably a variety of net.[763] The term si-NU×U appears first at ED IIIa Šuruppak. A related term U.NU from Ur III wool

763 Krebernik 1998: 307 n. 716.

texts denotes a work-consuming and elaborate type of spinning.[764] Civil compares the term si-NU×U with the ED IIIb Ĝirsu term si-ZI+ZI.U-saĝ and translates both as "thread, rope, net."[765] Si-U-NU and ^{eše2}si-NU are additional spellings in Presargonic and Sargonic texts.[766]

ED IIIa texts from Šuruppak record si-NU×U as discrete objects in either the sexagesimal or bisexagesimal system of numeration. As an example of the former practice, the total of TSŠ 424 mentions 977 si-NU×U-saĝ "nets" and x+3 "old" ones in obv. ii 2–4.[767] Other synchronous texts from Šuruppak resort to notating the quantities of the same objects in the bisexagesimal system.[768] This was used during the late 4th and at the beginning of the 3rd mill. BC to record grain. In contrast, Presargonic and later texts record this product as discrete objects with the indication of weight in minas using the ki-la_2-bi construction.[769] The calculations show that each piece had a mass of about 10–12 shekels. Some texts record si-U.NU nets simply in weight measures, such as "3 minas of *s*.-nets."[770]

Another commodity that often appears in early cuneiform sources in units of weight is gu, Akk. *qû*. This was spun thread from combed flax to produce linen (gada) textiles and ropes. An Early Dynastic document illustrates this: "1 mina of combed wool / 1/3 (mina) of (spud) flax thread (gu-gada)."[771] Two ED/ES documents also refer to gu(-gada) in minas. Their amounts are large: 60 minas in one case and 110 and 165 in another.[772] One Sargonic document mentions gu-gada in minas and shekels alike.[773]

Numerous Middle Sargonic texts from Adab published in CUSAS 20 and elsewhere record gu in talents/loads (gun_2) and bundles (sa).[774] The enormous amounts of hundreds of talents/loads of gu and the fact that it was measured by the imprecise one-talent stone weight suggest that this gu represented unprocessed flax stalks.[775] Nevertheless, we know that large amounts of gu-gada

764 Waetzoldt 1972: 120–122.

765 Civil 1987b: 313; see Visicato 1995: 86–87 for additional data.

766 E.g. CT 50 177 rev. 2 (CS Ĝirsu).

767 Other examples: FTP 88 obv. i 1, ii 1; TSŠ 430, 748; WF 142 (all ED IIIa Šuruppak).

768 DP 36; TSŠ 369, 415, 627, 736, 969 (all ED IIIa Šuruppak).

769 ITT 5 9231 obv. ii 2–3: 15 pieces = 3 minas; 9237 obv. i 1–2: 300 = 60 minas; 9240 obv. i 1–2: 340 = 60 minas; 9244 obv. i 1–2: 320 = 60 minas (all ED IIIb Ĝirsu).

770 ITT 5 9247 obv. i 1.

771 BIN 8 10 obv. ii 4–5 (ED IIIa/b): 1 ma-na siki-$garig_x$(ZUM×KASKAL)-ak, $^{šu2}1N_8$ gu:gada.

772 ECTJ 91 (ED/ES Nippur) and OIP 14 61 (ED/ES Adab).

773 STTI 33 (CS Ĝirsu).

774 See Chapter 2.

775 E.g. CUSAS 20 256: 229 gun_2, na_4 1 gun_2-ta.

were sometimes accounted in bundles similarly to a simple gu.[776] The Ur III evidence has a single term gu-gada. One document mentions 12 minas of "spun uncleaned" flax and 78 bundles of gu-gada weighing 18 talents.[777]

Less valuable and relatively easily obtainable minerals make up another group of weighed goods. Bitumen is the most common among them. Marten Stol (2012) provided a well-documented study of this material. Two aggregate states of bitumen appear in the corpus. **Esir$_2$-had$_2$**(UD)[778] "dry bitumen" was measured by weight whereas esir$_2$-A "liquid bitumen" was measured by capacity units. Both appear in *ED Practical Vocabulary A*.[779] The weight of bitumen appears in documents starting from the Sargonic period on. It appears only in talents/loads. This detail is very important. It shows that bitumen belonged originally to the less valuable goods measured by "loads" before and even after the introduction of the talent into the system of weight. Two texts from the archive of Ur-Inana of the Middle/Classical Sargonic period from Adab illustrate this argument.

Ur-Inana was a trading agent (ga:eš$_8$) who delivered various goods to a network of customers within the central economy of Adab during the reign of Naram-Suen. CUSAS 26 114 records the fact that he delivered 10 to 20 talents/loads of dry bitumen to several customers. CUSAS 26 115 documents a delivery of one talent/load of dry bitumen and one talent/load of a rush (ninni) to an official (šabra). Presargonic or Sargonic sources do not provide examples of the measurement of dry bitumen in minas or other smaller units, only Ur III records do.[780] The use of bitumen with gun$_2$ in the Sargonic period exemplifies a remarkable process of the transition of the "load" to the "talent" on the one hand and an inclusion of a material in the "family" of weighed goods on the other.

The same phenomenon underlies the measurement of an unidentified material **ANŠE/GIR$_3$-babbar$_2$** that appears in the same dossier. Seven "talents" are mentioned in the context of a resin (šim-gig), liquid bitumen, potash, and alum (al-la-ha-ru).[781]

The same rule applies to **im-babbar$_{(2)}$** "gypsum" = Akkadian *gaṣṣu(m)*.[782] It appears in "talents" only during the Sargonic period.[783] In contrast, it was

776 CUSAS 26 204 obv. 7 (CS "Lugal-ra archive"): 240 sa gu-gada.

777 AAICAB 1/1 pl. 71 1924–675 obv. ii 10–12 (Ur III Umma).

778 UD = had$_2$(ha$_5$) = *šābulu*, Š-stem of *abālu* "to be dry"; Stol 2012: 49.

779 Esir$_2$ is written LAGAB×AN instead of LAGAB×HAL there. Later terms for "liquid bitumen" are esir$_2$-e$_2$-a and esir$_2$ a ba-al-la (Civil 2008 nos. 319–320).

780 E.g. AUCT 2 168: 25 gun$_2$ 20 ma-na esir$_2$ hur-saĝ-ĝa$_2$.

781 CUSAS 26 111 obv. 10 (MS/CS Adab).

782 See Firth 2011 for a recent discussion; contra Waetzoldt 1972: 173 who interprets it as "fuller's earth." See Civil 2008 no. 348 for lexical data.

783 BdI 1 181: 4 "talents"; CUSAS 35 317: 1 "talent" (Ur-Inana's dossier).

included in the number of goods measured by other weight measures in the Ur III period.[784]

Še-gin$_2$, Akkadian *šimtu(m)*, a glue and a colorant, is perhaps another material belonging to this group.[785] No Early Dynastic or Sargonic evidence exists of its mensuration by weight. In contrast, Ur III records have talents, minas, and shekels of this material.[786] The way it was measured in previous periods is uncertain. An ED IIIb account TSŠ 782 obv. iii 9 f. mentions ten and five še-gin$_2$ without any units of mensuration.

In summary, these mineral goods were originally measured in the fashion of grass and reeds before and even during the Sargonic period. They were likely weighed by the imprecise one-talent stone weight in the manner flax was measured during this period. The Ur III period witnesses their complete inclusion into the number of goods measured by weight.

This list of weighed goods would be incomplete without bread, Sumerian **ninda**. Usually counted in pieces or measured by capacity measures, it appears sporadically in weight measures in cuneiform records. As with almost any type of weighed object, we have two practices for accounting bread. The first is to record the amount of bread in loaves and then state their weight. OIP 14 183 from Sargonic Adab is a good example of this. It mentions three sorts of bread: The "new year ... bread" (ninda ne-saĝ-UMBIN×LU) weighs about 55 shekels a piece, the "bread of one *sila*" weighs about 23–25 shekels, and a "large bread" is 60–65 shekels. The second practice avoids the number of pieces and notates only the weight of breads. For example, one ED IIIb sale document from Adab lists "10 minas of bread" among the presents for witnesses.[787] Sargonic texts mention numerous minas of bread before the Classical Sargonic period and talents and minas afterwards.[788]

10.11 Conclusions

In this chapter, I evaluated the data of 4th and 3rd mill. BC cuneiform records on the goods that were measured by weight. As a result, it has become possible

---

784 As in BIN 9 201 obv. 2 (Ur III Isin?).

785 CAD Š/3: 9.

786 BIN 5 107 obv. 4: 10 shekels; BPOA 1 505 obv. 3: 27 ½ minas (Ur III Umma); UET 9 378 obv. 1: 3 talents 1 mina (Ur III Ur).

787 CUSAS 35 1 obv. iii 1' ff. (ED IIIb Adab).

788 Nik 2 44 total: 333 minas of bread (ES Umma); PPAC 1 750 and 752: 1/3 mina to 5 talents (CS Adab).

to identify the "core goods": those substances whose mensuration triggered the emergence of a standardized system of weight measures in southern Mesopotamia. They are metals, wool, and resins.

Copper is the earliest material measured by weight according to written sources. Early Dynastic I–II and IIIa records witness two functions of this metal. First, it is a material for producing vessels and tools. Second, it represents the earliest metallic money. The ED IIIa period sale contracts exhibit the coexistence of copper and silver as metallic monies. Although silver gradually took superiority over copper during the ED IIIa period, legal sources from Zabalam suggest an important role of the latter in private transactions. Obviously, copper was the "middle-value money" in the middle of the 3rd mill. BC that stood between the cheap money (barley) and the expensive money (silver). The Sargonic period wiped out this function of copper. From then on, silver became the only metallic money. This was likely related to the expansion of the Akkadian state and its control over trade routes and booty of metals and luxury objects.

Similarly, ED I–II sources offer the first examples of objects made from copper whose weight was recorded. The original practice for notating the weight of objects was quite primitive. By the ED IIIa time, the scribes had introduced the construction ki-la$_2$-bi "its/their weight (is)" to avoid ambiguity.

The fact that the Sumerian words "merchant" and "mina" belong to the earliest layer of borrowings from the early Semitic is not accidental. Taken together, this may allude to the origins of weighing in early Mesopotamia as the response to the need to measure copper. The written and archaeological evidence of the second half of the 3rd mill. BC suggests Oman in the Persian Gulf as the main source of copper for the Sumerian south. However, the earliest references to copper and the measure ma-na in cuneiform accounts are at least 400 years older: the ED I–II period. Given the fact that the main sources of copper in Sumer during the Jemdet-Nasr and ED I–II periods lay elsewhere (Turkey and Iran), it is possible that weighing as an economic practice emerged on the trade routes populated by Semites to these regions and not to the Gulf.

The trade of metals and luxury goods in general illustrates the close link between the weight metrology and interregional trade. Coupling these data with the information on the regional standards of the mina (Chapter 7), it is arguable that the interregional trade has been one of the major factors in the emergence of the weight metrology at large.

Wool and cloth, textiles constitute the second group of "core goods." Although some scholars try to trace the use of the mina to as early as the Late Uruk period, the earliest certain examples of the use of the weight metrology in this case do not predate the ED IIIa period. The meager evidence of the trade in wool and textiles does not support the suggestion (in fact, almost an axiom) that southern Mesopotamia exported textiles in return for imports of metals and luxury objects. This detail shows no link between the emergence of the Mesopotamian weight metrology and interregional trade. We see wool in the context of 3rd mill. BC central households as mass production centers where weight metrology played a role in the accounting, thereby making weight metrology a "domestic" tool. In particular, the heavier woollen/textile standard of the mina represents two economic phenomena: the textile production and wool and textile allocations to the members of these households.

Written sources allow us to trace how accountants used specific weight measures for their needs. The most common unit during the Early Dynastic period for copper and wool was the mina. In contrast, the shekel and its fractions were used mostly for silver. This shows again the inclination of the ED scribes to avoid complicated measurements and calculations. Whereas Early Dynastic scribes put down entries such as "one axe of one mina" and "one cloth of three minas," Ur III scribes obsessively recorded the weight of goods up to 10 barleycorns in the case of cloths and to a single barleycorn (0.05 g) in the case of metals and metal objects. This does not indicate the gradual improvement of the precision of weighing. Rather, this is the sign of the increased control of resources in the central households.

The talent stands aside from other weight measures because its earliest use as a standardized unit of sixty minas did not predate the Sargonic reforms. Nevertheless, this unit played an important role in the expanding of the number of goods measured by weight. Originally, only metals, wool, and resins were measured in this fashion. In contrast, the primitive unit "load" was applied to a completely different set of goods. They included cheap and easily accessible bulk goods such as reeds, grass, fish, bitumen, etc. By the beginning of the Ur III period, we see that all these goods had been included in the family of weighed goods. The "load" turned into "talent" and played the role of the bridge for them to join the "family" of weighed goods.

These considerations highlight two main factors in the emergence of the weight metrology in southern Mesopotamia: (a) the beginning of the extensive use of metals and the long-distance trade related to it, and (b) the concentration of the wool and textile production within central urban households (palaces and temples) in the 3rd mill. BC. This provides a date of around 3000 BC as the earliest point at which a *standardized* system of weight measures may have appeared in Sumer.

A retrospect

Now it is clear that weighing was *an economic practice* deeply embedded in the society of early Bronze Age southern Mesopotamia. This practice reflected and influenced the creation and maintenance of new economic relations, and through this shaped the society. The practice of weighing as a cultural phenomenon included various related practices, agencies, interests, and relations on the one hand – all "ideal" representations of the culture – and many aspects of the "material culture" on the other.

The phenomenon of weighing in early Mesopotamia was both *unique* and a *model* at the same time. To begin with the latter, a certain level of political and socioeconomic complexity called "state" went hand in hand with new practices such as writing, sealing, the standardization of measures and weights, the regulation of prices, etc. This view goes back to Gordon Childe's characteristics of a "civilization" and is still maintained by many scholars.[789] However, the extensive use of writing and sealing as administrative practices in the Late Uruk "central households" does not make them into a "state."[790] Besides, no data suggest the use, not to mention the standardization, of the weight metrology there and then. The earliest definitely documented standardization of the weight measures in Mesopotamia was directly related to the rise of the first "real" state during the Sargonic period. This indicates that writing as an administrative tool did not necessarily correlate with the standardization of weights or the state. In general, a "high culture," an inappropriate segregationally concept, is not identical to the concept of state.

On a lower level, the model nature of the weighing in early Mesopotamia is discernible in numerous details, such as the role of the weighmaster in legal transactions, the names of the weight measures "load" and "barleycorn/grain," the use of balances and weights, the use of weight measures as "denominations" of metallic monies, etc. All these and other phenomena are characteristics of weighing practices in other "complex societies."

The uniqueness of the weighing in early Mesopotamia as a cultural phenomenon is evident in numerous details and practices too. They include the names of some measures ("counter/counted" and "axe"; Chapters 3–4), the sexagesimal background of their system, the unique phenomenon of the "little mina" (Chapter 5), the practice of weighing some goods that otherwise would be measured by other systems of mensuration, etc.

789 Mederos and Lamberg-Karlovsky 2004: 204–207; Hudson 2015: 658.
790 See Forest 2005, Stone 2013, and Ur 2014 for the critique of the "real" state prior to the Sargonic period.

https://doi.org/10.1515/9781501510267-011

In this concluding part of the book, I would like to address two more points. The first emphasizes the positive and new knowledge this study has brought on the weighing in early Mesopotamia. The second point is a short synthesis of the main theoretical argument of this book: how weighing as a practice simultaneously reflected and shaped the economy and social relations in early Mesopotamia.

What do we know about the weighing in early Mesopotamia? The backbone of the phenomenon is a system of relations between the individual weight measures. The earliest evidence of its use appears in script about 2800 BC in the context of copper as a material and, possibly, as a means of payment. This copper is measured in ma-na "minas" (480–510 g depending on the period and location). This word and the designations of its fractions "one-third" and "two-thirds" are borrowings or "wandering" words that originate in the early Semitic (Chapter 3). As a hypothesis, I relate this remarkable detail to the emergence of weighing in a cosmopolite milieu of merchants and interregional trade of the late 4th–early 3rd mill. BC: either the trade with the regions populated by Semitic-speaking people or the trade with Semitic-speaking merchants, which may have been the same.

At 2600 BC, we find abundant evidence on the existence of a fully developed and operational system of weight measures that included the units "mina," "shekel," and "little mina" (this reading is uncertain until ca. 2300). The unit "barleycorn" was not yet documented in the written data. But the role the "little mina" played in the system strongly suggests its existence and use. The numerical relations between the units were as follows: 1 mina = 60 shekels, one shekel = 3 "little minas" or 180 "barleycorns" (Chapter 6). These units were initially used to measure copper, silver, wool, and luxury goods such as resins (Chapter 10). The "Early Dynastic" stage is the earliest historically traceable system and I assume its existence as early as ca. 2800 BC or even earlier.

The founding of the Akkadian dynasty by Sargon led to the creation of a large territorial state (ca. 2350–2150 BC). Previously it has been argued that a complex set of reforms – which standardized the weight metrology, among others – took place during the second half of the reign of king Naram-Suen (2261–2206$^{\pm30}$ BC), Sargon's grandson. However, a detailed study of Sargonic documents reveals that the innovations commenced simultaneously with the establishment of the Akkadian administration in the Sumerian city-states. The example of the measure "load," transformed into the highest unit in the system of weight measures and defined as 60 correct minas (= ca. 28–30 kg) during the Early or Middle Sargonic period (the kings Sargon, Rimuš, and Maništusu), is most revealing (Chapter 2). Additionally, this process illustrates how a "primitive" measure became a part of a standardized system of measurement. The "load" of arbitrary and circumstantial capacity was used to measure low-value goods such as reeds, rushes, fish, etc. during the Early Dynastic period. The need for a unit larger than the mina in the system brought the accountants of the Early Sargonic period to the idea of "domesticating" this primitive measure. This resulted in a measure with a strictly defined mass, and from then on, a "load" was not a mass that a person carried but an "ideal" unit of weight not bound to any actual material object.

This process provides the only documented model of (a) how the system could have emerged and (b) what kind of practice must have preceded this. With regard to the former, it seems that various previously unrelated measuring practices joined a "core" unit one after another. Originally, these unrelated primitive measuring practices must have been represented by real objects playing the role of primitive weights used with a balance. These could be grains in the case of the "barleycorn," an axe-shaped metallic object in the case of the shekel (Chapter 4), and an ingot in the case of the mina. As a mental experiment, we can imagine the following procedure. An Uruk-period merchant did not need a system of interrelated units to calculate an amount of silver. He could use a silver "axe" of about 8–9 g and some barley grains. For example, this amount of silver could weigh "two axes and 20 barleycorns." This did not necessitate the numerical relationship "1:180" between these two primitive measures.

The question of the "core measure," the primitive measure to which all other measures were attached and through whose mass their masses were established, is challenging. The data suggest that the mina, the shekel, and the barleycorn must have represented these primordial unrelated weighing practices. The detail that one shekel is not 60 but 180 barleycorns excludes the latter measure as the unit par excellence of the system. This leaves us with the mina-shekel relationship "one to 60" as the original link and the "point zero" in the development of the first "standardized" Mesopotamian weight metrology. The masses of these units strongly suggest that its original purpose was the mensuration of metals. The term "standardized" is not related to any political actions in this case; it signifies the qualitative change when two measures with a background as real objects become "ideal" objects related to each other in terms of a numerical relation only ("1:60").

In contrast to this reconstructed "event" at a very early period, the written data document two state-run reforms of the weight metrology and writing in the latter half of the 3rd mill. BC. The first took place during the Sargonic period with its finished form appearing during the second half of Naram-Suen's reign. The reform of metrology aimed to create a logical symmetrical system of weight measures, which it did. However, due to its unpracticality and artificialness (the example with the "little shekel" in Chapter 6), it was abandoned once the Akkadian state had collapsed.

The second reform was claimed by king Ur-Namma of the 3rd Dynasty of Ur (ca. 2112–2095 BC) in his collection of laws. It is certain that major changes in the writing of weight measures occurred during his and his successor's (king Šulgi's) reigns. However, the data I have discussed show that the transition to the "Neo-Sumerian" stage in the development of the weight metrology happened immediately after the collapse of the Akkad state. The most important conclusion in this respect is that the state policy was not obligatory for a reformation of the system of weight measures: Each city-state returned independently to their local scribal traditions and to a radically simplified system of weight measures (the talent, the mina, the shekel, and the barleycorn). This system in this form existed until the end of the cuneiform written records (Chapter 6). This process shows that the weight metrology did not operate in terms of "core and periphery." The economic factor of the internal and intercity trade in Sumer must have been the major force in this phenomenon.

Chapters 7–8 use emic approach and combine their analyses to reveal the existence of various standards of the mina during the Early Dynastic period. The difference in their masses must be related to the practice of measuring certain goods with different weights and different types of weighing balances. The "correct stone" of ca. 480–510 g was used together with the "balance for copper," and the "stone for silver" with the "balance for silver," and the "stone for textiles" came in a pair with the "(large or small) balance for wool." In addition, we know about the "stone for wool allocations" of 680 g and a foreign "mina" of 720–750 g from the city of Der on the border with Iran.

The inclusion of the talent during the Early Sargonic period resulted in the use of large one-talent and heavier stone weights. They were imprecise, which forced the scribes to record this fact, for example, as "(measured) according to a one-talent stone" (Sargonic period) or "according to a stone of one talent and *x* mina" (Ur III period).

In the same vein, the written data show that weighing balances of different sizes and constructions were in use during the 3rd mill. BC (Chapter 8). The capacity of these balances is evident in terms such as "one-talent balance" and "30-mina balance" (Ur III). In contrast, the "balance to weigh out silver" likely represented the handheld type of balance without the base to place it on the surface. The main discovery of this chapter is that certain types of balances were used to measure certain types of goods, which allows the term "standard" to be used not only in the case of stone weights.

The issue of agency in the weighing practice and the localization of these agents in terms of "households" is dealt with in Chapter 9. This phenomenon had two sides: (a) the social one and (b) the operational one. The data allow a distinction to be drawn between (a) those who needed the goods to be weighed and (b) those who weighed these goods as their "job."

The first group of agents included the administrators of the central households who were in charge of supervising the issue and receipt of goods in and out of these organizations. Another group of people who needed weighing were those in the context of private economic transactions: sellers and buyers of land, houses, slaves, etc. Naturally, their interest in weighing was "egoistic": They needed to know whether or not they were paying too much or receiving enough.

The group of operational agents only rarely appears in script. The sources tend mostly to conceal the identity of the actual weighmasters. These people were professionals for whom the knowledge of the practice of weighing was part of their trade: mostly merchants and smiths. There are limited data indicating that officials operated weights and balances as well. The synthesis of these data suggests the social dichotomy of "illiterate vs. literate" and "production and trade vs. administration." It shows that weighing did not require literacy or direct involvement in the central households. This leads to the theoretical conclusion that weighing as a socioeconomic phenomenon did not necessitate any sort of central political authority and grew out of everyday practices such as trade and metalworking: Weighing did not require a "state," it required a buyer and a seller. The role of "authority" is mainly seen in the constant attempts to "standardize" the mass, the writing, and the weighing practices for the sake of uniformity, accountability, and control over goods and people who received them.

Written data are mostly nonexistent or very biased regarding the question of what the loci of weighing were, and where the weighing took place. Since all our data are from the archives of temple and palace households, they portray weighing as largely a "state" affair. Although the archaeological evidence of the weighing gear in private houses may be interpreted as officials weighing goods "at home," it is certain that weighing was not ghettoized in the palaces and temples. Merchants travelled abroad and between the cities with their portable scales and weights.

The question of what kinds of goods were originally measured by weight ("core goods") is addressed in Chapter 10. Its conclusions straightforwardly and unambiguously identify metals (primarily copper and silver, but also tin, lead, and other additives as well as gold), luxurious high-value goods, and wool as the goods whose mensuration led to the emergence of weighing. The selection of these materials and their use in the economy and society allows the identification of a number of factors in the origins of the weighing in early Mesopotamia.

The clearly visible factor was the interregional trade in metals and luxury goods. It is a well-known fact that metals were unavailable in southern Mesopotamian alluvium. The need for copper and additives to produce various bronzes was linked to the production of reliable tools and vessels.

Additionally, the elites longed for luxury goods that, due to their high value, were measured by weight. Luxury goods have been crucial in the emergence of the early Mesopotamian civilization. As Robert McCormick Adams accurately puts it, luxuries and exotics heightened the significance of rituals and enhanced elite status and detached social hierarchies from purely local levels of interaction.[791] Therefore, weighing was a mechanism that has contributed to the creation of elites and hierarchical socioeconomic order in early Mesopotamia. Another interesting aspect that requires emphasis and further research is the fact that most luxury goods sent as presents within and outside Sumer were measure by weight (jewelry, garments, etc.): Luxurious weighed goods created and cemented regional and international political networks.

The centralized production of wool and textiles in the central households of 3rd mill. BC Mesopotamia marks the turn of the economies of these households from a tributary (receiving from individual producers as obligations) to an *oikos* economy (organizing labor and collecting raw materials, producing, redistributing finished products). A reliable weighing practice was necessary to record the inputs and outputs of raw and finished goods *within* these households. Despite the axiomatic opinion of the scholarly community on the importance of the export of textiles produced in Sumer to other regions of the Near East, we do not have any substantial written evidence of the early 3rd mill. BC corroborating it.[792] This dismisses a hypothesis that weighing could have appeared as a result of the trade in textiles and garments.

The final factor that definitely influenced the emergence of weighing was also an internal one: the use of metals as *money*. The earliest written data on the use of copper around 2800 suggest its use as a value substitute for other goods. Extensively used as a form of money during the ED IIIa period (ca. 2600 BC), copper gradually ceded its position to silver, which became abundant during the Sargonic and Ur III periods. Both copper and silver were not fiat but monies with intrinsic value: Their value was identical to their value as materials for producing, say, tools and jewelry. The fluctuation in prices of copper and silver throughout the 3rd mill. BC attests to a gradual inflation of these

791 Adams 2001: 353.
792 See Laursen and Steinkeller 2017: 71–78 for the export of textiles during the Ur III period.

"natural monies." The weight measures "mina" and "shekel" and their numbers played a role equivalent to notes in the modern paper money.

The value of metals and the frequency of the attestations of a metal with a specific measure in the written data indicate that the "correct" mina of ca. 480–510 g must have been that originally related for the measurement of, and payment in, copper. In contrast, the smaller unit of ca. 8.3 g "shekel" was ideal for transactions with silver.

These individual conclusions lead to an understanding of how weighing *established value* and shaped society.

The concept of value in this context includes the subjects (interested parties, agents) on the one hand and the objects (weighed goods) on the other. Taking the example of the economy of the central households, their administrators were the subjects who required the weighing of goods as the means of accounting, responsibility, and control. From the standpoint of the recipients of the wool allocations or the payers of irrigation taxes in silver, weighing represented an essential economic practice as well. Weight measures and weighing were the "language" that defined how much wool they would receive to produce clothes to cover their backs and how much silver they needed to pay. Weighing is articulating value.

In the context of the economy of private households, weighing helped to maintain the economic relationships between sellers and buyers since purchases of land, houses, and slaves were performed with "expensive" metallic monies. The evolution of payment throughout the 3rd mill. BC shows the growing role of silver, which by the end of the 3rd mill. had become the money par excellence.

These considerations answer the question of how weighing shaped the society. Originally linked to several economic practices, such as trade in metals and accounting of wool in temple and palace households, weighing became an integral part of the economic and social life in early Mesopotamia. It maintained the economic relationships between individuals and their groups. It provided certain goods with their exact value in the eyes of these people. The trajectory of the development of the society in Mesopotamian cities of the 3rd mill. BC would have been completely different without the economic practice of weighing.

Although this study provides explanations regarding many previously obscure economic phenomena, we still lack two important prerequisites to arrive at a clear understanding of weighing in early Mesopotamia. The first concerns written sources from the first quarter of the 3rd mill. BC: their number, state of preservation, and the related factor of their historical eloquence remains unsatisfactory. Discovery of a considerable number of cuneiform documents excavated in the "Early Dynastic I–II" levels of Sumerian cities would clarify the remaining enigmas and uncertainties and refine the conclusions of this study.

Which brings us to the second point, the need for new archaeological excavations in southern Iraq, whose aim should be twofold: First, to yield the above-mentioned cuneiform tablets; second, there is still a lack of datable stone weights from Sumerian cities of the early 3rd mill. BC. The establishment of their context, date, and masses is another *sine qua non* for a comprehensive understanding of the origins of the weighing in early Mesopotamia.

Bibliography

Adams, Robert McC. 2001. "Complexity in Archaic States." *Journal of Anthropological Archaeology* 20: 345–360.

Algaze, Guillermo. 2005. *The Uruk World System. The Dynamics of Expansion of Early Mesopotamian Civilization*. Second Edition. Chicago: Chicago University Press.

Algaze, Guillermo. 2008. *Ancient Mesopotamia at the Dawn of Civilization. The Evolution of an Urban Landscape*. Chicago and London: University of Chicago Press.

Alster, Bendt. 1997. *Proverbs of Ancient Sumer: The World's Earliest Proverb Collections. Vol. 1.* Bethesda, MD: CDL Press.

Alster, Bendt. 2005. *Wisdom of Ancient Sumer*. Bethesda, MD: CDL Press.

Archi, Alfonso. 1987. "Reflections on the system of weights from Ebla" (and) "Weights found during 1981–1983 seasons." Pp. 47–89 in *Eblaitica: Essays on the Ebla archives and Eblaite language, Vol. I*, ed. by C. H. Gordon, G. A. Rendsburg, and N. H. Winter. Winona Lake, IN: Eisenbrauns.

Archi, Alfonso. 1988. "Zur Organization der Arbeit in Ebla." Pp. 131–138 in *Wirtschaft und Gesellschaft von Ebla. Akten der Internationalen Tagung, Heidelberg 4.-7. November 1986.* Heidelberger Studien zum Alten Orient Bd. 2, ed. by H. Waetzoldt and H. Hauptmann. Heidelberg: Heidelberger Orientverlag.

Archi, Alfonso. 2015. *Ebla and Its Archives. Texts, History, and Society*. Studies in Ancient Near Eastern Records 7. Boston/Berlin: De Gruyter.

Archi, Alfonso. 2017a. "Lapis Lazuli and Shells from Mari to Ebla." Pp. 34–47 in *Overturning Certainties in Near Eastern Archaeology. A Festschrift in Honor of K. Aslihan Yener*, ed. by Ç. Maner, M. T. Horowitz, and A. S. Gilbert. Leiden/Boston: Brill.

Archi, Alfonso. 2017b. "Metals in Third Millennium B.C. Standpoint Ebla." Pp. 163–172 in *Movements, Resources, Interactions. Proceedings of the 2nd Kültepe International Meeting. Kültepe, 26–30* July *2015*, Subartu XXXIX, ed. by F. Kulakoğlu and G. Barjamovich. Turnhout: Brepols.

Ascalone, Enrico, and Luca Peyronel. 1999. "Typological and Quantitative Approach to the Ancient Weight Systems. Susa, Persian Gulf and Indus Valley from the End of the III. Mill. to the Beginning of the II Mill. BC." *Altorientalische Forschungen* 26(2): 352–376.

Ascalone, Enrico and Luca Peyronel. 2006a. *I pesi da bilancia del Bronzo Antico e del Bronzo Recente*. Materiali e Studi Archeologici di Ebla VII, Rome: Missione Archeologica Siria.

Ascalone, Enrico and Luca Peyronel. 2006b. "Early Bronze IVA weights at Tell Mardikh-Ebla. Archaeological associations and contexts." Pp. 49–70 in *Weights in Context. Bronze Age Weighing Systems of Eastern Mediterranean: Chronology, Typology, Material and Archaeological Contexts. Proceedings of the International Colloquium. Rome, 22nd – 24th November 2004*, Studi e materiali 13, ed. by M. E. Alberti et al. Rome: Istituto Italiano di Numismatica.

Attinger, Pascal. 2005. "A propos de AK 'faire' (II)." Review of Å.W. Sjöberg et al., The Sumerian Dictionary of the University Museum of the University of Pennsylvania. Vol. 1 A Part III (Philadelphia 1998). *Zeitschrift für Assyriologie und Vordearasiatische Archäologie* 95: 208–275.

Bartash, Vitali. 2013a. *Miscellaneous Early Dynastic and Sargonic Texts in the Cornell University Collection*. Cornell University Studies in Assyriology and Sumerology 23. Bethesda, MD: CDL Press.

https://doi.org/10.1515/9781501510267-012

Bartash, Vitali. 2013b. Review of G. Chambon, Normes et pratiques. L'homme, la mesure et l'écriture en Mésopotamie (Gladbeck: PeWe-Verlag, 2011). *Bibliotheca Orientalis* LXX 3/4: 422–424.

Bartash, Vitali. 2015a. "New Texts from the Early Dynastic I-II Period." Review article of Camille Lecompte, Archaic Tablets and Fragments from Ur from L. Woolley's Excavations at the Royal Cemetery. Nisaba 25. Messina: DiCAM, 2013. *Rivista degli Studi Orientali* LXXXVIII: 119–127.

Bartash, Vitali. 2015b. "On Sumerian City UB-me^{ki}, the Alleged "Umma."" *Cuneiform Digital Library Bulletin* 2015:002: 1–7.

Bartash, Vitali. 2017a. *Sumerian Administrative and Legal Documents ca. 2900–2200 BC in the Schøyen Collection.* Cornell University Studies in Assyriology and Sumerology 35. Bethesda, MD: CDL Press.

Bartash, Vitali. 2017b. "Supervision over Weighing in Early Dynastic and Sargonic Mesopotamia." Pp. 79–87 in *Private and State in the Ancient Near* East. *Proceedings of the 58th Rencontre Assyriologique Internationale at Leiden 16–20 July 2012*, ed. by: R. de Boer and J. G. Dercksen. Winona Lake, IN: Eisenbrauns.

Bauer, Josef. 1989/1990. "Altsumerische Wirtschaftsurkunden in Leningrad." *Archiv für Orientforschung* 36/37: 76–91.

Becker, Cornelia et al. 2016. "The Textile Revolution. Research into the Origin and Spread of Wool Production between Near East and Central Europe." *eTopoi, Journal for Ancient Studies*. Special Volume 6: Space and Knowledge: 102–151. [http://journal.topoi.org]

Biga, Maria G. 2010. "Textiles in the administrative texts of the royal archives of Ebla (Syria, 24th century BC) with particular emphasis on coloured textiles." Pp. 146–172 in *Textile Terminologies in the Ancient Near* East *and Mediterranean from the Third to the First Millennia BC*, ed. by C. Michel and M.-L. Nosch. Oxford and Oakville: Oxbow Books.

Brunke, Hagan and Walther Sallaberger. 2010. "Aromata für Duftöl." Pp. 41–74 in *Why Should Someone Who Knows Something Conceal It? Cuneiform Studies in Honor of David I.* Owen *on his 70th Birthday*, ed. by A. Kleinerman and J. M. Sasson. Bethesda, MD: CDL Press.

Carter, Robert. 2013. "The Sumerians and the Gulf." Pp. 579–599 in *The Sumerian World*, ed. by H. Crawford. London/New York: Routledge.

Cavigneaux, Antoine. 1992. "LUL-bi = lib-bi." *Nouvelles Assyriologiques Brèves et Utilitaires* 1992 no. 109: 82.

Chambon, Gregory. 2006. "Weights in the documentation from Mari: The issue of the norm." Pp. 185–202 in *Weights in Context. Bronze Age Weighing Systems of Eastern Mediterranean: Chronology, Typology, Material and Archaeological Contexts. Proceedings of the International Colloquium. Rome, 22nd-24th November 2004*, ed. by M. E. Alberti et al. Rome: Istituto Italiano di Numismatica.

Chambon, Gregory. 2011. *Normes et pratiques. L'homme, la mesure et l'écriture en Mésopotamie. I. Les mesures de capacité et de poids en Syrie Ancienne, d'Ébla à Émar.* Berliner Beiträge zum Vorderen Orient 21. Gladbeck: PeWe Verlag.

Charvát, Petr. 2014. "Lambs of the Gods. The Beginnings of the Wool Economy in Proto-Cuneiform Texts." Pp. 79–93 in *Wool Economy in the Ancient Near* East *and The Aegean. From the Beginnings of Sheep Husbandry to Institutional Textile Industry*, ed. by C. Breniquet and C. Michel. Oxford: Oxbow Books.

Civil, Miguel. 1968. "Išme-Dagan and Enlil's Chariot." *Journal of the American Oriental Society* 88(1): 3–14.

Civil, Miguel. 1982. "Studies in Early Dynastic lexicography I." *Oriens Antiquus* 21: 1–26.

Civil, Miguel. 1987a. "Feeding Dumuzi's sheep: The lexicon as a source of literary inspiration." Pp. 37–55 in *Language, Literature, and History: Philological and Historical Studies Presented to Erica Reiner*. American Oriental Series 67, ed. by F. Rochberg-Halton. New Haven: American Oriental Society.

Civil, Miguel. 1987b. Review of A. Alberti and F. Pomponio, Pre-Sargonic and Sargonic texts from Ur edited in UET 2 Supplement (Studia Pohl: Series Maior 13). *Aula Orientalis* 5(2): 313–314.

Civil, Miguel. 1987c. "Sumerian riddles: A corpus." *Aula Orientalis* 5(1): 17–37.

Civil, Miguel. 1994. *The Farmer's Instructions. A Sumerian Agricultural Manual.* Sabadel/ Barcelona: Editorial AUSA.

Civil, Miguel. 2007. "Early Semitic loanwords in Sumerian." Pp. 11–44 in *Studies presented to Robert D. Biggs, June 4, 2004*, ed. by M. T. Roth et al. Chicago: Oriental Institute of the University of Chicago.

Civil, Miguel. 2008. *The Early Dynastic Practical Vocabulary A (Archaic HAR-ra A)*. Archivi Reali di Ebla. Studi 4. Rome: Università di Roma "La Sapienza."

Civil, Miguel. 2011. "The Law Collection of Ur-Namma." Pp. 221–286 in *Cuneiform Royal Inscriptions and Related Texts in the Schøyen Collection*, ed. by A. R. George. Cornell University Studies in Assyriology and Sumerology 17. Bethesda, MD: CDL Press.

Civil, Miguel. 2013. "Remarks on AD-GI$_4$ (a.k.a. "Archaic Word List C" or "Tribute")." *Journal of Cuneiform Studies* 65: 13–67.

Crawford, Harriet E. W. 1973. "Mesopotamia's Invisible Exports in the Third Millennium B.C." *World Archaeology* 5(2): 232–241.

Cripps, Eric. L. 2007. *Land Tenure and Social Stratification in Ancient Mesopotamia. Third Millennium Sumer Before the Ur III Dynasty*. BAR International Series 1676. Oxford: Archeopress.

Cripps, Eric. L. 2010. *Sargonic and Presargonic Texts in the World Museum Liverpool*. BAR International Series 2135. Oxford: Archaeopress.

D'Agostino, Franco, and Francesca Gorello. 2013. "The Control of Copper and Bronze Objects in Umma During the Ur III Period." Pp. 251–265 in *From the 21st Century B.C. to the 21st Century A.D. Proceedings of the International Conference on Sumerian Studies Held in Madrid, 22–24 July 2010*, ed. by S. Garfinkle and M. Molina. Winona Lake, IN: Eisenbrauns.

Damerow, Petr, Robert K. Englund, and Hans J. Nissen. 1988. "Die ersten Zahldarstellungen und die Enwicklung des Zahlbegruffs." *Spektrum der Wissenschaft*, März 1988: 46–55.

De Maaijer, Remco D., and Bram Jagersma. 2003/2004. Review of Sjöber, A.W. et al. The Sumerian Dictionary of the University of Pennsylvania. Vol 1: Part III. (Philadelphia 1998). *Archiv für Orientforschung* 50: 351–355.

Derksen, Jan G. 1996. *The Old Assyrian Copper Trade in Anatolia*. PIHANS 75. Leiden: Nederlands Historisch-Archaeologisch Instituut te Istanbul.

Edzard, Dietz O. 1968. *Sumerische Rechtsurkunden des III. Jahrtausends aud der Zeit vor der III. Dynastie von Ur*. München: Bayerische Akademie der Wissenschaften.

Edzard, Dietz O., Gertrud Farber, and Edmond Sollberger. 1977. *Die Orts- und Gewässernamen der präsagronischen und sargonichen Zeit*. Répertoire Géographique des Textes Cunéiformes I. Wiesbaden: Dr. L. Reichert Verlag.

Ellison, Rosemary. 1981. "Diet in Mesopotamia: The Evidence of the Barley Ration Texts (*c*. 3000–1400 B.C.)." *Iraq* XLIII: 35–45.

Englund, Robert K. 1990. *Organisation and Verwaltung der Ur III-Fischerei*. Berliner Beiträge zum Vorderen Orient 10. Berlin: B. Reimer.

Englund, Robert K. 1992. "Ur III Sundries." *Acta Sumerologica* 14: 77–102.

Englund, Robert K. 1998. "Texts from the Late Uruk Period." Pp. 15–233 in J. Bauer, R. K. Englund, and M. Krebernik, *Mesopotamien. Späturuk-Zeit und Frühdynastische Zeit*. Orbis Bibilicus et Orientalis 160/1. Göttingen: Vanderhoeck & Ruprecht / Freiburg, Schweiz: Universitätsverlag.

Englund, Robert K. 2001. "Grain accounting practices in Archaic Mesopotamia." Pp. 1–35 in *Changing Views on Ancient Near Eastern Mathematics*. Berliner Beiträge zum Vorderen Orient 19, ed. by J. Høyrup and P. Damerow. Berlin: D. Reimer Verlag.

Englund, Robert K. 2004. "Proto-cuneiform account-books and journals." Pp. 23–46 in *Creating Economic Order: Record-keeping, Standardization and the Development of Accounting in the Ancient Near East*, ed. by C. Wunsch and M. Hudson. Bethesda, MD: CDL Press.

Fink, Sebastian. 2016. "War or Wool? Means of Ensuring Resource-Supply in 3rd Millennium Mesopotamia." Pp. 79–92 in *Textiles, Trade and Theories: From the Ancient Near East to the Mediterranean*, ed. by K. Droß-Krüpe and M.-L. Nosch. Münster: Ugarit-Verlag.

Firth, Richard. 2011. "A Discussion of the Use of im-babbar$_2$ by the Craft Workers of Ancient Mesopotamia." *Cuneiform Digital Library Journal* 2011:2: 1–9.

Firth, Richard, and Marie-Louise Nosch. 2012. "Spinning and Weaving Wool in Ur III Administrative Texts." *Journal of Cuneiform Studies* 64: 65–82.

Forest, Jean-Daniel. 2005. "The State: The Process of State Formation as Seen from Mesopotamia." Pp. 184–206 in *Archaeologies of the Middle East. Critical Perspectives*, ed. by S. Pollock and R. Bernbeck. Malden/Oxford/Victoria: Blackwell.

Foster, Benjamin R. 1982a. *Administration and Use of Institutional Land in Sargonic Sumer*. Mesopotamia 9. Copenhagen: Akademisk Forlag.

Foster, Benjamin R. 1982b. "A postscript to the 'Letter of Gilgamesh'." *Anatolian Studies* 32: 43–44.

Foster, Benjamin R. 1982c. *Umma in the Sargonic Period*. Hamden: Archon Books.

Foster, Benjamin R. 1983. "Selected business documents from Sargonic Mesopotamia." *Journal of Cuneiform Studies* 35: 147–175.

Foster, Benjamin R. 1997. "A Sumerian Merchant's Account of the Dilmun Trade." *Acta Sumerologica* 19: 53–62.

Foster, Benjamin R. 2010. "Clothing in Sargonic Mesopotamia: Visual and Written evidence." Pp. 110–145 in *Textile Terminologies in the Ancient Near East and Mediterranean from the Third to the First Millennia BC*, ed. by C. Michel and M.-L. Nosch. Oxford and Oakville: Oxbow Books.

Foster, Benjamin R. 2016. *The Age of Agade. Inventing Empire in Ancient Mesopotamia*. New York: Routledge.

Foxvog, Daniel. 1980. "Funerary Furnishings in an Early Sumerian Text from Adab." Pp. 67–75 in *Death in Mesopotamia. Papers read at the XXVIe Rencontre Assyriologique Internationale*. Mesopotamia 8, ed. by B. Alster. Copenhagen: Akademisk Forlag.

Frayne, Douglas. 1992. *The Early Dynastic List of Geographical Names*. Americal Oriental Series 74. New Haven: American Oriental Society.

Frayne, Douglas. 1997. *The Royal Inscriptions of Mesopotamia. Early periods, Vol. 3/2: Ur III Period (2112–2004 BC)*. Toronto, Buffalo, London: University of Toronto Press.

Friberg, Jöran. 1990. "Mathematik." in *Reallexikon der Assyriologie und Vorderasiatischen Archäologie 7*: 531–585.

Friberg, Jöran. 1999. "Counting and Accounting in the Proto-Literate Middle East: Examples from Two New Volumes of Proto-Cuneiform Texts." *JCS* 51: 107–137.

Friberg, Jöran. 2005. "On the Alleged Counting with Sexagesimal Place Value Numbers in Mathematical Cuneiform Texts from the Third Millennium BC." *Cuneiform Digital Library Journal* 2005:2: 1–23.

Friberg, Jöran. 2007. *A Remarkable Collection of Babylonian Mathematical Texts*. Manuscripts in the Schøyen Collection: Cuneiform Texts I. New York: Springer.

Goetze, Albrecht. 1946. "Number Idioms in Old Babylonian." *Journal of Near Eastern Studies* 5(3): 185–202.

Gomi, Tohru. 1993. "A Note on gur, a Capacity Unit of the Ur III Period." *Zeitschrift für Assyriologie und Vorderasiatische Archäologie* 83(1): 31–41.

Gyllenbok, Jan. 2018. *Encyclopaedia of Historical Metrology, Weights, and Measures*. Vol. 2. Basel: Birkhäuser.

Hafford, William B. 2005. "Mesopotamian Mensuration Balance Pan Weights from Nippur." *Journal of the Economic and Social History of the Orient* 48(3): 345–387.

Hallo, William W. 1996. *Origins. The Near Eastern Background of Some Modern Western Institutions*. Studies in the History and Culture of the Ancient Near East VI. Leiden/New York/Köln: Brill.

Heimpel, Wolfgang. 1981. "The Nanshe Hymn." *Journal of Cuneiform Studies* 33(2): 65–139.

Heimpel, Wolfgang. 1987. "Das Untere Meer." *Zeitschrift für Assyriologie und Vorderasiatische Archäologie* 77: 22–91.

Heimpel, Wolfgang. 1998. "Netz. A. Philologisch." *Reallexikon der Assyriologie und Vorderasiatischen Archäologie* 9: 235–239.

Heimpel, Wolfgang. 2009. *Workers and Construction Work at Garšana*. Cornell University Studies in Assyriology and Sumerology 5. Bethesda, MD: CDL Press.

Heimpel, Wolfgang. 2011. "Twenty-Eight Trees Growing in Sumer." Pp. 75–152 in *Garšana Studies*, Cornell University Studies in Assyriology and Sumerology 6, ed. by David I. Owen. Bethesda, MD: CDL Press.

Helwing, Barbara. 2014. "Silver in the Early State Societies of Greater Mesopotamia." Pp. 411–421 in *Metalle der Macht – Frühes Gold und Silber. Metals of Power – Early gold and silver. 6. Mitteldeutscher Archäologentag vom 17. bis 19. Oktober 2013 in Halle (Salle)*, ed. by H. Meller, R. Risch, and E. Pernicka. Halle (Salle): Landesmuseum für Vorgeschichte.

Hudson, Michael. 2004. "The Development of Money-of-Account in Sumer's Temples." Pp. 303–329 in *Creating Economic Order: Record-keeping, Standardization and the Development of Accounting in the Ancient Near East*, ed. by C. Wunsch and M. Hudson. Bethesda, MD: CDL Press.

Hudson, Michael. 2015. "How the Organization of Labor Shaped Civilization's Takeoff." Pp. 649–664 in *Labor in the Ancient World*, ed. by P. Steinkeller and M. Hudson. Dresden: ISLET.

Jagersma, Abraham H. 2010. *A Descriptive Grammar of Sumerian*. Ph.D. thesis, the University of Leiden.

Jendritzki, Gert and Lutz Martin. 2018. "Ein bronzenes Rollsiegel aus dem Bīt Rēš in Uruk/Warka." *Mitteilungen der Deutschen Orient-Gesellschaft* 150: 7–18: 96–112.

Joannès, Frances. 1993–1997. "Metalle und Metallurgie. A. I. In Mesopotamien."*Reallexikon der Assyriologie und Vorderasiatischen Archäologie* 8: 96–112.

Joannès, Frances. 2010. "Silber." *Reallexikon der Assyriologie und Vorderasiatischen Archäologie* 12: 486–491.

Jursa, Michael. 2009. "Die Kralle des Meeres und andere Aromata." Pp. 147–180 in *Philologisches und Historisches zwischen Anatolien und Sokotra. Analecta Semitica in Memoriam Alexander Sima*, ed. by W. Arnold et al. Wiesbaden: Harrassowitz.

Ingham, Geoffrey. 2004. *The Nature of Money*. Cambridge: Polity Press.

Kalla, Gabor. 1998. "Nachlass B. Altbabylonisch." *Reallexikon der Assyriologie und Vorderasiatischen Archäologie* 9: 36–42.

Kaniuth, Kai. 2006. *Metallobjekte der Bronzezeit aus Nordbaktrien*. Archäologie in Iran und Turan 6. Mainz: Ph. von Zabern.

Karahashi, Fumi. 2000. *Sumerian Compound Verbs with Body-Part Terms*. Ph.D. thesis, University of Chicago.

Karwiese, Stefan. 1990. "Šiqlu, kite uns Stater. Der Weg zu einer neuen Metrologie des Altertums. I. Mesopotamien." *Res Orientales* II: 9–117.

Kienast, Burkhart. 2001. *Historische Semitische Sprachwissenschaft*. Wiesbaden: Harrassowitz.

Kisch, Bruno. 1965. *Scales and Weights. A Historical Outline*. Yale Studies in the History of Science and Medicine. New Haven: Yale University Press.

Kletter, Raz. 2009. "Weights and Measures." Pp. 831–841 in *New Interpreter's Dictionary of the Bible*, Vol. 5, ed. by K. Doob Sakenfeld. Nashville, TN: Abingdon Press.

Krebernik, Manfred. 1998. "Die Texte aus Fāra und Tell Abū Ṣalābīh." Pp. 237–430 in J. Bauer, R. K. Englund, and M. Krebernik, *Mesopotamien. Späturuk-Zeit und Frühdynastische Zeit*. Orbis Bibilicus et Orientalis 160/1. Göttingen: Vanderhoeck & Ruprecht / Freiburg, Schweiz: Universitätsverlag.

Krebernik, Manfred. 2016. "Etymological and Historical Problems Concerning Akkadian *tamkāru* 'merchant'." Pp. 119–129 in *Babel und Bibel 9. Proceedings of the 6th Biennial Meeting of the International Association for Comparative Semitics and Other Studies*, ed. by L. Kogan et al. Winona Lake, IN: Eisenbrauns.

Krebernik, Manfred, Horst Steible, and Fatma Yildiz. 2014. "Prä-Fāra-zeitliche Texte aus Fāra." Pp. in: 327–82 in *Studies in Sumerian Language and Literature. Festschrift Joachim Krecher*, Babel und Bibel 8, ed. by N. V. Koslova, E. Vizirova and G. Zolyomi. Winona Lake, IN.: Eisenbrauns.

Krispijn, Theo. 2016. "Early Silver: Thoughts About the Sign KU_3 in the Earliest Documents from Uruk." Pp. 1–10 in *Silver, Money and Credit. A Tribute to Robartus J. van der Spek on the Occasion of his 65th Birthday on 18th September 2014*, PIHANS 128, ed. by K. Kleber and R. Pirngruber. Leiden: Nederlands Instituut voor het Nabije Oosten.

Kulakoğlu, Fikri. 2017. "Balance Stone Weights and Scale-Pans from Kültepe-Kanesh: On One of the Basic Elements of the Old Assyrian Trading System." Pp. 341–402 in *Overturning Certainties in Near Eastern Archaeology. A Festschrift in Honor of K. Aslıhan Yener*, CHANE 90, ed. by Ç. Maner, M. T. Horowitz, and A. S. Gilbert. Leiden/Boston: Brill.

Lambert, Maurice. 1979. "Grand document juridique de Nippur du temps de Ur-zag-è, roi d'Uruk." *Revue d'Assyriologie et d'Archéologie Orientale* 73: 1–22.

Laursen, Steffen and Piotr Steinkeller. 2017. *Babylonia, the Gulf Region, and the Indus Archaeological and Textual Evidence for Contact in the Third and Early Second Millennia B.C.* Winona Lake, IN: Eisenbrauns.

Lecompte, Camille. 2014. See Nisaba 25.

Lehmann, Ulrich. 2016. *^{d}Šára-ì-sa$_6$ und ur-ba-gára. Untersuchungen zu den Verwaltungstexten der neusumerischen Lagaš II-Periode aus Ĝirsu*. Alter Orient und Altes Testament 420. Münster: Ugarit-Verlag.

Maekawa, Kazuya. 1990. "Cultivation methods in the Ur III Period." *Bulletin on Sumerian Agriculture* 5: 115–145.

Maekawa, Kazuya. 1996. “Confiscation of Private Properties in the Ur III Period: A Study of é-dul-la and níg-GA.” *Acta Sumerologica* 18: 103–168.

Maekawa, Kazuya. 1997. “Confiscation of Private Properties in the Ur III Period: A Study of é-dul-la and níg-GA (2). Supplement 1.” *Acta Sumerologica* 19: 273–291.

Maekawa, Kazuya. 1998. “Ur III Ĝirsu Records of Labor Forces in the British Museum (1).” *Acta Sumerologica* 20: 63–110.

Maiocchi, Massimo. 2005. “Sul valore ponderale del siclo “DILMUN” nei testi di Ebla.” *KASKAL* 2: 43–53.

Maiocchi, Massimo. 2015. “From Stylus to Sign: A Sketch of Old Akkadian Palaeography.” Pp. 71–88 in *Current Research in Cuneiform Palaeography Proceedings of the Workshop Organised at the 60th Rencontre Assyriologique Internationale, Warsaw 2014*, ed. by E. Devecchi, G. G. W. Müller, and J. Mynářová. Gladbeck: PeWe-Verlag.

Maiocchi, Massimo. 2016. “Women and Production in Sargonic Adab.” Pp. 90–111 in *The Role of Women in Work and Society in the Ancient Near East*, ed. by B. Lion and C. Michel. Studies in Ancient Near Eastern Records 13. Boston/Berlin: De Gruyter.

Marchesi, Gianni. 2015. “Toward a Chronology of Early Dynastic Rulers in Mesopotamia.” Pp. 139–156 in *Associated Regional Chronologies for the Ancient Near East and the Eastern Mediterranean*, ed. by W. Sallaberger and I. Schrakamp. ARCANE 3. History & Philology. Turnhout: Brepols.

Marzahn, Joachim, and Hans Neumann. 1995. “Eine altsumerische Urkunde aus Girsu über Silberzahlungen.” *Altorientalische Forschungen* 22(1): 110–116.

McCorriston, Joy. 1977. “Textile Extensification, Alienation, and Social Stratification in Ancient Mesopotamia.” Current Anthropology 38: 517–549.

McDonald, Daniel M. 1992. *The Origins of Metrology. Collected Papers of Dr. Daniel McLean McDonald*, ed. by Ch. Scarre. Cambridge: McDonald Institute for Archaeological Research.

Mederos, Alfredo, and Clifford C. Lamberg-Karlovsky. 2004. “Weight Systems and Trade Networks in the Old World (2500–1000 BC).” Pp. 199–214 in *Creating Economic Order. Record-keeping, Standardization, and the Development of Accounting in the Ancient Near East*, ed. by M. Hudson and C. Wunsch. Bethesda, MD: CDL Press.

Michalowski, Piotr. 1978. “Foreign Tribute to Sumer During the Ur III Period.” *Zeitschrift für Assyriologie und Vorderasiatische Archäologie* 68: 34–49.

Michalowski, Piotr. 1990. “The Shekel and the Vizier.” *Zeitschrift für Assyriologie und Vorderasiatische Archäologie* 80: 1–8.

Milano, Lucio. 2004. “Weight stones from Tell Beydar/Nabada.” *KASKAL* 1: 1–7.

Mille, Benoit, Roland Besenval, and David Bourgarit. 2004. “Frühes Gießen in verlorener Form in Baluchistan (Pakistan): das “Leopardengewicht” aus Shahi-Tump.” Pp. 274–281 in *Persiens Antike Pracht. Bergbau – Handwerk – Archäologie. Katalog der Ausstellung des Deutschen Bergbau-Museums Bochum vom 28. November 2004 bis 29 Mai 2005*, ed. by T. Stöllner, R. Slotta, and A. Vatandoust. Bochum: Deutsches Bergbau-Museum.

Molina, Manuel M. 1989. “Las piedras preciosas en los textos económicos de Ur de la tercera dinastía.” *Aula Orientalis* 7(1): 81–93.

Molina, Manuel M. 2014. See SCTRAH.

Monaco, Salvatore. 2012. “Loan and Interest in the Archaic Texts.” *Zeitschrift für Assyriologie und Vordearasiatische Archäologie* 102: 165–178.

Monaco, Salvatore and Francesco Pomponio. 2009. “L’impiego dell’argento nei testi mesopotamici dal periodo arcaico a quello paleoaccadico.” *Rivista di Storia Economica* 25: 19–50.

Moorey, Peter R. S. 1999. *Ancient Mesopotamian Materials and Industries. The Archaeological Evidence*. Winona Lake, IN: Eisenbrauns.

Muhly, James. 1993–1997. “Metalle. B. Archäologisch.” *Reallexikon der Assyriologie und Vorderasiatischen Archäologie* 8: 112–136.

Neumann, Hans. 2001. “Zu den Buchungseinträgen in den neusumerischen Handwerkerpräsenzlisten aus Ur.” Pp. 37–52 in *Changing Views on Ancient Near Eastern Mathematics*, ed. by J. Høyrup and P. Damerow. Berlin: D. Reimer Verlag.

Notizia, Palmiro, and Ingo Schrakamp. 2010. “Ein sargonischer Personenkauf aus dem British Museum, London (BM 103707).” *Altorientalische Forschungen* 37(2): 242–251.

Orel, Vladimir E., and Olga V. Stolbova. 1995. Hamito-Semitic *Etymological Dictionary. Materials for a Reconstruction*. Handbuch der Orientalistik. Erste Abteilung. Der Nahe und Mittlere Osten. 18. Band. Leiden: Brill.

Ouyang, Xiaoli. 2013. *Monetary Role of Silver and its Administration in Mesopotamia during the Ur III Period (c. 2112–2004 BCE). A Case Study of the Umma Province*. Biblioteca del Proximo Oriente Antiguo 11. Madrid: Consejo Superior de Investigaciones Cientificas.

Owen, David I. 2013. “Treasures of the Sacristy.” *Revue d’Assyriologie et d’Archéologie Orientale* 107: 29–42.

Paoletti, Paola. 2008. “Elusive Silver? Evidence for the Circulation of Silver in the Ur III State.” *KASKAL* 5: 127–158.

Paoletti, Paola. 2012. *Der König und sein Kreis. Das staatliche Schatzarchiv Der III. Dynastie von Ur*. Biblioteca del Proximo Oriente Antiguo 10. Madrid: Consejo Superior de Investigaciones Cientificas.

Paoletti, Paola. 2013. “The Manufacture of a Statue to Nanaja: Mesopotamian Jewelry-Making Techniques at the End of the Third Millennium B.C.” Pp. 333–345 in *From the 21st Century B.C. to the 21st Century A.D. Proceedings of the International Conference on Sumerian Studies Held in Madrid, 22–24 July 2010*, ed. by S. Garfinkle and M. Molina. Winona Lake, IN: Eisenbrauns.

Pasquali, Jacopo. 1997. “La terminologia semitica dei tessili nei testi di Ebla.” *Quaderni di Semitistica* 19: 217–270.

Parr, Peter A. 1974. “Ninḫilia: Wife of Ayakala, Governor of Umma.” *Journal of Cuneiform Studies* 26(2): 90–111.

Peterson, Jeremiah. 2018. “Thirty Shekels No More.” *Nouvelles Assyriologiques Brèves et Utilitaires* 2018/1: 3–4.

Pettinato, Giovanni. 1997. *L’uomo cominciò a scrivere. Iscrizioni cuneiformi della Collezione Michail. Catalogo della mostra (Milano, 29 ottobre–31 dicembre 1997)*. Milano: Electa.

Peyronel, Luca. 2014. “From Weighing Wool to Weaving Tools. Textile Manufacture at Ebla during the Early Syrian Period in the Light of Archaeological Evidence” Pp. 124–138 in *Wool Economy in the Ancient Near* East *and The* Aegean. *From the Beginnings of Sheep Husbandry to Institutional Textile Industry*, ed. by C. Breniquet and C. Michel. Oxford: Oxbow Books.

Peyronel, Luca. 2015. “Bronze Balance Pan from Southern Palace at Ebla.” *Studia Eblaitica* 1: 221–223.

Pollock, Susan. 1999. *Ancient Mesopotamia. The Eden that Never Was*. Cambridge: Cambridge University Press.

Postgate, J. Nicolas. 1992. *Early Mesopotamia: Society and Economy at the Dawn of History*. London: Routledge.

Pournelle, Jennifer. 2003. *Marshland of Cities: Deltaic Landscapes and the Evolution of Early Mesopotamian Civilization*. Ph.D. thesis, University of California, San Diego.

Powell, Marvin A. 1971. *Sumerian numeration and metrology*. Ph.D. thesis, University of Minnesota.

Powell, Marvin A. 1978. "A Contribution to the History of Money in Mesopotamia prior to the Invention of Coinage." Pp. 211–243 in *Festschrift Lubor Matouš*, vol 2, ed. by B. Hruška and G. Komoroczy. Budapest: Eötvös Loránd.

Powell, Marvin A. 1979. "Ancient Mesopotamian Weight Metrology: Methods, Problems and Perspectives." Pp. 71–109 in *Studies in honor of Tom B. Jones*, ed. by M. A. Powell and R. H. Sack. Alter Orient and Altes Testament 203. Kevelaer: Verlag Butzon & Bercker and Neukirchen-Vluyn: Neukirchener Verlag.

Powell, Marvin A. 1984. "Late Babylonian Surface Mensuration." *Archiv für Orientforschung* 31: 32–66.

Powell, Marvin A. 1990. "Masse und Gewichte." *Reallexikon der Assyriologie und Vorderasiatischen Archäologie* 7: 457–517.

Powell, Marvin A. 1992. "Timber production in Presargonic Lagaš." *Bulletin on Sumerian Agriculture* 6: 99–122.

Powell, Marvin A. 1996. "Money in Mesopotamia." *Journal of the Economic and Social History of the Orient* 39(3): 224–242.

Powell, Marvin A. 2000. "Gilgamesh's Elusive Thirty Shekels." Pp. 343–345 in *Assyriologica et Semitica. Festschrift für Joachim Oelsner anläßlich seines 65. Geburtstages am 18. Februar 1997*, ed. by J. Marzahn and H. Neumann. Münster: Ugarit-Verlag.

Prentice, Rosemary. 2010. *The Exchange of Goods and Services in Pre-Sargonic Lagash*. Alter Orient und Altes Testament 368. Münster: Ugarit-Verlag.

Proust, Christine. 2010. "Mesopotamian Metrological Lists and Tables: Forgotten Sources." Pp. 245–76 in *Looking at it from Asia: the Processes that Shaped the Sources of History of Science*, ed. by F. Bretelle-Establet. Boston Studies in the Philosophy of Science 265. New York: Springer.

Rahmstorf, Lorenz. 2006. "In search of the earliest balance weights, scales and weighing systems from the East Mediterranean, the Near and Middle East." Pp. 9–45 in *Weights in Context. Bronze Age Weighing Systems of Eastern Mediterranean: Chronology, Typology, Material and Archaeological Contexts. Proceedings of the International Colloquium. Rome, 22nd – 24th November 2004*, Studi e materiali 13, ed. by M. E. Alberti et al. Rome: Istituto Italiano di Numismatica.

Rahmstorf, Lorenz. 2010. "The concept of Weighing during the Bronze Age in the Aegean, the Near East and Europe." Pp. 88–105 in *The Archaeology of Measurement: Comprehending Heaven, Earth and Time in Ancient Societies*, ed. by I. Morley and C. Renfrew. Cambridge: Cambridge University Press.

Rahmstorf, Lorenz. 2014. "Early Balance Weights in Mesopotamia and Western Syria: Origin and Context." Pp. 427–441 in *Proceedings of the 8th International Congress on the Archaeology of the Ancient Near East, Warsaw, April 30th–May 4th 2012*, ed. by P. Bieliński et al. Wiesbaden: Harrassowitz.

Ratnagar, Shereen. 1981. *Encounters. The Waterly Trade of the Harappa Civilization*. Delhi: Oxford University Press.

Ratnagar, Shereen. 2003. "Theorizing Bronze-Age Intercultural Trade: The Evidence of the Weights." *Paléorient* 29(1): 79–92.

Reade, Julian. 2002. "The Early Iranian Stone 'weights' and an Unpublished Sumerian Foundation Deposit." *Iran 40*: 249–255.

Reiner, Erica, and Miguel Civil. 1967. "Another volume of Sultantepe Tablets." Review of O. R. Gurney and P. Hulin, The Sultantepe Tablets II (London 1964). *Journal of Near Eastern Studies* 26(3): 177–211.

Reiter, Karin. 1997. *Die Metalle im Alten Orient unter besonderer Berücksichtigung altbabylonischer Quellen*. Alter Orient und Altes Testament 249. Münster: Ugarit-Verlag.

Richter, Thomas. 2013. *Bibliographisches Glossar des Hurritischen*. Wiesbaden: Harrassowitz.

Roaf, Michael. 1982. "Weights of the Dilmun Standard." *Iraq* 44(2): 137–141.

Rubio, Gonzalo. 2016. "The Inventions of Sumerian: Literature and the Artifacts of Identity." Pp. 231–257 in *Problems of Canonicity and Identity Formation in Ancient Egypt and Mesopotamia*, ed. by K. Ryholt and G. Barjamovich. Copenhagen: University of Copenhagen, Museum Tusculanum Press.

Sallaberger, Walther. 1989. "Zum Schilfrohr als Rohstoff in Babylonian." Pp. 311–330 in *Der Orientalische Mensch und seine Beziehungen zur Umwelt. Beiträge zum 2. Grazer Morgenländischen Symposion (2.–5. März 1989)*, ed. by B. Scholz. Graz.

Sallaberger, Walther. 1994. Review of R. L. Zettler, The Ur III Temple of Inana at Nippur. Berliner Beiträge zum Vorderen Orient 11 (Berlin 1992). *Zeitschrift für Assyriologie und Vorderasiatische Archäologie* 84: 136–144.

Sallaberger, Walther. 1996a. *Der babylonische Töpfer und seine Gefässe*. Ghent: University of Ghent.

Sallaberger, Walther. 1996b. "Numbers and Metrology." Pp. 81–84 in *Administrative Documents from Tell Beydar (Seasons 1993–1995)*, ed. by F. Ismail, W. Sallaberger, Ph. Talon, and K. Van Lerberghe. Subartu 2. Turnhout: Brepols.

Sallaberger, Walther. 2004. "A Note on the Sheep and Goat Flocks. Introduction to Texts 151–167." Pp. 13–21 in *Third Millennium Cuneiform Texts from Tell Beydar*, ed. by L. Milano et al. Subartu 12. Turnhout: Brepols.

Sallaberger, Walther. 2014. "The Value of Wool in Early Bronze Age Mesopotamia. On the Control of Sheep and the Handling of Wool in the Presargonic to the Ur III Periods (c. 2400 to 2000 BC)." Pp. 94–114 in *Wool Economy in the Ancient Near East and Aegean. From the Beginning of Sheep Husbandry to Institutional Textile Industry*, ed. by C. Breniquet and C. Michel. Oxford/Philadelphia: Oxbow Books.

Sallaberger, Walther, and Ingo Schrakamp (eds.). 2015. *Associated Regional Chronologies for the Ancient Near East and the Eastern Mediterranean*. ARCANE 3. History & Philology. Turnhout: Brepols.

Schneider, Nicolaus. 1930. "Die Geschäftsurkunden aus Drehem und Djoha in den Staatlichen Museen (VAT) zu Berlin." *Orientalia Series Prior* 47–49.

Schrakamp, Ingo. 2006. "Kommentar zu der altakkadischen "Rüstkammerurkunde" Erm. 14380." Pp. 161–177 in *Babel und Bibel. Annual of Ancient Near Eastern, Old Testament, and Semitic Studies 3*, ed. by L. Kogan et al. Winona Lake, IN: Eisenbrauns.

Schrakamp, Ingo. 2012. "Zu den vor-Ur III-zeitlichen Keilschrifttexten des World Museum, Liverpool." *Journal of Cuneiform Studies* 64: 145–162.

Schrakamp, Ingo. 2013a. Review of CUSAS 11. *Journal of Cuneiform Studies* 65: 201–228.

Schrakamp, Ingo. 2013b. "Die "Sumerische Tempelstadt" heute. Die sozioökonomische Rolle eines Tempels in frühdynastischer Zeit." Pp. 445–465 in *Tempel im Alten Orient. 7. Internationales Colloquium der Deutschen Orient-Gesellschaft. 11.–13. Oktober 2009, München*, ed. by K. Kaniuth et al. Wiesbaden: Harrassowitz.

Schuster-Brandis, Anais. 2008. *Steine als Schutz- und Heilmittel. Untersuchung zu ihrer Verwendung in der Beschwörungskunst Mesopotamiens im 1. Jt. v. Chr.* Alter Orient und Altes Testament 46. Münster: Ugarit-Verlag.

Selz, Gebhard J. 1989. See FAOS 15/1.

Selz, Gebhard J. 1989/90. "Eine Urkude über Festgaben von Tempelverwaltern und anderen Notabeln aus dem Musée des Antiquités zu Rouen. (H.G. 12)." *Die Welt des Orients* 20/21: 35–44.

Selz, Gebhard J. 1993. See FAOS 15/2.

Selz, Gebhard J. 1995. "Der Wert des Fischmasses $EŠ_3$-ba-an." *Nouvelles Assyriologiques Brèves et Utilitaires* 1995 no. 118: 104–105.

Selz, Gebhard J. 1997. "TUN_3 = tun_3 bei Gudea." *Nouvelles Assyriologiques Brèves et Utilitaires* 1997 no. 36: 32–34.

Selz, Gebhard J. 2010. ""He put in order the accounts . . ." Remarks on the Early Dynastic Background of the Administrative Reorganizations in the Ur III State." Pp. 5–30 in *City Administration in the Ancient Near East. Proceedings of the 53e Rencontre Assyriologique Internationale*, Vol. 2, ed. by L. Kogan et al. Winona Lake, IN: Eisenbrauns.

Senior, Louise, and Harvey Weiss. 1992. "Tell Leilan 'Sila Bowls' and the Akkadian Reorganization of Subarian Agricultural Production." *Orient-Express* 2: 16–23.

Seri, Andrea. 2005. *Local Power in Old Babylonian Mesopotamia.* London: Equinox.

Sigrist, Marcel. 1983. *Textes économiques néo-sumériens de l'Université de Syracuse.* Paris: A.D.P.F.

Sjöberg, Åke W. 1965. Review of H. Limet, *Le travail du métal au pays de Sumer au temps de la IIIe dynastie d'Ur* (Paris, 1960). *Zeitschrift für Assyriologie und Vorderasiatische Archäologie* 55: 256–260.

Sjöberg, Åke W. 1988. "A Hymn to Inanna and Her Self-Praise." *Journal of Cuneiform Studies* 40: 165–186.

Sollberger, Edmond. 1948. "Documents cuneiforms au Musée d'art er d'histoire." *Genava* 26: 48–72.

Sollberger, Edmond. 1976. "Some Legal Documents of the Third Dynasty of Ur." Pp. 435–450 in *Kramer Anniversary Volume*, ed. by B. L. Eichler. Alter Orient und Altes Testament 25. Kevelaer: Verlag Butzon & Bercker.

Sommerfeld, Walter. 2006. "Die ältesten semitischen Sprachzeugnisse – eine kritische Bestandsaufnahme." Pp. 30–75 in *The Akkadian Language in Its Semitic* Context. *Studies in Akkadian of the Third and Second Millennium BC*, ed. by G. Deutscher and N. J. C. Kouwenberg. Leiden: Nederlands Instituut voor het Nabije Oosten.

Sommerfeld, Walter. 2012. "Hasselbach, Rebecca: Sargonic Akkadian. A Historical and Comparative Study of the Syllabic Texts. Ein Rezensionsartikel." *Wiener Zeitschrift für die Kunde des Morgenlandes* 102: 193–284.

Steible, Horst, and Fatma Yildiz. 1996. "Kupfer an ein Herdenamt in Šuruppak?" Pp. 149–159 in *Tablettes et images aux pays de Sumer et d'Akkad*: Mélanges offerts à Monsieur H. Limet, ed. by Ö. Tunca and D. Deheselle. Leuven: Peeters.

Stein, Peter. 2013. *Lehrbuch der sabäischen Sprache – 1. Tel: Grammatik.* Wiesbaden: Harrassowitz.

Steinkeller, Piotr. 1980. "Mattresses and Felt in Early Mesopotamia." *Oriens Antiquus* 19: 79–100.

Steinkeller, Piotr. 1981a. "The Renting of Fields in Early Mesopotamia and the Development of the Concept of 'Interest' in Sumerian." *Journal of the Economic and Social History of the Orient* 24(2): 113–145.

Steinkeller, Piotr. 1981b. "Studies in Third Millennium Paleography, 2. Signs ŠEN and ALAL." *Oriens Antiquus* 20: 243–249.

Steinkeller, Piotr. 1982a. "The Question of Marhaši: A Contribution to the Historical Geography of Iran in the Third Millennium B.C." *Zeitschrift für Assyriologie und Vorderasiatische Archäologie* 72: 237–265.

Steinkeller, Piotr. 1982b. "Two Sargonic Sale Documents Concerning Women." *Orientalia Nova Series* 51(3): 355–368.

Steinkeller, Piotr. 1986. "Seal of Išma-Ilum, Son of the Governor of Matar." *Vicino Oriente* 6: 27–40.

Steinkeller, Piotr. 1987a. "The Foresters of Umma: Toward a Definition of Ur III Labor." Pp. 73–115 *Labor in the Ancient Near East*, ed. by M. A. Powell. American Oriental Series 68. New Haven, CT: American Oriental Society.

Steinkeller, Piotr. 1987b. "On the Meaning of zabar-šu." *Acta Sumerologica* 9: 347–349.

Steinkeller, Piotr. 1987c. Review of B. R. Foster, Umma in the Sargonic Period (New Haven, 1982). *Wiener Zeitschrift für die Kunde des Morgenlandes* 77: 182–195.

Steinkeller, Piotr. 1989. *Sale documents of the Ur-III-Period. Freiburger Altorientalische Studien 17.* Wiesbaden: Franz Steiner Verlag.

Steinkeller, Piotr. 1991. "The Container *kabkūru*." *Nouvelles Assyriologiques Brèves et Utilitaires* 1991, no. 4: 3–4.

Steinkeller, Piotr. 1992. See MC 4.

Steinkeller, Piotr. 1995. Review of ZATU. *Bibliotheca Orientalis* 52(5/6): 689–713.

Steinkeller, Piotr. 2003. "An Ur III Manuscript of the Sumerian King List." Pp. 267–292 in *Literatur, Politik und Recht in Mesopotamien. Festschrift für Claus Wilcke*, ed. by W. Sallaberger, K. Volk, and A. Zgoll. Wiesbaden: Harrassowitz.

Steinkeller, Piotr. 2004a. "The Function of Written Documentation in the Administrative Praxis of Early Babylonia." Pp. 65–88 in *Creating Economic Order: Record-keeping, Standardization and the Development of Accounting in the Ancient Near East*, ed. by C. Wunsch and M. Hudson. Bethesda, MD: CDL Press.

Steinkeller, Piotr. 2004b. "Toward a Definition of Private Economic Activity in Third Millennium Babylonia." Pp. 91–111 in *Commerce and Monetary Systems in the Ancient* World. *Means of Transmission of Cultural Interaction. Proceedings of the Fifth Annual Symposium of the Assyrian and Babylonian Intellectual Heritage Project. Held in Innsbruck, Austria, October 3rd–8th, 2002*, ed. by Robert Rollinger and Christoph Ulf. Stuttgart: F. Steiner Verlag.

Steinkeller, Piotr. 2011. "Third Millennium Royal and Votive Inscriptions." Pp. 1–28 in *Cuneiform Royal Inscriptions and Related Texts in the Schøyen Collection*, ed. by A. R. George. Cornell University Studies in Assyriology and Sumerology 17. Bethesda, MD: CDL Press.

Steinkeller, Piotr. 2013. "An Archaic "Prisoner Plaque" from Kiš." *Revue d'Assyriologie et d'Archéologie Orientale* 107: 131–157.

Steinkeller, Piotr. 2015. "The Gutian Period in Chronological Perspective." Pp. 273–280 in *Associated Regional Chronologies for the Ancient Near East and the Eastern Mediterranean*, ed. by W. Sallaberger and I. Schrakamp. ARCANE 3. History & Philology. Turnhout: Brepols.

Steinkeller, Piotr. 2016. "The Role of Iran in the Inter-Regional Exchange of Metals: Tin, Copper, Silver and Gold in the Second Half of the Third Millennium BC." Pp. 127–150 in *Ancient Iran. New Perspectives from Archaeology and Cuneiform Studies. Proceedings of the International Colloquium held at the Center for Eurasian Cultural Studies, Kyoto University, December 6–7, 2014*, ed. by K. Maekawa. Kyoto: Nakanishi Printing Company.

Stieglitz, Robert R. 1987. "Ebla and Dilmun." Pp. 43–45 in *Eblaitica: Essays on the Ebla archives and Eblaite language, Vol. I*, ed. by C. H. Gordon, G. A. Rendsburg, and N. H. Winter. Winona Lake, IN: Eisenbrauns.

Stol, Marten. 2012. "Bitumen in Ancient Mesopotamia: The Textual Evidence." *Bibliotheca Orientalis* 69: 48–60.

Stone, Elizabeth. 2013. "The Organization of a Sumerian Town: The Physical Remains of Ancient Social Systems." Pp. 156–178 in *The Sumerian World*, ed. by H. Crawford. London/New York: Routledge.

Such-Gutiérrez, Marcos. 2003. "Überlegungen zu der sumerischen Zeichengruppe ŠÈ.KA." *Sefarad* 63(2): 394–410.

Such-Gutiérrez, Marcos. 2015. "The Texts from the 3rd Millennium BC at the Oriental Museum, University of Durham (England)." *Cuneiform Digital Library Journal* 2015:3: 1–49.

Süel, Aygül, and Oguz Soysal. 2003. "A Practical Vocabulary from Ortaköy." Pp. 349–365 in *Hittite Studies in Honor of Harry A. Hoffner Jr. on the Occasion of His 65th Birthday*, ed. by G. Beckman, R. Beal, and G. McMahon. Winona Lake, IN: Eisenbrauns.

Szarzyńska, Krystyna. 2002. *Sheep Husbandry and Production of Wool, Garments and Cloths in Archaic Sumer*. Warsaw: Agade.

Thesiger, Wilfred. 1964. *The Marsh Arabs*. London: Longmans.

Ur, Jason. 2014. "Households and the Emergence of Cities in Ancient Mesopotamia." *Cambridge Archaeological Journal* 24(2) (June): 249–268.

Vaiman, Aizik A. 1974. "Über die Protosumerische Schrift." *Acta Antiqua Academiae Scientiarum Hungaricae* 22: 17–22.

Vaiman, Aizik A. 1989. "Protosumerische Mass- und Zählsysteme." *Baghdader Mitteilungen* 20: 114–120.

Van de Mieroop, Marc. 1992. "Wood in the Old Babylonian Texts from Ur." *Bulletin on Sumerian Agriculture* 6: 155–161.

Van de Mieroop, Marc. 1999. *Cuneiform Texts and the Writing of History*. London/New York: Routledge.

Van de Mieroop, Marc. 2004. "Economic Theories and the Ancient Near East." Pp. 54–64 in *Commerce and Monetary Systems in the Ancient* World. *Means of Transmission and Cultural Interactio. Proceedings of the Fifth Annual Symposium of the Assyrian and Babylonian Intellectual Heritage Project. Held in Innsbruck, Austria, October 3rd–8th, 2002*, ed. by R. Rollinger and Ch. Ulf. Stuttgart: Franz Steiner Verlag.

Van de Mieroop, Marc. 2014. "Silver as a Financial Tool in Ancient Egypt and Mesopotamia." Pp. 17–29 in *Explaining Monetary and Financial Innovation. A Historical Analysis*, ed. by P. Bernholz and R. Vaubel. Cham: Springer.

Von Soden, Wolfram. 1990. Review of OSP 2. *Zeitschrift für Assyriologie und Vordearasiatische Archäologie* 80(1): 135–136.

Von Soden, Wolfram. 1995. *Grundriss der Akkadischen Grammatik. 3., ergänzte Auflage, unter Mitarbeit von W. R. Mayer*. Rome: Pontificium Institutum Biblicum.

Veldhuis, Niek. 2014a. "The Early Dynastic Kiš Tradition." Pp. 241–259 in *He Has Opened Nisaba's House of Learning. Studies in Honor of Åke Waldemar Sjöberg on the Occasion of His 89th Birthday on August 1st 2013*, ed. by L. Sassmanshausen. Leiden/Boston: Brill.

Veldhuis, Niek. 2014b. *History of the Cuneiform Lexical Tradition*. Guides to the Mesopotamian Textual Records 6. Münster: Ugarit-Verlag.

Verderame, Lorenzo. 2008. "Il controllo dei manufatti tessili a Umma." Pp. 111–133 in *The Management of Agricultural Land and the Production of Textiles in the Mycenaean and Near Eastern Economies*, ed. by M. Perna and F. Pomponio. Paris: Editions De Boccard.

Verderame, Lorenzo, and Gabriella Spada. 2013. "Ikalla, Scribe of (Wool) Textiles and Linen." Pp. 425–444 in *From the 21st Century B.C. to the 21st Century A.D. Proceedings of the International Conference on Sumerian Studies Held in Madrid, 22–24 July 2010*, ed. by S. Garfinkle and M. Molina. Winona Lake, IN: Eisenbrauns.

Verkinderen, Peter. 2006. "Les toponymes bàd^{ki} et bàd.an^{ki}." *Akkadica* 127(2): 109–122.

Visicato, Giuseppe, and Aage Westenholz. 2005. "An Early Dynastic Archive from Ur Involving the lugal." *KASKAL* 2: 55–78.

Waetzoldt, Hartmut. 1972. *Untersuchungen zur neusumerischen Textilindustrie*. Rome: Centro per le antlchità e la storia dell'arte del Vicino Oriente.

Waetzoldt, Hartmut. 1981. "Zur Terminologie der Metalle in den Texten aus Ebla." Pp. 363–378 in *La Lingua di Ebla. Atti del Convegno Internazionale (Napoli, 21–23 aprile 1980)*, ed. by L. Cagni. Napoli: Istituto universitario orientale.

Waetzoldt, Hartmut. 1984. "Zinn- und Arsenbronzen in den Texten aus Ebla und aus dem Mesopotamien des 3. Jahrtausends (mit H. G. Bachmann u. einem Beitrag von E. Pernicka)." *Oriens Antiquus* XXIII: 1–18.

Waetzoldt, Hartmut. 1985a. "Ölpflanzen und Pflanzenöle im 3. Jahrtausend." *Bulletin on Sumerian Agriculture* 2: 77–96.

Waetzoldt, Hartmut. 1985b. "Rotes Gold?" *Oriens Antiquus* XXIV: 1–16.

Waetzoldt, Hartmut. 1992a. "'Rohr' und dessen Verwendunsweisen anhand der neusumerischen Texte aus Umma." *Bulletin on Sumerian Agriculture 6*: 125–146.

Waetzoldt, Hartmut. 1992b. "Zu P. Steinkeller, *N.A.B.U.* 1991/4 "The Container kabkūru."" *Nouvelles Assyriologiques Brèves et Utilitaires* 1992 no. 15: 13.

Waetzoldt, Hartmut. 2007. "The Use of Wool for Production of Strings, Ropes, Braided Mats, and Similar Fabrics." Pp. 112–121 in *Ancient Textiles, Production, Craft and Society*, ed. by C. Gillis and M.-L. Nosch. Oxford: Oxbow Books.

Waetzoldt, Hartmut. 2009. "Schreiber. A. Im 3. Jahrtausend." *Reallexikon der Assyriologie und Vorderasiatischen Archäologie* 12: 250–266.

Waetzoldt, Hartmut. 2010. "*Ni-iK-Tum, Ni-Gi$_4$-Tum* und *Ni-iK-Tum al-la-ha-ru*." Pp. 295–300 in *DUB.SAR E$_2$.DUB.BA.A, Studies Presented in Honour of Veysel Donbaz*, ed. by Ş. Dönmez. Istanbul: Yayinlari.

Westenholz, Aage. 1987. See OSP 2.

Westenholz, Aage. 1995. Review of MC 4. *Journal of the American Oriental Society* 115(3): 535–537.

Westenholz, Aage. 1999. "The Old Akkadian Period: History and Culture." Pp. 17–117 in W. Sallaberger and A. Westenholz, *Mesopotamien: Akkade-Zeit und Ur III-Zeit*. Orbis Biblicus et Orientalis 160/3. Gottingen: Vanderhoeck and Ruprecht.

Westenholz, Aage. 2017. "Correction (1) to CUSAS 26." *Nouvelles Assyriologiques Brèves et Utilitaires* 2017, no. 88: 159–160.

Westenholz, Joan Goodnick. 1997. *Legends of the Kings of Agade. The Texts*. Winona Lake, IN: Eisenbrauns.

Westenholz, Joan Goodnick. 2010. "Drink Me Only with Thine Eyes." Pp. 463–484 in *Opening the Tablet Box. Near Eastern Studies in Honor of Benjamin R. Foster*, ed. by S. Melville and A. Slotsky. Leiden: Brill.

Wilcke, Claus. 1980. "Kauf. A. I. Nach sumerischen Quellen vor der Zeit der III. Dynastie von Ur." *Reallexikon der Assyriologie und Vorderasiatischen Archäologie* 5: 490–512.

Wilcke, Claus. 1996. "Neue Rechtsurkunden der Altsumerischen Zeit." *Zeitschrift für Assyriologie und Vordearasiatische Archäologie* 68(1): 1–67.
Wilcke, Claus. 2002. "Der Kodex Urnamma (CU): Versuch einer Rekonstruction." Pp. 291–333 in *Riches Hidden in Secret Places: Ancient Near Eastern Studies in Memory of Thorkild Jacobsen*, ed. by T. Abusch. Winona Lake, IN: Eisenbrauns.
Woods, Christopher. 2007. "The Paleography and Value of the Sign KIB." Pp. 323–339 in *Studies Presented to Robert D. Biggs, June 4, 2004*, ed. by M. T. Roth et al. Chicago: Oriental Institute.
Yildiz, Fatma. 1981. "A Tablet of Codex Ur-Nammu from Sippar." *Orientalia Nova Series* 50: 87–97.
Zaccagnini, Carlo. 1986. "The Dilmun Standard and its Relationship with Indus and Near Eastern Weight Systems." *Iraq* 48: 19–23.
Zaccagnini, Carlo. 1993. "The Dilmun standard again." *Nouvelles Assyriologiques Brèves et Utilitaires* 1993, no. 105: 89.
Zaccagnini, Carlo. 2018a. "Capital Investment, Weight Standards and Overland Trade at Emar." *Zeitschrift für Assyriologie* 108: 43–62.
Zaccagnini, Carlo. 2018b. "'Heavy Shekels' in Late Bronze Age Syria." *Annali, Sezione Orientale* 78: 3–18.
Zagarell, Allen. 1986. "Trade, Women, Class, and Society in Ancient Western Asia." *Current Anthropology* 27(5): 415–430.
Zettler, Richard L. 1992. *The Ur III Temple of Inanna at Nippur*. Berliner Beiträge zum Vorderen Orient 11. Berlin: D. Reimer.

General index: subjects, names, places, authors

Abu Salabikh (city) 7
Adab (city) 7, 64
Adams, Robert McC 234
alkali 190
alum 205, 226
amphora 19
apple tree 22
Arawa (Uru'a) (city) 130, 188
Archi, Alfonso 133
area mensuration 82
artisans 155

Baba (goddess) 134
balance
– for copper 129
– for wool 132
– made of bronze 149
– made of copper 149
– made of wood 149
– with 30-minas weight 147
– with metallic parts and inlays 149
– with one-talent weight 147
balance pans
– made of copper 149
balanced accounts 4
barley grains as primitive weights 84
barleycorn
– as principal unit in weight metrology 98
Bauer, Josef 163
beveled-rim bowl 20
Bible 1
Borger, Rykle 203
brass 178
bread 23, 227
bronze 178, 187
– tin bronze 188
bulbous plants (šum$_2$) 26
bundle (sa) 24
Burrows, Eric 61

capacity measures 3
Cavigneaux, Antoine 140
Chambon, Gregory 112
Civil, Miguel 115, 184, 204
copper 59, 137, 173, 183
– alloys 178
– as money 156, 174, 176, 228
"core goods" of weight metrology 227
coriander 26
culture 1n1
cuneiform numbers
– "pointed" 19, 39, 109
– "round" 50
cylinder seals 190, 214
cypress 207

D'Agostino, Franco 153, 167
Damerow, Peter 74
date palm 22
Deimel, Anton 60
Der (Tall ʿAqar) (city) 133, 160
Diakonoff, Igor 6
Dilmun 130
Dornauer, Aron 84n286
Dudu, temple administrator (saĝĝa) at ED IIIb Ĝirsu 132
Dudu, Ur III administrator of Arawa 130

Early Mesopotamia 1n1
Ebla (city) 7, 35, 51, 56, 198, 208, 214
Edzard, Dietz Otto 156
Ekur temple 182, 198
electrum 197
elites 160, 170, 179, 201, 217
Ellison, Rosemary 95
Englund, Robert 74, 179, 218
Enlilemaba archive 82, 214
Enmetena (ruler) 107

Falkenstein, Adam 12
fennel 207
fig tree 22
fir tree ^{ĝeš}še-du$_{10}$ 23
fir trees 208
flax 118
Foxvog, Daniel 156

https://doi.org/10.1515/9781501510267-013

Frayne, Douglas 106
Friberg, Jöran 12, 85, 116, 131

Garšana (city) 7, 146
garments 222
Gelb, Ignace 6, 101
gems 64, 214
Goetze, Albrecht 52
gold 157, 161, 183, 196
– purity 197
goldsmiths 157, 161
Gorello, Francesca 154, 167
governor (ensi$_2$) 163
grass (u$_2$) 25
Green, Margret 217
Gu'abba (site) 149
Gutians 104
gypsum 190

Hacinebi Tepe (site) 53
Hallo, William 178
Helwing, Barbara 179
horse 134
households
– palace and temple 160, 165, 167, 170, 175, 216, 229
– private 166

Indus culture 133
Irisaĝrig (city) 7
Isin (city) 7

Jagersma, Bram 44, 69
juniper 208
Jursa, Michael 201

Kaneš (city) 100
Karwiese, Stefan 98
Keš (city) 133
Kiš (city) 56
king 163
Kisch, Bruno 139
Krebernik, Manfred 61
Krispijn, Theo 179
kudurrus 181

labor division 164
lapis lazuli 64, 214
lead 189, 190
Leopard Weight (Leopardengewicht) 115n372
libripens (Roman weighmaster) 156
linkage
– barleycorn > shekel 83, 90
– mina > shekel 93
– mina > sila 11, 27, 107
– weight to area and capacity metrologies 94
literacy 167
little mina
– notation 101
little shekel 102
– in area and volume metrology 103
load (primitive measure) 16, 34, 226, 229
loan 4
loom 218
Lugal-ra archive 81, 145

Magan (Oman) 173, 187n621
Mama-ummi file 64
Maništusu (king) 30
Mari (city) 214
marshland 22
Maškan-ili-Akkade (Umm al-Hafriyat) (site) 145
mathematical texts 58n178
McDonald, Daniel 98
merchants 157, 159, 160, 174, 189
Mesag (governor) 166
Meskigala 31, 80
Meskigala archive 31
metals 137
metrogram 73
metrological reform 4
– Sargonic 11, 14, 54, 57, 81, 96
– Ur III 82, 105, 127
Middle Sargonic 30
mina
– application 59
– as the highest unit 59
– "exchange mina" 85, 89
– divided into five parts 52

– divided into six parts 51, 53
– heavy standard 135
– linkage to *sila* (capacity measure) 94
– origins 72, 174
Molina, Manuel 28n80, 146, 185, 215
Monaco, Salvatore 177
money 3, 71, 174
Moorey, Peter 190

Nabada (Tell Beydar) (site) 7, 95n300, 219, 221
Nagar (Tell Brak) (site) 198
nails 196
Naram-Suen (king) 95, 96
Neolithic revolution 3
Neumann, Hans 158
Nippur (city) 7, 57
Notizia, Palmiro 77n256
N-system (grain metrology, Late Uruk period) 74
numeration
– bisexagesimal 2, 23, 24n62, 218n745, 225
– decimal 35, 52
– sexagesimal 2, 11, 39, 73, 83, 128, 134, 218

officials 153, 156
oils 204, 211
Onion Archive 26
Owen, David 200

palaces as places of weighing 166
Paoletti, Paola 200
periodization of early Mesopotamia 7
pine 208
Pollock, Susan 217
Pomponio, Francesco 95, 177
poplar 22
potash 226
Potts, Daniel 188
Pournelle, Jennifer 22
Powell, Marvin 3, 10, 37, 50, 57, 69, 83, 94, 100, 172
presents 188, 197, 198, 206, 208, 217
prestige 179
primitive measures 2, 20, 27

Rahmstorf, Lorenz 165
Reade, Julian 62
reeds 22, 227
relation between capacity and weight metrologies 19
resins 64, 134, 200
– aggregate state 201
– wood in large blocks 207
Rimuš (king) 30, 200
Rubio, Gonzalo 5
rushes (ninni$_5$) 25, 190

Sagub (city) 7
sale documents 176
Sallaberger, Walther 33, 106, 158, 221
sar "garden plot" (area measure) 58
Sargon (king) 30, 95
Šarkališarri (king) 104
Schrakamp, Ingo 183
scribal tradition
– "standard" (Šuruppak, etc.) 56, 80
– of Ĝirsu 57, 79, 109
– of Isin 47, 66
– of Mugdan 66
– of Sippar and Mugdan 50
– of Šuruppak 45, 79
– of Umma 45, 80
– southern vs. northern 53
scribes 163
seed funnel 74
Selz, Gebhard 27, 163
Semites 174
shadoof 142
Shahi-Tump (site in Pakistan) 115n372
shekel
– "Dilmun shekel" 60n185, 72
– "silver shekel" (standard) 107
– "exchange shekel" 85
– 1/4 shekel 68
– application 71
– as 1/60 of a day 64
– as 1/60 of *sar* 70
– as 1/60 *sila* 64
– as primitive measures 65
– as the unit par excellence 72

– half-shekel in Hurrian 67
– hypothesis on its origins 62
– in Iron Age Judah 72
– of the Indus culture (13.65 g) 134
– one-fifth (nonexistent) 71
– origins 72, 198
– Phoenician 52
– Sumerian/Mesopotamian 60
– Syrian 52
Sherratt, Andrew 216n737
sila (capacity measure) 27
– of Enmetena 107
silver
– as money 134, 156, 157, 159, 181, 200n666
– extraction 179
– ingots 179
– rings 179, 183
– scrap 179, 183
Sippar (city) 50
smiths 155, 157, 161, 165, 167, 198
Sommerfeld, Walter 37
Spada, Gabriella 163
standardization 11, 21, 28, 73, 107, 130, 150, 168, 229
– barleycorn 97
– mina 14
– talent 97
state 6, 14, 168, 228
– emergence 179
Steinkeller, Piotr 68, 116, 156, 167, 219
Šulgi (king) 106
Šuruppak (city) 7, 42
system E (metrology, Late Uruk) 12

Tell Sweyhat (site) 165
temples 4, 166, 200
– as places of weighing 166
textile industry 167
textiles 143
– export 170, 216
– in bolts 218
– measurement 218
Thesiger, Wilfred 22
tin 189
trade 36, 59, 93, 170, 202, 228
– in copper 174, 228
– in lapis lazuli 214
– in resins 201
– in silver 182
– in textiles 228
– with Amorite tribes 207
– with Der 206
– with Elam 205, 211
tree ^{ĝeš}*zirum* 23
tribute 200

Umma (city) 7
Ur (city) 7, 8
Ur-Inana's archive (Sargonic Adab) 226
Ur-Namma (king) 106, 107
Ur-Ninmar, merchant in ED IIIb Ĝirsu 134
Uruk Expansion 53
Utu (god) 10

Vaiman, Aizik 12
value 113
– silver > arata$_x$ (a metal) 185
– silver > copper 85
– silver > gold 12, 197
– silver > MUŠ$_3^{uruda}$ 187
Verderame, Lorenzo 153, 163
Visicato, Giuseppe 95
von Soden, Wolfram 51

Waetzoldt, Hartmut 163, 205
weighing practice 33, 34, 71
weight metrology
– core goods 222
– core measure 231
– origins 168, 169, 217, 228
weights
– for silver 131
– for textiles 132
– for wool 132
– from diorite 127, 148
– from hematite 127
– heavy and light standards 127
– of Der 133

– one-talent 134, 227
– one-talent heavy weights 119
– one-talent, imprecise 32
– regular standard 127
Westenholz, Aage 198n657
Wilcke, Claus 107, 156
willow 22
Woods, Christopher 147
wool 119, 130, 137, 143, 215
– measurement 220
workshops 166
writing 2

Yildiz, Fatma 107

Zabalam (city) 7, 176

Signs and Sumerian words

$^{\text{šu2}}$1N$_8$ giĝ$_4$ 47
$^{\text{šu2}}$1N$_8$ NINDA$_2$ × ŠE giĝ$_4$ 80
2N$_8$ giĝ$_4$ 47
2N$_8$ ma-na 89
2N$_8$ NINDA$_2$ × ŠE giĝ$_4$ 80
$^{\text{šu2}}$*3N$_8$*^{ša} = kingusila "five-sixths" 109

a$_2$ "labor" 64
a$_2$ ĝeš-rin$_2$-na-ka ... gi.n 10
a$_2$-GAR-uruda 147
a-gar$_5$, a-bara$_2$ "lead" 190
a-gar$_5$-gar$_5$ 186
$^{\text{(šim/ĝeš)}}$ad$_2$ "myrtle" 201
agrig 163
^{uruda}alal$_x$(ŠEN)2 191
algameš 202
al-gazum$_x$(ZUM×LAGAB) 202
AN 179, 188, 226
an-na "tin" 188
– PA(kun$_2$)-na 189
^{šim}an/en-HAR 203
ANŠE/GIR$_3$-babbar$_2$ 226
$^{\text{na4}}$an-zu-gur$_4$-me, $^{\text{na4}}$an-zu$_2$-gul-me 215
arata$_x$(LAM.KUR.RU) 184
– arata$_x$ NI-na 185
– arata$_x$-BU 186
a-ru$_{12}$(EN)-da^{uruda} 175
AŠ (with talent) 109

BA 12, 50, 51, 67, 67n208, 164, 223
ba$_3$(EŠ$_2$) "half(-shekel)" 51
ba$_{15}$(BAR) "half" 50
/ba'a/ "half(-shekel)" 67
BAD 67
BAR 51, 67n208, 164, 223
– as half-shekel 66
– as ŠU$_2$ 48
bar "extra" 67n208
bar-dub$_2$-ba 164
$^{\text{(tug2)}}$bar-dul$_5$ 223
$^{\text{tug2}}$bar-dul$_5$ DU$_{\textit{gunû}}$-ma 223
$^{\text{tug2}}$bar-dul$_5$ tab-ba 223
bar-dul$_5$ uš-bar 223
bar-si(g$_9$) sa-dab$_6$ 223
bi$_2$-za-za 199
BU-ku$_3$ 199
bulug$_x$(ŠIM×UH$_3$) 203
BU^{uruda} kul-sa$_6$-ga / zabar 191

dam-gara$_3$ "merchant" 36
$^{\text{(šim)}}$dam-še-lu-um 204
DARA$_{4c}$ 218
^{ĝeš}dib-dib, water clock 94
dilim$_2$ ĝeš-rin$_2$ 141
– kul-sa$_6$-ga^{uruda} 191
DILMUN 60n185
du$_{10}$-gan 204
DUG×*AŠ* 19n37
DUG×UH$_3$ = ZATU123 200
DUG-uruda 41
DUN$_3$ 61
$^{\text{(kuš/ĝeš)}}$dun$_3$, a container for dry goods 62n192
^{uruda}dur$_2$ šen 191
dur$_{10}$-tab-ba 191

e$_2$-ĝidru 166
e$_2$-šu-šum$_2$-ma 119
eme-ĝiri$_2$-zabar 191
EN 12, 75
en-da 75
– sur$_x$(HUŠ)-ru$_{12}$ 75
eren$_2$ ku$_3$-la$_2$ 157
$^{\text{(šim/ĝeš)}}$eren(-UD(.UD)) "cedar" 204
ERIN$_2$ 204
^{ĝeš}erin$_2$ "yoke" 139
esir$_2$-had$_2$(UD) "dry bitumen" 226
eše$_2$ = *eblu(m)* "rope" 222

^{ĝeš}gab$_2$-il$_2$ 144
gab$_2$-la$_2$^{uruda} 191
GADA$_a$ 218
$^{\text{(uruda)}}$gag 191
GAL UMUN$_2$ KU 180
geme$_2$-gu 118n386
gi = *qashab* (Arabic) = *Phragmites australis* (Latin) 23
gi.n "to make firm, to confirm" 107
giĝ$_4$ "axe" 60

gi$\hat{g}_4$×N 63
gi$\hat{g}_4$-ba-gi$\hat{g}_4$ "shekel of its shekel" (1/216,000 of a *sar*) 103
gi$\hat{g}_4$-bi "its shekel" (1/60 of a shekel) 103
gi$\hat{g}_4$-DILMUN 72n236, 135
gi$\hat{g}_4$-tur "little shekel" 102
gi$\hat{g}_4$-tur (not "little shekel") 86
gi$\hat{g}_4$-zabar^{uruda} 60n184
gi-i$_3$, $^{(šim)}$gi "sweet reed" 204
GIN$_2$ 61, 158
GIN$_2$-la$_2$ 158
gi-ru-uš, a variety of reeds 34
GIŠ-ERIN$_2$ 139
gi-zi, green fodder reed 33
gu = *qû* "(spun thread from) combed flax" 225
gu(-gada) 30, 31, 225
GU$_2$ 17
gu$_2$ "neck" 17
GU$_2$-DU$_6$ 19
^{tug2}gu$_2$-gil$_2$(LAGAB) ku$_3$-babbar 199
gu$_2$-na "on his neck" 18
gu$_2$-sa-ma 75
gu$_2$-un "tribute" 18
gu$_2$-zi, Akk. *kāsu* "a bowl" 19n34
^{zabar}gu$_3$-zi 191
gug = *sāmtu(m)* "carnelian" 215
gu-gada 225
gun$_2$ 16
gur A-ga-de$_3$^{ki} 106
gur sila$_3$-zabar-ta 106
gur=sam$_2$=a(k) "exchange *gur*" 75
gur-^{d}Šul-gi-ra 106
gur-lugal 106
gur-sa$\hat{g}$-$\hat{g}$al$_2$ 106

$\hat{g}$eš-rin$_2$ "balance" 140
– a$_2$ $\hat{g}$eš-rin$_2$ "arm of the balance scales" 141
– e$_2$ $\hat{g}$eš-rin$_2$ "the box of the balance scales" 141
– $\hat{g}$eš-rin$_2$ 1 gun$_2$ 117, 140
– $\hat{g}$eš-rin$_2$ ku$_3$ (la$_2$) 144
– $\hat{g}$eš-rin$_2$ ma-na (la$_2$) 140, 158
– $\hat{g}$eš-rin$_2$-gaba 148
– $\hat{g}$eš-rin$_2$-ku$_3$-la$_2$-tur 149
– $\hat{g}$eš-rin$_2$-lub(-lub)-bi 140
– $\hat{g}$eš-rin$_2$-siki-gal-gal 142
– $\hat{g}$eš-rin$_2$-siki-tur-tur 142
– $\hat{g}$eš-rin$_2$-uruda 142, 143
$\hat{g}$eštug(-ku$_3$) 199
$\hat{g}$iri$_2$-udu-šum^{uruda} 191
$\hat{g}$uruš ku$_3$-la$_2$ 157

^{uruda}ha-bu$_3$-da 191
har ku$_3$-babbar 183
HAR.AN^{uruda} 191
har-hul$_3$-la 183
– ku$_3$ 199
^{uruda}har na$_4$ 1(*AŠ*) gun$_2$ 117
ha-zi-(in)^{uruda} 191
^{šim}hi(-ib) 205

ib$_2$-(ba)-du$_3$^{tug2} 223
igi/gu$_2$ $\hat{g}$eš-gid$_2$-da 191
igi...$\hat{g}$al$_2$ "to look upon/at" 69
igi-*3*-$\hat{g}$al$_2$ 79
igi-*5*-$\hat{g}$al$_2$ (never with weight measures) 109
igi-*6*-$\hat{g}$al$_2$ "one-sixth" 53
igi-*n*-$\hat{g}$al$_2$ "one-nth" 65, 69
igi-ni-ta 163
im-babbar$_{(2)}$ "gypsum" 226

kab$_2$-ku, a container 25, 26
ki ... la$_2$ = *napalšuhu(m)* "to fall to the ground" 173
$^{\hat{g}eš}$KIB 147
ki $\hat{g}$eš-rin$_2$-bi ... ak 149
ki $\hat{g}$eš-rin$_2$-na-ka ... gub 10
ki-la$_2$ "weight" 172, 173
^{uruda}kin/gur$_{10}$ 191
kingusila "five-sixth" 65
KU$_3$ = ZATU301 179
KU$_3$ UD 179
ku$_3$(-babbar) 178
– ku$_3$-luh-(ha) 183
KU$_3$-GAN 190
ku$_3$-la$_2$ 154
KU$_3$-NE 179
ku$_3$-sig$_{17}$ 197
– HI-da 197
– huš-a 197
– si-sa$_2$ 197

kul 145, 146
kul-sa_6-ga 145
$^{(šim)}$kur-gi-rin 205
KU-si-sa_2 189

la_2 "to weigh" 152, 162, 165, 167
– ba-la_2 118, 153
– in-la_2 154
LAK61 20, 147
LAK212 = $asal_x$ 22
LAK544 18n33
LAK610 147
LAK610-uruda 147
LAK666 62
LAK667 62
lid_2-ga (a capacity measure) 26
ligidba 205, 206
load (primitive measure) 20
lu_2 ĝeš-rin_2 dab_5-ba 150, 156, 160
lu_2-$^{(ĝeš)}$$erin_2$ 158
lu_2 ku_3-la_2(-a-bi) 156
lu_3-lu_3 "antimony(?)" 189
$^{(ĝeš/uruda)}$lub-bi 140

MA NA (personal name) 39
ma-na 36, 99, 100, 120, 127, 158
ma-na gi-na 120, 127
ma-na-gal "large mina" 100
ma-na-la_2 158
ma-na-tur "little mina" 99
MAŠ 51
maškim 162
ma-šum^{uruda} 191
$MUŠ_3$^{uruda} 115, 185, 186
$MUŠ_3$^{uruda} (luh-ha) "(pure) copper" 185

N_1 12, 74
N_2 49
N_7(N_1+EN) 12
N_8 12, 39, 49, 219, 220
N_8×*AŠ* 49
N_8×*DIŠ* 49
^{šu2}N_8^{ša}-tur 100
N_{14} 12
N_{24} 12
N_{34} = 60 23
N_{34}-*tenû* 23
N_{48} = 600 23
N_{51} = 120 23
NA_4 114
na_4 "stone (weight)" 113
na_4-BAD_3.AN^{ki} 133
na_4-gi-na ku_3 la_2-e-de_3 10
na_4-gu-la 135
na_4-ku_3(-babbar) 131
na_4-mah 134, 135
na_4-mah_2 135
na_4-siki-ba 132
na_4-si-sa_2 105, 127
na_4-$ša_3$-tug_2 132
NAM^{uruda} 191
^{ĝeš}ni_3-a_2-la_2 141
ni_3-gul^{uruda} 191
ni_3-gun_2-na "utensils" 18
ni_3-la_2^{tug2} 223
ni_3-luh^{zabar3} 191
ni_3-UD^{uruda} 176
$niĝ_2$-ib 205
NI-GAM^{uruda} 191
NI-na "tin" 188
ninda-UD 176n558
$NINDA_2$ 65, 74, 75, 76, 81, 82
$NINDA_2$ × $1N_1$ 74, 81
$NINDA_2$ × $1N_1$ + ŠE ma-na 81
$NINDA_2$ × 2(*AŠ*) NA 82
$NINDA_2$ × ŠE ^{šu2}$1N_8$$^{<ša->na}$ 82
$NINDA_2$ × ŠE + 10 + *5* 82
$NINDA_2$ × ŠE + 10 + *5* = *1/12 shekel = *1/4 little mina = 15 barleycorns 76, 82
$NINDA_2$ × ŠE + $1N_1$ (ma-na) 10 + *5* ($giĝ_4$) = 1/3 shekel (1 little mina) + 15 barleycorns = 75 barleycorns 76
$NINDA_2$ × ŠE + $1N_1$ ma-na = 1/3 shekel = 1 little mina = 60 barleycorns 76
$NINDA_2$ × ŠE + $2N_1$ ma-na = 2/3 shekel = 2 little minas = 120 barleycorns 76
$NINDA_2$ × ŠE + $2N_8$ = *2/9 shekel = 2/3 little mina = 40 barleycorns 76
$NINDA_2$ × ŠE + N_1 ma-na 75
$NINDA_2$ × ŠE + ^{šu2}$1N_8$ = *1/9 shekel = 1/3 little mina = 20 barleycorns 76
^{dug}$ninda_2$, Akk. *namaddu* "measuring vessel" 75

ninta(UŠ) (for $ninda_2$) 75
nir_3 = *ḫulālu(m)* "agate (?)" 215
nu-$banda_3$ 164

sa "bundle" 225
sa "bundle" and "net" 25
sa_9(MAŠ/BAN_2) "half" 50
sa_{10}(m) "to pay for, to buy, to sell" 74
saĝĝa 166
^{uruda}SAG×NI LAGAB×*U* 6-la_2 191
sal-la-um 184
SIG_2 = ZATU452 217
siki "wool" 217
siki-TUR-TUR 142n456
si-NU×U 24, 224
si-U-NU-saĝ 24
si-ZI+ZI.U-saĝ 225
su_3-GAN "antimony(?)" 189
sur/sur_3 "half (of a bread)" 191

^{tug2}$ša_3$-ga-du_3 223
^{tug2}$ša_3$-gi-da_5 223
$ša_4$(DU)-na-bi "two-thirds" 45
šagan-la_2 158
$šam_2$-ma-na 85
šanabi 52
ŠA-PI 56
$ŠE_3$-ba-an 21, 27
še-gin_2 62, 227
šembi(GU_2×SIG_7=LAK547) "kohl" 20
$šembi_3$(DUG×IGI-*gunû*)-babbar(UD)/ giggi(MI) 207
$šembulug_x$ 203
^{uruda}šen 191
šen-da-la_2/li_2^{zabar} 191
$^{(uruda)}$šen-gam(-e)(-zabar) 191
^{uruda}šen-$šu_2$ 191
ŠEN-šu-e_3 197
šim diri-*um* 204
šim mar-tu 207
šim $naĝa_3$(GAZ)^{ĝa2} 207
šim-IM 206
šim-MI 207
$ŠU_2$ 43, 44, 53, 56, 218
$ŠU_2$+N 44
$ŠU_2$+ŠA 56
$šu_2$-N_8-ša 54
šu-la_2^{uruda}, šu-ša-la_2-zabar 191
šum^{uruda} 191
šu-ri-a "half" 50
šurmen "cypress" 207
šuš "one-sixth" 53
šušana "one-third (mina)" 51

^{šim}tal_2-tal_2 "fennel" 207
TAR
– half-mina 67
– half-shekel 66
tug_2 = *ṣubātu(m)* "cloth, fabric" 218
tug_2 du_8-a banšur-ra 223
tug_2 gu_2-da_5 223
tug_2 guz-za 223
tug_2 ni_3-la_2 gu_2 anše 223
tug_2 ni_3-lam_2 (uš-bar) 223
TUG_{2a} 218
TUG_{2a}+BAD+BAD 218
tug_2-bur_2 223
tug_2-mug 223
TUN_3 12

U.NU 224
u_2-$kiši_{17}$ 201
^{ĝeš}u_3-suh_5 = *ašūhu* "a pine" 208
UD 204
UD+NI See NA_4
UET 2 sign list no.331 18n33
UR_2×HA 144
^{ĝeš}UR_2×HA.A 144
uri^{uruda}(-zabar) 191
urin-ku_3 199
uruda 41, 146, 161, 175, 184, 190
uruda a-$bara_2$ 190
uruda-kul-sa_6-ga 146
uruda-luh(-ha) 184
uruda ni_3-sahar-ra 161, 184
uruda sal-la-um 184
uruda-NI 41
uruda-sahar 184

uruda-sal 184
uruda-šen-til 184
^{ug2}uš-bar 223

ZA 114
za_3+N = fractions "1/nth" 108
^{ĝeš}za-ba-lum = *supālum* "a juniper" 208
zabar 185, 187, 191, 199
zabar ku_3(-babbar / luh-ha) 199
zabar-šu 191
zabar^{uruda} 185, 191
$zam_x(UH_3)$-da-ti^{uruda} "scrap metal" 186
^{uruda}za-ri_2-in 191
ZATU123 201n667
ZATU233 18n33
ZATU489 61
ZATU522 ($ŠENNUR_b$) 147
ZATU561 61
ZATU602 = URUDA 175
^{uruda}zi-ir 191

Akkadian words

aban kitti 120
'a$_3$-dam-um$^{\text{tug2}}$ 223
am-ru-um 202

ballukkum 203
baluḫḫum 203
biltum 16
bû, bā'um "half-shekel" 67

hā'iţu 158
ḫabšallurḫu 208
$^{\text{tug2}}$*ḫa-la-um* 223

itqūru "spoon, balance pan" 145

karpatum "pot" 25
ki-li-lum 199
kišādum "neck" 17
kuk(ku)rum 202
kurkānû 205

lulû "antimony(?)" 189

ma-an ṣa-ah-ru "little mina" 100
**manā'um* 38
manā'um "to count" 37

$^{\text{tug2/gada}}$*na-aš$_2$-pa$_{(2)}$-ru-um* 223
naruqqum "sack" 25
nikiptum 205

parras šiqlim 67
pāšu(m), an axe 60

sanāqum "to check, supervise, control" 173
su-ga-nu 199

šaqālum 162, 173
šāqil kaspi 158
šinipu "two-thirds" 53
šittān "two-thirds" 52
šuqultum "weight" 172
šurmēnum 207
šuššān "one-third" 51
šuššu "one-sixth" 53

tijāru 204

^{šim}*u$_9$-lu-lum* = *(h)ul(l)ulum* or *(ḥ)ul(l)ulum* 208

zūzu "half-shekel" 51

Cuneiform texts

A 4651 = Civil 1994: 190 64n201
Aa 35–38 lines 147–148 144n461
AAICAB 1/1 pl. 8 1928–439 54
AAICAB 1/1 pl. 18 1911-147 109n350
AAICAB 1/1 pl. 19 1911-150 132n425
AAICAB 1/1 pl. 45 1911-481 109n347
AAICAB 1/1 pl. 46 1911-483 188n628
AAICAB 1/1 pl. 53 1919–11a–b 33n104
AAICAB 1/1 pl. 59 1924–553 32n98
AAICAN 1/1 pl. 67–68 1924-667 109n352
AAICAB 1/1 pl. 71 1924–675 226n777
AAICAB 1/2 pl. 117 1951-81 219n753
AAICAB 1/3 pl. 203 Bod B 8 221n761
AAICAB 1/3 pl. 206-207 Bod S 138 124n401
AAICAB 1/3 pl. 206–207 Bod S 138 33n101
AIHA 44 76n248, 81n272
Aleppo 439 109n350
Archaic Lu A 32 180
Archaic Metals 60, 179, 189, 217n744
Archaic Metals 8 217n744
Archaic Vessels and Garments 90–116 217n744
ARET 2 3 57
ARET 2 4 35n111
ARET 2 11 67n211
ATU 1 218 13
ATU 3 pl. 68 (W 20266,10) 61
ATU 5 pl. 38 (W 9168,a) 180n581
ATU 5 pl. 69 (W 9579,bk) 13n22
ATU 6 pl. 27 (W 13946,a) 60n186
AUCT 1 701 109n349
AUCT 2 168 226n780
AUCT 3 192 32n98

Bdl 1 13 118n386, 177, 177n564
Bdl 1 29 155, 161
Bdl 1 32 77n256, 81n274
Bdl 1 40 30n91
Bdl I 42 30n91
Bdl 1 88 82n278, 84n285
Bdl 1 95 188n627
Bdl 1 139 118n386
Bdl 1 181 190, 226n783
Bdl 1 215 196
Bdl 1 221 82
Bdl 2/1 61 214n726
Berens 89 119n392, 149n479
BIN 3 617 34n106
BIN 5 107 227n786
BIN 6 193 100n311
BIN 6 944 100n311
BIN 8 10 31n95, 166n535, 175, 177, 180n582, 184, 225n771
BIN 8 35 27n76, 67n208, 79n266, 82n279, 89n292, 98, 98n305
BIN 8 37 54, 67n208
BIN 8 39 67n208, 185
BIN 8 43 67n208, 76n246, 81n271
BIN 8 46 177n564
BIN 8 51 166n535
BIN 8 53 50n150, 66n206
BIN 8 72 196
BIN 8 100 31n95, 175
BIN 8 101 184
BIN 8 103 177
BIN 8 105 180n582
BIN 8 107 180n582
BIN 8 109 166n535
BIN 8 135 190n640
BIN 8 167 67n208
BIN 8 175 79n267, 81n271, 82n278, 84n285
BIN 8 180 76n248, 81n272
BIN 8 300 212
BIN 8 309 31n95, 54, 175
BIN 8 319 212
BIN 8 332 164
BIN 8 340 70n233
BIN 8 356 27n76
BIN 8 368 132, 165n530, 219n750
BIN 8 392 185
BIN 9 201 227n784
BM 94366 131n421
BPOA 1 505 227n786
BPOA 6 997 34n109

Canonical Ea VIII 17
CBS 8800 39n122
CHEU 53 184n605
Cripps 2010 no.41 23n54, 25n65
CST 11 161, 164n524, 184n605
CST 207 33n102
CST 570 117n382
CT 10 pl. 20–23 BM 14308 34n110
CT 50 4 63, 66n206, 181, 182n593
CT 50 5 181
CT 50 8 101n316, 188n626, 220n754
CT 50 8a 220n754
CT 50 9 50n148
CT 50 16 220n757
CT 50 47 66n206
CT 50 72 23n52, 50n152, 54
CT 50 73 103n321
CT 50 83 101n316
CT 50 137 58n180, 58n182
CT 50 177 225n766
CUNES 47-12-176 75, 82, 85, 99
CUNES 50-04-077 186
CUNES 50-08-001 = Friberg 2007, 419–425 102n319
CUSAS 3 706 162n517
CUSAS 3 1372 33n100, 124n398, 127n407, 142n454, 146n471, 148
CUSAS 11 15 54, 177
CUSAS 11 59 220
CUSAS 11 68 206n705, 212
CUSAS 11 77 54
CUSAS 11 109 198
CUSAS 11 112 31n95, 175
CUSAS 11 140 132n428
CUSAS 11 147 54
CUSAS 11 168 77n258, 80n268
CUSAS 11 189 166n536
CUSAS 11 224 131n423
CUSAS 11 240 25
CUSAS 11 242 186
CUSAS 11 254 77n258, 80n268
CUSAS 12 6.3.1 44, 54
CUSAS 13 2 76n247, 80n269, 81n273, 160n510
CUSAS 13 4 71n235, 188n627, 198, 198n658
CUSAS 13 7 67n208
CUSAS 13 46 198
CUSAS 13 47 198n658
CUSAS 13 48 188n627
CUSAS 13 106 58n182
CUSAS 13 162 203, 212
CUSAS 13 168 = CUSAS 27 184 145n464
CUSAS 13 203 160n510
CUSAS 14 177 166n535
CUSAS 17 19 116n376
CUSAS 19 213 23n53
CUSAS 20 18 30n90
CUSAS 20 172 31n93
CUSAS 20 254 26n70
CUSAS 20 255–256, 260 118n387
CUSAS 20 255–260 30n90
CUSAS 20 256 31n97, 225n775
CUSAS 20 260 118n388
CUSAS 20 396 186
CUSAS 23 77 58n178, 58n182
CUSAS 23 115 142n456
CUSAS 23 197 135
CUSAS 26 111 226n781
CUSAS 26 114 226
CUSAS 26 115 226
CUSAS 26 151 = Pettinato 1997 no.3 154n490, 157
CUSAS 26 175 81n275
CUSAS 26 204 226n776
CUSAS 26 207 25
CUSAS 26 265 29n84
CUSAS 26 293 82
CUSAS 27 209 100n314
CUSAS 33 171 54
CUSAS 33 220 176n561
CUSAS 33 221 130n414, 176n561
CUSAS 33 224 66n202
CUSAS 33 225 66n203
CUSAS 33 226 176n560
CUSAS 33 228 66n203
CUSAS 33 233 66n203
CUSAS 33 234 176n561
CUSAS 33 236 66n203
CUSAS 33 240 177
CUSAS 33 241 197n654
CUSAS 33 256 176n560
CUSAS 35 1 166n536, 227n787
CUSAS 35 2 30n92, 70n232, 155n491, 187n622, 203n684

CUSAS 35 7 47, 60n184, 197n654
CUSAS 35 8 47, 166n536
CUSAS 35 9 78n263, 81n270
CUSAS 35 88 166n536
CUSAS 35 134 166n536
CUSAS 35 169 166n536
CUSAS 35 192 166n536
CUSAS 35 207 155n491
CUSAS 35 227 203n684
CUSAS 35 250 30n92
CUSAS 35 251 30n92
CUSAS 35 261 187n622
CUSAS 35 301 223
CUSAS 35 302 166n533
CUSAS 35 314 118n386
CUSAS 35 317 226n783
CUSAS 35 321 107n341
CUSAS 35 337 107n341
CUSAS 35 360 198
CUSAS 35 364 187n623
CUSAS 35 386 182n589
CUSAS 35 418 177n562
CUSAS 35 419 76n253, 78n261, 80, 89n291
CUSAS 35 427 150n482
CUSAS 35 450 184n602
CUSAS 35 451 164
CUSAS 35 458 183
CUSAS 35 469 181
CUSAS 35 470 181
CUSAS 35 500 58n177
CUSAS 35 514 95n298, 204n685, 208, 212
CUSAS 35 515 222

DP 36 24n63, 225n768
DP 38 54
DP 40 27n76
DP 53 164n524
DP 57 27n76
DP 59 22n48, 70n230
DP 171 29n84
DP 192 132n429, 165n530
DP 194 29n84, 165n530
DP 283 27n76
DP 284 27n76
DP 418 26n73
DP 429 70n231
DP 491 23n50
DP 509 124n397, 129, 132, 142, 166
DP 512 29n84
DP 513 70n229, 160, 206
DP 516 163
DP 517 165n530
DP 518 130n414, 130n415, 133n432
DP 519 70n229
DP 594 70n230
DPA 36 104n327

Ea I 342 ff. 48
Ebla Sign List 18, 74
ECTJ 51 31n94, 198
ECTJ 65 58n181
ECTJ 91 29n83, 30n89, 225n772
ECTJ 100 54
ECTJ 108 54
ECTJ 149 54
ECTJ 153 146n469, 162
ECTJ 198 197
ED Metals 121–122 197
EDPV A 37, 102 197
EDPV A 101 135
EDPV A 136 115
EDPV A 142 186
EDPV A 145–146 188
EDPV A 223 207n713
EDPV B 140 115
EDPV B 145 150, 185
EDPV B 140 44, 115, 185
ELTS 11 = Blau Plaque 219
ELTS 13 219
ELTS 15 50n148, 182n593
ELTS 16a 54
ELTS 20 = Enhegal Tablet 29, 175
ELTS 21 = Lupad Statue 176
ELTS 36 54
ELTS 40 = Maništusu Obelisk 30, 68, 99, 182
ELTS 41 = Sippar Stone 68
ELTS 43–44 100n309
ELTS 123 220n755
ELTS 125 76n245
Englund 1992: 99 no.1 110n354
ETB 2 72 198n659

FAOS 15/1 300 29n85, 209n720
FAOS 15/2 66 27n76
FAOS 19 Um 6 185n612
Foster 1997 p.54 130n414
Foxvog 1980 156n492
FTP 83 25
FTP 84 171, 220n756
FTP 88 225n767
FTP 96 58n178, 63
FTP 98 76n245, 182

Genava 26 1 23n51

Hendursaĝa A 10
Hirose 322 34n107
HSS 4 5 149
HSS 4 6 148n475
HSS 10 169 54

Imgula 3/1 57 100n314
Inana's Descent to the Netherworld 234 140
Instructions of Šuruppak 72
ITT 1 1070 100n314, 103n320
ITT 1 1091 81n276, 98n304
ITT 1 1282 205n695
ITT 1 1422 187n621
ITT 2 631 34n108
ITT 2 909 124n403, 148
ITT 2 2852 196n647
ITT 2 4369 100n314, 175
ITT 2 4461 203, 212
ITT 2 4573 206n707
ITT 2 4598 200
ITT 2 5728 189
ITT 2 5799 130n414
ITT 4 7052 104n330, 104n332
ITT 4 7441 104n333, 105n334
ITT 4 7466 104n332
ITT 4 7522 222n762
ITT 4 7560 104n331
ITT 5 6670 189n633
ITT 5 6671 81n276, 103n323, 189
ITT 5 6676 189n632
ITT 5 9231 165n530, 225n769
ITT 5 9237 225n769
ITT 5 9240 225n769
ITT 5 9245 165n530
ITT 5 9246 63, 221n760
ITT 5 9247 165n530, 225n770
ITT 5 9249 184n608
ITT 5 9260 190n640
ITT 5 9276 145n462, 189n633, 190n640, 215n731
ITT 5 9317 162
ITT 5 9323 54

Krebernik, Steible, and Yildiz 2014 no. 10 171n539

Lambert 1979 48n140
Laws of Ur-Namma (LUN) 135-149 106

MAD 1 50 100n309
MAD 1 166 100n314
MAD 1 188 54, 58n177
MAD 1 195 100n314, 101
MAD 1 286 207
MAD 1 303 100n314, 183n596
MAD 4 2 54
MAD 4 65 183
MAD 4 71 146n470
MAD 4 124 61
MAD 5 9 54
MAD 5 17 99n307, 100n314
MAD 5 23 102n317
MAD 5 52 54n171
MAD 5 66 66n207
MAD 5 82 66n207
MAD 5 84 103n325
MAD 5 86 100n314
MAD 5 88 66n207
MAD 5 101 54
MAD 5 108 81n275, 98n304
MAD 5 110 145n463
Maekawa 1997 no. 15 149n478
Maekawa 1997: 291 119n390
MARI 5 1 72n236
MARI 5 2 54
MC 4 4 48n139, 66n207
MC 4 27 56n174
MC 4 28 56n174

MC 4 48 66n207
MC 4 61 156, 160
MC 4 69 98n304
MLVS 918 64
MS 2515 40n124
MS 4576 See *CUSAS 17 19*
MSVO 4 80 40n124
MVN 3 1 48n139, 54, 71n235, 100n309, 100n310, 129n412, 160
MVN 3 10 71n235, 100n309, 100n310, 129n412, 160
MVN 3 13 48n139, 54
MVN 3 36 67n208
MVN 3 59 67n208
MVN 3 102 100n309
MVN 3 108 100n310
MVN 5 155 149
MVN 7 34 = ITT 4 7634 190n640
MVN 8 179 76n249
MVN 10 85 58n178
MVN 14 471 26
MVN 16 1042 26
MVN 16 1226 34n105

N 6119 10n9
Nabnītu E 67–68 142n453
Nabnītu IV–IVa 361 62n194
Nabnītu XVII 236, 238 67n212
Nanše A 10
NBC 2565 130
NBC 10262 99n307, 101n316
Nik 1 282 26n73
Nik 1 295 165n526
Nik 1 299 133n433
Nik 1 300 165n530
Nik 1 301 130n413, 212
Nik 1 305 165n530
Nik 1 310 57n175
Nik 2 44 227n788
Nik 2 51 166, 219n750
Nik 2 52 30n91
Nik 2 55* 166
Nik 2 56 43n130, 163
Nik 2 58 54
Nik 2 76 166n532
Nik 2 77 166n532
Nik 2 78 98n305
NISABA 15 656 124n404
NISABA 25 6 24n58
NISABA 30 77 32n99
Notizia and Schrakamp 2010 160n510
NRVN 1 78 109n351
NTSŠ 154 172

OAIC 5 101n316
OAIC 7 31n94, 188n628
OAIC 10 162
OAIC 36 131n 424
OB Nippur Ura 1 436–441 140
OB Nippur Ura 4 178-206 121
OB Proto Ea 718 62n193
OB Sippar Ura 197–205 121
OB Ura I 144 94n296
OIP 14 49 = ELTS 32 76n251
OIP 14 61 30n89, 225n772
OIP 14 66 54
OIP 14 70 77n260, 78n264, 80, 86, 88, 89
OIP 14 111 185n613
OIP 14 156 188n627
OIP 14 157 76n247, 80n269, 81n273, 186
OIP 14 183 227
OIP 97 2 54, 171n541
OIP 99 33 175n555
OSP 1 17 77n254, 81n274, 214n723
OSP 1 96 197
OSP 1 97 196
OSP 1 109 29n84
OSP 1 127 54, 55n172
OSP 1 131 77n254, 81n274
OSP 2 17 100n314
OSP 2 22 100n314
OSP 2 23 100n314
OSP 2 25 182
OSP 2 32 188n628
OSP 2 44 31n95, 54, 175, 175n554
OSP 2 48 145n466, 184n603
OSP 2 49 146n469, 214n727
OSP 2 51 215n729
OSP 2 52 76n246, 81n271
OSP 2 55 82n277
OSP 2 59 54, 76n246, 81n271
OSP 2 61 82n278, 84n285
OSP 2 62 162
OSP 2 63 64, 77n255, 81n274, 214n725

OSP 2 128 26n75, 159n508
OSP 2 130 159n508
OSP 2 183 98n305

P000151 19n35
P003729 19n35
P201714 117n384
P271220 77n258
P271238 66n203
P388147 117n383
Parr 1974 p. 100 212
PBS 9 72 54
PDT 209 34n105
PPAC 1 666 189
PPAC 1 750, 752 227n788
PPAC 1 752 54
PPAC 1 1121 54
PPAC 4 291 119n393
PPAC 5 279 77n259
Prisoner Plaque (Steinkeller 2013) 114
Proto-Ea 116 17, 67n209

RIME 1.9.9.13 131n420
RIME 1.14.14 206n706
RIME 2.1.2.6 200n662
RIME 3/2.1.04.22 131n421
RTC 9 220n757
RTC 14 77n257
RTC 15 182n594
RTC 19 29n82
RTC 20–21 205
RTC 21 205n694
RTC 23 116n379, 161, 184
RTC 24 184
RTC 25 31n94, 165n530
RTC 27 164, 166n531
RTC 100 188n627
RTC 101 54
RTC 182 105n335, 130, 130n414
RTC 183 130n414
RTC 202 54
RTC 209 130
RTC 239 116n379
RTC 255 31n94
RTC 263 109n346, 134n440

SAT 3 1274 32n98
Schneider 1930 no.463 124n402
SCTRAH 59 31n93
SCTRAH 103 24n59
SCTRAH 115 118n389
SCTRAH 116 26n71, 118n388
SCTRAH 206 54
SCTRAH 221 166
SCTRAH 224–238 185n614
SCTRAH 225 185
SCTRAH 228 146n467
SCTRAH 229 146n467, 187
SCTRAH 237 146n467
SCTRAH 269 224
SEL 19 1–4 46n136, 54
Selz 1989/90 p.37 25n65
SF 20 44, 54, 185n611, 186
SLT 12 205n693
Song of Release 67n215
SP 3 10n9
SP 4 10n9
SP 5 10n9
SP 13 10n9
STA 1 110n354
Statue B of Gudea 208
Steible and Yildiz 1996 220n755
StPohl SM 13 1 68n216
StPohl SM 13 25 68n217
STTI 26 58n177, 98
STTI 27 212
STTI 33 225n773
STTI 46 76n248, 81n272
STTI 49 163
STTI 107 58n177, 189, 200
STTI 110 76n248, 81n272
STTI 135 156
STTI 162 58n177
STTI 170 103n322
STTI 181 58n177
Subartu 2 6 221n759
Such-Gutiérrez 2015: 3 131n421
Sumerian King List 30
Syracuse 452 149n477
Š 692 42